MW00443720

Inventory Management Explained

A focus on Forecasting, Lot Sizing, Safety Stock, and Ordering Systems

David J. Piasecki

www.opspublishing.com

ISBN-13:   978-0-9727631-1-0

ISBN-10:   0-9727631-1-2

Printed and bound in the United States of America

Ops Publishing
P.O. Box 580150
Pleasant Prairie, WI 53158

www.opspublishing.com

Table of Contents

3. Forecasting Part 1: Basic Concepts and Techniques   45

4. Forecasting Part 2: Now It Gets Complicated   75

Before you go any further:

Go to **http://inventoryexplained.com** to check for updates, extras, and corrections. You'll also find Cut&Paste formulas you can use to help set up some of the more complicated examples from the book.

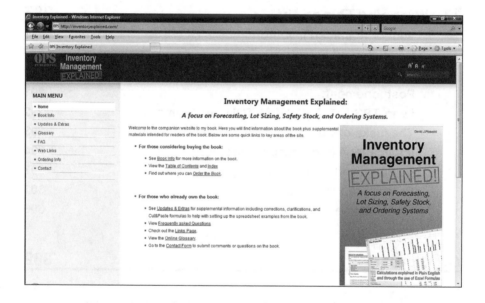

The Basics and the Big Picture

Over the years, it has become very apparent to me that most aspects of business are far more complicated than they seem on the surface. Businesses are complex and diverse, and assumptions of simple processes and standard solutions rarely hold true. So the first mistake you want to avoid is oversimplifying your problem or solution. On the other hand, some processes and solutions that at first may seem incredibly difficult and complex will become much easier once you take the time to try to understand them. Therefore, the second mistake you want to avoid is assuming you are incapable of understanding or utilizing certain solutions or technologies. This isn't to say that you won't occasionally run into solutions or technologies that are beyond your current skills, only that you should not assume they will be. In addition, there are very few universal truths in business, so the third mistake you want to avoid is blindly accepting any solution, technology, or strategy just because the "experts" say so. And yes, that includes my comments in this book. And finally, the techniques we use to manage our inventories are full of flaws, and while you should do your best to identify and eliminate these flaws, you will likely find it impractical to eliminate all of them. So the final mistake you want to avoid is letting fear of an imperfect system prevent you from implementing improvements.

Mistakes to avoid:

Oversimplifying your problem or solution.

Assuming you are incapable of understanding or utilizing certain solutions or technologies.

Blindly accepting any solution, technology, or strategy just because the "experts" say so.

Letting fear of an imperfect system prevent you from implementing improvements.

If you take this balanced approach to reading this book and tackling your inventory management tasks, you will find that managing inventory can be incredibly challenging, interesting, and rewarding. To be fair, I should also mention that managing inventory can also be incredibly aggravating, unappreciated, and has been shown to shorten the life spans of lab rats in clinical studies.

Alvin's story.

In an effort to hypocritically capitalize on the soap-opera/cutesy-fairy-tale approach to business education that has become annoyingly popular in recent years, I've put together the following little story. This is simply a quick story that helps to demonstrate how seemingly simple inventory-related decisions are actually more complex once you start to consider additional factors. The goofy parts are included purely for my own amusement—and to keep me from gagging at the thought of including a factory fable in my book. Oops, did I say that out loud?

Ever since that "Got Milk?" ad campaign featuring supermodels and celebrities started several years ago, Alvin has become a regular consumer of dairy products, drinking about a pint of milk every day. During full-contact-team-speed-walking race season, Alvin's drinking buddies come over on weekends to watch the competitions on the Make-Up-Your-Own-Sports channel and consume large quantities of—you guessed it—milk and cookies. Alvin's buddies aren't satisfied with just any milk and cookies; they want whole milk and homemade chocolate chip cookies with nuts. In addition, Alvin has a weird uncle who just shows up periodically and, of course, also likes to have a cold one. Alvin wants to keep his uncle happy because his uncle is both wealthy and old, and Alvin's career plan basically consists of doing well in his Uncle's will.

So what does this odd little story tell us about inventory management? Let's start with managing Alvin's milk supply. Alvin has many options for buying his milk. These options include various sized containers (pints, quarts, half-gallons, gallons) with associated price breaks (lower cost per pint) at each successive size increase. He also has choices of where to buy the milk; he has a small convenience store within a mile of his apartment or he can go to the large grocery store five miles away. Not surprisingly, the cost per unit at the convenience store is higher than at the grocery store.

Alvin's neighbor works in inventory management and hooked Alvin up with some industry magazines. After reading them, Alvin is convinced that he either needs to source his milk overseas, or source locally and go with a just-in-time strategy. Since he has no idea how to source milk overseas, he decides he should go with the just-in-time strategy and only buy what he needs for that day. This way he won't be burdened with all that extra inventory that—based on the articles in the magazines—would prevent him from being world class. Though he isn't quite sure what "world class" is, he thinks it sounds like something he would like to be. Since this just-in-time strategy would result in Alvin having to go to the store to buy milk every day, he would be more likely to use the convenience store even though the prices are higher. Alvin understands that the smaller quantities purchased daily at the convenience store will cost more, but he is confident those folks that write the magazine articles must know what they are talking about, so he prepares to move forward with his "strategy".

Is this the most cost-effective way to manage Alvin's milk inventory? Probably not; but how do we know for sure? We can start by looking at the costs associated with procuring milk. These include the various price breaks for larger sized containers, the price differences between the convenience store and the grocery store, and the costs associated with traveling to and from the convenience store and grocery store. If we just look at these costs, we will likely find that buying the largest container available at the grocery store is the best option. In fact, we may also inquire into sizes larger than the one-gallon container. Alvin could go to a commercial 5-gallon container of milk or maybe even look into getting his own tank installed and have his milk delivered directly from the dairy via a tanker truck. This would certainly have the lowest cost per unit.

From a practical standpoint, most would say that this last scenario is obviously absurd—though Alvin's drinking buddies would be way impressed. But why is it absurd? There must be other factors that need to be considered. What is the cost of purchasing the tank and having it installed? What are the ongoing costs of maintaining and refrigerating the tank? Alvin lives in an efficiency apartment. Where is he going to put a tank? What are the costs associated with buying significant quantities of milk well in advance of actual need? Does Alvin even have access to enough money to buy milk in these quantities? And, of course, milk has a limited shelf life; so how much milk will spoil before Alvin and his buddies can consume it?

These additional factors seem obvious at the tanker level or even at the five-gallon commercial level, but they also exist to a lesser extent at the lower price-break levels. Buying gallons of milk will have a greater risk of spoilage than buying smaller quantities, and, Alvin may not even have enough room in his refrigerator to store gallons of milk. We also have changing demand patterns. Remember that during race season Alvin is buying significantly more milk than during the rest of the year. Not only is this significant increase in demand limited to a specific time of year, but also to specific days of the week. This predictable calendar-based demand variability is known as seasonality, and will change the quantities that Alvin requires at any given time. The process of quantifying future demand (including seasonality) is known as forecasting.

So if we take all these costs, constraints, and forecasted demand into consideration, we can determine the most effective quantity to buy, and the most effective source. But is that all? Have we now achieved effective inventory management? Well, not quite yet. We now know where Alvin will purchase the milk and the quantities (known as order quantities or lot sizes), but we need to know when Alvin should purchase the milk. Should Alvin just wait until he runs out and then run to the store? Let's not forget about Alvin's weird uncle; Alvin needs to keep enough "extra" milk to accommodate the fact that his uncle could show up at any time. This extra milk used to compensate for demand that is not predictable, is known as safety stock. In addition, Alvin may not be able to go to the store every day. This means that he needs to evaluate his milk inventory every time he goes to the store to see if he has enough to last until his next opportunity to go to the store. And what if he did choose to go with the option of ordering in commercial quantities? He would then need to compensate for the extra time it takes to receive his milk after placing an order. This is known as lead time.

Though this is getting more complicated, it is still a very simple inventory management example. To complicate things further, let's say that Alvin is actually a binge drinker. Though he averages drinking one pint per day, he actually will go for several days without drinking any milk and then drink a half-gallon or more in a single day. In addition to this, the consumption of milk and cookies during the speed-walking competitions varies depending on how many of his drinking buddies show up and whether or not their team is winning. Because of this, forecasting demand becomes more difficult. Alvin will need to plan more safety stock to accommodate his drinking binges unless he can predict when he will binge. He will also need to use safety stock to buffer for the variable demand of milk during the speed-walking competitions unless he can predict the outcome of the event and how many of his buddies will show up. This demonstrates the importance and complexity of forecasting.

And, we haven't yet talked about the cookies. Since the requirement is for homemade cookies, Alvin must plan to have all the necessary ingredients to bake the cookies. Since Alvin pretty much lives on microwave dinners and take-out, he normally doesn't have ingredients around for cooking anything. Though he could try to independently predict the demand of each ingredient based on historical usage, this would prove to be less than effective. What he needs to do is predict the independent demand of the cookies, and then use this forecast combined with the cookie recipe to calculate the dependent demand of the ingredients. We call the demand for the ingredients "dependent" because the demand is dependent on the demand for the cookies. If you know how many cookies you will consume and how much of each ingredient it takes to make a single cookie, you can now calculate how much of each ingredient you will need to meet the total demand for cookies. If there was also independent demand for an ingredient—such as Alvin periodically consuming a bag of chocolate chips during one of his drinking binges—you would need to forecast this demand independently and add it to the dependent demand calculated through the recipe.

Alvin also needs to determine if he is going to bake cookies each week prior to the speed-walking competition or if he can make larger batches less frequently. After all, baking cookies is a lot of work (especially for Alvin) and making larger batches less frequently requires less setup and cleanup time. Once again, issues like spoilage and the investment in more cookies than are immediately needed will need to be considered.

Alvin may also choose a hybrid process whereby he makes large batches of cookie dough and then freezes or refrigerates them, adding the final ingredients (chocolate chips and nuts), and baking smaller batches of cookies right before each game. This is a concept known as postponement.

We also need to determine how much of each ingredient to buy and when to buy it. Sure, we know how much is needed, but is that the best quantity to buy? We'll again need to consider quantity price breaks, various sources, storage considerations, financial implications, and potential spoilage. We may even find that ingredients with longer shelf lives allow Alvin to take advantage of sales that occur well in advance of need. Inventory bought in advance of need because of price variability is known as hedge inventory.

And what if everyone does not want the same type of milk? Alvin's buddies want whole milk, but Alvin's clogging arteries do not allow him to drink whole milk throughout the week. And Alvin's uncle has developed a preference for buttermilk. Now, Alvin needs to balance the problems associated with carrying more types of milk (known as product proliferation or SKU proliferation) against the potential ramifications of only carrying one type.

Well there you have it. A complex look at the seemingly simple issue of Alvin's milk and cookies. Through this exercise, we've quickly touched upon some of the key concepts and challenges of inventory management. So should Alvin invest in computer software and spend numerous hours planning and managing his milk and cookies? I think not. The benefits are not worth the effort. But it would help that Alvin at least understands these concepts and makes some informed buying decisions. However, in real businesses—where inventory is a significant resource—investing time, money, and effort into managing inventory can prove to be a strategic necessity. So let's move beyond milk and cookies, and start discussing inventory management in business environments.

> **Alvin's story introduced us to:**
>
> Sourcing
>
> Order quantities
>
> Lead time
>
> Seasonality
>
> Forecasting
>
> Safety stock
>
> Dependent demand
>
> Independent demand
>
> Postponement
>
> Hedge Inventory
>
> SKU proliferation

What is inventory management?

Inventory management is the control of inventory in a manner that best achieves the business objectives of your organization. It not only involves the physical management of inventory, but also the management of the data used to describe the inventory, and the systems used to process the data.

Inventory management ultimately comes down to having the right inventory in the right form in the right quantity in the right place at the right time at the right cost. In order to achieve this you must be able to answer the questions:

- What is the right inventory?
- What is the right form?
- What is the right quantity?
- Where is the right place?
- When is the right time?
- What is the right cost?

These are not simple questions to answer. Let's take a shot at answering, "What is the right inventory?" Some may say that it is merely inventory that has marketing potential. In other words, something you can expect to sell. This is often marketing's approach as they look at inventory as something that generates revenue. Therefore, any inventory that generates revenue is the "right inventory" to have. Unfortunately, just because something generates revenue—and probably sales commissions—does not mean that it has generated a profit. Since the ultimate objective of business is to generate profits, you would probably want to define the right inventory as inventory that generates profits; so now it just comes down to simple math. If the cost of procuring, managing, and processing the inventory is less than the sell price, then it must be the right inventory; and if the cost is greater than the sell price, it is the wrong inventory. Right? Well, it's not quite that simple either. While it is correct to state that the right inventory is inventory that ultimately generates profits, it's not necessarily a matter of simple math to determine this. For example, you may have individual items that—in a simple calculation—do not generate profit by themselves; however, they do generate profits by generating sales of related items or services. Some equipment manufacturers have built business models whereby they make minimal, if any, profit from the equipment they manufacture (thereby not meeting the simple profit calculation), but instead, profit through servicing the equipment and the sale of repair parts and consumables. You may also choose to stock "unprofitable" items to generate increases in market share or brand recognition, which will ultimately lead to greater sales in profitable items. Or, you may choose to produce or purchase "unprofitable" items to consume excess capacity, reduce waste of raw materials, or obtain greater discounts from vendors. While individually these items do not appear to be profitable, they are contributing towards the ultimate profitability of the company by increasing sales of profitable items or reducing overhead and material costs.

As you can see, just trying to answer one of these questions brings up a whole subset of additional questions. Inventory management is not simple. If it were, more companies would be good at it. And trust me, they're not. And though inventory management is not simple, it's not unattainable either. While you may never achieve perfection at getting the right inventory in the right form in the right quantity in the right place at the right time at the right cost, you can at least achieve competency in it. And achieving just a minor level of competency in inventory management can put you well ahead of most businesses. Throughout this book we will be exploring ways to answer some of these questions.

> *Inventory management ultimately comes down to having the right inventory in the right form in the right quantity in the right place at the right time at the right cost.*

Why manage inventory?

Inventory is one of the largest—if not the largest—investment many businesses will ever make. Too much inventory or too early inventory results in added expenses related to storage costs, handling costs, risk of obsolescence, risk of damage, and cost of money (interest). Too little inventory or too late inventory can result in lost sales, poor customer service, and added costs related to production delays, expediting, and order processing. With ever-increasing competition in virtually every industry, businesses cannot afford to have any weaknesses. In this context, proper management of inventory could be the difference between a business's success and failure.

What is inventory?

Well I guess before you can attempt to manage inventory, you need to know what inventory is. I define inventory as any quantifiable item that you handle, buy, sell, store, consume, produce, or track. Though most can easily equate inventory with saleable goods and raw materials used to produce saleable goods, inventory can also include many other items. The pens in an office supply cabinet, the bottled water for the water cooler, packaging and shipping materials, lubricants and repair parts for production equipment, disk space on a web server, computer forms, water in a city's water system, trees in a forest, and software licenses can all be considered inventory. This isn't to say that you should manage all types of inventory the same. The methods you choose and the level at which you manage the different types of inventory should be based on the costs involved and the importance of the inventory in meeting your business objectives.

In addition to knowing that something is inventory, there are many ways to categorize inventory. These categories may be related to the physical state of the inventory, the location within the supply chain, the intended use of the inventory, the owner of the inventory, or the specific quantity of inventory. A common method of classifying inventory involves breaking it down based upon its primary purpose.

Vocabulary Notes: Items, Products, SKUs, Units, Unit-of-measure.

Just to clarify some vocabulary, I use the terms, "items", "products", and "SKUs" (Stock Keeping Units) interchangeably. They all refer to unique things you track and manage as part of your inventory. The only difference is, the term "products" is generally used to describe finished goods.

The term "units" is used to describe the individual pieces of physical inventory that make up an item (assuming pieces is the unit-of-measure). Unit-of-measure is used to describe what it is that constitutes a unit (quantity of one) of an item. For example, if I sell candy bars and have two different sizes of a particular candy bar, each size would be considered a unique item or SKU. If the unit-of-measure is pieces (or eaches, or bars), it would mean that each individual candy bar is a unit. Therefore, if I had 150 of the large candy bars, and 100 of the regular candy bars, I would have two items with a total of 250 units (pieces). If, however, I were a wholesaler and used cases as my unit-of-measure, and there were 50 candy bars per case, I would then have 2 items with a total of 5 units (cases). Other examples of units-of-measure would include gallons, pounds, pallets, linear feet, square feet, and so on. The "stocking unit-of-measure" is the main unit-of-measure used by your inventory system and is generally (though not always) the smallest unit-of-measure you would sell or consume.

For example, if I am selling candy bars at a convenience store, it would not make sense to have "cases" as my stocking unit-of-measure since I sell the individual candy bars. However, if my supplier sold the candy bars to me using cases as the unit-of-measure, I would need to have a "purchasing unit-of-measure" in my system set to cases, and then have a conversion to tell my system how many individual candy bars (my stocking unit-of-measure) make up a case.

Just to make it clear here, if my supplier has cases as his unit-of-measure, it means that when I order from him I create a purchase order showing how many cases I want, not how many candy bars I want. However, if my supplier uses "eaches" as his unit of measure, but requires I order in case quantities (multiples), it means that when I order from him I create a purchase order for the number of candy bars I want, but need to make sure my total quantity is an exact multiple of the case quantity.

Finished goods.

Though the definition of finished goods seems obvious, it is not necessarily so. People often assume a finished-goods classification is based solely on an item's physical state. A complete automobile is a finished good, and rolls of steel are unfinished goods, right? Well this would be correct if the automobile and rolls of steel were in an automobile manufacturing plant. However, what if the rolls of steel were in a plant that manufactures and sells rolls of steel?

A simple definition of a finished-goods item is one that is in a saleable or ble state within a given environment. This means that the same item will be sified differently based upon its location within the supply chain. For exam castings produced at a foundry would be a finished good at the foundry, yet whe the casting arrives at a machine shop it becomes an unfinished good. The machine shop may machine the casting, at which point the machined casting becomes a finished good at the machine shop. Once the machined casting arrives at a final assembly plant, it is once again an unfinished good. However, if the same business owns the foundry, the machine shop, and the final assembly plant, they will likely only consider the final assembled item to be finished goods, and all other forms as unfinished goods.

Sometimes an item can be both a shippable item and an item used to produce other items within the same facility. For example, a bicycle manufacturer may separately sell wheels, forks, frames, pedals, and other components, as well as use them to produce complete bicycles. Should these saleable components be considered finished goods or unfinished goods? Actually, they could be either or both. If the saleable component usage is very small, they will likely be considered unfinished goods. If the saleable component usage is greater, they may be considered finished goods, or you may set up an additional category for saleable components. You may even set up separate item numbers for the saleable portion of component inventory.

What is important to note here is that the finished-goods classification is essentially a management tool. How you classify an item should be based upon how you intend to use the classification in business decisions. You need to develop a consensus within your organization about what management wants to consider a finished good, and then make sure you are consistent in applying this classification.

Unfinished goods.

Once you figure out what your finished goods are, you will likely also have a pretty good idea of what your unfinished goods are. Unfinished goods are items that are used to produce finished goods items. Unfinished goods are often called components, ingredients, raw materials, semi-processed materials, and subassemblies. Each of these names is somewhat descriptive of groups of unfinished goods, however, as with other classifications, these can also be interpreted differently in different environments. Let me give some brief descriptions of each.

Components. These would usually be items that are used in an assembly process. A rim, spokes, and a hub, would be examples of components used to assemble a bicycle wheel.

Ingredients. These are generally bulk materials that are mixed or otherwise processed to create another product.

Raw materials. These are materials that will undergo some type of a physical change. Examples would include bar stock that will be machined, sheet

cut or formed, plastic pellets that will be melted and

rials. These would be stockable items (meaning they
item number) that have gone through some process-
be later pulled from stock and undergo additional processing.

Subassemblies. These are stockable items that have been assembled, but will later be used to assemble other products.

As previously mentioned, these categories are not always black and white. Items that would be considered ingredients in one industry may be called raw materials in another. A subassembly that has been purchased (rather than assembled in-house) may be considered a component. Once again, it's important to note that these classifications are management tools and should be assigned based upon your expected use of the classifications. If you really don't care whether something is a component versus a raw material versus a semi-processed material, then just keep them all under a single classification. Alternatively, if you feel that you need to break down your unfinished goods into even more categories, by all means, do so. Examples would include categories such as roll stock, bar stock, sheet goods, bulk materials, castings, blanks, hardware, electronic subassemblies, and pump subassemblies.

Maintenance, repair, and operating (MRO) inventory.

This is that "other" inventory. It includes your office supplies, maintenance supplies, repair parts, and other consumables. A common mistake made with MRO inventory is placing responsibility for it in the hands of people with little or no education, training, or experience in inventory management. Office supplies are managed by the office manager or whoever is available, maintenance supplies are managed by the maintenance person, janitorial supplies by the cleaning personnel, and so on. Now don't get me wrong here, I'm not saying that these people can't or shouldn't manage these inventories; only that they may not be prepared to manage the inventory, there may be someone else better suited to manage it, or it may not be the best use of their time to manage the inventory. When evaluating MRO inventory, you need to consider the total investment in the inventory, the time it takes to manage it, the tools available to manage it, and the capabilities of the personnel available.

Work-in-process (WIP).

WIP is very different from the other classifications of inventory that have already been discussed, and is probably the most misunderstood inventory classification. WIP is an inventory account; it is the summarized value of in-process materials. WIP basically works like this: The value of materials issued to a production order, the value of labor reported against a production order, and the value of overhead applied to a production order (usually tied to labor or machine hours reported) are all added to the WIP account. The value of the finished materials (good and scrap) reported against a production order are deducted from the WIP account. Hence, what's left in the WIP account should be the dollar value of in-process materials.

I need to clarify a little further what is and is not considered "in-process materials" within the context of WIP. In-process materials are materials that no longer exist as specific stockable items. Subassemblies or semi-processed materials that can be tracked by an item number do not fall under this category and are not considered as WIP, provided they have not yet been issued to a production order. The WIP classification is the result of your bill-of-materials structure. Let me use an example of a casting that gets machined, and then has bushings, bearings, and grease fittings added to it. If your bill-of-materials structure is set up such that the casting, bearings, bushings, and grease fittings, are a single-level bill, and your manufacturing process performs the machining and the assembly steps all under the same production order, these materials will be part of WIP from the time they are issued to the production order until the time the finished item is produced. However, if your bill-of-materials structure is setup so that the casting is on a bill that only has the machining process, and there is a stockable item number set up for the "machined casting" that is on another bill along with the bushings, bearings, and grease fittings that is used to assemble the finished item, the machined casting is now a "stockable" item and is therefore not part of WIP (that is, it is not part of WIP from the time it is reported as being produced, until the time it is issued to another assembly production order).

This is probably the biggest misconception among shop-floor personal (management and general workforce) about WIP. They tend to think it is based solely on the physical state of the materials, when, in fact, it is based upon the structure of the bills of materials and the transactional status of the materials. The transactional status of the materials is a result of the issuing process. If I pick materials and issue them to production orders as I deliver them to the production area, they are now part of WIP. However, if I deliver those same materials to the production area, but they are not issued until they are used, they are not part of WIP until they are issued.

> ## Vocabulary Note: Issue
>
> When I say "issued to a production order", I'm referring to the transactional process that deducts the materials from your perpetual inventory system and adds the value (cost) of those materials to the WIP account.

Therefore, WIP categorization is highly dependent upon the specific environment in which materials are consumed. If you are a planner or work on the shop floor and find this to be rather confusing, that's because this classification is not intended for your use. WIP is an accounting classification, and in that context it makes perfect sense.

Why do we carry inventory?

Understanding why you carry specific quantities of inventory is an important step in managing your supply chain.

Current-demand inventory.

This is inventory carried to meet immediate expected demand, for example, the inventory that will be shipping in today's orders. The definition of "current demand" is somewhat subject to interpretation since you must apply a time period to determine what is considered "current demand" as opposed to "future demand".

Safety stock.

Safety stock is primarily used to buffer against variation in demand; however, it may also be used to buffer against supply variability or process variability. You have safety stock because you can't predict future events with 100% accuracy. The amount of safety stock you carry will depend upon the accuracy of your forecasts, the consistency of your supply and processes, and your desired service level. Safety stock is simply a quantity used in replenishment calculations; it does not require that units be physically separated from the regular inventory.

Lot-size inventory.

Lot size inventory is the result of ordering or manufacturing more inventory than is required to meet your current demand and safety stock. Despite the emphasis in recent decades on just-in-time inventory practices, the fact remains that cost savings may be realized through ordering or manufacturing in larger quantities than is immediately needed. This "extra" inventory is considered lot-size inventory.

Anticipation inventory.

Anticipation inventory can also be thought of as capacity inventory because it is usually the result of inadequate capacity to produce the inventory during peak seasons. If you have a seasonal product and limited capacity, you may need to build inventory prior to your busy season in "anticipation" of demand during the busy season. This is a common practice in highly seasonal industries.

Transportation inventory.

Transportation inventory is the amount of inventory that is currently in-transit. That is, it is the inventory that has left the shipper's facility (either an owned facility or a supplier's facility) and has yet to arrive at the consignee's facility (may be an owned facility or a customer's facility). Though tracking transportation inventory for inventory planning purposes is rather straightforward, trying to place a financial value on transportation inventory can be much more complicated. This is where legal ownership and financial tracking of transportation inventory are often out of sync. For instance, if a supplier ships product to you "F.O.B. Origin" (which means that transfer of ownership occurs when the shipment leaves the shipper's dock), you essentially own the inventory at that point, however, the inventory will probably not show on "the books" until the inventory is received.

Distribution inventory.

Though it sounds similar to transportation inventory, distribution inventory is the result of a distribution network and the increases in inventory required to operate out of multiple distribution points. When you decide to have two or three or more strategically located distribution centers rather than a single centrally located distribution center, you will generally increase your overall inventory levels. The reason for this is you are now breaking up your demand among three locations. When demand is broken up (disaggregated) you will usually find greater variability in the demand at each location. This increase in variability results in increases in safety stock in order to meet desired service levels. This increase in safety stock is essentially your distribution inventory. Some practitioners consider all inventory in the distribution network to be distribution inventory. I disagree with that definition, since much of that inventory would exist regardless of the distribution network.

Hedge inventory.

Hedge inventory is inventory that is purchased to protect against or take advantage of price fluctuations. The price fluctuations may be the result of seasonal or cyclical variations that result with imbalances in supply and demand (supply exceeds demand or vice versa), changes in exchange rates with international purchases, or even special promotions. In some industries, monitoring prices and managing hedge inventory can be an extremely important part of inventory management. This is especially true in industries that consume massive amounts of certain raw materials. It's essentially taking the stock-market approach and applying it to inventory management. In wholesale and retail it equates to "buying low and selling high", while in manufacturing it would be "buying low and consuming high".

I need to mention that trying to segregate and calculate exactly how much inventory you have in each category can be a challenging undertaking, and is not something that is done on a regular basis. However, depending on your business model, you may need to at least be able to make a reasonable estimation of certain categories in order to make certain types of business decisions.

Manufacturing and procurement strategies.

So what is a manufacturing and procurement strategy? In the broader sense, it can be many things, but in this context I am referring to various inventory management strategies that seek to provide the most effective means of meeting customer demand while minimizing costs. Before we discuss these strategies we need to talk about lead time and cumulative lead time. Lead time is the period of time that occurs between the time an order is placed and the time the goods or services are received. When I order a pizza from my local pizzeria, it takes about an hour to arrive; therefore the lead time for a pizza from that specific pizzeria is one hour. If I call my local auto repair shop to get some work done and it takes a week to get an appointment and then another two days to complete the repair, the total lead time is nine days (one week plus two days). Lead time to the customer is a critical factor in decisions related to manufacturing and procurement strategies. Cumulative lead time describes the longest lead time necessary to cover all individual lead times related to the manufacturing or procuring of a product. It is the sum of the longest consecutive lead times (shorter concurrent lead times are not added) within the process. It represents the length of time in advance of need of the finished item that the first actions need to occur.

So let's see how lead time relates to the following strategies.

Make-to-stock/procure-to-stock.

This is the most common inventory strategy. In a make-to-stock/procure-to-stock strategy you must carry adequate finished goods inventory to meet upcoming forecasted demand. The reason this stocking strategy is so common is not that it is the most cost-effective inventory strategy overall, but rather it is a necessary strategy when market conditions require shipment of goods quicker than you can manufacture or procure them. A grocery store is a good example of a procure-to-stock environment because the grocery store must keep inventory on the shelves to meet their customers' immediate needs. The customers are not providing any advance notice about what their needs will be; therefore the grocery store must anticipate (forecast) customer demand and procure inventory based on this forecast. As another example, a manufacturer of electric motors would likely use a make-to-stock strategy if their customers were primarily small repair shops that used the electric motors in the repair of various types of equipment. However, if the manufacturer was supplying large quantities of motors to a manufacturer of appliances, the electric motor manufacturer would be more likely to use a make-to-order strategy (discussed next). In a make-to-stock/procure-to-stock environment, your lead time to your customers consists of the time it takes to process the order and the transportation time to the customer.

Make-to-order/procure-to-order.

In this strategy, you do not manufacture or procure your product until after you receive actual orders from your customers. The primary advantage to this strategy is that you do not have to carry finished goods inventory. This means you do not have the costs associated with warehouse space, the capital investment in the inventory, and the risk of obsolescence that would normally go along with stocking finished goods inventory. This strategy does not necessarily result in zero inventories. Many make-to-order manufactures will forecast and procure some raw materials and components in advance of receiving orders in an effort to reduce the lead time to their customers. For example, if I am running a local print shop, I will likely stock commonly used paper stock to reduce the lead time for common print jobs such as business cards and brochures.

Configure-to-order.

Configure-to-order exists somewhere between make-to-stock and make-to-order. In this strategy, all or most components are generally stocked in anticipation of customer orders. Partial processing—such as production of subassemblies—is often done in advance of customer orders. All that remains are the final assembly or final processing activities. Configure-to-order is most commonly used when a product is sold with a great variety of options available. A direct-to-consumer manufacturer of personal computers is likely to use the configure-to-order strategy. In this scenario, the manufacturer would forecast demand for the specific components in advance of customer orders and then do the final assembly of a "custom" PC after the customer places an order specifying the processor, memory, drives, software, and other options. Since I had mentioned that make-to-order manufacturers often forecast and stock commonly used components and raw materials in advance of actual orders, you may be thinking—and rightly so—that this sounds very similar to the configure-to-order strategy just described. In fact there is no specific point at which make-to-order becomes configure-to-order. It may make more sense to think of configure-to-order as a variation of make-to-order rather than a unique strategy. The term postponement is often used to describe configure-to-order processes, since you are putting off (postponing) part of the process until the last moment before the product ships. Generally, when the term postponement is used, it is describing a configure-to-order process where the final process is a very quick and simple process such as brand-name packaging, kitting, or a quick final assembly.

Engineer-to-order.

This is yet another variation of make-to-order. An engineer-to-order strategy is used when the end product is truly custom. In this strategy, design or engineering tasks must be completed after the customer places the order. This strategy has the longest lead time to the customer, but is necessary since the detailed specifications of the product are not known in advance.

Direct shipping.

This is a procurement strategy that allows a company to sell product without ever stocking or even handling the product. When a customer places an order with a seller, the order is passed on to the seller's supplier who will then ship the product directly to the customer. The customer may or may not be aware that a direct shipment is taking place. In the past, direct shipping was very common with large expensive items or with very slow moving items such as repair parts. However, with

Lead Time and Inventory Implications of Manufacturing & Procurement Strategies

Strategy	Lead Time to Customers	Internal Cumulative Lead Time	Inventory Investment
Procure-to-stock	Includes only processing and transportation time.	Lead time from suppliers.	Significant investment in finished goods inventory.
Make-to-stock	Includes only processing and transportation time.	Manufacturing lead time plus cumulative lead time of components.	Significant investment in finished goods and component inventories.
Procure-to-order	Includes processing and transportation time plus lead time from supplier.	Lead time from suppliers.	No inventory investment.
Make-to-order	Includes processing and transportation time plus manufacturing lead time and cumulative lead time of components.* *The manufacturer may choose to stock some or all components to shorten lead-time to customers.	Manufacturing lead time plus cumulative lead time of components.	Does not require any inventory beyond temporary stocks of component inventory for the orders currently being processed. * *Unless the manufacturer chooses to stock components to shorten lead times.
Configure-to-order	Includes processing and transportation time plus manufacturing lead time of the final assembly process.	Manufacturing lead time plus cumulative lead time of components.	Investment in component and sub-assembly inventory.
Engineer-to-order	Same as Make-to-order, but also includes engineering time and may also require time to source components.	Same as Make-to-order, but also includes engineering time and may also require time to source components.	Same as Make-to-order

the growth of catalog and Internet-based businesses, direct shipping is expanding to cover much broader product lines. In a pure direct-shipping environment, the business is primarily a sales operation, not requiring facilities, equipment, and resources to manufacture, store, or distribute the inventory. Sweet deal, eh?

Consignment and vendor-managed inventory.

These are subsets of a procure-to-stock strategy. Consignment refers to the timing of transfer of ownership of the inventory, while vendor-managed inventory (VMI) refers to a process where the supplier is responsible for managing the inventory at the customer's facility. I'll be covering both of these in a little more detail later in this book.

Which is the best strategy for you? This depends on your particular industry, your inventory characteristics, the expectations of your customers, your supply chain, your manufacturing processes, your competition, and your facilities and distribution capabilities. In other words, there is no single best strategy that works for everyone. In fact, it's very common to use several strategies within the same business. A reseller may use procure-to-stock for their fast moving product and use procure-to-order or direct shipping for slower movers and oversized items. A manufacturer may use a combination of make-to-stock and make-to-order, as well as use vendor-managed-inventory for some of their components, and consignment inventory for some repair parts for their manufacturing equipment.

Some of these strategic decisions are rather simple. For example, if you produce custom machinery you can assume that you will be using an engineer-to-order strategy. However, when multiple options are available, you must balance the costs or cost savings associated with each against the potential impact on sales. There is no doubt that in most industries, being able to provide the shortest lead time to your customers can be a significant strategic advantage. So the trick is to determine which method(s) ultimately provide the highest profits. Note that I am using the word "profit" rather than "margin" or "revenue". Profits are the result of margin and revenues (sales); and business decisions that increase revenues will sometimes reduce margins (and vice versa). Therefore maximizing either margin or revenue does not necessarily maximize profit.

Inventory tracking methods.

Periodic review system.

A periodic review system has two different (though related) definitions. When referring to inventory tracking methods, a periodic review system means that you do not keep track of inventory transactions and current inventory balances. Instead, you periodically physically count your inventory to see how much you have. When referring to replenishment systems, periodic review means that you have a fixed schedule (not daily) where you review inventory levels and place replenishment orders. For example, if you have a fixed replenishment schedule with a supplier where you place one order every Friday for a Wednesday delivery, this is a periodic review replenishment system. However, if you need to actually go to the shelf every Friday to determine how much inventory you have, this is a periodic review inventory tracking system. You may be operating both a periodic review inventory tracking system and a periodic review replenishment system, but they are not mutually inclusive.

Perpetual inventory system.

A perpetual inventory system refers to a system where you track inventory balances and process individual inventory transactions whenever inventory is received, consumed, sold, transformed, scrapped, etc. This means that at any given point in time (based on the timeliness of the transactions) you should be able to inquire into your inventory system to determine your current inventory levels. As an added note, when I use the term "inventory system", it can be assumed that I am referring to a computer system designed to track and manage inventory.

Most businesses that have significant inventory-related activities use perpetual inventory systems. Though periodic review inventory tracking systems are still used, their use has become much more limited as access to computers has increased.

Inventory management tasks.

And now to the specific activities associated with inventory management. This is where the tires meet the road and to which most of the remainder of this book is dedicated. Shortcutting these processes is where most companies fail in effectively managing their inventory. I am not going to attempt to imply that doing these activities well is easy. It's not! It takes time, effort, knowledge, and even a bit of creativity. But the rewards are well worth it.

Forecasting.

Forecasting is the process of predicting future demand. Forecasting is likely the most difficult, most imprecise, and most beneficial activity related to inventory management. If you think you do not need to forecast, you are mistaken. Everybody forecasts, even if they don't know they are doing it. Businesses invest a significant amount of time, effort, and money into reacting to unknowns; therefore, the more unknowns you can make into knowns (or reasonable approximations) the better. And therein lies the benefits of forecasting.

There are a seemingly endless variety of forecasting techniques that range from simple period-averaging techniques to complex applications of indexes and the incorporation of educated guesses. We will be covering some of these in detail in subsequent chapters.

Calculating safety stock.

Safety stock (also known as buffer stock) is carried to compensate for uncertainty in supply or demand. In the case of demand uncertainty (the primary use of safety stock), safety stock makes up for inaccuracies in your forecasts. The more accurately you can forecast demand, the less reliant you are on safety stock. Safety stock calculations are essentially supplemental forecasting techniques, but rather than trying to predict demand, they attempt to quantify and assign probability to demand variability. Because of this, the most effective safety stock calculations are adapted from statistical models.

Lot sizing.

Lot sizing is the activity of determining how much to make or buy each time you make or buy something. Lot sizing techniques are primarily financial calculations that look to determine the order quantity that will result in the least cost to the company. The most well known calculation is known as economic order quantity (EOQ). EOQ is designed to achieve the lowest annual cost by calculating the best balance of order cost and carrying cost. Most lot sizing techniques are variations of the EOQ technique. The key to proper lot sizing is getting the right costs in the right formula. And while costs are the primary driving factor in lot sizing decisions, other factors such as capacity or cash flow may also need to be considered.

Ordering/Replenishment.

Ordering/replenishment is the inventory management activity that tends to get the most attention. It's the activity that "makes things happen" and therefore must occur (usually on a daily basis). It's also the most frequent activity and tends to require the most resources. Ordering/replenishment techniques take forecasted demand, actual demand, safety stock, lot sizing, and on-hand balances, and converts them into orders (manufacturing orders, purchase orders, transfer orders) with quantities and dates. Once again, there are many techniques used to do this, including fixed reorder point, time-phased reorder point, periodic review, Kanban, material requirements planning (MRP), and distribution requirements planning (DRP). The mechanics of these various techniques are fairly standardized and are rather simple. Unfortunately, the effectiveness of each technique is dependent on the data inputs, which are the results of the more difficult and more complex calculations related to forecasting, lot sizing, and safety stock.

Transactional control.

Transactional control is an important part of inventory management as it ensures that the data used to make inventory management decisions is both accurate and current. "Accurate" and "current" are somewhat relative terms since absolute accuracy is probably impossible and absolute real-time transactions are not always practical—or necessary. What is important, is maintaining reasonable and consistent levels of accuracy, and maintaining policies as to when and how transactions are to occur. To maintain transactional control you need to understand what a transaction is. Basically, a transaction is any action that changes your inventory system data. This would include entering a receipt, completing a shipment, disposing of scrap, entering or changing a purchase order or manufacturing order, updating inventory counts, as well as making any changes to planning data (such as changing lead times or inventory classification codes or updating forecasts). Transactional control policies and procedures must dictate who is authorized to make transactions, under what conditions transactions are to occur, how transactions are processed, and when transactions must be executed.

Inventory analysis.

Inventory analysis is the task that likely gets the least attention in your organization. In many companies, inventory analysis does not get beyond high-level measurements such as total inventory valuation, fill rates, and inventory turns. To best manage your inventory, you need to understand its characteristics. How many SKUs (items) do you have? What are your top sellers? How many SKUs make up the majority of your sales? How many SKUs have had no activity in the last month? Three months? Year? What drove you to procure or manufacture inventory that is now obsolete? What are your spoilage and scrap rates? How accurate is your inventory and how is your accuracy affecting inventory management decisions? How frequently do you need to expedite orders? What are your inventory levels by commodity? Inventory type? Vendor? Customer? Planner/buyer? Activity code? How have your inventory characteristics changed over time? These are just some of the questions you should be asking when making inventory management decisions. Inventory analysis provides information that allows you to make better inventory management decisions and helps to point out problems with current processes.

Hype, history and the real deal.

Anyone who has been involved in business management for an extended period of time can attest to the constant bombardment of hype related to business philosophies, strategies, techniques, software products, and equipment that are deemed to be the "next new thing" every business must have to succeed. Some have clever names, many have acronyms, and some even provide titles to those involved in their use. The biggest thing they all have in common is that someone expects to profit by convincing others to implement these ideas and products. And that's where the hype begins.

If you are new to operations, you may not have mapped a value stream or experienced a quality circle, kaizen event, or team-building workshop. You may not know what Total Quality Management (TQM), Just-in-time (JIT), Theory of Constraints (TOC), Quick Response, or Six Sigma are. You probably don't understand the benefits of cellular manufacturing or drum-buffer-rope scheduling. You may not know what Enterprise Resource Planning (ERP), Manufacturing Resource Planning (MRP), Manufacturing Execution Systems (MES), Distribution Requirements Planning (DRP), Warehouse Management Systems (WMS), Advanced Planning and Scheduling (APS), Transportation Management Systems (TMS), Customer Relationship Management (CRM), and Supply Chain Management (SCM) software products do or why they need to be robust, modular, and scalable. You certainly don't know why some people call themselves Jonahs and Black Belts. And you struggle to figure out why you need to be collaborative in real-time, how you can tell if you are world class, where best practices come from, how web services will help your manufacturing capabilities, and what exactly are paradigms and why they are always shifting and changing.

The fact is we live in a society that loves hype. Why is it that one year every kid in America wants the same toy and the following year millions of that toy are collecting dust in closets, attics, basements, and garages? It's because kids are very susceptible to next-new-thing hype. This doesn't mean that the original product had no value, only that it did not live up to the hype. It was not as "new", "revolutionary", or "essential" as it first appeared. Give it about a decade and it's likely the same product will reappear with new packaging and new hype, and the cycle repeats.

The business world is no different. Put out a product or idea and make it look shiny and new, and managers and executives become kids in toy stores. When interest drops off after a few years, someone will repackage it (probably change it slightly and give it a new name) and here we go again.

For the most part, the fundamental principles of modern business developed and documented during the first three quarters of the twentieth century still hold true. The Management-Science / Operations-Research movement during the middle part of the century provided enough mathematical models to keep computer programmers busy for decades to come. The last few decades have primarily provided us with computer processing capabilities to automate processes and communicate more effectively. Other than that, most everything else is simply new packaging and hype. If you believe that it never occurred to plant managers to focus efforts on their bottleneck operations prior to the introduction of the Theory of Constraints, or that prior to the Toyota Production System everyone thought that large component and work-in-process inventories were a good thing, you are sorely mistaken. Not to take anything away from those that developed and documented these strategies. I simply see them more as a means of education and effective reminders of good practices rather than revolutionary ideas. Certainly, information technology is having a significant positive effect on business processes, but in reality it is just providing speed and automation to already known calculations and business practices.

I'll readily admit that there is nothing really "new" or "revolutionary" about the basic calculations and concepts outlined in this book. I am primarily gathering existing techniques and ideas that I feel work (or don't work), and providing explanations about what they are, how to use them, and where they are effective. And while there are some variations on calculations in this book that I have developed independently, I think it would be presumptuous to try to claim I "invented" all of them since many are just logical mathematical solutions to common inventory problems. So in some respects, this book is a repackaging of old ideas. My primary contributions are my interpretation and insights, tips based on my experience and analysis, and my charm and wit. OK, maybe you're not impressed with my charm and wit, but I stand by my interpretations and insights.

In my experience, every strategy, technique, or product has some value as well as some weakness. They are never universal, are rarely new, and rarely live up to the hype. What you need to do is try to cut through the hype and evaluate the underlying substance, and how it could potentially benefit your operations. Realize that just because a strategy or product works for company A, does not mean it will work for company B. But also, realize that just because—as a whole—it doesn't quite fit company B, does not mean that company B cannot benefit from utilizing parts of the strategy, technique, or product.

The Big Picture.

In my first book, *Inventory Accuracy: People, Processes, & Technology*, I repeatedly referred to the question, " What is the best way to do this that takes into account the customer service, productivity, quality, accuracy, capacity, safety, and financial objectives of your organization?" All too often, people make process changes and business decisions that optimize a specific business objective that relates to their area while unintentionally sacrificing the organization's ability to meet other objectives. This isolationist decision-making is often unwittingly promoted by the organization through individual and department performance measures that place too much focus on certain aspects of the business. This is a flawed business philosophy known as local optimization. Most of us have done this to some extent both knowingly and unknowingly. It's hard to do the right thing for the company when doing the right thing results in missing out on a bonus.

Global optimization requires that decisions be made within the context of the overall objectives of the entire organization or even beyond. This is extremely important in inventory management since decisions made here will affect manufacturing, distribution, sales, and finance. Inventory management is one of the biggest balancing acts in business, and a constant focus on the big picture is essential. That said, some aspects of inventory management can get rather complicated and it's not always practical to "globally optimize" them. The reality is, many of our inventory calculations could be interpreted as local optimization calculations. Using local optimization is not inherently wrong, it's just potentially wrong. When using local optimization, you should at least consider the global consequences, and in doing so, you may be able to set parameters within the local optimization process that help to adjust it to global factors.

Significant gains can be made in inventory management through competent execution of the basics. However, to competently execute the basics, you must not only understand the basics, but also the overall objectives of your business and the interrelationships of the basics within the confines of the big picture.

A quick note on the impact of lead times and lot sizes.

I can't overstate the impact lead times and lot sizes have on inventory management. If you would like to achieve higher fill rates, lower inventory investment, and lower risk of obsolescence, while at the same time reduce the amount of work that goes into managing the inventory, you need to look good and hard at ways to reduce your lead times and lot sizes. This isn't to imply that you should just blindly reduce lot sizes or lead times as some "industry experts" would suggest. But rather, you should understand the implications of lead times and lot sizes and make smart decisions on achieving the shortest lead times and smallest lot sizes that make economic sense for your specific operation. We will revisit this topic throughout the book.

2

Tools of the Trade

Not to intentionally frighten you, but the most important tool you will use in inventory management is your brain, or more specifically, your knowledge of inventory management, your industry, business processes and systems, and your ability to apply this knowledge to real-world situations you encounter. That being said, there are more tangible tools to discuss.

Computer systems.

I think I can safely say the days of managing inventory on index cards or in large journals are behind us—though there are undoubtedly a few holdouts. Today, inventory management is performed on computers; and inventory managers must not only understand inventory management methods, but also must understand the data that describes their inventory and the programs that utilize this data to automate inventory management tasks. This collection of data and programs is what I refer to as your "inventory system". Inventory systems can vary widely in their functionality, complexity, and cost. In its most minimal form, an inventory system must be able to maintain inventory quantity and basic ordering information (reorder point, lot size) by item. At the other end of the spectrum are software products that automatically generate forecasts and optimize inventory levels across extended supply chains.

Now just because your company didn't invest millions of dollars in high-end supply chain software does not mean you cannot effectively manage your inventory using computer technology. Nor should you assume those high-end systems will magically manage your inventory for you. In the end, inventory management success is more dependent on the knowledge of the inventory manager than it is on the functionality of the software. Don't get me wrong, there are some fantastic software products out there that can prove to be valuable inventory management tools, but without the knowledge to fully utilize their advanced functionality you may just as well be using low-end software. This is a common scenario in large companies that purchase these high-end systems only to find that they did not achieve the improvements they had expected. In most cases, this is not as much a reflection on the shortcomings of the software they purchased—though software vendors do tend to overstate the benefits of their systems—as it is the lack of knowledge of those setting up and using the software.

And, for those of you with low-end inventory systems, you should know that there is a lot you can do with low-cost desktop software (spreadsheet programs and database programs) to supplement the functionality of your inventory system. So stop blaming your inventory system for your inventory problems. Ultimately, it's your responsibility.

There are many terms used to attempt to classify business software products. Unfortunately, this terminology is constantly changing as software vendors try to portray their software as something "New" and "Innovative".

ERP systems / software suites: a little history lesson.

ERP is an acronym for Enterprise Resource Planning, the poster child for the business software gold rush of the late 1980s and 1990s. During this period, companies were convinced by the software industry, consultants, and industry magazines that an ERP system was the solution to all their problems. Though ERP had already existed for over a decade, it had been confined to very large companies that could afford the large computers and staffs of programmers required to maintain and run it. In fact, ERP was designed specifically for very large companies with multiple divisions (hence the term "enterprise") in an effort to get all aspects of the company on the same system.

When the big ERP push for mid-sized and smaller business ensued, nearly all mid-sized to large companies and many smaller companies were already using computers to manage certain aspects of their businesses. The software industry started using the term "legacy system" to describe the systems these companies already had. The term "legacy system" implies an outdated system that is either a homegrown (custom built) system, a purchased system that has likely been modified over the years, and/or a hodgepodge of various disconnected software systems. In reality, some of the systems that were being referred to as "legacy" systems by the software industry already had much of the functionality of the ERP systems that were being promoted to replace them.

ERP was portrayed as the highly functional fully integrated replacement to this ineffective mixed-bag of outdated standalone systems. And to some extent, this is an accurate portrayal of ERP since ERP is essentially a single system (made up of multiple modules) that manages the company's financials, sales, distribution, manufacturing, and human resources. All data exists in a single database (usually) and the various modules have a common user interface and are tightly integrated with each other. For example, when a receiving clerk received an item at the dock, the warehouse inventory system would be updated, the product would immediately be available for sale, accounts payable could match the vendor invoice to the receipt, and all financial accounts would be appropriately updated.

This fully integrated transactional system and database is the core of ERP systems. In fact, the transactional system is so much the core of ERP systems that many have referred to these systems as glorified accounting systems. This description of ERP is arguably valid and tends to be the source of complaints by us non-accountants who are looking to the ERP system to help in the operational aspects of the business.

So why are ERP systems—and virtually all other business management software suites—built around accounting systems? Well, maybe because accounting is such an essential part of running a business. There, I've said it! Business is about making money; it's that simple. In order to manage a business, you need measurements of where, when, and on what the money is being spent; and where, when, and on what the money is being made. This is called accounting, and even though accounting by itself does not generate profits, it is a critical part of the business. And since virtually every major business activity needs to interact with the accounting system, it makes sense that the accounting system would be the central part of the business software system.

When businesses started implementing these packaged software suites, they quickly encountered a variety of problems.

- These software systems are very complex and require significant resources to set up and implement. With very large companies, implementations could take several years and millions of dollars.

- Failure to properly set up and implement these systems could be disastrous. Stories of businesses being forced to shut down business operations due to poorly implemented systems were commonplace. Even the bare essentials—like having the ability to take an order and ship product—failed during the go-live stage of far too many implementations.

- In an effort to properly account for business activities (a key objective of implementing these products), businesses found that many of their processes became more complex and time consuming. This was a rather unwelcome surprise to those who thought implementing these computer systems would reduce clerical tasks.

- The new system couldn't do things their old legacy system did. This was especially true with manufacturing processes, which tend to be unique to specific industries.

With the exception of the failed or flawed implementations—which are the fault of those implementing the system—these issues are essentially the nature of the beast. In order to design a business software system that can be effectively implemented in a variety of environments, you must create a complex system with numerous configurable options. The greater the diversity of functionality offered, the greater the complexity of system setup required. And even the most highly configurable systems cannot be designed to be able to meet every possible business practice. Conversely, systems designed for smaller businesses must often sacrifice flexibility and functionality in order to provide a system that can be implemented with the limited resources of smaller business.

In the end, the reality of ERP was nowhere near the hype of ERP. Due to the negative perception of ERP that has grown over the years, software companies have slowly been migrating away from using this term to describe their enterprise software suites, instead, choosing to use terms like supply chain software, enterprise system, or simply referring to their products as "solutions". Regardless of what they call it, these business software suites are still glorified accounting packages. That being said, having a glorified accounting package as your core business system is not a bad thing. Though ERP didn't live up to the hype (what does?), it does provide the company-wide integrated business software backbone it was intended to provide. That is, ERP provides the integrated transactional system and centralized database that is critical to an effective business system. Beyond this, ERP provides a variety of additional functionality related to managing, planning, and executing business activities. This additional functionality can vary greatly from one ERP system to another and is where many ERP systems fall short of user expectations. Though there certainly are some poorly designed software products out there, the functional deficiencies of ERP systems tend to be more the result of the near impossible task of trying to balance functionality with complexity within the context of an endless variety of business practices currently in use.

This brings me to another "benefit" of ERP that ultimately proves to be a double-edged sword. The claim that "ERP will help to standardize business practices" is undoubtedly true, however, it is debatable whether or not standardizing your business practices is good for your business. For the most part, ERP systems are designed around a core set of standard business practices and process flows. These "standard business practices" were obviously influenced by business practices that have been taught in business schools for decades (standardized accounting practices), but were also highly influenced by decisions made by those who pioneered the use of computers in business. These pioneers typically worked for very large manufacturing companies and therefore the standard practices were heavily influenced by these environments. As the business software industry grew, many new products were introduced, but they all tended to follow the initial business-practice roadmaps created by the earlier systems. This shouldn't be surprising since the key people in many of the new software companies were people who previously worked for one of the other software companies. While this core set of standardized business practices has evolved somewhat over the years, the changes have been rather minor.

Since ERP packages are built upon the assumption of "standard business practices", their functionality is severely limited when it comes to non-standard business practices. For companies implementing these systems, it forces them to either change their non-standard processes to work within the constraints of the system, modify the system, use a separate system for these processes, or develop offline workarounds. At a high level, changing the processes to work within what ERP considers standard business practices makes a lot of sense. Many businesses develop non-standard business practices as they grow, not because the practices were the best means of accomplishing the task, but rather, because those instituting the practices didn't know any better or simply didn't really think through the process. In these cases, adopting standard business practices

> ## ERP Systems \ Software Suites
>
> Fully integrated.
>
> Common database.
>
> Common user interface.
>
> Highly functional.
>
> Highly configurable.
>
> Standardized business practices.

may not only improve the process, but also can make it easier for new employees, customers, vendors, and other outside parties to interact with your processes.

On the flipside, many non-standard business practices are put in place because they are the best means of accomplishing a specific task in a specific environment. Remember, there is significant diversity in business and just because a practice works well for many businesses doesn't mean it will work well for all businesses. In some cases, changing these processes to fit the system may not be substantially less effective than the non-standard process. In other cases, you may find that standard practices simply don't apply or that the standard practice is so functionally deficient to the non-standard practice, that using it would create substantial additional costs or reduce your ability to meet business requirements. In my experience, most businesses will have at least one critical practice that falls into this latter category. This isn't to imply that they are doing something completely unique, but rather, they are doing something that is not common enough for ERP vendors to incorporate the functionality into their systems.

Generic or industry specific?

Though I'm quite certain you will not encounter a software vendor referring to his product as "generic", the term does arguably fit the type of ERP systems previously described. These systems are designed to work in a variety of industries (not necessarily all industries) and follow the standard-business-practice model. On the other hand, industry-specific software products have a much narrower focus and therefore are more likely to have functionality designed for non-standard business practices that are unique to their target industry. Certainly there are varying degrees of industry specificity; some products have a very narrow focus (such as a software product designed specifically for the construction equipment rental industry) while others will focus on a larger class of industries. Even the generic packages will have some industry specificity to them, in that they tend to be shaped over the years by the requirements of the industries they serve, although not with the same focus of a product designed for a single industry or small group of similar industries.

Even though industry-specific products are still based on standard business practices, they are based on standard business practices for a specific industry, which are not necessarily the same as standard business practices for general industry. The benefits of industry-specific software include functionality for non-standard business practices that are unique to an industry, and quicker, less expensive implementations. The reason industry-specific products are easier to implement is a result of a smaller set of configuration options. The idea is that since it is designed for a specific industry, there is no need to have functionality not common to that industry; and, since it doesn't have this additional functionality, it doesn't require the setup complexity of products designed for multiple industries.

As you may have guessed, the downside of industry-specific products is a lack of flexibility. If your business practices don't follow what the software vendor determined were standard business practices for your industry, it is highly unlikely the software will be configurable enough to meet your needs. As businesses grow, they often expand into other industries or adopt business practices from other industries. In these situations, you would be far more likely to find some of this added functionality in a generic software product than an industry-specific one. In other words, generic software products tend to have significantly more functionality than their industry-specific counterparts do. When using a generic product, you are generally utilizing only a small percentage of the overall functionality of the product, therefore, as you find a need for additional functionality that may not be commonly required in your industry, you are more likely to find it already exists in the generic product. Whereas, when using an industry-specific product, you are generally utilizing a larger percentage of the product's less extensive functionality and therefore have limited capabilities when it comes to incorporating business practices not common to that industry. I know it's a bit redundant, but it's an important point.

> ## Industry-specific software
>
> Focused on business practices of a specific industry.
>
> Quicker implementations due to fewer configuration options.
>
> Less likely to have functionality for business practices not common to the specific industry in which they are focused.

Though not universally true, the smaller your business is, the more likely you are to use an industry-specific product. Conversely, the larger your business is, the more likely you are to use a product focused on general industry or a larger class of industries. Some exceptions would include large businesses in industries with very unique business requirements (such as a large oil refinery) or small businesses in industries with very generic business practices (such as a general wholesale distributor).

Best of breed.

As previously discussed, software suites (ERP systems) are comprised of a set of modules. Each module encompasses a functional area of the business. For example, a software suite may offer financials, purchasing, inventory management, sales-order processing, distribution, warehouse management, and manufacturing as separate modules. This means you can purchase and implement only the modules you want (although there may be some dependencies). The term best of breed became widely used as people started realizing that certain modules within their software suite were inadequate to meet their needs, and started looking at separate software products to replace these modules. Software vendors, trade magazines, and consultants started using the term best of breed to categorize these highly functional, independent software modules (or sets of modules). The idea is that a single software suite cannot possibly have the best modules for every functional area of your business, therefore, rather than settling for the mediocre functionality in some modules just because you liked the functionality in other modules, you could build your system from the best modules from two or more software vendors. And purely from a functionality standpoint, this is a very valid consideration.

The downside to the best-of-breed approach is the need for integration with other modules, and the introduction of dissimilar user interfaces across modules. Though integration is getting easier, it is still a substantial undertaking and adds a level of risk related to data integrity. And, depending on how the modules are integrated, you may sacrifice some of the real-time data synchronicity across modules you would otherwise have with a fully integrated software suite from a single supplier. In addition, you now may have users that need to be trained on several user interfaces because their job requires them to use multiple modules that are not provided by the same software vendor. So weren't these the same reasons we had to all get off those legacy systems back in the 1980s and 1990s and get a fully-integrated enterprise system? You betcha. To be fair, integration capabilities today are far superior to those of decades past and user interfaces today tend to share more similarities than differences; but it is highly unlikely a best-of-breed approach will result in the same level of integration and ease of use as a packaged software suite from a single vendor.

> **Best-of-breed**
>
> By mixing modules from various vendors, you can get the functionality that best meets your specific needs.
>
> Will not have a common user interface.
>
> Integration can be problematic.

Software specific to inventory management.

The following are brief descriptions of software products and generalizations about the functionality they may provide. This is only meant to be a quick introduction to the variety of products and functionality offered. Some of this functionality will be covered in much greater detail in subsequent chapters. Also, be aware there are no firm standards for software functionality. Therefore just because a software vendor calls his software a demand planning/inventory optimization package doesn't mean it has the same functionality I consider part of a demand planning/inventory optimization package.

Basic inventory management.

This functionality comes with most software suites, and at a minimum will provide the ability to track inventory items (quantity and cost tracking) and link a supplier and a fixed reorder point to the item. In some small business software products, this is about all you get.

A little better inventory management.

This functionality would include the ability to utilize a forecast and to calculate a time-phased reorder point. It may provide some basic tools for generating the forecast and calculating order quantities (basic EOQ). This type of functionality should come with most software suites designed for all but the smallest businesses.

Demand planning / inventory optimization.

This functionality is most likely part of an add-on software product, but may be available as an option in a high-end software suite or one with a greater-than-average focus on inventory management. This functionality would include more advanced forecasting capabilities and more advanced calculations for determining order quantities and safety stock. It may or may not have the functionality to optimize inventory across multiple facilities.

Material requirements planning.

MRP is used in manufacturing operations to plan the component/raw materials inventory. The key to MRP is the calculations used to cascade demand through a bill-of-materials structure, and time-phase this demand based on time requirements for the manufacturing process. MRP functionality is very standardized and should be available for any software suite designed for manufacturers.

Manufacturing resource planning.

Also known as MRPII, manufacturing resource planning extends the capabilities of MRP to include capacity requirements planning (CRP) and master production scheduling (MPS).

Multi-plant planning.

Multi-plant MRP extends the planning capabilities of MRP to include planning across multiple facilities by utilizing plant relationships and lead times between plants. Distribution requirements planning (DRP) uses the same logic to plan across multiple facilities in a distribution environment. Multi-plant planning functionality provides the ability to time-phase demand across plants, but does not necessarily provide tools for generating forecasts or optimizing the inventory levels across plants.

Advanced planning and scheduling.

APS is most likely an add-on product but may be available with some higher-end software suites. APS is a step beyond MRPII and is somewhat more difficult to define, but generally includes capabilities for finite capacity scheduling and reacting to rapidly changing demand.

Supply-chain optimization.

Like advanced planning and scheduling, supply-chain optimization software is difficult to clearly define. The term generally implies considerable functionality related to inventory management, transportation management, and multi-facility planning. But, more importantly, it should include advanced optimization algorithms to optimize supply chain decisions by considering the key variables of a complex supply chain.

Desktop software.

In most environments, the starting points to effectively managing inventory include the ability to generate a reasonably accurate forecast, determine the lowest safety stock levels that meet your business requirements, and calculate cost-effective order quantities. Unfortunately, your business software (your specific glorified accounting package) likely does a lousy job or is totally incapable of doing these tasks. The reasons for this are mostly related to the diverse nature of inventory management needs resulting in the seemingly impossible task of creating single software programs that meet the needs of a variety of businesses. And, if you did create such a miracle program, the skill set required to set up and run it would likely be well beyond that of the intended users.

The good news is, the inventory management needs of a single business are dramatically less complex than the inventory management needs of all businesses. And, the tasks described above can be inexpensively accomplished with the help of desktop software and/or some custom programming. I frequently have people admit to me with a sense of shame that "we do our inventory management in spreadsheets". Well good for them. The fact is, spreadsheets are extremely powerful tools for making inventory management decisions, and there is no shame in using them. I think it would be more correct to say you should be ashamed if you are NOT utilizing a desktop spreadsheet program to help in your inventory management decision-making.

I have included spreadsheet examples throughout this book to help demonstrate the use of a desktop spreadsheet program in inventory management. I think you'll find that this not only helps in understanding the use of spreadsheet applications in managing inventory, but also greatly helps in understanding the calculations themselves. While there are other very capable spreadsheet programs, I have chosen to use Microsoft Excel for the examples in this book. Though the syntax and functions may be different in other spreadsheet programs, the core logic is still the same. But, before you go any further, I strongly recommend you first go to **www.inventoryexplained.com** to check for corrections, updates, and extras related to the examples in this book.

> *You should be ashamed if you are NOT utilizing a desktop spreadsheet program to help in your inventory management decision-making*

Spreadsheet modeling.

For the purposes of this book, a model is a mathematical representation of a business problem (a set of circumstances that require a decision to be made). Since businesses are expected to make money, many mathematical models used in business are cost-based models used to evaluate the financial impact of decisions. For example, if a small business needed to purchase a delivery truck to perform local deliveries, they may have several makes and models from which to choose. They could build a simple mathematical model that includes the cost of each truck combined with a depreciation schedule, the capacity (to determine the number of trips), the labor costs for a driver, the expected delivery distances and the expected fuel mileage. They could then use this model to show the financial impact of each vehicle over a period of several years. If they wanted to be more precise, they may also attempt to include ongoing maintenance costs, insurance costs, and expected resale value. To complicate things further, they should also evaluate purchase options versus lease options, new versus used, and even the option of outsourcing their deliveries to a trucking company.

A spreadsheet program is the perfect tool for this type of modeling. You simply place your costs and other variables in individual cells in the spreadsheet, and then begin to build your mathematical relationships. Though the total calculation requirements for the model may seem daunting, the spreadsheet allows you to build your model out of a series of smaller simple calculations. For example, you compare the number of pallets delivered each day to the capacity of each vehicle to determine the number of trips back to the warehouse to reload. Each return trip would add miles and time to the total daily mileage and labor. The total daily mileage will then be divided by the expected fuel mileage of each vehicle and multiplied by the expected cost per gallon of fuel. The labor hours would be multiplied by the labor rate (which may be different for different models of trucks). You do similar calculations for the other cost variables and then extend them to calculate total one-year, two-year, and three-year costs.

Spreadsheet modeling with optimization.

Simply put, optimization is the process of getting the "best" result from a stated problem. A typical optimization model would be made up of a value that you would like to optimize (minimize or maximize), one or more changeable values that have a mathematical relationship to the value you want to optimize, and one or more constraints (limits).

To demonstrate a total lack of imagination on my part, I will use the "product-mix decision" as an example (I believe the product-mix decision has been used as an example for optimization in every management science textbook published in the last fifty years). Though there are endless variations on the product-mix decision, it essentially involves a choice of products to make or purchase, where the different products have different profit potential and there are constraints present that prevent you from purchasing or manufacturing an unlimited supply. The constraints would be a limited amount of money to purchase the items or a limited amount of capacity to manufacture them, as well as the forecasted demand for each item. In other words, you cannot sell more than your customers are willing to buy or more than you can manufacturer or purchase. The value that you would want to optimize would be "profit". The mathematical relationships involved would include item costs, item sell price, capacity requirements (if manufactured), and possible relationships among products (for example, in order to sell one product you must also sell another product). As a quick side note, most of you will never actually use the classic product-mix decision. Though it sounds logical in text books, its practical use in general business is rather limited.

So far the math is pretty simple here. The quantity to make or buy multiplied by the difference between cost and sell price equals the gross profit for each item. The quantity to make or buy multiplied by the item cost results in the total cost (investment) for each item, and the quantity to make or buy multiplied by the item capacity requirements (per unit) results in the total capacity requirement for each item. We also know the maximum we can sell of each item (based upon forecast), any relationships between items, the total manufacturing capacity available, and/or the total amount of money we can invest. But how do we put this all together to calculate the specific product mix that provides the greatest profit? Hmm, let me think. Oh, I know, we can use spreadsheet modeling with optimization.

But wait, you say. I didn't explain the mathematical science behind optimizing the value? That's right; and I'm not going to. Well, not in the technical sense. That's because—thanks to readily available computer programs—you don't need to know the technical details of the various optimization algorithms in order to utilize spreadsheet modeling with optimization. You do, however, need to at least have a minimal understanding of the capabilities and limitations of the specific optimization program and settings you use.

There are numerous optimizations methods used in optimization programs. My understanding of these methods and programs is rather limited, but I'll take a shot at trying to give a rough explanation of them. Some methods use "conventional mathematics" to find the best solution to certain types of problems. These methods tend to provide highly accurate solutions, but are limited to certain types of problems. Other methods are more of a mathematically structured guessing program. They replace your variable data elements (the values you tell it that can be changed) with values (guesses), and then compare the change in the value of the data element you told it to optimize to see if the result is "better" or "worse" than the results received with other guesses. It then uses this to decide which "guesses" to try next. At some point, it will decide that it has a good answer (set of variables that provide a better enough answer when compared with other guesses that it decides to stop guessing).

Herein lies the tricky part. Depending upon the specific mathematical model (problem) and the optimization algorithm used, the "good" answer may or may not be the best answer. So how do you know if you are using the right optimization tool for your model? Well, to know with absolute certainty you would need an understanding of mathematics that is well beyond the scope of this book (and my capabilities). However, with some basic understanding of optimization and very thorough testing (an emphasis here is on the testing, which can help to compensate for a lack of complete understanding of the optimization tool and model being optimized), you may be able to effectively use these types of tools for inventory management decisions. Now I do need to warn here that you can also get into a lot of trouble playing with things you don't understand. But hell, that's half the fun.

The simplest optimization algorithms work best with smooth linear relationships. An example of a smooth linear relationship would be the relationship of freight costs to order quantity when freight costs are a simple fixed cost per pound. As the order quantity increases, so does the freight cost; and, if graphed, the lines would follow the same pattern. But if the freight cost per pound was not fixed and instead dropped at specific points (for example the cost per pound was less after 50 lbs, 100 lbs, etc.) and your supplier offered you free freight on orders over a specific amount, you no longer have the same simple linear relationship. The free-freight example is especially tricky in an optimization algorithm because it uses a conditional statement in the mathematical model. A conditional statement means that something happens only if a specific condition exists, otherwise something else or nothing happens. This is commonly known as IF-THEN-ELSE logic. In the free-freight example, the statement may go something like IF the order amount is greater than $500, THEN freight cost = 0, ELSE freight cost = units multiplied by unit weight multiplied by cost per pound.

A simple linear optimization algorithm will not work with a conditional statement (at least that has been my experience). This is where more advanced algorithms such as genetic or evolutionary algorithms can be tried. But more importantly, this is where your thorough testing of the output of the specific optimization algorithms against your model should tell you whether or not the algorithm is working. Just because a program spits out a solution, does not mean that it worked (well, technically it worked but that doesn't mean it provided an optimal solution). Testing the output can include trying to manually find a better solution and/or comparing the outputs of several different optimization algorithms to see if they find the same solution.

The programs commonly used to perform optimization within a spreadsheet program are actually add-ins designed to be used with the specific spreadsheet program you are using. Microsoft Excel comes with an add-in called Solver, which is a "lite" version of the commercially available Solver program produced by Frontline Systems, Inc. To install the add-in click Tools>Add-Ins> Solver Add-in in Excel 2003 or earlier, or Office Button>Excel Options>Add-Ins>Manage Excel Options>Go>Solver Add-in in Excel 2007 or later. The version that comes with Excel has limited functionality but gives you a good idea how to use a spreadsheet optimization program. If you're serious about using spreadsheet modeling with optimization you will probably want to purchase the full version of Solver or a similar product (Palisade Corporation has an advanced optimization add-in product called Evolver). But be aware, the more advanced optimization programs are also more complex.

We'll cover the use of spreadsheet modeling with optimization again in the chapter on order quantities / lot sizing.

Spreadsheet statistical tools.

Spreadsheet programs contain a significant number of statistical functions that can also be very useful in inventory management. We will cover these in more detail in the chapters on forecasting and calculating safety stock.

Data analysis tools.

Data analysis is a critical part of managing inventory. Modern business software systems contain massive amounts of transactional and descriptive data that can be incredibly useful in making inventory management decisions. Unfortunately, most inventory management professionals lack the motivation and skills to properly access and analyze this data. Note that I said "lack the motivation and skills" and not "lack the tools". The tools are there just waiting to be used. Most business software products come with at least some simple reporting or querying capabilities. On top of that there are add-on custom reporting and query programs (such as Crystal Reports), and data analysis tools in desktop products (such as Microsoft Access) and—of course—your favorite spreadsheet program. Most current business software products will provide ways for either directly accessing the data or exporting the data to these types of desktop applications.

A lack of adequate data analysis is a bit of a pet peeve of mine. I've frequently gone into companies and sat in a conference room for hours taking notes as the people responsible for making decisions in the company describe the intricacies of their inventory and operations to me. I then ask for a data dump and do some analysis on my own and frequently find that their descriptions don't jive with the data. In some cases the differences are minor yet still important, while in others, the differences between what they think and what is actually occurring (according to the data) are significant.

So how can these people be making business decisions without understanding the business? Easy, they don't know that they don't understand the business so they just chug along making bad decisions and blaming poor results on circumstances beyond their control. Alright, maybe I'm being a bit too sarcastic here, but the data is there and the tools are there so please Use Them! And no, you don't need to invest in a "data warehouse" or "business intelligence" software to be able to pull meaningful information from your data. In fact, if you can't scrounge up enough initiative to utilize your current data-analysis tools, I doubt that a more advanced analysis toolset would be anything more than a pretty new icon on your computer desktop. Oops, there goes that sarcasm again.

Does this mean I will be manually performing all these inventory management tasks in desktop programs?

Probably not. In some cases, your volume may be so low that it makes sense to just occasionally perform some of these tasks manually in a spreadsheet or other desktop program. In others, you will find that you can have someone with some programming knowledge introduce some simple scripting that can help to automate the task within the desktop applications. In still others, you will take the logic of the desktop application and have a programmer create or modify a program to fully automate the task within your inventory management system.

People sometimes start to cringe when I start talking about custom programming for their inventory system. The fact is, custom programming does not have to be expensive. Certainly programming time can be expensive, but it does not have to take a lot of programming time to write a program. In fact, the reason custom programming is often expensive is more related to a lack of clear specifications than to the amount of actual time needed to design and write the program. Programmers can spend a significant amount of time trying to figure out what it is you want—or will want after you figure out what you asked for doesn't really meet your needs. That's where your desktop spreadsheet model comes into play. If you built the model and tested it and tweaked it, and retested it and retweaked it, you should have a pretty good idea if it meets your needs. In addition, your model clearly shows the inputs, outputs, and everything that happens in between. A programmer couldn't ask for anything more—though you probably won't hear him admit it. Even if you based your model around an optimization add-in program, many of these spreadsheet add-ins are also available as part of a developer tool that programmers can incorporate into a custom program (so they don't have to recreate from scratch the optimization algorithm you used).

I think it's extremely wasteful to start to spec out a custom program if you haven't first tested the calculations against your actual data first. And the easiest way to do this is in a desktop application such as a spreadsheet program.

A note on zeros.

Some of the calculations we use in inventory management don't like zeros. Any regular user of spreadsheet programs has probably encountered a "divide by zero" error at some point. When you are putting together your calculations, you need to keep this in mind whenever a zero or null value is possible for a variable. In most cases you will probably just want to add a simple IF statement saying that if the value is zero, do this, otherwise do this. In an effort to try to keep the calculations in this book reasonably simple (to better communicate the logic behind the various methods) I will not be including this (or other validations) in every calculation that may encounter zeros.

Negative values are another issue with some calculations. Once again, I may not include references about how to handle negatives in specific calculations, so you need to keep in mind that if negative values are possible, you need to set up your calculations to handle them appropriately for your requirements.

What's good enough?

One of the most difficult questions to answer related to business decision-making is "How far do you go?" There can be seemingly endless variables that may potentially impact inventory management decisions. In the following chapters, we will cover a variety of calculations and analysis methods used to help make these decisions. As you read on, you may notice that I have a propensity for taking a seemingly simple calculation and exposing a much greater level of complexity. In fact, much of this book is dedicated to pointing out complexities that are often overlooked in typical inventory management education programs. But you should also notice there are points at which I just stop further expanding the complexity of a specific solution. That's because there are practical limitations as to just how far you take a solution—as well as limitations as to just how much I can stuff into this book.

When evaluating techniques for managing your inventory you need to make decisions related to the potential benefits of the techniques. More complex techniques usually require more time and effort to implement and manage. This time and effort translates into added costs for the business. If these added costs exceed the incremental cost savings gained from the use of the technique, it would not be wise to use the technique—even though it is a "better" technique. Since these techniques are generally implemented in the form of software (either purchased software packages or modifications to existing systems), you need to determine the level of software support that is appropriate for your business. For a very small business, some relatively simple calculations performed in a desktop spreadsheet program may be all that is warranted. On the other hand, a very large complex business may be able to justify a multi-million dollar optimization solution to effectively manage their supply chain. It may be that the multi-million dollar optimization solution is only 5% more effective at managing inventory than what could be done with more basic software, however that 5% improvement is huge when you are dealing with many millions of dollars in inventory.

Fortunately, many of these technique/system decisions can be made on an incremental basis. In my experience, most companies can gain significant improvement in inventory management with relatively minor software modifications, and even through the use of separate calculations in desktop spreadsheet programs. As should be obvious by now, I am a strong proponent of inventory managers first testing potential techniques in a spreadsheet program. This allows you to more quickly and economically assess the potential value of the change, as well as work the bugs out of the calculations. If the savings are proven, you can then implement the techniques in the form of a modification or software purchase. In reality, there is not much that cannot be tested in a spreadsheet program. The only difference between calculations in the spreadsheet program and those in your primary inventory management software is the automation and direct access to your system data.

The reality is, the systems we use to manage our inventories are flawed. In the following chapters, I will point out many of these flaws and offer solutions to some of them. My intent here is not to push you towards a "perfect" system, nor is it to discourage you from using a flawed system. Instead, it's to help you understand the flaws, and to help you determine the appropriate level of imperfection for your specific environment.

And while I accept and even promote imperfect practices, there are practices that I feel are so flawed that I don't think anyone who is serious about managing their inventory should be using them, or are so misunderstood that I think far too many people are misusing them. Surprisingly, some of these practices are very commonly used (or misused) and promoted in inventory management, and you will see that I don't mince words when discussing them. Some may even feel that my approach towards those who use or promote these practices is a bit harsh. Well, get over it. There are some practices that are simply ridiculous, and if the logic I present isn't enough to keep people from using them, I'm not averse to shaming people into more effectively managing their inventory.

So I guess what I am really saying is there is a level that I feel should not be acceptable for any business, beyond that, "good enough" is different for different operations, but is also not static. As technology changes, as your business changes, as your expertise changes, and as you experience successes and failures with current systems, your definition of "good enough" will also change. You should not assume that just because you are a large company, you must have a highly sophisticated inventory management system, nor should you assume that just because you are a small company, you are relegated to using very simplistic inventory management techniques. In addition, you should not be content that what is good enough today will be good enough tomorrow, nor should you get overwhelmed in trying to build the perfect inventory management system your first time out. You'll find that evolution tends to ultimately provide a better result than revolution.

A note on "cheats".

Though mathematics by its very nature is considered a precise science, a particular mathematical calculation is not necessarily precise or even logical. It's very important to understand this since inventory management is full of what I refer to as "cheats". These include mathematical calculations designed to provide a particular wanted result, but the means of getting that result may not be mathematically correct or even logical. In some cases these cheats are used because a mathematically correct means of getting the result is impractical due to significant data requirements, processing limitations, or a lack of mathematical knowledge by those setting up the system (we all have our limitations). In other cases, there simply is no mathematically correct means of getting the result.

Cheats (as I describe them) are not necessarily bad things. In fact, they can be very useful and even necessary in inventory management. My point in referring to them as cheats, is to make it very clear that there likely is a lack of preciseness associated with them and they may even be completely wrong (or wrong for your application). People often see a mathematical formula in an inventory book and incorrectly assume it to be both precise and logical simply because it is expressed as a mathematical formula and it is in a book. They then proceed to start using the calculation and potentially making a mess of their inventory system because they don't understand what it is they are implementing. I will revisit the topic of cheats throughout this book as a way of pointing out logic or calculations that deserve some level of scrutiny. Don't assume them to be wrong; just don't assume them to be correct either.

The changing role of inventory managers...

First, let me apologize for the heading of this section. I know whenever I see a magazine article that starts out with "The changing role of …", I can usually assume the article will contain more hype than substance and is likely not worth the effort required to read it. However, in the case of those responsible for managing inventory, their roles must change to take advantage of advances in technology.

Inventory management consists of a series of decisions. At the top levels, these decisions relate to choosing inventory strategies, designing distribution networks, and setting inventory policies. In the middle, are decisions related to system setup, lot-sizing, forecasting methods, replenishment methods, and safety stock. At the most detailed level, these decisions are related to whether or not on a given day you need to order a given item, and, if so, how much should be ordered.

Currently, most of the labor investment in inventory management is focused on this execution-level decision-making. This daily, time/item dependent decision-making is where inventory planners are spending most of their time. What companies need to realize is these are the types of decisions that are easily handled by computers. These high-volume, highly repetitive mathematical decisions are where computers excel. Sure, inventory planners are using their computers to assist in this task, but ultimately, far too many of these daily decisions are being made—or individually reviewed—by human beings.

The changing role requires inventory planners to migrate their efforts from the daily execution decisions to the mid-level system setup and control decisions. They should be conducting group-level (I'm referring to groups of items) analysis and making group-level decisions related to how the system will treat the individual items within these groups. They then need to let the system execute the bulk of the daily decision-making. Humans should only interact with this daily execution on an exception basis.

What are the benefits of this? These changes focus on utilizing information technology to not only better manage inventory, but also to do it faster at a lower cost. This is what computers are good at. Rather than having the computer tell you when a task needs to be done, you describe to the computer (through system and item setup) how to make the inventory decisions and how to perform the tasks, and then let the computer do it.

So why is this not happening? It's a combination of "this is how we've always done it" thinking, distrust of computer systems, lack of management focus, lack of knowledge of inventory systems, and lack of the short-term resources required to conduct the initial analysis and setup. Contrary to popular belief, it is not the result of inadequate computer capabilities. Most mid to high-end business software products already have these capabilities and many lower-cost products do as well.

> *The changing role requires inventory planners to migrate their efforts from the daily execution decisions to the mid-level system setup and control decisions.*

The scope of this book.

Up to this point I've provided a general overview of inventory management. While many of these topics deserve a more in-depth treatment, to do so would result in a book so massive that I doubt too many of you would ever actually read it. This book focuses on the planning aspects of inventory management (forecasting, calculating safety stock, calculating lot sizes, and ordering systems) and I think you will soon realize why I found it important to narrow the focus to these critical topics. The first two chapters are primarily here to provide context for the remainder of the book.

My intent with the following chapters is to provide enough detailed information on the key topics to allow you to develop a true understanding of these topics. Learning a little terminology and some simple calculations is not what I consider "understanding". There are far too many books that quickly gloss over key topics, leaving the reader knowing just enough to be dangerous. Understanding a topic means you no longer need to accept standard business practices or recommendations made by "experts" at face value. Understanding a topic means you are capable of identifying the potential problems and advantages of whatever "new" technique or strategy is thrown at you. Understanding a topic means you can start to develop your own solutions that take into account your own specific business needs.

And while much of this book seems to focus on the solutions (the actual calculations used to make inventory management decisions), the truth is, I am using my explanations of the solutions to help describe the requirements of the problem. Therefore, even if you choose not to use a specific solution I describe, you should have gained a much better understanding of the problem itself, and should be able to use that understanding to evaluate or develop other solutions.

I'm also hoping that as your eyes are opened to the complexity of the topics I cover here, you will use this experience to better prepare yourself as you tackle other related topics. As I said before, inventory management is not simple. If it were, more companies would be good at it.

3

Forecasting Part 1:
Basic Concepts and Techniques

It all starts with the forecast. Now some of you may be thinking, "but we don't forecast". I frequently run into this comment, so let me explain forecasting a little more. Whenever you procure or manufacture inventory without having pre-existing firmly-booked demand (such as actual customer orders), you are forecasting. If an office worker notices that he is running low on paperclips and decides to pick up more at the office supply store, he is forecasting. He has decided that he does not have enough paperclips to last until his next opportunity to go to the office supply store. In order to determine that he does not have enough, he must predict how many he will use in that period of time. Though he may not have performed a precise calculation or even realized he was performing any type of calculation, this is a forecast. If an inventory planner orders more inventory when inventory drops below a preset order point, he is using a forecast. In this case, the forecast is represented by the order point. The order point states a quantity whereby anything less may not be enough to last until the next opportunity for an order. Again, this is a forecast. If an inventory planner uses an average demand quantity (average monthly demand, average weekly demand, etc.) to make inventory ordering decisions, he is also using a forecast. In this case, the forecast assumes the future will be the same as the past (average demand quantity).

So, even though these may not represent formal forecasting processes, they are still forecasts. Unfortunately, the use of informal forecasts—such as someone looking at a quantity and deciding, "We need more"—tend to be problematic due to a lack of consistency or sound quantitative-based logic. If you were to review informal planning decisions from three planners using the same data, you will likely find three different planning decisions. At best, only one of these decisions is an optimal decision, at worst, all are ineffective. This is not to say there is no place for judgment in forecasting and planning decisions, but rather, you should not rely on individual judgment when you can more effectively calculate the decision. Over the next few chapters, we will be covering more formal forecasting techniques.

Before we get into specific forecasting techniques, we need to cover some terminology and some generalizations relative to forecasting.

Forecasting terminology.

Forecast period.

A forecast period is a specific span of time described by a forecast quantity. For example, if I forecast demand of 500 units each week for the next six weeks, each week is a separate forecast period. Forecast periods are sometimes referred to as "time buckets", though that can get confusing since some systems have time buckets that are different from the forecast period.

Forecast interval.

A forecast interval is the length of time over which each forecast period is based. If I use the previous example, the forecast interval is seven days (one week). Forecast intervals usually follow standard cumulative measures of time (years, quarters, months, weeks, days). There is not a single best forecast interval for all forecasting applications. The term forecast interval is sometimes used inter-changeably with forecast period because the descriptions are similar. To clarify, forecast interval is the length of time each forecast period is based on.

Forecast horizon.

The forecast horizon is the length of time into the future over which the forecast is based. Forecast horizons vary greatly based on the characteristics of the product, the supply chain, and manufacturing process. As a general guideline, your fore-cast horizon must be at least as long as the cumulative lead time of the product being forecast. But, forecast horizons beyond the cumulative lead time may be needed to plan for lot sizing, manufacturing capacity, cash flow, facilities, labor, etc. You may even have different forecast horizons (and use different forecasting techniques) depending upon the intended use of the forecast (short term inventory planning versus long term facilities planning). Some definitions of forecast horizon would also include the period of time into the past over which historical demand was used to produce the forecast. This can get confusing when using forecasting techniques such as exponential smoothing; so, for the purposes of this text, we will only consider future time periods as part of the forecast horizon.

If you are a little confused about the difference between forecast period, forecast interval, and forecast horizon, think of it this way. If today is December 31st and I have calculated a forecast for each month through June, then my forecast horizon is six months, my forecast interval is 1 month, and January's forecast would be an example of a specific forecast period.

Forecast basis.

This is the data and information that is used to produce the forecast. In most cases, this is the historical demand for the product.

Forecast consumption.

Forecast consumption is the process of depleting the forecast as actual orders are received. For example, if I have a forecast of 1,000 units for the month of May and receive a firm order in April for 300 units to ship in May, my inventory system needs to know how to calculate total demand. If I tell the computer to reduce the forecast by the actual order quantity, this is known as consuming the forecast. If I don't consume the forecast, the system will treat this as a total of 1,300 units demand. Forecast consumption options may also include the ability to have demand from one period consume the forecast in previous or subsequent periods.

Trend.

Trend is a gradual increase or decrease in demand over a period of time. Graphically represented, trend will appear as a straight line or curve. For example, if you have experienced a five percent increase in sales each of the last three years, you have experienced a straight-line trend (depending on how you calculated the increase percentage). If you experienced sales increases of two percent, five percent, and nine percent respectively over three years, you have experienced a curved-line trend. The value of identifying a trend lies in extending the line to project future sales.

Seasonality.

Seasonality describes fluctuations in demand that repeat with the same pattern over equivalent time periods. The most common representation of seasonality occurs with changing demand patterns measured weekly, monthly, or quarterly, that repeat annually. For example, demand for ice cream is greater in the summer months than winter months.

Noise.

Noise is the unpredictable variation in demand. The best way to describe noise would be to create a hypothetical product that is not subject to seasonality and has not experienced any trend (annual sales have been flat). I should mention that I have never run across a product that was not subject to some level of seasonality or trend. Anyway, back to our hypothetical product, since we sold 5200 units last year, we can expect to sell 5200 units this year (remember sales are flat), and if we expect to sell 5200 units this year and there is no seasonality, we should expect weekly sales to be 100 units (5200 units divided by 52 weeks). When we monitor actual sales for three weeks we see we have sales of 87 units, 118 units, and 95 units, respectively. These variances of 13 units, 18 units, and 5 units are known as noise because they represent random variability in demand that does not follow a predictable pattern (such as seasonality or trend).

Level (also known as normalized demand or base demand).

Level is your starting point for a forecast. It can be a confusing term because people sometimes think of it as a flat line, when in reality level changes over time (the result of trend). I find it's easiest to think of level as your current demand after seasonality and noise have been removed. You will subsequently adjust your level by future expectations of trend and seasonality to produce your final forecast.

Forecasting generalizations.

Now that we've gotten the terminology down, let's cover some forecasting generalizations. These generalizations are often referred to as "Rules" though I prefer not to think of them as absolutes. To better describe these generalizations, I'm going to use weather forecasts as an analogy.

Forecasts are always wrong?

This is by far the most repeated and most abused "rule" of forecasting. Consultants, instructors, and practitioners just love to repeat this whenever the topic of forecasting comes up. They sometimes enunciate it as though it were some cosmic truth the rest of us have somehow missed. My problem with this statement is twofold. First, it sometimes frightens decision-makers away from utilizing forecasts to their fullest potential. Second, I have repeatedly heard this used by consultants to preach the evils of MRP (discussed later). The statement usually goes something like this, "MRP is forecast driven therefore it is flawed from the outset". Gimme a break! Of course MRP has flaws, just as every alternative to MRP has flaws. This doesn't mean you shouldn't use them. And certainly forecasting is imperfect, but to say that a forecast is always wrong is a bit of an overstatement. If a weather forecast predicts that it will be sunny with a high of 75 degrees and winds out of the South, and it ends up being sunny with a high of 73 degrees and winds shifting from South to Southeast, do we say the forecast was wrong? Does imperfection in weather forecasting make it of no value? Of course not. Every estimation of future events has some level of uncertainty. If I forecast sales of 200 units for a given week and actual sales ends up being 185 units, I think you'll agree that even though the actual sales quantity did not match exactly, it still came relatively close to the forecast quantity. And while the forecast was not absolutely accurate, designating it as being wrong does not adequately describe the situation. Therefore, rather than saying forecasts are always wrong, we'll say all forecasts have some level of uncertainty.

Forecasts are more accurate at the aggregate level than at the detail level.

There is a greater risk of uncertainty as a forecast is broken down into greater levels of detail. Using the weather analogy, you would likely be more accurate at forecasting the total rainfall for a specific month than you would for each day of the month. Or, you could more accurately forecast the number of tornados to occur in the state of Oklahoma in a given year than you could forecast the number of tornadoes to occur in each county or city. With inventory forecasts, this means you will likely be more accurate at forecasting groups of items than individual items, and monthly sales than daily sales. For a more specific example, an electronics store will likely be more accurate at forecasting sales of all TVs than sales of 27-inch TVs, or all models of 27-inch TVs than each specific model of 27-inch TVs. Now before you start thinking that you should be focusing all your efforts on aggregate forecasting, you need to realize that forecasts tend to be more useful at the detail level. Once again, inventory managers need to balance conflicting factors and decide which level of forecasting is most appropriate for the given task.

Forecasts are more accurate for nearer time periods.

Uncertainty increases the further an event occurs in the future. Back to the weather analogy, the first day in a seven-day forecast will likely be more accurate than the seventh day. In inventory management, the first week in a multi-week forecast horizon will likely be more accurate than the second, the second more accurate than the third, etc. This is one forecast generalization that is well understood but sometimes underappreciated. Since forecasts are less accurate the further into the future the time period occurs, inventory management decisions will also be less accurate if they are based on forecasts further in the future. This helps to show the benefits of shorter lead times. So for those of you looking to increase forecast accuracy, reduce inventory, and just plain make life easier, you should be looking good and hard at your lead times and investigating what can be done to reduce them.

Mathematical forecasting methods.

Now that we've gotten the formalities out of the way, it's time to start covering some specific forecasting methods.

Last-period demand.

The simplest of techniques is that of using demand from the previous period to forecast demand for subsequent periods. For example, if last week's demand was 250 units, I would assume that next week's demand would also be 250 units. Ah, if only it were that simple. The problems with last-period demand include an inability to remove noise from the forecast and a tendency to lag in both trend and seasonality. The severity of these problems will vary based on the amount of noise, trend, and seasonality present as well as the length of the forecast interval. A longer forecast interval will naturally reduce the amount of noise but increase the effect of a lag in trend and seasonality. If we use weekly demand of 87 units, 118 units, and 95 units, you can see that a last-period demand would leave you significantly short during the second week (87 units would have been forecasted for the week that resulted in 118 units demand).

Last-period demand							
	Week 1	Week 2	Week 3	Week 4	Week 5	Week 6	Week 7
Demand	270	235	286	301	270	315	
Forecast		270	235	286	301	270	315

Figure 3A. All we're doing here is setting the forecast equal to the demand for the previous week.

Last-relative-period demand.

Also a very simple technique, last-relative-period demand uses the relative period (usually from the previous year) to forecast demand. For example, where last-period demand would use January's demand to forecast February's demand, last-relative-period demand would use February's demand from the previous year to forecast February's demand for the current year. Last-relative-period demand naturally accounts for seasonality, but still does not remove noise or account for trend.

Last-relative-period demand						
	January	February	March	April	May	June
2009 Demand	857	795	804	957	1126	1078
2010 Forecast	857	795	804	957	1126	1078

Figure 3B. Here we simply set our 2010 monthly forecast equal to the monthly demand from 2009.

Moving average.

The moving average is probably the most well known forecasting method. Whenever you base planning decisions on an average demand number, you are almost certainly using the output from a moving average calculation. A moving average calculates the average demand over a fixed period of time relative to the date the forecast is generated. For example, if I am calculating a three-month moving average on July 1st, I will calculate the average demand over April, May, and June. Subsequently, on August 1st, I would use May, June, and July demand for the calculation. In a simple moving average forecast, the forecasted demand for each subsequent period within the forecast horizon will be the same (the moving average).

The assumption of a moving average forecast is that future demand will be the same as recent demand. Moving average does a good job of removing noise, but will lag in trend and either lag or totally ignore seasonality. This varies based upon the number of previous periods and the forecast interval used for the forecast. If I use a three-week moving average, I will eliminate some of the noise and only slightly lag in trend and seasonality. However, if I use a twelve-month moving average, I will significantly eliminate noise but will have a substantial lag in trend and have no allowance for seasonality.

Three-week moving average							
	Week 1	Week 2	Week 3	Week 4	Week 5	Week 6	Week 7
Demand	270	235	286	301	270	315	
Forecast				264	274	286	295

Figure 3C. Here you can see the forecast for week #4 is the average of demand from weeks #1, #2, and #3. The forecast for week #5 is then the average of demand for weeks #2, #3, and #4. If you were to set this up in Excel, with the week #1 demand of 270 in cell B3, the formula you would enter for the week #4 forecast would be =AVERAGE(B3:D3)

Weighted moving average.

A weighted moving average seeks to take advantage of the noise-reducing properties of a moving average while increasing its ability to accommodate trend and seasonality (though it will still lag both). In a standard moving average calculation, all periods are treated equally (given equal weight). With weighted moving average, you are allowed to apply varying degrees of importance (weight) to the periods. In a standard moving average calculation, you simply sum the demand for the periods and then divide by the number of periods. You could restate this equation as dividing the number 1 by the number of periods and then multiplying each period's demand by the resulting fraction. For example, in a four-period moving average, you would divide 1 by 4 (resulting in 0.25) and multiply each period's demand by this number, and then add the results together to get your forecast.

With a weighted moving average, rather than multiplying each previous period's demand by the same factor, you could use a larger number for some periods and a smaller number for others. This is known as weighting the periods. The sum of the weights for all periods must be equal to one (the number 1). So where a four-period moving average used the same weight for all periods (0.25 + 0.25 + 0.25 + 0.25 = 1), a weighted moving average allows a variety of weights to be used, provided they total 1. Examples would include using 0.20 for the first three periods and using 0.40 for the final period (0.20 + 0.20 + 0.20 + 0.40 = 1) or using 0.15 for the first period, 0.20 for the second, 0.30 for the third, and 0.35 for the fourth (0.15 + 0.20 + 0.30 + 0.35 = 1). A three-period moving average may use 0.25 for the first period, 0.32 for the second, and 0.43 for the third (0.25 + 0.32 + 0.43 = 1).

The objective of the weighted moving average is to apply greater weight on nearer periods, thus maintaining more of the effects of trend and seasonality from recent periods. However, since it is solely based on recent periods, it is not actually projecting trend or seasonality, only repeating a portion of what has already occurred (lagging). And the greater the difference between the weighting of periods, the greater risk of noise impacting the forecast.

Three-week weighted moving average (0.20 , 0.30 , 0.50)							
	Week 1	Week 2	Week 3	Week 4	Week 5	Week 6	Week 7
Demand	270	235	286	301	270	315	
Forecast				268	283	283	299

Figure 3D. Here we have a three-week weighted moving average using weights of 0.20, 0.30, and 0.50 respectively. If you were to set this up in Excel, with the week #1 demand of 270 in cell B3, the formula you would enter for the week #4 forecast would be =(B3*0.2)+(C3*0.3)+(D3*0.5)

Exponential smoothing.

Now we're getting fancy. Well, not really. Exponential smoothing is a great example of something that sounds far more complicated than it actually is. Exponential smoothing is essentially a variation of weighted moving average; in fact, because it has fewer inputs, exponential smoothing is easier to calculate than a weighted moving average. This is because you need not maintain any data beyond the previous period's demand and the previous period's forecast for simple exponential smoothing to work. This minimal data requirement has historically given exponential smoothing a significant advantage over other methods (such as moving averages and weighted moving averages). Since advancements in computer technology have greatly increased both processing capacity and storage capacity, these advantages are no longer a significant issue—though programmers still like it for its simplicity.

The only data inputs to the exponential smoothing calculation are the previous period's demand, the previous period's forecast, and a smoothing factor (also known as a smoothing constant). The smoothing factor is a number between zero and one (0.01, 0.02, . . . 0.99) that is used to weight the most recent period's demand against the forecast for that period to produce the next period's forecast. This is very similar to the weighting conducted in the weighted moving average calculation. The primary difference here is that rather than applying additional weights against a fixed number of previous demand periods in the calculation, you simply use the previous period's forecast to represent the additional historical demand. This works because the previous period's forecast is essentially a calculation of previous demand. Since, as in the weighted moving average calculation, the sum of the weights must equal the number 1, and you are only applying weights to two numbers (previous period's demand and previous period's forecast), the calculation will automatically calculate the weight to apply to the previous period's forecast by subtracting the smoothing factor from the number 1.

Confused yet? Here's an example. April sales forecast was for 1000 units, actual April sales were 1200 units, and the smoothing factor was set at 0.20. I would multiply 1200 by 0.20 resulting in 240, then multiply 1000 units by 0.80 (1 minus 0.20) resulting in 800. I would then add 240 to 800 to get my exponentially smoothed forecast of 1040 for the next period. Now, if the next period's actual sales were 1100, I would start the process again by multiplying 1100 by 0.20 and adding it to the result of multiplying 1040 by 0.80. This gives me the next period's forecast of 1052.

You may be wondering where the original forecast for April came from. With exponential smoothing, you need to start with an initial forecast. In most cases, you will just use the previous period's sales as the forecast to start the exponential smoothing process. Since it takes several periods for the smoothing to become effective, you should go several periods into history to initialize the exponential smoothing process. The amount of time you need to go back is relative to the smoothing factor used. As a general guideline, you should divide the number one by the smoothing factor, and then go back at least this many periods (usually add a couple of periods to the result). For example, if my smoothing factor is 0.20, I would go back at least five periods (1 divided by 0.20 equals 5) so that a reasonable amount of smoothing has taken place prior to the forecast that will be used. Remember, this is just used to start the process; once your calculation is up and running, all you need is the previous period's forecast and previous period's demand to calculate your forecast.

Exponential smoothing (smoothing factor 0.30)							
0.30	Week 1	Week 2	Week 3	Week 4	Week 5	Week 6	Week 7
Demand	270	235	286	301	270	315	
Forecast		270	260	267	278	275	287

Figure 3E. Here we have an example of exponential smoothing using a smoothing factor of 0.30. If you were to set this up in Excel, with the week #1 demand of 270 in cell B3, you would need to start by plugging the week #2 forecast (make it equal to the demand from week #1). You can see I put the smoothing factor of 0.30 in a cell (it would be cell A2 in Excel). This allows me to reference it in my formula. I can now set the formula for my week #3 forecast to =(C3*$A2)+(C4*(1-$A2)) . The $ is in there because I want to be able to copy and paste my formula for the week #3 forecast (cell D4) into my subsequent forecast cells (cells E4 through H4), but don't want the reference to cell A2 to change (this is known as an absolute cell reference).

As with the factors used in a weighted moving average, the smoothing factor used in exponential smoothing determines how much smoothing occurs. In fact, if you were switching from a weighted moving average to exponential smoothing, you would likely start by using the weighting factor for the most recent period's demand from your weighted moving average calculation as the smoothing factor for your exponential smoothing calculation. A low smoothing factor will result in a highly smoothed (significant amount of noise removed) forecast, however, it will also be very slow to react to changing demand patterns. Alternately, a high smoothing factor will react quickly to changing demand patterns but will be highly susceptible to noise.

The previous example is the simplest form of exponential smoothing. As with the other forecasting techniques discussed, simple exponential smoothing forecasts will also lag changes in demand that result from trend or seasonality. Over the years, numerous variations of exponential smoothing have been used to help account for this deficiency. Among these are double exponential smoothing, triple exponential smoothing, adaptive smoothing, and the lesser known double-secret exponential smoothing (highly touted by Dean Wormer of Faber College, although the actual calculation has never been revealed). Exponential smoothing variations will be discussed in greater detail in subsequent chapters.

The most interesting—though admittedly not very important—characteristic of an exponentially smoothed forecast is the fact that all previous demand (since the initiation of the exponential smoothing process) has a potential impact on the current forecast. For example, if I started using exponential smoothing on an item back in 1975, that 35-year-old demand is still part of my 2010 forecast (assuming I am still selling the same item). Did I hear a "You're freakin' me out, man"? Are you gettin' bummed because your forecasts are based on a time when 8-track tapes and pastel-colored double-knit polyester leisure suits were popular? Well mellow out dude, it's not like that old demand is totally bogarting your new forecast. In reality, that 30-year-old demand has such a light weighting applied to it (that's the whole "exponential" part of exponential smoothing) that its true impact would likely be imperceptible—though it could theoretically occasionally affect the rounding up or down to the nearest whole unit.

Seasonality and seasonality indexes.

I have yet to encounter a business that did not have some level of seasonality. Anytime you have changing demand patterns that repeat based upon fixed time cycles, you have seasonality. While snow shovels, school supplies, and air conditioners are obvious candidates for seasonality, you will also likely have seasonality with less obvious items such as medical supplies, automotive supplies, or aluminum poles (during Festivus). So why would medical supplies be seasonal? Certain types of injuries such as sport-related injuries, insect bites/stings, and sunburns are more likely during certain times of the year. Certain infectious diseases such as the flu or colds are more likely to occur during certain times of the year. In addition, certain types of elective surgery such as cosmetic surgery or joint replacement are more likely to occur during the winter months in preparation for the summer.

You also have seasonality related to business cycles and business measures. Budgetary cycles usually result in greater expenditures at the beginning (money just became available) and end (spend it or lose it) of the cycle. Time-based incentive programs (annual, quarterly, monthly) will often cause peaks at the end of each time period as customers or sales reps seek to meet a specific incentive level. Re-

Example of weighting resulting from exponential smoothing (smoothing factor 0.20)		
Period	Weight	Cumulative Weight
Current Period	20.000000000%	20.000000000%
Period -1	16.000000000%	36.000000000%
Period -2	12.800000000%	48.800000000%
Period -3	10.240000000%	59.040000000%
Period -4	8.192000000%	67.232000000%
Period -5	6.553600000%	73.785600000%
Period -6	5.242880000%	79.028480000%
Period -7	4.194304000%	83.222784000%
Period -8	3.355443200%	86.578227200%
Period -9	2.684354560%	89.262581760%
Period -10	2.147483648%	91.410065408%
Period -11	1.717986918%	93.128052326%
Period -12	1.374389535%	94.502441861%
Period -13	1.099511628%	95.601953489%
Period -14	0.879609302%	96.481562791%
Period -15	0.703687442%	97.185250233%
Period -16	0.562949953%	97.748200186%
Period -17	0.450359963%	98.198560149%
Period -18	0.360287970%	98.558848119%
Period -19	0.288230376%	98.847078495%
Period -20	0.230584301%	99.077662796%

Figure 3F. The table above shows the weighting that results from exponential smoothing. This example uses a smoothing factor of 0.20, which results in a 20% weighting of the current period (we are assuming we are at the end of the current period, this would be referred to as the previous period in the calculation). You can see the weighting for Period -1 (one period prior to the current period)) is 16%, and each previous period has a progressively smaller weighting. The "Cumulative Weights" column represents the total weight applied to all periods up to that point. For example, by the time we get to period -20 (20 periods prior to the current period) we have accounted for over 99% of our forecast. In other words, the total weight of all periods beyond 21 periods in the past, is less than 1%. If I were to continue this table, you would see that period -100 (100 periods prior to the current period) has a weighting of 0.000000004%. So even though it is still technically affecting our forecast, the weighting is so small that the affect is negligible.

peating promotions will also contribute to seasonality. Examples would include an annual catalog mailing or a special discount (sale) that occurs at the same time each year. If you are a distributor to retailers that get most of their sales on the weekends, you will likely find that your customers are more likely to place orders on certain days during the week (depending upon transportation times) to get their orders just before the weekend. While some may feel that getting to the day-of-the-week level is going too far, there are businesses that can benefit from this level of forecasting.

Most seasonality is caused by outside forces (forces beyond the control of your operation), however, there can be a significant amount of seasonality that is generated by your own internal business practices. This phenomenon—I like to refer to this as self-induced seasonality—occurs when your incentive policies create end-of-month, end-of-quarter, and end-of-year peaks in volume that are unrelated to market demand. These business practices have become so standardized that it's rare to encounter a business that doesn't use them to some degree. They are also so entrenched in business management philosophy that I'll admit it may be a losing battle to try to get businesses to change. There is no getting around the fact that seasonality is disruptive, and while forecasting can help in dealing with seasonality, it does not completely eliminate the disruptive effects seasonality has on a business. Therefore, wouldn't it make sense to try to eliminate seasonality wherever practical? I certainly think so. This doesn't mean you cannot have incentive policies, but rather you should consider alternatives that achieve the same benefits of your incentive policy without all the disruption to your business. Consider breaking your sales staff or customers into groups and creating staggered dates for the incentive periods. Sure, this makes it a little more difficult to manage the incentive policy, but if it avoids stock-outs, overtime, and inventory increases, isn't it worth the effort?

And now back to seasonality basics. Though I had mentioned that some of the previous forecasting techniques can adapt somewhat to seasonal changes, they tend to be less than effective at it. The best way to incorporate seasonality into a forecast involves developing a seasonality index. The index consists of a number for each specific forecast period that describes the relationship of each period's demand to the average demand (level) over the complete seasonal cycle. The average demand is represented by the number one. If seasonality for a period results in demand greater than the average demand, it will be represented by a number greater than one. For example, if December's sales were, on average, 30% greater than the average monthly sales for the year, you would have a seasonality index of 1.3 (1 plus .30) for December. If January's sales were, on average, 20% less than the average monthly sales for the year, you would have a seasonality index of 0.8 (1 minus .20).

To calculate a seasonality index you require at least a full seasonal cycle's demand history broken down by forecast period. For example, the most common types of seasonality occur at certain times of the year, resulting in a seasonal cycle of one year. If you use months as your forecast interval, you would require the demand history for the previous year broken down into monthly time periods. You would calculate the average monthly demand over the 12 months (total annual demand divided by 12) and then divide each month's demand by the average monthly demand to find your seasonality index for each month. For example, if my 2008 demand averaged 200 units per month, and my January, February, and March demand was 190, 200, and 210 respectively, I would have seasonality indexes of 0.95, 1.00, and 1.05 respectively.

Seasonality index

	Jan	Feb	Mar	Apr	May	Jun	Jul	Aug	Sep	Oct	Nov	Dec
Demand	857	795	804	957	1126	1078	973	908	934	879	891	833
Index	0.93	0.86	0.87	1.04	1.22	1.17	1.06	0.99	1.02	0.96	0.97	0.91

Figure 3G. Here is an example of a seasonality index based on one year's history. If you were to set this up in Excel, with January demand of 857 in cell B3, your formula for the index for January (cell B4) would be =B3/AVERAGE($B$3:$M$3). You could then copy B4 and paste it into cells C4 through M4 to get the remainder of your indexes.

In practice however, you generally wouldn't want to create a seasonality index using the history of just one item for just one seasonal cycle (as in the previous example). Since we understand forecasts are more accurate at the aggregate level than the detail level, we should apply this to creating a more accurate seasonality index. You can do this by using more years and/or more items in the calculation. By using two or more years (three tends to work pretty well) in the calculation, you will reduce the impact noise has on your seasonality index. Also, by calculating the index over groups of items rather than single items, you will reduce noise even further. To achieve this you must designate groups of products that share the same seasonality profiles. You could do this mathematically by calculating seasonality indexes for each item and then grouping items that have similar seasonality indexes. This can be problematic—especially for slower movers—due to the impact of noise on the calculation. A better way is to use a combination of judgment and math. For example, if I am in the beverage distribution industry, I can make some generalizations about product groups. I could probably assume that all sport drinks (all brands and flavors) would follow similar seasonal patterns. I could then test the assumption by creating a seasonality index based upon the entire group and then review demand from some individual items to validate my assumption. Can I assume the same for all carbonated beverages? I'm not so sure. I would probably experiment a little here by creating smaller groups based on flavor (colas in one group, fruit flavors in another, etc). I would also check to see if there is a seasonality difference between diet and non-diet beverages because I suspect diet beverages may get a boost in sales in January or early spring. I may also look at the container size to see if it affects seasonality (I would probably look at this for the sports drinks as well).

One of the issues that comes up when calculating seasonality indexes across groups of products, is the question of whether to use units, dollars, or some other measure in the calculation. When calculating for groups of similar products, units (individual pieces) tends to work pretty well. In the beverage example, units (cans, bottles, etc.) would probably work—though you may want to try converting all units to gallons to see if this has an effect on the index.

When calculating against widely dissimilar products, you may find that using units creates problems. For example, if you are a distributor of repair parts and have parts that vary from large expensive electronic assemblies sold one at a time, to nuts and washers sold in large quantities, you may find that noise in the demand for the nuts and washers is so significant (due to the larger order quantities) that these items skew the seasonality calculation. In this case, you may want to try calculating the index using dollars rather than units. However, using dollars can create similar problems if you have a few items that are extremely expensive. In addition, you may need to back out price increases to ensure they are not skewing the results. So what is the best solution? There are numerous variations you can try: Exclude the extremely expensive items and then calculate the index by dollars, or exclude the small items sold in large quantities and calculate based on units. Or, calculate both ways and combine the indexes.

Seasonality index

	Jan	Feb	Mar	Apr	May	Jun	Jul	Aug	Sep	Oct	Nov	Dec
Year 1	857	795	804	957	1126	1078	973	908	934	879	891	833
Year 2	960	910	920	1115	1250	1240	1130	1075	1054	993	1057	954
Year 3	901	837	840	1030	1195	1104	1022	950	990	915	938	880
Total	2718	2542	2564	3102	3571	3422	3125	2933	2978	2787	2886	2667
Index	0.92	0.86	0.87	1.05	1.21	1.16	1.06	1.00	1.01	0.95	0.98	0.91

Figure 3H. Here our seasonality index is calculated over three years. If you were to set this up in Excel, with January demand of 857 in cell B3, your formula for the index for January (cell B7) would be =B6/AVERAGE($B6:$M6) .

How do you know if you got it right? You can compare different calculations to see if the indexes end up being similar. For example, break a large group into two smaller groups and perform the calculation against each group. If the results for each smaller group are similar to the large group, you should feel pretty good about the calculation. Another way is to test it against another time period. For example, if you used the previous two years' demand to create the index, calculate it again using the two years prior to that. Once again, if the results are similar, you probably have a pretty good index.

Though this seems like a lot of work, the benefits of calculating an accurate seasonality index far outweigh this effort. In addition, since seasonality patterns tend to be relatively consistent, you can use the same seasonality index year after year—though you may want to review it every few years to ensure it is still valid.

Trend adjustments.

As previously stated, trend is a gradual increase or decrease in demand over a period of time. Though some of the previously discussed forecasting techniques react to trend, they all will lag because they are simply taking into account the effects of trend that have already occurred, rather than extending trend to predict future increases or decreases in demand. For example, in all the previous techniques, if you had increased demand for each consecutive period in a series, the forecasts for subsequent periods would never be greater than the demand from the previous periods. I feel pretty confident in saying that if most of us looked at a five-week period that had demand of 5, 10, 15, 20, 25, units respectively, we would likely come to the conclusion that the following week's demand would be greater than 25 units (assuming seasonality is not an issue). Therefore, we need to do something in addition to the previously discussed techniques to handle trend.

Trend-lag example						
	Week 1	Week 2	Week 3	Week 4	Week 5	Week 6
Demand	5	10	15	20	25	
Forecasts						
Last-period		5	10	15	20	25
Moving average (3-week)				10	15	20
Weighted moving average				12	17	22
Exponential Smoothing		5	8	11	16	20

Figure 3I. Here we see four different forecasting methods used on demand that has an obvious trend. The three-week weighted moving average uses weights of 0.20, 0.30, and 0.50 respectively, and the exponential smoothing forecast uses a smoothing factor of 0.50. The obvious trend suggests that the forecast for week #6 should be 30, yet none of these forecasting techniques will provide a forecast greater 25.

So how do we account for trend in a forecast? That depends on the forecasting technique used, but basically consists of identifying and tracking changes from one forecasting period to the next, and adjusting future forecasting periods accordingly. In the previous example, the trend is an increase of 5 units for each period (trend can be expressed as units, percentages, or more complex formulas).

Unfortunately, trends are rarely as obvious or consistent as the previous example. As with all forecasting calculations, you need to consider noise in your trend calculation. Looking at a five-week period that had demand of 8, 7, 19, 12, 27 respectively, it appears that there may be a trend, but there is also a significant amount of noise and/or seasonality. And, even if you identify an obvious trend, you still need to take into account that the trend may not continue or may change. If we go back to the 5, 10, 15, 20, 25 example and consider that this item has a lead time of ten weeks, we now need to make a decision whether or not the five-per-week demand increase will continue ten weeks into the future. That would result in a forecast of 75 units for the tenth week, and a total forecasted demand of 525 units for the upcoming ten-week period (the sum of the projected demand during the lead time). So, if you have fewer than 525 units in stock, do you order more? And if so, how much? Also remember, your order will be for the demand beyond ten weeks into the future. If you assume the trend will continue and order accordingly, you will have excess or obsolete inventory if the trend flattens out or turns into a downward trend. The same would occur if what appeared to be a trend was, in fact, just noise. However, if you don't order according to the trend, and the trend does continue, you will end up being unable to meet future demand. Welcome to the world of inventory management.

As you should have deduced from the previous example, decisions related to how you identify and use trend are, to some extent, a form of gambling. As with most forms of gambling, you are balancing risk and reward. You are also using your knowledge of your business (the game) to help minimize risk. The greater your knowledge, the greater your chances of success. The way you play the game and the level of risk to which you can expose yourself need to be adapted to your specific business characteristics. Characteristics such as margins (difference between cost of an item and sell price), risk of obsolescence, and effects of stock-outs, will all contribute to forecasting decisions. For example, if your product has very large margins and stock-outs are likely to result in lost sales opportunities, you would want to be fairly aggressive at identifying and projecting positive trends. Even if you are occasionally wrong, the rewards associated with having these high-margin items available to meet all demand exceed the risks associated with excess or obsolete inventory. Alternately, if you are operating on minimal margins, your product is highly prone to obsolescence, and your customers accept backorders (meaning you are not losing the sale), you will probably take a much more conservative approach to positive trends.

I also want to take this opportunity to once again mention the benefits of minimizing lead times. If we go back to the previous example and were able to find a supplier that could provide the same product in two weeks rather than ten weeks, how much have we reduced risk? How much more quickly can we adapt to changing demand?

Forecast error measurement.

Forecast error/accuracy measurement is one of the most important tools used in managing your forecast. Though there are numerous ways of measuring forecast error, the most common is to represent forecast error as a percentage. And, to add some confusion, there are several different ways to calculate this. Below are the two most commonly used calculations.

([Forecasted Sales]-[Actual Sales]) / [Actual Sales]

([Forecasted Sales]-[Actual Sales]) / [Forecasted Sales]

The first calculation is usually the preferred method (though both methods are quite common) because you would generally want to know your accuracy relative to actual sales. It is best explained by using a significant forecast error as an example. If your forecast was for 200 units and actual sales were 100 units, the first calculation would result in a forecast error of 100%, while the second calculation would give an error of 50%. So, the first calculation states that the forecast was 100% greater than actual sales, while the second states that sales were 50% less than the forecast. In other words, the first calculation represents how inaccurate your forecast was at predicting sales, while the second represents how inaccurate sales were at meeting the forecast. Though the first is the more logical representation of forecast error, I think either method is OK provided you are consistent, and those using the measurement understand what it represents. For the remainder of this book, we will use the first calculation.

The previous calculations only determine the forecast error for specific forecast periods. While this is useful, what you ultimately want to do is track the accuracy of forecasts over a series of forecast periods. This is especially true when using smaller forecast intervals such as weeks. You can do this by introducing three additional calculations that are applied to a series of forecast errors.

Multi-period forecast error amplitude measurements (MPFEAM).

Alright, I made up this term and the corresponding acronym so don't worry about trying to memorize it. These measurements quantify the size of the forecast error over multiple forecast periods.

Mean absolute deviation (MAD). To calculate mean absolute deviation, you calculate the average of the absolute values (change all negative values to positive values) of each period's forecast error. For example, if you had forecast errors of -20%, +10%, and -6% for three periods, you would ignore the negative signs (treating all three values as positives) and calculate the average of the three values. Your result would be a mean absolute deviation of 12%. In other words, on average, your period forecasts were 12% off from your actual period demand. Mean absolute deviation is sometimes referred to as average absolute forecast error.

Exponentially smoothed absolute deviation (ESAD). Similar to MAD, you use the absolute forecast error, but instead of averaging the periods, you apply a smoothing factor to them the same way you did in an exponentially smoothed forecast.

Forecast bias measurements.

Forecast bias describes the tendencies of forecasts to be high or low. Whereas the mean absolute deviation calculation ignored positives and negatives, the forecast bias uses these values (signed errors) to determine if your forecasts are more likely to be high (a positive bias) or low (a negative bias) and to what level they are high or low. There are several ways to calculate forecast bias.

Cumulative forecast bias (Sum of forecast errors). To calculate a cumulative forecast bias you simply add up each period's forecast error for a series of forecast periods. In the previous example where we had forecast errors of -20%, +10%, and -6% for the three periods, we would sum the three values and get a result of -16%.

Average (mean) forecast bias. Forecast bias may also be measured as an average (rather than a sum) of forecast errors. In the previous example, that would result in -5.333%

Exponentially smoothed forecast bias. And, of course, you can exponentially smooth the forecast bias. This calculation is exactly the same as the exponential smoothing calculation used for forecasting, except you will be using the forecast error in place of sales (demand).

Tracking signal.

Tracking signals are important parts of many forecasting systems. The basic idea here is to create a calculation that describes the overall health of the forecast relative to trend. The tracking signal can then be used to initiate changes to the forecasting technique or parameters. Though I've encountered several ways to calculate tracking signals, I have found the most useful to be dividing the absolute value of the forecast bias measurement by the multi-period amplitude measurement. This would include either dividing the absolute value of your average forecast bias by your mean absolute deviation, or dividing the absolute value of your exponentially smoothed forecast bias by your exponentially smoothed absolute deviation.

To use the previous example where we had forecast errors of -20%, +10%, and -6% for three periods, resulting in an average forecast bias of -5.333% and a mean absolute deviation of 12%, we would divide 5.333 (the absolute value of your bias) by 12 to get .444. So what does .444 tell us? It's basically a ratio that describes the relationship between the bias and the forecast error. The higher the number (the closer this number is to 1), the more likely it is that you are not adequately accounting for trend. A lower number (closer to 0) suggests that the forecast error is more likely the result of noise or an inadequate seasonality adjustment.

In the next chapter, we will cover the use of a tracking signal in adaptive smoothing.

Forecast Error Measurements

		Jan	Feb	Mar	Arp	May	June
Demand		857	795	804	957	1126	1078
Forecast	0.4		857	832	821	875	976
Forecast Error (Units)			62	28.	-136	-251	-102
Forecast Error (Percentage)			7.80%	3.51%	-14.22%	-22.26%	-9.50%
Absolute Error (Percentage)			7.80%	3.51%	14.22%	22.26%	9.50%

Multiple-Period Forecast Error Amplitude Measurements (MPFEAM)

Mean Absolute Deviation (MAD)					8.51%	13.33%	15.33%
Exponentially Smoothed Absolute Deviation (ESAD)	0.4		7.80%	6.08%	9.34%	14.51%	12.50%

Forecast Bias Measurements

Cumulative Forecast Bias					-2.91%	-32.97%	-45.98%
Average Forecast Bias					-0.97%	-10.99%	-15.33%
Exponentially Smoothed Forecast Bias	0.4		7.80%	6.08%	-2.04%	-10.13%	-9.88%

Tracking Signals

Tracking Signal (Averages bias / MAD)					0.11	0.82	1.00
Tracking Signal (Exp. Smoothed bias / ESAD)			1.00	1.00	0.22	0.70	0.79
Tracking Signal (Cum. bias / Mad)					0.34	2.47	3.00

Figure 3J. Here I've created a table showing all the measurements previously covered. The Mean Absolute Deviation, Cumulative Forecast Bias, and Average Forecast Bias are all based on a 3-month moving time period. All exponential smoothing calculations are using a smoothing factor of 0.40. Notice how our tracking signals increase in April through June, reflecting repeated periods where our forecast was not adequately accounting for trend.

I've also included a 3rd Tracking Signal calculation that consists of dividing the Cumulative Forecast Bias by the Mean Absolute Deviation. I don't particularly like this calculation, but included it because you may see it referenced in other publications. Obviously this tracking signal is not limited to a number between zero and one.

Doin' it in Excel.

Create a spreadsheet based on the previous table and fill in all the labels, the demand numbers, and the smoothing factors (the cells with 0.4 in them). Make sure you set up your spreadsheet so the January Demand of 857 is in Cell C3

In D4 enter =C3

In E4 enter =($B4*D3)+((1-$B4)*D4)

>   Copy E4 and paste into F4 through H4

In D5 enter =D4-D3

>   Copy D5 and paste into E5 through H5

In D6 enter =D5/D3

>   Copy D6 and paste into E6 though H6

In D7 enter =ABS(D6)

>   Copy D7 and paste into E7 though H7

In F9 enter =AVERAGE(D7:F7)

>   Copy F9 and paste into G9 though H9

In D10 enter =D7

In E10 enter =($B10*E7)+((1-$B10)*D10)

>   Copy E10 and paste into F10 through H10

In F12 enter =SUM(D6:F6)

>   Copy F12 and paste into G12 through H12

In F13 enter =AVERAGE(D6:F6)

>   Copy F13 and paste into G13 through H13

In D14 enter =D6

In E14 enter =($B14*E6)+((1-$B14)*D14)

>   Copy E14 and paste into F14 through H14

In F16 enter =ABS(F13)/F9

>   Copy F16 and paste into G16 through H16

In D17 enter =ABS(D14)/D10

>   Copy D17 and paste into E17 through H17

In F18 enter =ABS(F12)/F9

>   Copy F18 and paste into G18 through H18

Format cells to appropriate number formats

Important note:

With all the syntax and calculations I've included in this book, it's possible that that some errors will get through. Please go to www.inventoryexplained.com to check for corrections and updates. Also, if you come across an error, please report it.

A common mistake in forecast error measurement.

There is, however, one significant flaw in most forecast error/accuracy measurements. It seems logical that the calculations are based on comparing the forecast to the actual demand for a forecast period. But which forecast do you use? A forecast is generally not static, therefore, a forecast for a specific period will change as time passes and more current data becomes available. For example, at the end of week one, I may calculate forecasts for periods two through ten (forecast interval = one week). After week two, I will then recalculate periods three through ten and add a forecast for week eleven. By the time I get to week ten, I have had nine forecasts for that week, and may have made planning decisions based on one or more of those forecasts. Yet surprisingly, most forecast error measurements are based solely on the most recent forecast.

To go back to my weather forecast analogy, what if on Monday I checked the 7-day weather forecast, and, based on a forecast for favorable skiing conditions, I made arrangements for a ski trip over the upcoming weekend. By Friday, the weekend forecast has changed, and the original favorable-conditions forecast is now a forecast for a rain/ice storm. Sure enough, on Saturday the rain starts falling. So based on the Friday forecast for Saturday, the forecast was very accurate, but that doesn't do me much good since I based my plans on Monday's forecast for Saturday.

So to get a more accurate picture of forecast error, you would need to take some forecast snapshots (maintain a forecast history) and use them to create a measurement that shows forecast error/accuracy relative to the number of periods into the future the forecast was created.

I also want to note that it's common to state forecast error measurement in terms of a "forecast accuracy" measurement. So a forecast error measurement of 5% would be stated as an accuracy measurement of 95%. I think you can figure out the math here.

Regression analysis.

Before moving on to the next chapter, I want to cover Regression Analysis. Like exponential smoothing, the term regression analysis sounds pretty sophisticated. For example, if you were to ask someone about their forecasting technique and they answered "Oh yeah, we do some regression analysis and then throw in a little quadruple exponential smoothing to boot" (This can sound really funny if you imagine Barney Fife running his hand across his nose as he says it to Floyd, the barber) wouldn't you be impressed? Well, unlike exponential smoothing—which just sounds sophisticated— regression analysis is actually rather sophisticated.

Regression analysis can be used to determine a mathematical relationship between two or more sets of data where one or more sets of data is thought to be able to predict the other set of data. The data used to predict is known as the Predictor Variable. In our case, the data being predicted is our forecast.

For example, there is likely a mathematical relationship between changes in the price of oil and changes in demand for certain automobile models (cars with better gas mileage sell better as gas prices increase). Another example would be a relationship between interest rates and sales of certain home improvement products. Both of these examples show a causal relationship between the predictor variable and variable being predicted; however, this is not always the case. You may find a predictor variable that has no causal relationship to the variable being predicted, but is instead affected by forces that also affect the variable being predicted. For example, you may find that increases or decreases in sales of stationary exercise equipment in the winter tend to predict changes in the sales of bicycles in the spring. In this case, the sales of exercise equipment are not causing the sales of bicycles, but instead are affected by people's interest in exercise, which also affects the sales of bicycles.

So how does someone without a degree in mathematics and statistics go about calculating this relationship? Fortunately, you probably already have access to a software product that can do this. Microsoft Excel comes with an add-in called the "Analysis ToolPak" that has a function for conducting regression analysis. As with other free Excel add-ins, the functionality is somewhat limited, but it does allow you to conduct some simple regression analyses and give you a feel for how regression analysis works. If you want to go further than you can with the add-in provided by Microsoft, there are more advanced add-ins available for purchase from third parties.

Doin' it in Excel.

To see if the add-in is already installed and loaded click Tools>Add-Ins in Excel 2003 or earlier, or Office Button>Excel Options>Add-Ins>Manage Excel Add-Ins>Go in Excel 2007 or later. If you don't see it on the list, check the Microsoft documentation on installing and loading the Analysis Toolpak.

Once you have confirmed you have the Analysis Toolpak installed and loaded, create a spreadsheet with historical values for the predictor variable, and historical values for the variable you want to predict. For example, we'll use values of 1054, 1502, 2007, and 1375 for the predictor variable and values of 54, 75, 98, and 60 for the variable being predicted.

	A	B	C
1	**Historical Data**		
2	**Predictor**	**Sales**	
3	1054	54	
4	1502	75	
5	2007	98	
6	1375	60	
7			

Figure 3K. Set up spreadsheet as shown.

Set up your spreadsheet as shown in Figure 3K.

In Excel 2003: Click Tools>Data Analysis>Regression.

In Excel 2007: Click Data>Data Analysis>Regression

You'll now see the Regression popup window. Click the field labeled "Input Y Range:" and then click and drag through the values for the variable to predict.

Next click the field labeled "Input X Range:" and click and drag through the values for the predictor variable.

If you included the column headings as you clicked and dragged through the values, you need to click the "Labels" check box.

Now click the "Output Range:" check box, and then click in the field next to it. Now click a cell in an open area of your worksheet (we'll click cell A12).

The Regression popup window should appear as in Figure 3L.

Click OK.

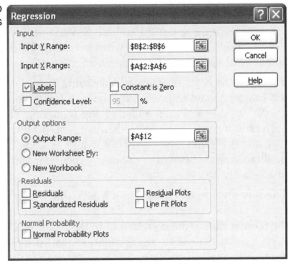

Figure 3L. Regression popup window

Excel will write the output to the area of the worksheet we set (as shown in Figure 3M).

	A	B	C	D	E	F	G	H	I
1	Historical Data								
2	Predictor	Sales							
3	1054	54							
4	1502	75							
5	2007	98							
6	1375	60							
7									
8									
9									
10									
11									
12	SUMMARY OUTPUT								
13									
14	Regression Statistics		Correlation						
15	Multiple R	0.974600589							
16	R Square	0.949846309		Intercept					
17	Adjusted R Squar(	0.924769463							
18	Standard Error	5.376554087							
19	Observations	4		X Variable					
20									
21	ANOVA								
22		df	SS	MS	F	gnificance F			
23	Regression	1	1094.935	1094.935	37.87742	0.025399			
24	Residual	2	57.81467	28.90733					
25	Total	3	1152.75						
26									
27		Coefficients	andard Err	t Stat	P-value	Lower 95%	Upper 95%	ower 95.0%	pper 95.0%
28	Intercept	0.146665236	11.94092	0.012283	0.991315	-51.231	51.52428	-51.231	51.52428
29	Predictor	0.048233974	0.007837	6.154464	0.025399	0.014513	0.081955	0.014513	0.081955

Figure 3M. Regression analysis output.

At the bottom, you'll see a column labeled "Coefficients". Beneath this, you'll see values for the Intercept and the X Variable (the label will read "X Variable" if you didn't select the labels when selecting the data, otherwise it will read the actual label for the predictor variable).

These are the key values for our mathematical relationship. What this says is that the value we want to predict will be equal to the predictor variable multiplied by the X Variable and then added to the Intercept. Therefore, if the new value for our predictor variable is 950, then we would multiply 950 by 0.048233974 and then add 0.146665236. The result would be 45.96894054. In other words, if our predictor variable is 950, we should expect our variable being predicted to be approximately 46.

The other value we want to look at is the value labeled "Multiple R", which represents the correlation. Simply put, the closer this value is to the number 1.0, the more accurate the correlation. In the example I provided, I purposely created datasets that have a strong correlation just to make it easier to understand the regression analysis process.

So you're probably wondering what all those other values are for. Did you ever take something apart and then after putting it back together realize you have a few extra parts yet the thing you "fixed" seems to work OK. Well, that's what all those other values are. Just kidding. The truth is I don't know what all that other stuff is (I know what some of it is and given enough time can probably figure out the rest). My intent here is not to comprehensively cover regression, but rather to give an introduction to it and discuss how it can potentially be used within forecasting. I'm not going to spend a whole lot of time on regression analysis because most of you will not actually ever incorporate regression analysis in a real-world automated forecast. Sure, you should experiment with it a bit and you may use it in some higher-level decision-making or as an input to the forecasting process (with human intervention), but using it in an automated forecast in the real world is not as practical as it first seems.

The biggest problem with regression analysis is finding an effective predictor variable. A variable that has a direct correlation to your sales is not necessarily a predictor variable. For example, it may sound perfectly logical that the amount of snowfall during a particular period has a direct impact on snow blower sales, and therefore would be a great application for using regression analysis. Unfortunately, by the time the snow falls, it's probably too late to use this information for the purposes of manufacturing. So even though the snowfall occurs before the snow blower sales, and, in fact, is a causal factor for snow blower sales, it may not occur enough in advance to provide useful information for the manufacture of snow blowers. That doesn't mean that a short-term weather forecast for heavy snows in a particular area of the country cannot be used to try to position your snow blower inventory (I'm talking about the physical location of the inventory) so you can quickly replenish your reseller's inventory.

Now, let's go back to the example of using the price of oil to predict sales of specific models of automobiles. Sounds like a slam-dunk, right? Well, not necessarily. Certainly there is a strong cause-and-effect relationship here; however, you once again need to know about changes in the price of oil far enough in advance to be able to not only change the production schedule, but also to possibly retool plants in order to increase the capacity of specific models. I would agree that evaluating the forecasted price and supply of oil over the next few years or more could be useful in planning product lines in the automotive industry, that is, if you can somehow manage to get a reasonably accurate forecast of future oil prices.

Therefore, in order to effectively use regression analysis, you must find a predictor variable that is known (or reasonably accurately forecasted) in a time frame prior to your forecast great enough to make it useful. In addition, the accuracy in using the predictor variable to forecast demand must be better than other forecasting techniques available. This second point is very important since you rarely find a predictor variable that has a strong enough correlation that it can outperform less-sophisticated forecasting techniques (like those covered in these chapters). This is especially true if you have reasonable lead times and flexible capacity (if you are a manufacturer). In these cases, simple level, trend, and seasonality-based forecasts will likely outperform regression analysis.

The regression analysis used in the previous example is single-variable linear regression. The "linear" part means the calculation looks for a best-fit straight line that describes the correlation between the sets of data. The "single-variable" part means that we used only one predictor variable. There are also non-linear regression techniques and ways to use multiple predictor variables. Multi-variable regression (also known as multiple regression) takes two or more predictor variables and looks to find a mathematical relationship between them and a single variable to predict. For example, you may want to try using a combination of gas prices, interest rates, and disposable income to predict sales of automobiles. The Excel plug-in used in the previous example is also capable of multiple linear regression (though I'm not going to go through another example).

Before we move on, I want to talk about using historical demand as the predictor variable, and introduce the Excel Forecast function. When I first started playing with regression, it occurred to me that I could use my own historical demand as the predictor variable for my future demand. Though this sounds a little strange, what I am doing is using my historical demand as both the predictor variable and the variable being predicted. However, I am offsetting the demand by one period. In other words, I would use my January, February, and March demand as the predictor variable input (Input X Range), and my February, March, and April demand as the data for the variable being predicted (Input Y Range). This can provide a forecast that does a real nice job of accounting for trend. In fact, if we went back to the earlier trend example where we had a five-week period that had demand of 5, 10, 15, 20, 25, units respectively, we could use regression to get us that 30-unit forecast we were looking for.

However, rather than using the Regression add-in to do this, we are going to use the Excel Forecast function. The Forecast function in Excel uses linear regression to predict the next value (our forecast for the next period). See Figure 3P.

G4			f_x	=FORECAST(F3,C3:F3,B3:E3)		
	A	B	C	D	E	F	G
1	Trend example using Forcast function.						
2		Week 1	Week 2	Week 3	Week 4	Week 5	Week 6
3	Demand	5	10	15	20	25	
4	Forecast						30
5							

Figure 3P. Here you can see how the Forecast function can be used to predict demand for the next period based on demand from the previous period. In this example, the formula in cell G6 is =FORECAST(F3,C3:F3,B3:E3) , where F3 (Week #5 demand) is the value we are using to predict our demand for Week #6, C3:F3 represents the existing data for the values being predicted (our known Y values), and B3:E3 represents the existing data for the predictor values (our known X values).

So the Forecast function in Excel essentially does the linear regression stuff and builds our calculation behind the scenes so we can skip a step. While this is a great little function, I need to caution you not to get too excited about it. Our example used demand with a very clear sustained trend, no noise, and no seasonality. If these other factors were present, we would need to find a way to make separate adjustments for them. For example, if noise were present, we would probably have to smooth the demand before using it as an input to the Forecast function. And, as you'll see in subsequent chapters, I have a whole bunch of other stuff I like to build into my forecasts.

A note on relevant history.

For the purposes of forecasting, relevant history is the amount of data recorded under business conditions similar enough to current and future conditions, such that it can still be effectively used to forecast future demand. The relevance of historical data tends to degrade over time; this degradation may be a gradual change or occur suddenly relative to the significance of changes to business conditions.

In addition, the relevance of data is related to its use in the forecasting process. For example, three-year-old data may no longer be useful in directly calculating current trend, but may still be useful for calculating seasonality, variability, or creating models of events that may occur again in the future.

Bullwhip effect?

I guess no discussion of demand would be complete without mentioning the infamous bullwhip effect. Let me start by saying that, in my opinion, the bullwhip effect is probably as much bull as it is whip. The basic concept behind the bullwhip effect is that demand variation becomes amplified as it progresses up through the supply chain. It's based on the assumption that an increase in demand at a low level in the supply chain (such as a retail store) will trigger a series of overreactions (in the form of safety stock or aggressive forecasts) at each subsequent level in the supply chain. So, where Newton's third law states that for every action there is an equal and opposite reaction, the bullwhip effect assumes that for every action there is a series of overreactions. In theory it goes something like this, a retailer sees an increase in demand for a certain product so he orders twice as much (let's say 4 cases instead of 2) on his next order from his supplier (probably a distributor). The distributor sees this increase in demand and then increases his next order (let's say from 30 cases to 50 cases) from the manufacturer. The manufacturer sees this increase in demand from the distributor and increases his production quantity (from 500 cases to 700 cases). His increase in production quantity changes the demand of all components and raw materials, which in turn triggers overreactions by all his suppliers for these materials. And on and on it goes until those 2 additional cases of product at the retail level eventually result in the entire world economy crumbling down around us. Hmm?

When I see mentions of the bullwhip effect, it is often described as a phenomenon that has been "observed" by supply chain experts. Yeah, and last week I "observed" Elvis and Bigfoot playing fetch in a local park. I'm not denying there is a possibility of the bullwhip effect occurring, BUT, I think it's more of a theoretical possibility than it is a commonly observed reality. First of all, the nature of supply chains (especially retail) usually consists of a many-to-one relationship between customers and suppliers. So if I am a distributor and one of my many customers doubles his normal order, I probably won't even notice the change in demand since it is small in relation to my overall demand (due to my many customers), therefore, the whip basically never materializes. But let's say for the sake of argument that the increase in demand occurred at all the distributor's retail customers at the same time, thereby creating a noticeable increase in demand at the distributor. Well in this case, I would hope there would be a reaction at the distributor level, but my experience (based on my "observations") is that the distributor will more likely be slow to react, under react, or not react at all. He is probably using some type of smoothing in his forecasting system that will reduce the impact of this demand change on his forecast, and if he is using an overly simplistic safety stock calculation (as many businesses do), the demand change will have little to no impact on his safety stock. Although, if he is using a statistically based safety stock calculation (discussed later), it should eventually increase his safety stock to reflect the demand variability. But, will his change in safety stock amplify the demand variability or just more accurately reflect it? Once again, I think it is just as likely that his change in safety stock level will actually be equal to or less than the actual demand variability. However, even if it is greater than the actual variability, it is very unlikely that it would be substantially greater than the observed variability.

So this process will then repeat at each level of the supply chain, and you are supposed to accept that each level is going to result in an overreaction. I think a scenario that is just as likely—or more likely—is that smoothing will occur at each level (or some levels) of the supply chain, therefore the outcome is actually the opposite of the bullwhip effect. Meaning, a sudden dramatic change in demand at a low level in the supply chain may have a smaller impact as the demand progresses up the supply chain. Ya know, I bet my little theory here would catch on if I could just come up with a clever little name for it.

The fact is, different supply chains, different levels within the same supply chain, and even different planners at the same point of a supply chain may react differently to changes in demand. So a demand ripple at one level may be repeated, amplified, attenuated (diminished), or completely ignored at other levels of the supply chain.

Though I don't think bullwhip is as common or dramatic as we have been led to believe, I do find bullwhip to be an effective teaching tool in demonstrating the "potential" problems of a disconnected supply chain. A disconnected supply chain is one where the only visibility a supplier has to demand consists of the orders placed on him from his customers. In the previous example, the distributor only sees the orders from the retailers, not the actual demand that resulted in the creation of those orders. The manufacturer then only sees the orders from the distributors, not the orders from the retailers or the demand at the retail level. So in effect, what the distributor and manufacturer see as demand is not the end-user demand, but instead are the reactions to that demand.

Is there a solution to the disconnected supply chain? Well if disconnected is bad, then maybe connected is better? This is where collaborative planning and forecasting come into play. Collaborative planning involves sharing information between customers and suppliers and then using this shared information to make planning decisions. This will be discussed a little more in subsequent chapters.

4

Forecasting Part 2:
Now It Gets Complicated

In the previous chapter we covered common forecasting techniques and terminology. So now that you know how to calculate a moving average, seasonality index, exponential smoothing, and forecast error, you should be set to start forecasting. Well, are you? Unfortunately, many inventory management books and courses never get beyond the basic calculations covered in the previous chapter, and some don't even get that far. That's a shame, because they are essentially telling you that you are now ready to start forecasting without actually providing you with enough information to effectively use these tools. Think of it as quickly showing someone how a saw, hammer, level, and tape measure work, and then expecting them to build a house. Even providing them with the latest and greatest in carpentry technology—like pneumatic nail guns, laser levels, and saws with laser guides—won't help them to overcome the fact that they have never been introduced to basic framing techniques, load calculations, weatherproofing techniques, proper materials, etc. Sure they may be able to build something, and they may even call it a house, but I doubt it will be a well-built house—or even meet minimum code requirements.

The same is true of forecasting—and inventory management in general. Sure, you can take the basic tools and start pounding out a forecast, but without considering a number of additional factors, you are unlikely to produce a highly effective forecast.

Trend revisited.

One of the most significant challenges in forecasting is trying to differentiate trend from noise. Another is then trying to determine how far to extend trend into the forecast. Let's start with differentiating trend from noise. Given a sustained trend over an extended period of time, I think most people would be fairly effective at identifying the trend. However, the longer you wait to identify trend, the less effective your forecasting becomes. On the other hand, if you are too aggressive in attributing a change in demand to trend, you will undoubtedly find that you sometimes misidentify noise as trend.

This is why it's so important to understand trend and, more specifically, the trend characteristics of the specific items you are forecasting. An item's demand may be affected by various factors that could be categorized as trend. Let's take a look at some of them.

Product life cycles. Product life cycle represents the period of time in which a specific item is considered an active saleable item. More specifically, product life cycle (for our purposes) starts when a product is first introduced, and ends when a product is removed from active status. Some items, such as hand tools, fasteners, repair parts, or other industrial items, may have product life cycles of many years or even decades; while other items, such as high-tech consumer goods, may have product life cycles measured in months or weeks. The general nature of a typical product life cycle consists of an initial increase in sales, then a plateau, followed by a decrease in sales until the item is no longer viable (has lost its profit potential) or is replaced by a new model. Though most product life cycles follow the same general pattern, the details of specific products' life cycles may vary significantly. For example, one product may start out with very high initial demand, which quickly plateaus then gradually decreases. Another product may start out with rather low demand, which gradually increases then suddenly has a sharp increase to a plateau and then quickly decreases. While yet another may have relatively steady demand that only sees a modest increase in demand over a long period of time, and then has a similarly very slow gradual decrease in demand.

Though most products follow this general increase-plateau-decrease pattern, there are other patterns, such as products that start with a peak and gradually decrease, or others that have several increases, peaks, and decreases throughout their product life. The latter is often due to changes in pricing or competition.

Overall market conditions. Most businesses find that when the overall economy is doing well, demand for their products increases. Obviously, the opposite also occurs when the economy does poorly.

Popularity of product line or specific category of product. Though this is often cyclical, it is different from product life cycle in that it is relative to demand for groups of products, for example, an increase in the popularity of hybrid vehicles due to increases in fuel costs. These changes in demand would affect all products within the group.

Market share. This includes demand changes relative to a company gaining or losing market share. For example, a consumer-goods manufacturer getting a contract to sell to a large retail chain should result in increased demand for the products they sell because their products are very likely displacing a competitor's product on the store's shelves. Cost competitiveness or increases in brand recognition or brand reputation will often result in gains in market share. Conversely, increases in a competitor's brand recognition or introduction of a new competitor into your market will likely result in a loss of market share.

Events. Certain events may trigger changes (positive or negative) in demand. For example, if a company or specific product becomes the focus of a news story, is reviewed on a web site, mentioned in a book, or used by a celebrity, it's very likely there will be an immediate impact on demand. The "Colbert bump" is a classic example of how certain types of publicity can have an immediate impact on the popularity of a product. Other events, such as wars, natural disasters, lawsuits, legislation, international trade agreements, or the introduction of a competing product, can also significantly impact demand. Even a change in the search algorithm of a popular search engine can result in significant changes in demand.

It's very possible that a single product's demand is being affected by all these factors at the same time. This results in a trend that is actually a composite of multiple trend elements that follow different trend cycles and have varying degrees of impact on the product's demand. In fact, it is possible and sometimes necessary to track these trend elements separately and then combine them for your forecast.

Separating trend elements.

Since it's obviously much easier to just track trend as a single factor, why would someone want to track these various trend elements separately? The answer lies in being better able to predict longer-term changes in trend and making item-based decisions. For example, you may have a product that appears to be experiencing a very gradual modest increase in sales; however, most of your other products are experiencing much more significant increases. What you may actually have is a product that is being affected by upward trends related to overall market conditions and gains in market share, while at the same time is in the declining sales phase of its product life cycle. History has shown that (for this type of product) once it starts into the declining sales phase of its product life cycle it is generally just a couple of months away from becoming obsolete. If you were only tracking trend as a single factor, you would probably not recognize that this product is nearing the end of its product life cycle since the other trend factors are masking the declining relative demand for this product. Another example would be if you had information that your market share was going to change (increase or decrease) and needed to adjust your forecasts accordingly. At first, you may think you could just manually apply a trend to all items that reflects this change in market share, however, this would not take into account the fact that your individual products are also being affected by other trend elements.

Recognizing that your product is affected by various trend elements is a good first step, but the real key lies in understanding the potential impact the various trend elements can have on your product's demand during the forecast horizon. This once again brings me back to the benefits of short lead times and small lot sizes. If my lead times are short enough, and my lot sizes are small enough, most of these trend elements probably will not have a significant enough impact on demand during the forecast horizon to make a difference. For example, if I'm ordering product from a local distributor that gets the product to me in one day, and I generally only order the equivalent of two week's demand at any given time, do I really need to consider separately the trend associated with product life cycle if the product life cycle for this type of product is generally three years or more and is characterized by very gradual changes in demand? And how volatile would demand changes related to overall market conditions, product line popularity, or market share need to be to justify tracking them separately? Certainly an event could have an impact, but do I need to track event trend separately? Probably not.

But what if my lead time was six months and I ordered the equivalent of six month's demand. Now I need to be able to forecast demand (including trend) over the next twelve months. How much more likely is it that product life cycle, overall market conditions, product line popularity, market share, and/or potential events can significantly impact demand during this much longer forecast horizon? What could potentially happen if I just took the recent overall trend and extended it over the next twelve months? Can I effectively forecast this item if I don't have some understanding of the potential impact of each trend element? I doubt it. This doesn't mean that I absolutely need to separately forecast each trend element, only that I at least need to understand the potential each may have during this forecast horizon. For example, if this is a product with a very long product life cycle in a stable industry, it may be fine to just track trend as a single element and extend it over the forecast horizon.

How does one go about separating and then combining the trend elements to get a forecast? I'll admit this is both tricky and problematic. First, you need more information than just the historical demand of the item in question. Let's look at calculating a couple of trend elements individually. For simplicity's sake, we'll assume this product is only subject to trend related to changes in market share and product life cycle.

> **Important note:** The following pages cover a complex approach to treating trend. And even though many of you will probably never need to break down trend into its various elements for your forecasts, it is important to understand these factors. Later in this chapter and the following chapter, we will cover more conventional ways of dealing with trend in forecasting.

Product life cycle index.

In the case of the trend element related to product life cycle, you need to look at the historical demand of similar items that have already completed (or are well into) their product life cycle. Rather than breaking the demand down by specific periods (actual dates), you break the demand down by numbered periods relative to the product life cycle. For example, if your forecast interval is one month, the first month that specific product was available for sale would be listed as forecast period #1, regardless of which month the product was actually released. This way you can take demand from multiple items released at various times during the year, and align their demand into forecast periods relative to their product life cycle. You can now combine their demand (either in units or dollars) by forecast period, and create a product life cycle index for the product group by dividing each period's demand by the average period demand throughout the product life cycle. See figure 4A for an example of calculating an index for a product group with a product life cycle of 15 periods.

Product life cycle index for a product group

Period	1	2	3	4	5	6	7	8	9	10	11	12	13	14	15
Item #1	10	15	20	25	30	40	50	60	40	20	10	10	5	5	5
Item #2	15	28	35	45	50	70	90	105	70	35	15	13	8	7	5
Item #3	7	12	15	20	23	30	25	45	30	12	8	6	3	4	3
Total Demand	32	55	70	90	103	140	165	210	140	67	33	29	16	16	13
Index	0.41	0.70	0.89	1.15	1.31	1.78	2.10	2.67	1.78	0.85	0.42	0.37	0.20	0.20	0.17

Figure 4A. Here we just aligned the demand for three items over their product life cycles, and then calculated an index the same way we calculated our seasonality indexes. This gives us a product life cycle index we can use on similar products.

Now that you have a product life cycle index, you could apply that to the expected overall sales for a new item to get your initial forecast. For example, if you are introducing a new product that you expect to sell 600 units over it's 15-period product life cycle, you would divide 600 by 15 to get an average demand of 40 units, which can then be multiplied by each period index to get the expected sales during that period. If we used the index created in figure 4A, we would have a first-period forecast of 16 (40 times 0.41), a second-period forecast of 28 (40 times 0.70), and so on. Where did the 600-unit forecast come from? An initial estimate of sales for a new item is generally based on analysis of sales of similar items, combined with some qualitative assessments as to changes in market conditions, features of the new product, and expected pricing. This can be as much art as science and is therefore not relegated to a simple mathematical calculation.

When analyzing product life cycles, you may find they are gradually changing (shrinking or expanding). Once again, you need a lot of history to determine this, but if you do determine that product life cycles are changing, you should change your product life cycle index to reflect this before applying it to future forecasts.

You may have noticed that the product life cycle index calculation is very similar to the seasonality index calculation covered previously. This is not a coincidence; in fact, product life cycles and seasonality are very similar. That is, they both demonstrate cyclical patterns of changes in demand that are relative to a specific period of time. Whereas a seasonality index represents changes in demand that are relative to time periods in a conventional calendar (demand changes repeat same time each year, quarter, month, etc.), a product life cycle index represents changes in demand that are relative to the entire period of time the product is active. Wouldn't it be great to sit around for hours arguing about whether product life cycle should be considered a form of seasonality versus a form of trend? Naah. Even though it has more similarities to seasonality, it is more likely that you will treat demand changes related to product life cycle as a form of trend, therefore we'll call it trend for now.

Market share index.

To calculate a trend index for changes related to market share you would generally analyze the history of a much larger group of products. In many cases, this would include all products sold by your business. Unlike the index we created for product life cycle—where the index for each period is relative to the demand during the entire product life cycle—our market share index (and most other trend indexes) represents the demand change in one period relative to the demand in the previous period (period-to-period index). For a very simple example, you could take total sales (in either dollars or units, depending upon the type of product) for all products you sell, and combine them by month. Then divide the most recent complete month's sales by the previous month's sales. So, if November's sales were 5,000, and December's sales were 5,500, you would have a trend index of 1.10 (represents a 10% increase in sales). You could now multiply December's sales of 5,500 by your trend index of 1.10 to get a forecast for January of 6,050. I know this is an oversimplification, but it is enough to get us through the next section.

Combining your product life cycle index and your trend index.

Our first problem here is that we have two indexes that are based on different demand elements. The product life cycle index is based on the demand over the entire product life cycle, while the market share trend index is based on the demand of the previous period. What we want to do here is to change the product life cycle index so that it reflects the change in demand from one period to the next, rather than one period relative to all other periods. This is actually rather easy. You simply divide the index for each period by the index for the previous period.

Converting product life cycle index to period-to-period index

Period	1	2	3	4	5	6	7	8	9	10	11	12	13	14	15
Original Index	0.41	0.70	0.89	1.15	1.31	1.78	2.10	2.67	1.78	0.85	0.42	0.37	0.20	0.20	0.17
Period-to-Period		1.71	1.27	1.29	1.14	1.36	1.18	1.27	0.67	0.48	0.49	0.88	0.54	1.00	0.85

Figure 4B. Converting a cycle-based index to a period-to-period index is as simple as dividing the index of one period by the index of the previous period.

For example, period 3 had a product life cycle index of 0.89 and period 4 has an index of 1.15, so you would divide 1.15 by 0.89 to get a period-to-period index of 1.29, which represents period 4's demand relative to period 3. So now, if we have actual or forecasted demand for period 3, we can multiply it by 1.29 to get forecasted demand for period 4. But wait, there's more. Multiplying period 3's demand by 1.29 only gets us a forecast that takes into account product life cycle demand changes. What we really want to do is multiply period 3's demand by 1.29 and then by 1.10 (our market share trend index) to get forecasted demand for period 4 that takes into account product life cycle demand changes and demand changes related to market share. In fact, we can combine as many trend indexes as we want this way. So if we had a product life cycle index, a market share index, an overall market index, a product line index, and an event index, we would take period 3's demand and multiply it by our first index, then take the result and multiply it by the second index, then take that result and multiply it by our third and so on.

You can then repeat this for subsequent periods using the resulting forecast as the basis. In other words, once you have multiplied period 3's demand by all your period 4 indexes to get your period 4 forecast, you can then multiply your period 4 forecast by your period 5 indexes to get your period 5 forecast and so on. So essentially, once you have all your indexes set up you can create the calculations that allow you to simply enter in the demand for any period and get an immediate forecast for all subsequent periods. It's almost like magic.

Combining trend indexes in a forecast

Period	1	2	3	4	5	6	7	8	9	10	11	12
Demand	100											
Forecast		299	266	216	344	491	579	735	502	246	123	110
Product life cycle index		1.71	1.27	1.29	1.14	1.36	1.18	1.27	0.67	0.48	0.49	0.88
Product line index		0.98	0.98	0.98	0.98	0.98	0.98	0.98	1.00	1.00	1.00	1.00
Market share index		1.00	1.00	1.05	1.05	1.05	1.00	1.00	1.00	1.00	1.00	1.00
Market index		1.02	1.02	1.02	1.02	1.02	1.02	1.02	1.02	1.02	1.02	1.02
Event index		1.75	0.70	0.60	1.33	1.00	1.00	1.00	1.00	1.00	1.00	1.00

Figure 4C. Here I've produced a forecast for the next 11 periods using the demand from period #1 and five trend indexes (all indexes are period-to-period indexes). If you were to set this up in Excel, with Period #1 demand of 100 in cell B3, your formula for the forecast for period #2 would be:

=IF(ISBLANK(B3),B4*C5*C6*C7*C8*C9,B3*C5*C6*C7*C8*C9)

The "=IF(ISBLANK" stuff is there to determine if I have demand for a period. If I don't have demand, I will use the previous period's forecast to calculate my next period's forecast.

As wonderful as this sounds, you need to be very careful not to get fooled into believing that this seemingly magical creation of your future period forecasts is going to reflect actual demand through the entire product life cycle. As we had previously discussed, forecasts (and more specifically, trends) are more accurate for nearer periods of time. Because of this, our forecasts will be more accurate if we recalculate them as more demand history becomes available.

When trends collide.

To be more precise, this should be titled: when trends and seasonality collide. If you were paying close attention, you may have noticed that even though I gave examples of calculating a couple of trend elements and then combining them to create a forecast, I didn't exactly explain how to cleanly extract various trend elements and seasonality from historic demand when multiple similar trend elements and seasonality are present at the same time. For example, if you suspect your demand is being affected by trends related to general market conditions as well as trends related to market share, how would you identify each? Or, if you calculate a seasonality index based upon the past two year's history, and trend was present during this period, wouldn't your seasonality index be skewed by the trend(s) present during this time?

I would like to say that there is a simple mathematical calculation that can separate these factors, but there isn't. In fact, the process for doing this can range from a little tedious to virtually impossible depending upon the demand characteristics of the products, and the amount of relevant history available. It's best to start with what you "know" about your business and use that knowledge to identify the most important factors as well as the factors that can most accurately be isolated. When I say start with what you know, you should be aware that what you think you know may not be accurate. Don't worry about that for now because we're just using what you think you know to try to save some time in this process. We will test the data to verify your assumptions.

The process for disaggregating trend elements essentially involves aggregating demand into groups and time frames that are most likely to accurately isolate a specific factor. Then once that factor is isolated (calculated), we then disaggregate demand and remove the now known factor from the disaggregated demand and then reaggregate the demand into new groups that are most likely to accurately isolate another factor. Ouch! That hurt me as much to write as it probably did you to read.

For example, one of the first things you probably want to identify is a seasonality index. In many cases, we can hide the impact of some other factors by simply aggregating demand. If you have many products that were introduced at different times you'll probably find that by aggregating demand into very large product groups you'll mask most of the effects of demand changes related to individual product life cycles (you'll have a good mix of products at various stages in their product life cycles). This same logic may very well also mask demand changes due to the popularity of specific product groups or even events that were specific to certain products or smaller product groups.

You're now left with aggregated demand that still may be affected by trends related to overall market conditions, market share, and seasonality. Since the seasonality index only impacts time periods of less than one year, we can aggregate demand into yearly buckets to try to isolate trend related to market share and overall market conditions (I know we were trying to calculate seasonality, but this will make sense shortly). It's pretty easy now to calculate the overall demand changes (at this point I really don't care if it was from overall market conditions or market share) from year to year (note: if you use sales dollars for this calculation, you should first adjust them for any inflation/pricing changes that may have occurred). Now a little bit of educated guesswork comes into play. You need to use your knowledge of your business to make assumptions about whether the overall demand change (trend) that occurred in a given year was a steady gradual change or followed a different pattern. If it was a steady gradual change, you can equally spread the demand change over smaller periods of the year (months or weeks) and then adjust each period by this trend to provide a "trendless" set of data to use for your seasonality calculations.

For example, if your demand change from 2008 to 2009 was an increase of 24% and you want to create a seasonality index based on months, you need to spread the 24% over the 12 months of the year and remove this demand increase from your monthly demand data. We are going to keep things simple here and not worry about whether the percentage demand change from period to period was compounding (it won't make a whole lot of difference anyway). So, if we divide the annual percentage increase by the number of periods on which we are going to base our seasonality index, we will have the information we need to adjust our demand history. For our monthly index we need to divide 24 (the annual percentage increase) by 12 (the number of months in a year) to get 2%. We can now start adjusting our monthly demand. The twelfth month would have had the full 24% increase (124% of sales from the same month in the prior year) therefore we need to divide the 12 month's demand by 1.24 (the decimal equivalent of 124%). For the 11th month, we need to deduct 2% from the 24% and therefore we would divide the 11th month's demand by 1.22 (the decimal equivalent of 124% minus 2%). Continuing with the other months, we would divide the 10th month's demand by 1.20, the 9th by 1.18, and so on.

Removing trend

	Jan	Feb	Mar	Apr	May	Jun	Jul	Aug	Sep	Oct	Nov	Dec
Demand with trend	153	179	194	190	163	157	155	178	193	215	287	210
Trend index	1.02	1.04	1.06	1.08	1.1	1.12	1.14	1.16	1.18	1.2	1.22	1.24
Demand with trend removed	150	172	183	176	148	140	136	153	164	179	235	169

Figure 4D. We can remove the trend by dividing the demand by the trend index.

This completes removing our overall market conditions and market share trend from the 2009 data. We now need to repeat this entire procedure (starting with determining the annual demand change for each specific year) for the remaining data we will use for our seasonality index. We don't need to worry about removing multiyear demand changes. For example, if we are basing our seasonality index on 2007, 2008, and 2009 data and we had annual demand changes of 30%, 28%, and 24% respectively, we do not need to remove 82% (the demand changes for all three years) from the 2009 data, or 58% from the 2008 data (the demand change for 2007 and 2008) to keep them in line with the 2007 data after the 30% trend is removed. We only need to remove the demand change (trend) that occurred in each specific year.

Now that you have removed the trend from all three years, you can calculate your seasonality index(s) as described in the previous chapter. Once you have your seasonality index(s) you can compare the index for the three-year period to each specific year to see if the pattern is similar. If the patterns aren't similar, it may signal that your trend during one or more years was not as smooth as you had assumed. In this case, you could either go back to that specific year and try to reallocate trend to match the pattern you are observing, or you can just remove that specific year from the seasonality index calculation.

Take your time trying to get your seasonality indexes as accurate as is practical. As mentioned in the previous chapter, seasonality indexes generally don't change very much from year to year (or even decade to decade in some industries) therefore once you get it calculated, you can reuse it year after year (with periodic reviews).

We can now go back to our raw data and remove our seasonality (divide the demand by the seasonality index), then reaggregate this de-seasonalized demand into groups that make it easier to identify other trend factors. In fact, we would likely start again from scratch on trend related to overall market conditions or market share. The trend calculations we previously conducted were really just aimed at getting us our seasonality indexes (which are extremely important), but don't do us much good for future forecasts. In order to separate trend related to overall market conditions and trend related to market share, we need some outside information. I'd like to note here that many (if not most) businesses don't need to (or simply can't) do this. For those businesses, you would instead aggregate (probably for all product) your de-seasonalized demand and calculate your overall trend from that data.

For those of you who want to utilize separate trend indicators for overall marked conditions and market share, you need to first identify these indicators. This means that you need an outside indicator that reflects overall market conditions, and an outside indicator that allows you to calculate market share. Let me first state that, based on my experience with the inconsistencies and inaccuracies in how organizations manage and report their data, combined with their reluctance to share this information, I tend to be rather skeptical of "industry indicators" supposedly based on this stuff. That being said, you don't have a whole lot of alternatives here. You can try the industry data and see if your forecasts using the data are better than your forecasts not using the data. Depending upon your industry, the sources of this information may be government agencies, an industry-specific trade organization, or a consulting organization that focuses on accumulating this data for your specific industry. And you're not just looking for "current state" information here. You need historical data in order to build a correlation with your historical trend, and then you need industry forecasts or other predictor variables to make use of this correlation.

To build your correlation, you can use regression analysis or simply look for an obvious mathematical relationship (sometimes you get lucky). Incorporating two indicators (one for overall market conditions and one for market share) requires multi-variable regression (also know as multiple regression). The concept and output are similar to that of the single-variable regression technique detailed in the previous chapter (you will need to check the documentation of the specific regression software product you use to understand how to set up the inputs and interpret the outputs). What you are doing is comparing changes in trend from your indicator variable's historical data, to changes in trend in your historical data, then applying the output from your regression analysis against forecasts of overall market conditions and market share to create a trend forecast. Realize you will not output a separate market share trend and a separate overall market conditions trend. Instead, you will get a single trend forecast that is based on these two factors and therefore can be independently influenced by changes in either factor.

It's very likely that you will calculate these high-level trend factors manually in a spreadsheet program and then later manually (or semi-automatically) input them into your forecasting system. It generally makes sense to do this manually because it's easily done in a spreadsheet program, and since this is done at an aggregate level (usually for all sales or large groups of items), the calculation will not be repeated hundreds or thousands of times (which would make it a candidate for automation). It's very important that someone knowledgeable is reviewing this calculation and its output because it's quite possible that the inputs and/or outputs of this will need to be manually adjusted. For example, forecasting changes in market share is likely going to require input from people within the organization responsible for high-level strategic decision-making and those most knowledgeable in your market.

You also need to convert the relationships between overall market conditions, market share, and trend into a simple period-to-period percentage change that can be used by your forecasting system. Most people will probably find it less confusing if they just stick with period-to-period percentage changes throughout the trend calculation process. Therefore, whether you calculate your overall trend manually or through the use of regression analysis, you will first convert all inputs to period-to-period percentage changes. So rather than using a dollar amount (such as total industry revenue for each period) and comparing that to total revenue for each period for your company, you would first calculate the change in total industry revenue from period to period as a percentage, and compare this percentage change to the period-to-period percentage change in your company's revenue. In other words, rather than looking for how January's revenue for your industry of 500 million dollars compares to your January revenue of 3 million dollars, you would compare (through regression analysis or other method) the percentage change between December and January revenue for your industry to the percentage change between December and January revenue for your business.

Let me once again mention that many of you will probably never need to break down trend into its various elements for your forecasts. I felt it was important to cover this for those who may need to go to this level, but also to help the rest of you to develop a better understanding of the complexities of trend.

Exponential smoothing revisited.

We've already covered simple exponential smoothing, but forecasters have taken exponential smoothing far beyond simply smoothing historical demand. Terms like double exponential smoothing and triple exponential smoothing are somewhat misleading since they seem to imply you are somehow re-smoothing the historical demand over and over again, when in reality you are applying the smoothing technique to additional elements of the forecast (though some re-smoothing does occur in some methods). So rather than focusing too much on catchy names for particular variations, I'm going to show the logical progression in using smoothing in forecasts. By the way, these same concepts can be applied to other smoothing techniques (moving averages or weighted moving averages).

Smoothing trend.

So you have your simple exponential smoothing calculation all put together, but you realize your forecast always lags in trend. What do you do? You add trend to the calculation. Since trend is a gradual change in demand over time, we can look to quantify trend as the change in demand from one period to the next. However, since actual period-to-period demand variability tends to consist of a lot of noise, we need to find a way to eliminate as much of this noise as possible. And how do we do that? Well, we smooth it, of course. But, instead of taking the difference in actual demand from one period to the next and then smoothing it, how about we take the difference in the forecasts created from one period to the next (which is already smoothed to some extent) and then smooth that? Well that would make it double smooth wouldn't it? Hmm, I wonder what would be a good name for something like that?

In other words, we are taking the results of our simple exponentially smoothed forecast, then looking at the difference between the previous period's forecast and the next period's forecast, and then applying a smoothing factor to that to get a smoothed trend, which we can now add to the forecast to better account for trend. Essentially we are running two separate-but-related exponential smoothing calculations (one for the base demand forecast, and one for the trend forecast) and then combining the results for our finished forecast. So if our basic exponentially smoothed forecasts (note this is forecast, not actual demand) for the last two periods were 50 and 55 respectively, and our next period's basic exponentially smoothed forecast is 58, the trend numbers that go into our trend exponential smoothing calculation are 5 (55 minus 50) and 3 (58 minus 55). So to get our smoothed trend, we would multiply 3 by our smoothing factor (does not necessarily have to be the same smoothing factor used in the base forecast) and then multiply the previous period's forecasted trend by 1 minus the smoothing factor, and add the two together. But, since we don't yet have a previous period's trend forecast, we will just use the previous period's actual trend (5) for the calculation. Therefore, if our smoothing factor is .40, we multiply 3 by .40 to get 1.2, then multiply 5 by .60 (1 minus .40) to get 3. We then add 3 to 1.2 to get a smoothed trend of 4.2. The seemingly obvious next step would be to add 4.2 to the next period's base forecast of 58 to get a next period's trend-adjusted forecast of 62.2. Or would it?

Smoothing trend

Period		1	2	3	4	5	6	7
Demand		50	62	63	70	83	79	95
Smoothed demand	0.4		50	55	58	63	71	74
Trend				5	3	5	8	3
Smoothed trend	0.4			5	4	4	6	5

Figure 4E. Here we used exponential smoothing to smooth our demand and then again to smooth our trend. Since we based our trend calculation on the smoothed demand, some smoothing has already occurred. So by smoothing the trend that is already based on smoothed demand, we can say we are double-smoothing our trend.

Well this is where many exponential smoothing calculations go wrong. As has been previously covered, exponential smoothing (and all other smoothing calculations) will lag in trend due to the smoothing process. So even though we developed a nice little calculation for producing a smoothed period-to-period trend number (4.2 in the previous example), the smoothed base forecast that we are adding this to is already lagging current demand. Exactly how much it is lagging depends upon the smoothing factor used.

Figure 4F shows how the lag varies depending upon the smoothing factor used. The demand shown has a consistent trend of 25 units increase per period, with absolutely no noise. This is an unrealistic demand pattern but works to demonstrate lag in trend. I think most planners could look at this demand and be able to predict that the demand for period 20 will most likely be 975 units. But as you can see, the basic smoothed forecast for period 20 using a smoothing factor of 0.20 is 852 units, which essentially represents the demand that occurred 5 periods back. So even if we added the unsmoothed trend quantity of 25 to the 852, we get 877 which is still lagging by about 4 periods. Now if you look at the calculation that used a smoothing factor of 0.60 (which is a rather high smoothing factor), you can see that even if you add the unsmoothed trend of 25 units to the basic smoothed forecast of 933, you get 958 which is still almost one period behind.

Trend-lag example

Period	Demand	Smoothing factor 0.20		Smoothing factor 0.60	
		Smoothed	Trend	Smoothed	Trend
1	500				
2	525	500		500	
3	550	505	5	515	15
4	575	514	9	536	21
5	600	526	12	559	23
6	625	541	15	584	24
7	650	558	17	609	25
8	675	576	18	633	25
9	700	596	20	658	25
10	725	617	21	683	25
11	750	638	22	708	25
12	775	661	22	733	25
13	800	684	23	758	25
14	825	707	23	783	25
15	850	730	24	808	25
16	875	754	24	833	25
17	900	779	24	858	25
18	925	803	24	883	25
19	950	827	24	908	25
20		852	25	933	25

Figure 4F. This example shows two exponential smoothing calculations based on demand with an obvious trend. The first calculation uses a smoothing factor of 0.20, the second uses 0.60. You can see that both calculations eventually calculate the appropriate trend of 25 units per period, but the trend-lag of the smoothed demand is so significant that adding the trend to it still does not provide us with an accurate forecast.

Some of the "double-exponential smoothing" calculations I have seen published, will add the previous period's smoothed trend into the basic forecast before calculating the smoothed trend for the next period, which will then be added into the forecast for the final trend-adjusted forecasted. So what they are sort of (though not exactly) doing, is adding the trend into the forecast twice. And while this provides a better forecast than the previous example I've shown, it still isn't completely taking into account the forecast lag relative to the smoothing factor used (though it is compensating for it to some extent). In other words, this is a simple "cheat" to make the results of the calculation more closely match what you would expect the output to be. Though this is a useful cheat, I think we can do a little better.

Now if we go back to my example in figure 4F and then recall how the smoothing factor in exponential smoothing works similarly to the weighting used for the most recent period of a weighted moving average, we can see that a smoothing factor of 0.20 means that the most recent period's demand will account for 20% (or one-fifth) of the forecast. Now let's remember that the forecast without the trend adjustment had a lag of approximately five periods. Hmmm, one-fifth weighting results in a five-period lag? I think we've found something here. So if I divide one (the number 1) by the smoothing factor and then multiply the trend by this (we'll call this the trend multiplier), I should be able to add this to the basic smoothed forecast to get a trend-adjusted forecast that takes into account trend lag relative to the smoothing factor used. So back to the initial example, I would divide 1 by 0.20 giving me a result of 5. I then multiply 25 by 5 to get 125, and add this to 852 to get a forecast of 977 for period 20 (in the actual calculation, it would be closer to 975, but since I used rounded numbers, it comes out higher). Now let's try it with the example that used a smoothing factor of 0.60. Divide 1 by 0.60 to get 1.67, which multiplied by 25 results in 42, which added to 933 results in a final forecast of 975. Now that's more like it.

Or is it? We previously noticed that a smoothing factor of 0.2, which translates to a one-fifth weighting being placed on the most current period, also resulted in an approximately five-period delay in trend. Well, the five in one-fifth and the five in five-period delay kind of jumps out at you. So we made an assumption that seemed logical, then we tested our logic with a smoothing factor of 0.6 and received similar positive results. We then jumped to the conclusion that our assumption was correct. But, if you rethink this from the perspective that if the most recent demand accounted for one-fifth of the weighting, wouldn't trend lag by 2.5 periods (one half of 5)? This would be true if we were using equal weighting for all periods (such as a five-period moving average), However, with exponential smoothing, the previous periods' weights decrease exponentially for each subsequent previous period. Therefore, the lag in trend for an exponentially smoothed forecast that placed one-fifth weighting on the most recent period would be longer than if using a five-period moving average.

In essence, dividing one by the smoothing factor to give us a trend multiplier is just another cheat. That doesn't mean it won't provide useful results, only that these useful results were not provided by a mathematically correct calculation. But then again, forecasting itself cannot be mathematically correct because we are dealing with a level of uncertainty. If you consider the smoothing methods we've covered so far, although the basic smoothing calculations are mathematically correct, their application to forecasting is basically a "cheat". Since we cannot accurately identify noise when trend is also present, we use these smoothing calculations to remove variations in demand that are likely to be noise. In other words, these smoothing calculations provide results that look like the kind of results we would want.

Trend-adjusted forecast				
		0.20		
Period	Demand	Smoothed	Trend	Forecast
1	500			
2	525	500		
3	550	505	5	530
4	575	514	9	559
5	600	526	12	587
6	625	541	15	615
7	650	558	17	642
8	675	576	18	668
9	700	596	20	695
10	725	617	21	721
11	750	638	22	747
12	775	661	22	772
13	800	684	23	798
14	825	707	23	823
15	850	730	24	849
16	875	754	24	874
17	900	779	24	899
18	925	803	24	924
19	950	827	24	949
20		852	25	975

Figure 4H. This example shows a trend-adjusted forecast using the trend-multiplier cheat previously discussed. If you were to set this up in Excel, with Period #1 demand of 500 in cell B4, your formula for the period-3 forecast (cell E6) would be =C6+((1/C$2)*D6) .

So is there a mathematically correct means of determining the trend multiplier? Probably, but I don't know how to do it because it is beyond my mathematical skill set. Hey, I'll admit it. What I know about mathematics is very small in comparison to what is knowable about mathematics. I know that there must be a mathematically correct means of doing it because I have a good understanding of how exponential smoothing works, and since the exponential smoothing calculation itself is a mathematical calculation, there has to be a mathematically correct means of determining a characteristic (the trend lag) of the output of exponential smoothing. But once again, because we are dealing with uncertainty here, a mathematically precise calculation for trend lag very well may not provide better results than my "cheats". So in an effort to more accurately reflect the practical realities we often face in setting up our inventory systems, I'm just going to stick with my little cheat.

Period	Demand	Smoothed Demand	Trend	Smoothed Trend	Forecast	Error %
		0.3		0.4		
1	53					
2	42	53				
3	75	50	-3	-1	45	-40%
4	82	57	8	2	65	-21%
5	67	65	7	4	79	18%
6	78	65	1	3	75	-4%
7	75	69	4	3	80	7%
8	96	71	2	3	80	-17%
9	88	78	8	5	94	7%
10	105	81	3	4	94	-10%
11	98	88	7	5	106	8%
12	113	91	3	4	105	-7%
13	112	98	7	5	115	3%
14	120	102	4	5	118	-2%
15	123	107	5	5	124	1%

Figure 4I. Here we have a trend-adjusted forecast where we also used exponential smoothing on the trend (using a different smoothing factor). I've also included a column for the forecast error. Though this example does contain noise, the trend is rather consistent so it's still pretty easy to forecast. If we had more variation in our trend we would need to use a larger smoothing factor to allow our forecast to more quickly adapt to the changing trend.

Smoothing seasonality?

Three times is the charm, right? We've smoothed demand and trend; why not apply exponential smoothing to the seasonality index as well. Well, it's easy enough to do. There are a couple of different approaches to applying exponential smoothing to seasonality. One would be to apply the exponential smoothing process to the actual demand, resulting in smoothed demand for each forecast period within the seasonal cycle (usually a year). Then create the index from this smoothed demand. The other would be to create an index for each previous seasonal cycle and then smooth the index.

Let's use a typical annual seasonal cycle with a forecast interval of one month. In the first method, we would be applying the exponential smoothing technique to demand from all relative time periods. So basically we are running twelve separate exponential smoothing calculations (one for each month). Therefore, for January we would be using actual demand from the most recent January, and the smoothed output from the previous years' Januarys. We would then do the same for February, March, and so on. Once we have smoothed demand for each month, we divide the smoothed demand for each month by the average smoothed demand for all months to get our exponentially smoothed seasonality index.

The second method would start by dividing each month's actual demand (un-smoothed) by the average demand for all months in the year to get an unsmoothed index for the most recent year. Then we would be applying the exponential smoothing technique to the indexes from all relative time periods. For January, we would use the unsmoothed index from the most recent January and the smoothed output from the previous years' Januarys' indexes. We would then do the same for February, March, and so on.

Either method should provide similar results. I'm not a big fan of applying exponential smoothing to seasonality for one simple reason. Seasonality tends to be relatively static and therefore any of the smoothing techniques (moving average, weighted moving average) tend to provide very similar results. So in many cases, exponentially smoothing your seasonality index is simply unnecessary (though it really doesn't hurt). However, if your seasonality is trending, it would make sense to use a technique that can account for these changes. What I mean by trending is there is a noticeable pattern (trend) in how your seasonality changes from one seasonal cycle to the next. For example, if you are an online retailer of consumer goods and you notice that your big Christmas rush starts a little earlier each year, you could apply to your seasonality calculation the same exponential smoothing and trend adjustment methods that we previously covered for demand and trend in the forecast. This way, you would project the trend you have observed in sea-

Why Seasonality and Trend Adjustments?

It's unlikely your inventory is not subject to some level of seasonality and trend. If you do not build seasonality and trend into your forecast, you will be forced to use safety stock to compensate for it. The problem with using safety stock to compensate for seasonality or trend is you will end up carrying more inventory than you would if you built these into your forecast. That's because seasonality and trend have valleys as well as peaks, so by forecasting these elements, you are able to carry less inventory during the lower periods of demand.

sonality into the next seasonal cycle. But then again, you don't need exponential smoothing to apply trend (you can incorporate a trend calculation into a moving average or weighted moving average calculation to provide similar results).

Adaptive smoothing.

Adaptive smoothing is the ultimate fix for smoothing addicts. The basic concept behind adaptive smoothing is you create logic that monitors your forecast and automatically adjusts your smoothing factor(s) on the fly to provide an appropriate smoothing factor for that particular forecast on that particular day.

So how does this wonder of modern forecasting work? For the most part, adaptive smoothing techniques will take one or more forecast error measurements (see forecast error measurement in the previous chapter) and incorporate them into a calculation to adjust the smoothing factor. The simplest (and not very useful) method I have encountered is to use the absolute value of the previous period's forecast error as the smoothing factor for the next period. So if your last period's forecast was for 100 units and your actual sales were 130 units, you would subtract 130 from 100 and then divide the result (-30) by 100 to get a forecast error of -30% (or -0.30). The absolute value of -0.30 would be 0.30. So you would use 0.30 as the smoothing factor for your next period's forecast. You would have to put some limits in place here since a forecast error can possibly be more than 100 percent, resulting in a smoothing factor that is greater than 1 (remember that a smoothing factor must be a number between zero and one). This method rarely provides respectable results so I only include it here to help explain the concept.

A better method of adaptive smoothing uses the tracking signal (discussed in the previous chapter) as the basis for the smoothing factor. A tracking signal is a better input to adaptive smoothing because a tracking signal helps to distinguish between noise and trend. So since a higher tracking signal suggests that the forecast error is more likely due to the forecast inadequately accounting for trend, and a lower tracking signal suggests that noise is the predominant contributor to forecast error, it would make sense that you would want to use a higher smoothing factor when you have a higher tracking signal (and vice versa). Therefore, if we took the tracking signal example in the previous chapter that resulted in a tracking signal of 0.444, we would then use 0.444 as the smoothing factor for the next period's forecast. You would generally build in limits to prevent the smoothing factor from being too high or too low (for example, limiting it to a number between 0.20 and 0.70).

Be aware that the tracking signal is not necessarily the optimal smoothing factor. It's just another "cheat" that works in some environments. And this leads us to an even better method that uses the tracking signal to change the smoothing factor. In this method, you would analyze demand patterns, smoothing factors, and tracking signals to determine which smoothing factors tend to provide the best results relative to the tracking signal. In other words, you would build a table that says when the tracking signal is X, use Y as the smoothing factor, or, when the tracking signal is X, adjust the smoothing factor by Y.

And then can I smooth that? You bet you can. You can take the smoothing factor created by one of the previous (or other) techniques and smooth it against the smoothing factors created for previous periods. This can help to keep your smoothing factors from jumping all over the place. And it doesn't end here; there are all kinds of other forecast measurements, limits, and overrides, you can add to your logic to tweak it to your liking. But be careful out there, sometimes you can clever yourself into something really stupid.

Black-box forecasting.

Adaptive smoothing is a nice lead-in to black-box forecasting. The basic idea of black-box forecasting is that you input data, magic happens, and the most phenomenal stupendous magnificent awesometacular forecast mankind has ever known is spit out. Your "black box" is essentially a piece of forecasting/demand planning software, and not only do you not know what goes on inside, you probably don't want to know what goes on inside. These programs are designed for inventory managers that are basically lazy, lack curiosity and initiative, and are intent on not taking responsibility for anything. In other words, there's a big market for these puppies.

Alright, I'll play nice. There are legitimate reasons for using these types of products and there are legitimate reasons why you may not understand exactly what is going on within them. What is probably happening inside, is your data is being run through various forecasting techniques with various configurations, and the results are then automatically compared to see which configuration and technique seems to provide the best results given your demand patterns. Why you may not understand exactly what is going on inside is possibly due to the fact that the various combinations of techniques and algorithms built into the box are considered "top secret" intellectual property by the software provider and they don't want their hard work being stolen by other software companies (or by potential clients). In addition, some of what goes on inside may be so complex that there is no easy way to explain it to the laymen, even if the software company wanted to. In fact, there may only be a handful of people at the software company who truly understand what goes on in the box.

My basic problem with black-box forecasting is that I believe you get the best results when knowledgeable inventory managers use their knowledge of their business in combination with technology. Black-boxes often take the inventory manager out of the process. My other issue is, that based on my experience, business software products in general are often far less sophisticated than we are led to believe. Therefore, what's going on inside, may not be capable of providing respectable results.

That being said, these "black boxes" may very well perform better than the forecasting logic many companies are currently using. But more importantly, if you combine the advanced logic of a packaged forecasting system with the ability to input parameters from knowledgeable users, you may very well have the optimal solution for your forecasting needs. Therefore, I'm not saying that packaged forecasting systems are inherently flawed, but rather the implementation of a packaged forecasting system as a black box that just "does everything automatically" is a flawed approach.

Human input.

Despite the focus on various mathematical forecasting techniques, human input is a very important part of forecasting. I guess the best way of saying this is that sometimes a human needs to tell the computer what it doesn't know. So far we've covered various mathematical methods that look at what has happened in recent history, and then mathematically extend what has happened into a prediction of what will happen. And this works fine provided the factors that impacted your sales remain fairly constant or gradually change. However, there are times when we (humans) have new information the computer doesn't know about. Therefore, we need a way of telling the computer that something different is going to happen that will affect demand.

What kind of events are we talking about here? Promotions, are a prime example. It boggles the mind how companies can run a promotion and never get around to adjusting their forecasts (and therefore their inventory) to account for the upcoming promotion, but it happens with regularity. Other examples would include sudden changes in fuel prices or interest rates (though you could build it into your system to monitor these), natural disasters, wars, changes in trade agreements, pricing changes by you or a key competitor, one of your products being featured in a magazine or on a television show, an ad campaign, the introduction of a competing product from another supplier, or some government official getting on TV and telling people they can protect themselves from terrorist attacks by stocking up on duct tape and polyethylene sheeting. It's not like your computer is watching the news and hanging around in sales meetings. I think a prime example is when many companies saw sudden dramatic downturns in demand during 2000 and 2001. As this was happening, I kept thinking that there are a lot of inventory systems out there that are not going to react appropriately to this. And sure enough, over the following months and years, reports started to trickle out how many companies got stuck with excessive inventory. Some of these companies were the same companies that years earlier were being showcased in industry magazines as leaders in supply chain management.

So what happened? The multi-million dollar systems these companies were using had been set up and tweaked to perfection (or so we were led to believe) during a time when gradual and consistent growth was the norm. These automated systems didn't know what to do when things suddenly changed, because these systems had never experienced this before. Therefore, they initially treated the sudden drop in demand as noise, then as the drop continued, they gradually worked it into the forecast. The key word here is "gradually". What this basically resulted in was that as demand was dropping off dramatically, these systems kept ordering more inventory (based on previous trend). Somebody needed to jump in and tell the computer to stop.

Well let me go back to the comment I made on black-box forecasting systems that were "designed for inventory managers that are basically lazy, lack curiosity and initiative, and are intent on not taking responsibility for anything." These dumbasses (when a highly paid manager exhibits this level of incompetence, he deserves to be called a dumbass) either assumed their fancy system would somehow handle this (obviously not understanding how their system works), or they didn't know how to stop what was happening (again, not understanding how their system works), or they didn't want to stick their neck out by overriding their fancy system, or they just didn't have a clue that anything was happening.

Any forecasting system should have (this doesn't mean they do have) a means of overriding the system-generated forecast. The most basic would be allowing for manually entering an override forecast. For example, I would go into the system for item X and manually enter a forecast for periods 3, 4, and 5. The system would use my manually entered forecast for these periods and then take over again at period 6. Other methods may include the ability to adjust the forecast for a group of items by a specific percentage, or enter an override trend (as a percentage) for a group of items. Another option would be to build several forecasting models based upon specific demand characteristics; when you suspect that a sudden change in demand is or will be occurring, you switch over to a model designed for this type of demand (you may still want to use some type of override in combination with this). For known temporary events such as promotions, you would want a means to apply an index (somewhat like a seasonality index) over a specific number of periods to adjust for the promotion. These types of overrides are covered in the next chapter.

Then there are forecasts that are almost entirely based on human input. An example would be where each salesperson tells you what he expects to sell and then you accumulate this into aggregate forecasts. I'll admit this scares the hell out of me; unfortunately, some businesses have no choice but to do this. It's more likely though that this type of forecasting is used for higher-level planning such as financial, capacity, labor, and facilities planning, or for longer term strategic plans. There are various methods for accomplishing this, including systems designed with various forecasting levels involved where higher-level forecasts from management are compared to aggregated lower-level forecasts from sales people or branch managers, adjustments are made, and information is passed back and forth in an organized manner until consensus is achieved.

It can be very challenging to get biases and general incompetence out of these types of subjective forecasts. If sales people are held accountable for meeting their projections, they are likely to provide a conservative forecast so as not to be caught underperforming. On the other hand, if there is no accountability, sales people will likely provide an inflated forecast to ensure they aren't hindered by stock shortages. Then there are sales people who simply don't have a clue as to how to put together a forecast. The characteristics of a good sales person (depending on the industry) do not necessarily include good analytical skills (or even basic math skills in some cases). I'm not trying to pick on sales people here, but as I mentioned previously, this type of forecasting scares the hell out of me. So if at all possible, look for some way to at least try to validate the information provided by this type of forecasting against something that is a little more analytical.

Forecasting Part 3:
Putting It All Together

Setting up your forecasting system requires you to make quite a few decisions, some that can easily be changed later, and others that are much more difficult to change once your forecasting system is running. In this final chapter on forecasting, we will go over some of these decisions and show how the various forecasting components and techniques previously covered can fit into a complete forecasting system. We'll also briefly cover some additional topics related to forecasting.

Setting up a forecasting system.

Selecting a forecast interval.

One of the key early decisions that has to be made is the selection of a forecast interval. The forecast interval determines the length of your forecast periods (also called time buckets). For the most part, this means selecting between monthly or weekly forecasts. This is a rather important decision since changing forecast intervals later can be rather complicated and troublesome. In most systems, the forecast interval will also be reflected in the "time buckets" used throughout the system to summarize planning data (historic demand, future orders, etc.).

Monthly forecasts are usually easier to implement and manage, but weekly forecasts offer some distinct advantages in many environments. In making this decision, you need to understand how your forecast interval affects various aspects of your inventory management system.

> **Safety stock and lead time.** This will be covered in detail in the next chapter, but for now I'll just state that the forecast (and therefore, the forecast interval) is a critical component of any statistical-based safety stock calculation, as is your lead time. Therefore, it can be advantageous to have a forecast interval that is close to your typical lead times. So, if your typical lead times are less than two weeks, you would have a strong reason to consider a weekly forecast interval over a monthly one.

Lot sizes / order quantities. Although not quite as important as safety stock and lead time, lot sizes or order quantities should also be considered here. If you are typically ordering less than two week's demand at a time, you should also consider weekly forecast intervals.

Seasonality. In all likelihood, your seasonality index will be based on your forecast intervals. Therefore, your seasonal patterns should be analyzed under multiple forecast-interval scenarios to determine if there is a significant advantage for using a smaller forecast interval. For example, if you are a mail-order retailer of consumer goods, you may find that you have a significant Christmas peak that covers the last two weeks in November and the first two weeks of December. With a seasonality index based on monthly intervals, you would not see that the last two weeks of November have significantly more demand than the first two, or that the first two weeks of December have significantly more demand than the last two weeks. This very well could result in replenishing inventory too early in November or too late in December.

Trends. Shorter forecast intervals will allow you to identify sudden changes in trend more quickly. This can be a huge advantage in businesses with fluctuating trends or where a sudden significant trend change is likely.

It's important to note here that some of these factors are impacted by other factors. Let's go back to that Christmas seasonality issue. If I am an importer and have long lead times, it is possible that I may have had to place my order for the entire Christmas season several months earlier, and will have the entire season's inventory delivered by early November. Therefore, it really doesn't make a difference if I have seasonal fluctuations within the November-December season. The same would hold true of trend, in that if I have long lead times and large lot sizes, my ability to react to a sudden change in trend is very limited anyway.

Is there a downside to weekly forecasts? This is a valid question since there are some obvious benefits to weekly forecasts—and you could always just accumulate the weekly forecasts into monthly buckets if you wanted to. In that respect, there is no downside to weekly forecasts as far as the results you can get from them. The downside is more related to implementing and maintaining weekly forecast intervals. The most significant is related to developing a seasonality index. With monthly time buckets and annual seasonal cycles, there is a clear relative period from one seasonal cycle to the next (January of last year is relative to January of this year). And even though a month in one year may not have the same number of working days or sales days as the same month in previous years, the impact is not usually significant (though you may want to take this into account). But with weekly time buckets, you are basing your time periods on a fixed set of seven days that always starts on a specific day and ends on a specific day (such as Sunday through Saturday). While this sounds like it should be easy, the fact is, specific events (such as holidays and month ends) that can have a significant impact on sales for the week, will not always occur in the same relative weekly period from year to year. Therefore, your seasonality index just got a hell of a lot more complicated.

Creating your seasonality index(es).

So how many seasonality indexes do you need? If you've read other inventory management books or taken courses on inventory management, you are probably under the impression that you calculate a seasonality index for each item you need to forecast. But, if you were paying attention a couple of chapters ago, you should remember that I recommended calculating seasonality indexes at the group level. This comes back to the idea that forecasts are more accurate at the aggregate level. Therefore, by using the demand history of a group of products that are similarly impacted by seasonal cycles, I should be able to get a more accurate (less impacted by noise) seasonality index than if I tried to calculate a seasonality index for each item in the group individually. Keep in mind that when I talk about product groups relative to seasonality indexes, I am talking about a group of products that share the same seasonal sales patterns. This grouping of products may be different from product groups used for other purposes, so it may be easier to think of these as seasonality categories rather than product groups, but I'm going to continue to call them product groups.

Let's start with a hypothetical regional retailer that has about a dozen large hardware stores, and one of the big product lines is lawnmowers. Calculating a separate seasonal index for each model of lawn mower would be problematic since models frequently change and therefore I wouldn't have enough relative history on each model to get an accurate index. In addition, the generally low sales for each individual model also make the demand highly susceptible to noise. Therefore, going to a product-group based index makes a lot of sense here. The next issue I need to resolve is whether lawnmowers can be fit into the seasonality index of a larger product group. For example, would all my "lawn and garden" products have the same seasonality index? My suspicion here is that although they may have somewhat similar indexes to other lawn and garden products, there may be enough of a difference to justify a separate index. To take this further, I also suspect there may be some differences in seasonality indexes for different subcategories of lawnmowers. Primarily, I would want to compare indexes for rider-type lawnmowers to the standard walk-behind types. Why would I suspect differences here? The rider-type lawnmowers are a larger investment for the customer and therefore I suspect these purchases are planned well in advance, while the purchase of the lower cost walk-behind lawnmowers are more likely to be purchased spur-of-the-moment—like when you go to cut your grass the first time and find out you can't start your lawnmower and the service lead time at the local repair shop is running about six weeks. Also, since some rider-type mowers can be fit with optional equipment (such as snow plows), and may even end up as Christmas gifts, they may have a seasonality index that includes a winter spike. And then there's demand from the riding lawnmower racing crowd—oh yeah!

Now I need to start to crunch the numbers to test my assumptions and put together my indexes. This is where we come back to forecast interval. If you are using monthly forecast intervals, this is pretty easy, and for the sake of testing the assumptions (about product groups) I find it's sometimes easier to just start with a monthly index even if you will eventually need a weekly index. First, I would want to clean up demand history if necessary. For example, I would try to remove the trend from the demand as described in the previous chapter, and make adjustments for promotions or other events that may skew the seasonality index. I would then calculate my index the way I described in Chapter 3 for each product group, and then compare them (the product groups) to see if some share the same or very similar indexes. I may even create some additional product subgroups just to see if there are differences in the index. I can now analyze my monthly indexes and combine product groups that share a similar index before creating my actual indexes.

Let's assume now that I am using weekly forecast intervals, and therefore need a seasonality index based on weekly time buckets. This is where things can get a bit messy. Weekly forecast periods are based on calendar weeks (Sunday through Saturday, Monday through Sunday, etc), but seasonality tends to based more on specific dates, such as specific times of the year, holidays, month-ends, etc. And since specific dates do not fall an the same day or necessarily within the same week from year to year, I do not have a clean way of relating specific weeks in one year to specific weeks in the next year for the purposes of calculating my indexes. For example, if my business pushes out a lot of sales at the end of each month (self-induced seasonality), I should see a spike in my seasonality index for weeks that occur at the end of the month. But when I compare calendars, I find that the last day of September sometimes falls in week 39 and sometimes falls in week 40. Therefore week 40 from one year may not share the same index value as week 40 from another year, and since each calendar year consists of 52 whole weeks plus a fraction of a week, I can't really create a nice little table that lists the relative weeks by year the way I can with months.

So what I really need to do here is to disaggregate my demand to create a daily seasonality index based on calendar date, and then reaggregate my date-based index into specific weekly time periods. The most obvious way to do this is to simply group your demand by date over several years and create your index this way. For example, if my average daily demand for a product group over a three-year period was 50 units per day, and my demand on January 1st for the three-year period was 40 units, 50 units, and 45 units, I would have an average January 1st demand of 45 units (40 plus 50 plus 45, divided by 3) divided by an average daily demand of 50 units,to get a January 1st index of 0.90 . I would then continue and calculate an index value for each day of the year. Now to reaggregate the index into weeks, I would determine which specific dates fall into which specific weekly time buckets, and then calculate the average of their values to get my index values for each week. Therefore, if the seven days that fell into a particular weekly time bucket have indexes of 0.90, 0.92, 0.93, 0.95, 0.87, 0.88, 0.90, I would get an index of 0.907 for that week.

Another way to do this is to "stack indexes". Let's say for example you have various product groups that have unique seasonality patterns, but the seasonality differences are not all that significant from month to month, and, all your product groups are equally impacted by the same month-end sales push—and subsequent beginning-of-the-month sales slump. You could create unique monthly indexes for each product group and then create a single index within each month that represents the daily changes in demand during that month for all products. For example, each month tends to start out slow and then peak at the end of the month, so you may end up with an index that roughly starts around 0.70 for the first few days of the month and ends around 1.50 for the last couple days of the month (the index could be different for each month, or you could use a generic month index). You could then multiply the daily index values from this generic (all items) index by the monthly index value for each specific product group, to get a daily index for each specific product group. Therefore, if product group "A" had a January index of 0.90 and your daily index within the month of January for all products had a value of 1.50 for January 31st , you would multiply 0.90 by 1.50 to get a January 31st daily index for product group "A" of 1.35 .

What this is doing, is taking the fact that for this product group, sales during the month of January tend to be slower by 10% (resulting in index of 0.90) than average monthly sales during the year, and sales for all products on the last day of January tend to be 50% higher (resulting in index of 1.50) than average daily sales for the month of January. Therefore you can combine these indexes (by multiplying them) to get an index of 1.35 that says sales for the date of January 31st for this specific product group tend to be 35% higher than average daily sales for the year.

You could then do this for each day and then reaggregate the days into weeks the same way we did previously. You can stack as many indexes as you like as long as they are useful to your forecasting. For example, if you want to get down to the daily forecast level and you have significant differences in demand on specific days of the week, you can create another index that represents the day of the week and apply that. So, if Fridays are busier than Mondays and month-ends are busier than the beginning of the month, and March is your busiest month, and this March 31st happens to fall on a Friday, you can multiply your March index value by your month-end index value and then by your Friday index value, to get an index value for what should be your busiest day of the year. The main thing you need to be careful of here is that you don't stack an index that is already represented in another index. For example, if you calculated your daily index based on actual demand on specific dates as we did in the first example, you would not want to later try to stack a month-end index value onto it since it already took into account month-end demand changes. We'll also do a little more index stacking later when we cover events like promotions.

There may be additional adjustment needed for your index depending on how your business is impacted by specific events. For example, some holidays don't fall on the same date each year, so if your demand is impacted by these holidays you will need to adjust your index to reflect the actual dates of these events.

Date functions

Date	Month	Day of Month	Day of Week	Week #
1/1/2009	1	1	5	1
1/2/2009	1	2	6	1
1/3/2009	1	3	7	1
1/4/2009	1	4	1	2
1/5/2009	1	5	2	2
1/6/2009	1	6	3	2
1/7/2009	1	7	4	2
1/8/2009	1	8	5	2
1/9/2009	1	9	6	2
1/10/2009	1	10	7	2
1/11/2009	1	11	1	3

Figure 5A. This example shows how you can use Excel functions to extract date information you may need for your seasonality calculation. If the date of 1/1/2009 is in Cell A3 in Excel, the formula for Month would be =MONTH(A3), the formula for Day of Month would be =DAY(A3), the formula for Day of Week would be =WEEKDAY(A3), and the formula for Week# would be =WEEKNUM(A3). You would then use this date information as keys to facilitate matching specific indexes with specific dates.

Seasonality index example (combining indexes)

Date	Month Index	Day of Month Index	Day of Week Index	Holiday Index	Combined Index
1/4/2009	0.90	0.88	1.28	0.99	1.00
1/5/2009	0.90	0.88	0.73	0.99	0.57
1/6/2009	0.90	0.90	0.88	0.99	0.71
1/7/2009	0.90	0.90	0.92	0.99	0.74
1/8/2009	0.90	0.90	0.99	0.99	0.79
1/9/2009	0.90	0.90	1.03	0.99	0.83
1/10/2009	0.90	1.00	1.17	0.99	1.04
				Week #2 index	**0.81**

Figure 5B. Here I've taken the date information from the previous table (I added a holiday index for this example) and associated indexes for each day during week #2 (Sunday through Saturday). I then multiplied the indexes to get a combined index for each specific date. I then averaged the indexes for the 7 days to get my index of 0.81 for week #2 in 2009. This is just one example of how you could use various calendar-based indexes to create your seasonality index. There are numerous possible variations, so you need to build the index that makes the most sense for your specific business.

I should note that you would not actually use a day-of-week index if you were ultimately going to consolidate your daily indexes into weekly indexes as I did in this example. It basically negates any effect of your day-of-week index (the day-of-week index nets out to nothing). I included it in this example just to remain consistent with the previous example.

The holiday index I added represents any seasonality that is not reflected in the other indexes. This would most likely be due to holidays, but could be used for any date-based events that impact demand but are not already accounted for by the other indexes. In this example, our day-of-month index is generic (represents all months) therefore, seasonality that occurs relative to a specific date will not be reflected here unless we add another index.

Once you have your seasonality indexes created for your various product groups, you can then apply the indexes to your forecasts for the individual products within each group. Though I highly recommend you consider creating seasonality indexes at the group level (as has been described here) because I believe it provides a much more accurate and functional seasonality input to your forecasts, there are times when it makes sense to calculate seasonality indexes at the item level. If your products are very diverse (meaning you don't have many items that would share seasonality patterns with other items), AND the items have reasonably consistent demand (low noise), AND you have enough relative sales history for the items (usually at least a couple of years), you may be able to calculate a reasonably accurate seasonality index at the item level. This can work with moderate-to-fast moving items, but is usually problematic with slow movers since demand patterns associated with slow movers tend to have a much larger amount of relative noise than demand patterns of faster movers.

De-seasonalizing your demand.

Before we get to the next steps of smoothing and adding trend to our forecast, we must first use our seasonality indexes to de-seasonalize our demand history. In other words, we are removing the seasonality affect on our demand. Removing known factors from demand is sometimes referred to as "normalizing demand". We must remove the seasonality effect on our demand in order to more accurately identify noise and trend. If we didn't remove the seasonality, any smoothing technique we applied to the forecast would incorrectly treat seasonal demand changes as either noise or trend (depending on seasonal patterns and other factors). Remember, the object here is to identify all predictable elements of your demand so you can use these in your forecast. So once you have a predictable element (such as seasonality), you can remove it, then analyze your demand to see what other predictable elements can be identified.

To de-seasonalize demand, we simply divide the demand for each previous forecast period (time bucket) by the corresponding seasonality index for that period. So, if January's demand was 250 units and we had a seasonality index of 0.90 for January, we would divide 250 by 0.90 to get "normalized" demand of 277.78 units. Yes, it really is that simple.

Figure 5C shows how I have started to assemble a forecast in a spreadsheet. You can see that I have the historical demand and the seasonality index, and have used those to create a Normalized Demand (de-seasonalized demand) column. I'll keep adding to this spreadsheet to create a finished forecast that includes additional functionality.

	A	B	C	D	E	F	G	H	I	J	K	L	M	N
1	**The Forecast**													
2														
3	Period	Demand	Seasonality Index	Normalized Demand										
4	1	95	0.85	112										
5	2	103	0.87	118										
6	3	113	0.92	123										
7	4	120	0.98	122										
8	5	149	1.12	133										
9	6	162	1.20	135										
10	7	158	1.18	134										
11	8	158	1.15	137										
12	9	146	1.07	136										
13	10	148	0.99	149										
14	11	147	0.87	169										
15	12	138	0.88	157										
16	13	138	0.86	160										
17	14	188	0.87	216										

Figure 5C. We start our forecast by removing seasonality from the historical demand. First, fill in the values in columns A, B, and C. Then, in cell D4 enter =B4/C4 then copy and paste into the cells below.

Smoothing your de-seasonalized demand.

Now we are ready to use any of the smoothing methods (average, moving average, weighted moving average, exponential smoothing) previously discussed to try to separate our base demand from noise. If there were no trend present and you had a long history of this product's demand, this would be easy. You would simply calculate the average de-seasonalized demand over as long a period of relative history as was available. This could mean calculating over several years. In reality, there is almost certainly going to be some trend present, and as mentioned in the previous chapter, one of the most significant challenges in forecasting is trying to differentiate trend from noise.

We eliminate noise by smoothing; the more we smooth, the more noise is eliminated, BUT, the more we smooth, the more likely we are also masking our visibility to changing trends. To be honest, if you know what you are doing you can get a pretty good forecast by starting with any of the smoothing methods (it's the trend adjustments that tend to make or break the forecasts), so you shouldn't get too freaked out over whether you should use moving average, weighted moving average, or exponential smoothing. But, because exponential smoothing has become very much entrenched in the professional forecasting and programming community, I think it's probably a good idea to just go that route.

In Figure 5D, I've added a column that represents the smoothed de-seasonalized demand. I just used the basic exponential smoothing calculation described in Chapter 3. Since we are starting from scratch with this forecast, I need to plug the first forecast value (used period #1 de-seasonalized demand as the period #2 forecast). I've used a smoothing factor of 0.40 for this example.

	A	B	C	D	E	F	G	H	I	J	K	L	M	N
1	**The Forecast**													
2					0.40									
3	Period	Demand	Seasonality Index	Normalized Demand	Smoothed Forecast									
4	1	95	0.85	112										
5	2	103	0.87	118	112									
6	3	113	0.92	123	114									
7	4	120	0.98	122	118									
8	5	149	1.12	133	120									
9	6	162	1.20	135	125									
10	7	158	1.18	134	129									
11	8	158	1.15	137	131									
12	9	146	1.07	136	134									
13	10	148	0.99	149	135									
14	11	147	0.87	169	141									
15	12	138	0.88	157	152									
16	13	138	0.86	160	154									
17	14	188	0.87	216	157									
18	15		0.85		180									

Figure 5D. Next we smooth our normalized demand. In cell E2 enter 0.40 , in cell E5 enter =D4 , then in cell E6 enter =(E$2*D5)+((1-E$2)*E5) , then copy and paste into cells below. Note I've added a row for Period #15.

Calculating and smoothing trend.

Next we are going to calculate the period-to-period trend and then smooth it. To calculate the base period-to-period trend, all we need to do is subtract the basic smoothed forecast for the previous period from the basic smoothed forecast for this period. Since we are calculating our trend from the already smoothed forecast, our trend inherently has some smoothing in it, so it's possible we could just use this trend for our trend-adjusted forecast. This tends to work better when you are using a lower smoothing factor (therefore more smoothing has already occurred), but since we are using a moderate-to-high smoothing factor (and weekly time buckets), we are going to smooth our trend again.

Smoothing the trend (see chapter 4) works pretty much the same as smoothing the demand. First, we need to plug the first value (we'll use the period 3 trend as the period 3 smoothed trend), then we can start calculating our smoothed trend (using a smoothing factor of 0.60). If you look at Figure 5E, you can see the calculated period-to-period trend and the smoothed trend.

	A	B	C	D	E	F	G	H	I	J	K	L	M	N
1	**The Forecast**													
2					0.40		0.60							
3	Period	Demand	Seasonality Index	Normalized Demand	Smoothed Forecast	Trend	Smoothed Trend							
4	1	95	0.85	112										
5	2	103	0.87	118	112									
6	3	113	0.92	123	114	3	3							
7	4	120	0.98	122	118	3	3							
8	5	149	1.12	133	120	2	2							
9	6	162	1.20	135	125	5	4							
10	7	158	1.18	134	129	4	4							
11	8	158	1.15	137	131	2	3							
12	9	146	1.07	136	134	3	3							
13	10	148	0.99	149	135	1	2							
14	11	147	0.87	169	141	6	4							
15	12	138	0.88	157	152	11	9							
16	13	138	0.86	160	154	2	5							
17	14	188	0.87	216	157	3	3							
18	15		0.85		180	24	16							

Figure 5E. Next we calculate our trend and then smooth it. In cell G2 enter 0.60 , in cell F6 enter =E6-E5 , then copy and paste into cells below. In cell G6 enter =F6 , then in cell G7 enter =(F7*G$2)+(G6*(1-G$2)) , then copy and paste into cells below. Note that I've added a row for Period #15.

Adjusting for trend lag.

To incorporate the trend and compensate for trend lag due to smoothing, I'm using the calculation discussed in the previous chapter. Let me note again that this is just a "cheat" I came up with a while back when trying to find a better way to account for lag than I had found in published exponential smoothing calculations. I've found it to work pretty well with a variety of demand patterns, but use at your own risk.

All we're doing here is dividing the number one (1) by the smoothing factor to get our trend multiplier, then multiplying the smoothed trend by the trend multiplier and adding the result to the basic smoothed forecast. We now have our forecast with trend adjustment. See Figure 5F.

Adjusting for seasonality.

Next, we need to apply our seasonality index to the forecast. We just multiply our trend-adjusted forecast by the seasonality index. We now have our forecast with trend and seasonal adjustments. See Figure 5F.

	A	B	C	D	E	F	G	H	I	J	K	L	M	N
1	**The Forecast**													
2					0.40		0.60							
3	Period	Demand	Seasonality Index	Normalized Demand	Smoothed Forecast	Trend	Smoothed Trend		Forecast with Trend Adjustment	Seasonally Adjusted Forecast				
4	1	95	0.85	112										
5	2	103	0.87	118	112									
6	3	113	0.92	123	114	3	3							
7	4	120	0.98	122	118	3	3		125	123				
8	5	149	1.12	133	120	2	2		126	141				
9	6	162	1.20	135	125	5	4		135	162				
10	7	158	1.18	134	129	4	4		139	164				
11	8	158	1.15	137	131	2	3		138	159				
12	9	146	1.07	136	134	3	3		140	150				
13	10	148	0.99	149	135	1	2		139	138				
14	11	147	0.87	169	141	6	4		151	132				
15	12	138	0.88	157	152	11	9		173	152				
16	13	138	0.86	160	154	2	5		165	142				
17	14	188	0.87	216	157	3	3		165	144				
18	15		0.85		180	24	16		219	187				

Figure 5F. Next we calculate our trend-adjusted forecast and adjust it by our seasonality index. In cell I7 enter =E7+((1/E$2)*G7) , then copy and paste into cells below. In cell J7 enter =I7*C7 , then copy and paste into cells below. Leave column H empty for now.

Extending the forecast.

What we've done so far has produced a forecast for the next period, but in real life you need to produce a forecast for several periods in advance to account for lead times and lot sizing. We'll start out simple here and just extend the forecast using the current trend. To get the next period's trend-adjusted forecast, we just add the current smoothed trend to the current trend-adjusted forecast. We can then continue this as far into the future as is necessary. We then adjust for seasonality the same way we did before. See Figure 5G.

While this may seem to make perfect sense on paper, in practice there can be problems with this method. This is most notable when you have fluctuating trends and use an aggressive smoothing factor to adapt to the trend changes (which would be a typical approach for demand with fluctuating trends). Though you probably want to incorporate the most recent trend in your short-term forecast, you may have concerns about extending it too far into the future. For example, let's say we have a product that had somewhat flat sales for the first 10 weeks of the year, then started trending up dramatically. You have found that historically your products generally tend to not sustain these changes in trend for more than four to six weeks; after that, they tend to either flatten out or trend back to previous demand levels. In addition, you have an eight-week lead time on this product

	Period	Demand	Seasonality Index	Normalized Demand	Smoothed Forecast	Trend	Smoothed Trend		Forecast with Trend Adjustment	Seasonally Adjusted Forecast
					0.40		0.60			
1	95	0.85	112							
2	103	0.87	118	112						
3	113	0.92	123	114	3	3				
4	120	0.98	122	118	3	3		125	123	
5	149	1.12	133	120	2	2		126	141	
6	162	1.20	135	125	5	4		135	162	
7	158	1.18	134	129	4	4		139	164	
8	158	1.15	137	131	2	3		138	159	
9	146	1.07	136	134	3	3		140	150	
10	148	0.99	149	135	1	2		139	138	
11	147	0.87	169	141	6	4		151	132	
12	138	0.88	157	152	11	9		173	152	
13	138	0.86	160	154	2	5		165	142	
14	188	0.87	216	157	3	3		165	144	
15		0.85		180	24	16		219	187	
16		0.92				16		235	216	
17		0.95				16		251	238	
18		1.01				16		266	269	
19		1.04				16		282	293	

Figure 5G. Here we've extended our forecast five weeks into the future. To do this we need to go back and change some of our formulas to account for the fact that we will not have any new demand or trend numbers for these periods.

In cell G7 enter =IF(ISBLANK(B6),G6,(F7*G$2)+(G6*(1-G$2))) , then copy and paste in cells below.

Then in cell I7 enter =IF(ISBLANK(B6),G7+I6,E7+((1/E$2)*G7)) , then copy and paste it into cells below.

You'll also need to manually enter in the seasonality index values for the future periods.

Notice how the sudden demand increase in period #14 affects our forecast in future periods. This is a good example of where we would probably not want to extend this sudden increase in trend too far into the future. As we continue with our forecast you will see that this increase was actually the result of an event, and we will therefore adjust for it another way.

and often purchase lot sizes equivalent to a six-month supply. This means that your ordering decision is being based on what you expect to sell in the next eight months (8-week lead time plus the lot size of 6 months).

Using the simple method of extending the forecast under these conditions would likely result in a significant overestimation of demand in the long term, and subsequently result in a substantial amount of excess inventory. What you can do here (there are actually many options) is run a parallel forecast that is designed specifically for long-term forecasts. One way to do this would be to calculate a separate forecast or trend using exponential smoothing but using a smaller smoothing factor than your short-term forecast. You would do this exactly the same way as described so far in this chapter, but instead of using a moderate-to-aggressive smoothing factor (such as 0.40 and 0.60 used in the example), you would use a smaller smoothing factor (like possibly 0.10 or even less). You would then build logic into your final forecast that says, if the specific forecast period is X (a number of your choosing) or fewer periods in the future, use the short-term forecast, but if it is greater than X periods in the future, use the long-term forecast. Though this may seem a bit complicated, it's actually very easy to do since you are just duplicating what you have already done and adding some fairly simple decision logic. You could even go further and create multiple forecasts for short-term, mid-term, and long-term depending on your needs.

Another option for the long-term forecast would be to use the more complex trend calculations discussed in Chapter 4. This is where we created a composite trend based on various trend elements—such as product life cycles, product line popularity, market share, market conditions, etc. Once again, you would just run this as a parallel forecast and set up logic to use this forecast for periods greater than X periods in the future.

Other simpler options would include just flattening out your forecast after a certain number of periods in the future. For example, use the standard trend calculation up to 5 weeks in the future, then just use the 5th week's forecast for all subsequent weeks. There are endless variations that can incorporate additional elements such as fixed caps on demand relative to historical demand, a fixed index that automatically decreases the trend over a preset period of time, or a fixed trend used for long term forecasts.

Promotions and other events.

Promotions and other events that impact demand are common in so many industries, yet many forecasting systems have no way to incorporate these into the forecast (other than possibly through an override forecast) despite the fact that the logic is very simple. My preference for incorporating events into the forecast is to build indexes for the particular events common to your business.

Let's use a typical promotion as an example. Let's say you are an Internet retailer and periodically run a Free Shipping promotion for a one-week period. You find that your sales increase by 40% during that week over what you would normally have without the promotion. A simplistic approach would be to increase your forecast for that week by 40%. However, you'll probably find the impact on your demand from this type of promotion is more complicated than that. It's possible that what you actually get is a 40% increase in demand during the promotion week, but then have a decrease in demand during subsequent weeks due to customers moving their expected purchases into that promo week. What you need to do is conduct some analysis of demand during previous promotions, and build an index that represents the demand increases and demand decreases resulting from the event. What you may end up with is something like:

Week 1	1.40
Week 2	0.85
Week 3	0.95
Week 4	0.98

Week 1 is the promo week, and represents a 40% increase in sales for that week. Week 2 represents a 15% decrease in sales (relative to normal sales for that week). Week 3 represents a 5% decrease, Week 4 a 2% decrease. If your customers are aware of a promo in advance (some salesmen just can't keep their mouths shut), you very well may have a decrease in sales in the period(s) before the promo as well. For example, you may end up with an index of 0.95, 1.25, 0.90, and 0.95 respectively, where the 2nd index value represents the promo period. Unlike a seasonality index, the values in a promo index should not average out to the number one. If they did, that would mean that you didn't actually have any sales gain due to the promo.

As was done with the seasonality index, you will also need to "de-event" your demand as part of the forecasting process. In other words, you need to remove the impact of the event on your demand history to prevent it from skewing future forecasts. To do this, we just divide our demand by the event index. So, where we have a seasonality index present and a promotion/event index, we would divide the demand for a period by the seasonality index for that period, and then divide the result of that by the index we created for the promotion or event.

Then, to apply the index to your forecast, you just multiply your forecast by the index for the period relative to the promotion. You'll see an example of this later in Figure 5H.

It's important to note that different product groups may be impacted differently by an event. Some additional analysis (and knowledge of your business and customers' buying habits) will be needed to determine how your product groups are impacted. For example, you may find that when you run a percentage discount promo (such as a 15%-off sale), your customers stock up on particular items they know they will use (fast movers, stock items, common consumables), therefore you will see a significant increase in sales of these items and a more modest (if any) increase in sales of other items.

Also note that the event index functionality you incorporate into your forecasting system can be used for far more than just your own promotions. You can also use it to adjust for the promotion of a competitor that may temporarily negatively impact your demand, or any event that has an impact on your demand. This could include events such as a mention of your product on a news show or in a magazine, or weather events, acts or terrorism, or other events that will likely have a measurable impact on your demand.

Overrides and adjustments.

Though it can be thought of as a normal part of the forecast in businesses where events occur on a regular basis, the event index covered previously is sort of an example of a forecast override, in that it allows a temporary manual adjustment of the normal forecast. Overrides are an incredibly important part of the forecasting process because they allow humans to tell the forecasting system something it doesn't know. The promotions/events index is very useful for this, but you may find you need some additional functionality for greater flexibility in how you override your forecast.

The simplest forecast override comes down to just putting a number in the system that represents what you want your forecast for a specific period to be. An example of a fixed forecast override would be manually entering 150 as the forecast for forecast period #10. The logic for the final forecast for period #10 should then use this as the final forecast and ignore all other calculations. Even the most basic forecasting systems should allow for a fixed forecast override, in fact, that's all you get in many inventory systems (a field to enter in a forecast number).

Another common override would be some type of trend override. Though there are various ways to do this, I'm rather partial to using a period-to-period trend percentage override. This allows you to specify your trend as a percentage change from one period to the next. So rather than using the smoothed trend, we would multiply the basic smoothed forecast by our trend override percentage to get our trend in units. Then we would apply the same trend-lag calculation we would otherwise use with the smoothed trend, to incorporate our trend override into the forecast. The trend override percentage can be useful for events, but is more useful to apply a group trend to all items within the group. This is especially useful with slow movers where it is difficult to otherwise calculate a trend.

Another useful override consists of incorporating an additional index much like the event index. The main reason I would want this would be to more easily adjust for multiple events possibly occurring at the same time. For example, if I regularly run promotions, the main event index would be used primarily for this. But then, if some other event occurred, I could just input the new event index separately, and the system could calculate the forecast using both the promotion index and the separate event index. Otherwise, I would need a way to find out which items were impacted by both events and manually calculate a composite index. Another difference is that I may choose to not have the 2nd index as part of the "normalized demand" calculation. In other words, where I divided the demand by the seasonality index and the event (promotion) index to normalize the demand, I may not want to do the same with my 2nd event index. This way I could use it for events that I do want to impact my long-term forecasting. Let's say that one of my competitors goes out of business and I want to immediately adjust my forecasts to prepare for an increase in market share that would likely be the result of this event. The normal event index is designed for events that only have a short-term impact on demand, which is why we de-event the demand to normalize it for future forecasts. But, this gain in market share should be sustainable and therefore we do want the demand changes to impact future forecasts. The reality is, you could incorporate several of these index adjustments in your forecast and have some of them set up to normalize demand, and others to not normalize demand, depending on the specific type of event. See figure 5H.

	A	B	C	D	E	F	G	H	I	J	K	L	M	N
1	**The Forecast**													
2					0.40		0.60							
3	Period	Demand	Seasonality Index	Normalized Demand	Smoothed Forecast	Trend	Smoothed Trend	Trend Override %	Forecast with Trend Adjustment	Seasonally Adjusted Forecast	Event index	Forecast Override Index	Fixed Forecast Override	Final Forecast
4	1	95	0.85	112							1	1		
5	2	103	0.87	118	112						1	1		
6	3	113	0.92	123	114	3	3				1	1		
7	4	120	0.98	122	118	3	3		125	123	1	1		123
8	5	149	1.12	133	120	2	2		126	141	1	1		141
9	6	162	1.20	135	125	5	4		135	162	1	1		162
10	7	158	1.18	134	129	4	4		139	164	1	1		164
11	8	158	1.15	137	131	2	3		138	159	1	1		159
12	9	146	1.07	136	134	3	3		140	150	1	1		150
13	10	148	0.99	149	135	1	2		139	138	1	1	150	150
14	11	147	0.87	169	141	6	4	3.5%	153	133	1	1	150	150
15	12	138	0.88	157	152	11	9	3.5%	165	145	1	1		145
16	13	138	0.86	169	154	2	5	3.5%	167	144	0.95	1		137
17	14	188	0.87	173	160	6	5	3.5%	174	151	1.25	1		189
18	15		0.85		165	5	5		178	152	0.95	0.90		130
19	16		0.92				5		184	169	0.95	0.90		144
20	17		0.95				5		189	179	1	0.95		170
21	18		1.01				5	1.0%	191	193	1	0.95		183
22	19		1.04				5	1.0%	193	200	1	0.95		190

Figure 5H. Here I've added an event index and several additional overrides. You'll have to manually enter in the override values in columns H, K, L, and M. Then we need to go back and change some of our previous formulas.

In cell D4 enter =B4/C4/K4 , then copy and paste into cells below. This allows us to use our event index to normalize our demand.

In cell I7 enter =IF(ISBLANK(B6),(IF(ISBLANK(H7),I6+G6,(H7*I6)+I6)),E7+(1/E$2)*(IF(ISBLANK(H7),G7,H7*E7))) , then copy and paste into cells below. This takes our trend override % and incorporates it into our trend-adjusted forecast.

In cell N7 enter =IF(ISBLANK(M7),J7*K7*L7,M7) , then copy and paste into cells below. This incorporates our event index, forecast override index, and fixed forecast override into our final forecast.

You can see that as we add functionality to our forecast, some of our formulas start to get rather complicated. But you can also see the flexibility this gives us in producing a forecast that best meets the needs of our business.

Another useful override is a demand override. Why would someone want to override demand? Probably the most common reason would be to remove demand for a significant one-time shipment from the demand history your forecasting system is using. Though I wouldn't say these occur frequently, I would say that they occur occasionally in many businesses and therefore it would make sense to provide functionality to deal with them. What you don't want to happen, is to have a one-time significant shipment impact your future forecasting. Like the fixed forecast override, you can simply add a column for a demand override and then set up the logic of your system to use the demand override instead of actual demand. Another method would be to add a column for a "demand adjustment" in which case you would enter a negative number in the column for the quantity of the shipment you want removed from demand history. I should also point out you could just use your event/promotion index for this purpose, provided your event index is set up as part of the normalized demand calculation. You may also want to override demand history if you eliminate an item that is identical or similar to another item you sell, or if a new item is replacing a similar item that is being discontinued (you would probably want to combine the historic demand for both items under the item you are keeping active).

More Forecasting Stuff.

Group forecasting logic.

It should be evident by now that I like grouping products as part the forecasting process to help increase the overall accuracy of the forecast. We've already covered this relative to seasonality indexes but it also applies to other aspects of forecasting.

Using trend groups allows you to take a group of items that are theoretically equally impacted by the same trend forces, and use the demand history of the group to calculate the overall trend, then apply this trend back to all items within the group. You would generally calculate the trend here as a period-to-period percentage change and then incorporate it into your forecast the same way we used the "trend override %" discussed previously. You would want to use a group trend calculation when noise is a significant issue with individual item demand.

The most commonly used group logic for forecasting is simply grouping your products to apply a specific forecasting method or configuration. If you take the exponential smoothing forecast we've used in this chapter, you may find that even though all your products can use the same forecasting logic, they may not have the same demand profiles and therefore may require some different configuration of the forecast. The most obvious configuration change is the smoothing factor used. Higher smoothing factors work best with demand with relatively low noise and a history of significant trend variability. Lower smoothing factors work best with demand with relatively high noise and either low trend or constant trend.

It's very likely that you have products that fit into both of these categories. Slow movers are an example of a group of items that tend to require their own forecast configuration. The lower demand per period for slow movers (sometimes zero demand in some periods) generally results in a high level of noise and therefore tends to require some significant smoothing (a very low smoothing factor) and may also fit well into using trend groups for calculating trend. The higher demand levels of fast movers generally result in lower noise and therefore can more effectively use a higher smoothing factor, especially if variable trend is present. New items generally require a more trend-oriented smoothing factor, as well as some forecast overrides. Grouping products based on their product life cycles is very useful for forecasting and especially for how you calculate the long-term forecast.

Though changing the forecast configuration for specific groups is often enough, sometimes you may even need to use completely different forecasting techniques for different groups. Don't assume that all your products fit the same demand profile and therefore work within the same forecasting model. That said, be careful to not go overboard here. You're going to have to manage all these separate groups and forecasting techniques, so don't make this more complex than it needs to be.

Dependent demand and forecasts.

Dependent demand is demand that is created as a direct result of another item's demand. For the most part, this is the demand for components and raw materials used in manufacturing, assembly, or kitting processes, but may also be the result of demand flowing through a multi-facility planning system (such as DRP). Conversely, independent demand is demand that is not the direct result of demand of another item or facility. Demand for sales orders is the most common form of independent demand, but demand for internally used service parts may also be considered independent demand (though it is also possible to treat service parts as dependent demand).

The general rule of thumb is that you should not forecast dependent demand. Instead, you should calculate dependent demand based on the independent demand (probably forecasted) for the end items or downstream branches. For example, if I am manufacturing desk chairs and needed to determine demand for the casters (wheels), there should be no need to forecast the demand for the casters since I am already forecasting the demand for the chairs and I know (through the bill of materials) how many casters it takes to build each chair. The same would be true in a multi-facility environment where one facility provides products to one or more other facilities. For example, if I have 20 retail stores and a central distribution center that supplies these stores, and have forecasts at the store level, I could just calculate demand at the distribution center based on the forecasts at the stores. Though I could optionally create a forecast at the distribution center rather than forecasting at the store level, I would generally not want to do both.

And while it's generally a good idea to follow this rule of thumb, there are some complications and exceptions. In some cases, an item may have both dependent demand and independent demand. Back to the casters example, I would also have independent demand for the casters if I sold them separately as replacement/repair parts. And in the store/distribution center example, if my distribution center also sells product directly, I would also have independent demand at the distribution center. So in both these examples, I have both dependent and independent demand for the same item in the same facility.

There are also some circumstances where I may choose to forecast dependent demand. For example, if I am a manufacturer, and the majority of the components and raw materials I use have lead times of less than 30 days, however, I have a couple of components that have lead times of six months. Under the "rule of thumb" I would need to forecast the independent demand of the finished goods (the items that use the components) out at least six months into the future (actually at least six months plus the manufacturing lead time of the finished items). In some cases this is probably the best way to go, but, if these specific components are used in many different finished items, it may be easier and more accurate to forecast the demand for just these long-lead-time components out at least six months into the future than to forecast the demand for all the finished items out that far.

How do you go about setting up combinations of non-forecasted dependent demand and forecasted independent demand for the same item, or forecasted dependent demand for just some items? This depends on your inventory/forecasting system. This can get a bit complicated and, to be honest, many systems may not even be capable of doing this. This is why it's extremely important that you understand the capabilities and setup requirements of your specific system.

Managing demand history.

I had previously covered the use of a demand override to adjust historic demand under certain circumstances (large one-time shipments, combining or replacing items), but there is another significant issue related to demand history. Contrary to the logic in many business software systems, demand history is not necessarily a compilation of product shipments. As the name implies, demand should reflect when your customer wanted (demanded) an item, not when you shipped or invoiced the order. Therefore, demand should (from a systems standpoint) be tracked based upon Requested Date, rather than Shipped Date, Invoiced Date, or Ordered Date. The reason for this is best demonstrated with backorders. Backorders refer to specific items and quantities on orders that could not be filled on the requested date. In most cases, backorders are caused by inadequate inventory to fill the order. Failure to properly manage your demand history in regards to backorders can create some serious problems with forecasting and safety stock calculations.

For example, if item "A" normally sells 50 units per week (using a forecast interval of one week), and I run out of item A at the end of week #1 and am out of stock for 3 weeks, and then get a shipment in that allows me to fill all backorders and new orders in week #5, my shipment history will show something like shipment quantities of 50, 0, 0, 0, 200 respectively for weeks 1-5. Now if I were to use this as my demand history (as many systems do), how do you think this would affect the results of my forecasts over this period and future periods? Remember, your forecasting system doesn't know that you are/were out of stock during this period; so after showing demand go from 50 per week to zero for three weeks in a row, I would expect many forecasting calculations would be treating this as a significant downward trend in demand. Then when suddenly showing demand of 200, any systems set up to aggressively react to trend would possibly see this as a dramatic upswing in trend.

In addition, when we get into our safety stock calculation, the significant differences between our forecasts and shipments for these periods will appear as demand variability. Subsequently, we may end up setting up excessive safety stock for this item.

If you are in a business where your customers generally accept backorders and allow you to take the order and then just ship when the inventory comes in, you need to make sure you use the requested date (the date your customer wanted the item) to compile your historical demand used for forecasting purposes. Unfortunately, it's not quite this simple for many businesses. Sometimes a customer will just purchase this item from one of your competitors, resulting in a lost sale. Sometimes, they will just keep checking back and then maybe purchase the item when you get inventory. Sometimes, they will purchase a similar product from you in its place. Sometimes all these scenarios are being played out every day within the same business. To further complicate matters, the clues to any of these things happening may be spread across various systems. For example, the clues to what is happening may be based on requested dates on orders, or based on cancelled lines on orders, or on abandoned shopping carts on web stores, or a measurable increase in sales on similar items when you are out of stock, or a measurable decrease in sales when you are out of stock, or a measurable increase in sales when the item gets back into stock, or a combination of any of these.

There is no simple generic solution for dealing with this. You need to look at your specific business and determine how much of an impact backorders have on your demand and what you can do within reason to make your demand history reflect actual demand. For some businesses, this may mean doing nothing; for others, it may be a manual process of evaluating demand history for anything that has been out of stock for more than a specific length of time; and still others may require some very sophisticated custom programming just to manage the demand history.

Another often-neglected part of managing demand history is related to customer returns. This one can also get a bit tricky since different industries are impacted differently by returns, and even different types of returns within the same industry may have different demand management requirements. For example, if a customer orders the wrong item—and especially if the order quantity is large in respect to the normal demand for this particular item—and then returns the item in another demand period, how will this affect your demand history and subsequently your forecasting system? If the original demand was left in the demand period in which it occurred and then demand was reduced by that quantity in the period in which the return occurred, you would end up showing unusually high demand for one period and unusually low (possibly negative) demand for a later period. The better solution here would be to reduce the demand by the return quantity within the period in which the original demand occurred.

On the other hand, what if you are a retailer that has significant sales during the Christmas season and subsequently has a large number of returns after the Christmas season? If you reduced your pre-Christmas demand by the post-Christmas return quantities, and subsequently use this demand history to plan your next Christmas season, you will likely come up short on inventory during the next season since this same demand/return scenario is likely to repeat again. So in this case you would probably be better off leaving the initial pre-Christmas demand as is, and reducing demand in the period in which the return occurred. Oh, but I think I can complicate this a bit further. What if your returns—or a portion of your returns—are not in saleable condition (meaning you cannot resell them as new items)? In this case, you would not want to have the returns (or the unsalable portion of the returns) have any effect on demand history. Once again, you need to determine how returns affect your specific business before determining how to best handle the demand related to them.

Managing demand variability.

Up to this point, we've covered ways to adjust our forecasts for demand variability through seasonality indexes and trend adjustments, or minimize the impact of noise through smoothing techniques. But, in some cases you may actually be able to eliminate some of this demand variability. I had previously mentioned self-induced seasonality, a situation that results from certain business practices such as calendar-based incentive programs. Fortunately, if you can't eliminate self-induced seasonality, you can at least adjust your forecast for it as part of your seasonality index. But you may also have self-induced demand variability that is not based on specific events, but rather based on order policies that you impose on your customers. Quantity discounts, minimum order quantities, and even freight policies can potentially result in demand variability.

These policies result in your customers purchasing larger quantities less frequently than they would if the policies were not in place. On the surface, this does not sound like a bad thing since it probably reduces some operating costs, but in practice this can result in "lumpy" demand (noise). This is especially true for slower moving products or products that sell to a limited number of customers. For example, let's take a product that has average demand (no trend or seasonality present for this example) of 10 units per week (your forecast interval). But either through a minimum order policy or quantity discount policy, your typical customer order for these is for a quantity of 100 units. When you look at your demand history, you see that most weeks show demand of zero units, with a small number of random periods showing demand of 100, 200, or even 300 units, which means you will need to keep a significant quantity of inventory on hand (mostly in the form of safety stock) to meet this demand, or risk backorders. So in the end, you may end up holding more inventory and being at greater risk of stockouts, without effectively increasing your overall sales. I want to make it clear, I am not suggesting that you shouldn't have these types of policies, but you should be smart about which products you put under these policies.

You may even find that sometimes you encounter similar demand patterns on items that don't fall under these policies. For example, you may be looking into the reason for a stockout, and notice that even though the product normally has reasonably steady demand, occasionally a customer orders an unusually large quantity on a single order. And every time he does this, you run out of stock and incur either backorders or lost sales as a result. Upon contacting this customer you may find that he either doesn't really know why he orders in such large quantities and therefore may be able to change his system to reflect smaller more frequent order quantities in the future, or that he may be able to provide you advance notice for those shipments, in which case you can make sure you have adequate inventory on hand. This advanced notice would most likely come in the form of "future orders". Future orders are customer orders that are placed well in advance of need to help ensure product availability on the required date.

And while we're on the topic of future orders, you may find that it is beneficial to separate firm future orders from history and forecast. This could be used where you have multiple sales channels for the same products, and different needs for the different channels. For example, for a specific product you occasionally get some very large orders from a small set of manufacturers, but always get these orders well in advance, while the remaining demand for this product is consumer-level demand that comes in the form of smaller but more regular orders requesting immediate shipment. Provided the future orders are placed well enough in advance to appropriately affect your ordering decisions, there is no need to try to "predict" (forecast) this demand since it is "known". In this case, you would want to remove these orders from the demand history used for your forecasts (part of the normalize demand process) and create a forecast based solely on the demand of the non-future orders. Your ordering system must then have logic to take into account your future orders in addition to your forecast to come up with your expected demand for those periods.

Forecast consumption.

This brings us back to forecast consumption. You should recall that forecast consumption is the process of depleting the forecast as actual orders are received. On the surface, this would seem to be a simple process, but there may be many options for how you consume your forecast. In the previous example, where we wanted to separate some firm future orders from the forecasting process, we would also want to make sure that these orders do not consume the forecast when they are processed. We also need to tell the system whether dependent demand (discussed previously) should consume the forecast.

And to complicate things further, you may want to allow demand from one period to consume the forecast from another period. Sound crazy? In fact, this is a very common requirement. Remember the "lumpy demand" example discussed earlier, where we would occasionally get unusually large orders? Let's say that we had a similar situation but were unable to convert these large orders to firm future orders, and therefore unable to remove them from the forecasting system. So we now have an item that we have a forecasted weekly demand of 25 units that includes the demand for the large orders, but our actual demand for weeks 1 through 3 was 10, 0, and 75, respectively. Discrete-period forecast consumption would consume 10 units from week 1 then 0 units from week 2 and then ignore the remaining unconsumed demand. So when week 3 came up, the forecast was still for just 25 units. Week 3 would then consume the entire forecast of 25 units and ignore the additional 50 units of demand that occurred in that period. Weeks 4 and 5 would then still show forecasted demand of 25 units each. A smart person familiar with this demand pattern would probably be thinking after week 2, that since they haven't had a big order in a couple of weeks, they were probably close to getting one and would therefore want to show a larger forecast. Then, after week 3, would likely think that since they just shipped a big order of 75 units, they probably have a little time (at least another week) before expecting another big order. The way you would get your forecasting system to "think" like this is to set it up to roll some of the unused (unconsumed) forecasts from previous periods into future periods and allow some excess demand to consume forecast in future periods. Welcome to the world of forecast consumption rules.

Exactly how you go about setting this up will vary based on your specific system, but a common way of doing this is to set up forward and backward consumption days (or periods). The logic will probably go something like this:

1. If there is adequate remaining forecast quantities within the forecast period in which the demand occurred, it will consume from this period.

2. If there is inadequate remaining forecast quantities within the forecast period in which the demand occurred, it will look to see if the backward consumption days set up are great enough to go back into a previous period. Then, if that previous period(s) has unconsumed demand, it will consume that.

3. If there is still inadequate remaining forecast quantities within the forecast period in which the demand occurred or previous periods relative to the backward consumption days set up, it will look to see if the forward consumption days are great enough to go into a future forecast period and consume from that.

This covers how you can take excess demand from one period and consume from previous or future forecast periods, but doesn't address how you can roll unused forecast quantities from one period into future periods. This is somewhat less standardized functionality but may have a similar setting that allows your demand planning system to include unconsumed forecast quantities from a predefined number of previous periods into the demand calculation for future periods. Technically, it probably would not actually be changing forecast quantities in future forecast periods, but rather just including the unconsumed forecasts in the calculations for reordering.

And, of course, we need to tell our system which types of demand consume the forecast and which types do not. Remember that in our "future order" scenario, we wanted to run these firm future orders outside of our forecasting system, therefore we would also not want them to consume the forecasts. Similarly, we need to make sure our dependent demand is either consuming or not consuming forecasts based upon how we intend to plan dependent demand.

Forecast consumption is another one of those areas where it is very important that you read any documentation for your planning system on forecast consumption, and then test, test, test, to make sure it is doing what you wanted it to do. This is one of those situations where a single setting (like incorrectly setting up how dependent demand is handled) can create enormous problems with your planning systems.

Treating negative trends differently from positive trends.

This is a rather interesting practice. The idea here is that you may want to intentionally bias your forecast. The most likely approach is that you would want your forecast to react more aggressively to positive trends than to negative trends (though you could go the other way). In a high-margin industry where out-of-stocks would generally result in lost sales, you may want to consider this. I'm not going to go into detail on this one because it is a rather unusual practice, but I thought I'd throw it out there to provide another example of just how creative a process forecasting can be. I should note though, that when you start getting creative with your forecasting it's very important to thoroughly understand the impact this creativity will have. In the chapter on safety stock, we will revisit biased forecasts.

Composite forecasts.

For another example of creative forecasting, enter the realm of composite forecasts. Let's say you experimented with various forecasting techniques, and variations of techniques, and in the end just couldn't decide which one to use. Well, why not just use them all. Think of it as just adding one more layer of smoothing to your forecast. What you're doing here is running two or more parallel forecasts and then averaging or using a weighted average on the results to produce your final forecast.

Running multiple forecasts.

For a more adventurous approach, how about running multiple parallel forecasts (as in the composite forecast example), but rather than averaging the results, switch among the various forecasts based upon changes in demand patterns.

Summary.

For the most part, all history-based mathematical forecasting techniques are "cheats". Smoothing techniques do not actually identify and eliminate noise. Instead, they eliminate certain characteristics of a series of numbers; and it just so happens these characteristics are similar to the characteristics of noise we see in demand. Similarly, the mathematical techniques covered in these chapters cannot predict future trend. They can only help to quantify an approximation of past trend and provide tools to assist in extending past trend into the future to whatever level you choose. The basic idea in forecasting is to find a clever little mathematical calculation (or series of calculations) that makes the forecast do what you want it to do. In that respect, forecasting is a "creative" process that utilizes mathematics as a tool.

Ultimately, forecasting is an educated guess as to future demand, and is therefore inherently subject to inaccuracies. So why do we forecast? Because forecasting is better than not forecasting. For most businesses, there really is no effective alternative to forecasting. Certainly there are ways to lessen the need for forecasting (make-to-order, shorter lead times, etc.) and you would be well advised to explore these. But at the end of the day you will probably still need to do some forecasting. Although this is the final official chapter on forecasting, we will keep revisiting forecasting through the remaining chapters because the forecast is a key input to just about everything we do in managing inventory. As I said before, it all starts with the forecast.

OK, first I'll smooth the demand, then I'll smooth the trend, then the seasonality...

6

Safety Stock

What is safety stock and why do I need it? Some might say safety stock is used to compensate for unknown events, but that's not exactly correct. If we were truly trying to compensate for "unknown events", we would have no way of knowing how much safety stock is needed since we obviously have no idea what it is we are trying to compensate for (cuz it's like not known). So it's more appropriate to say safety stock is used to compensate for events that are known to occur; we just don't know exactly when they will occur. That isn't to say that we don't get some level of protection against unknown events with safety stock. If an unknown event occurs and the impact of the unknown event is within the range of the known events we plan for, we will get some protection there; we are just not able to specifically plan for these events.

Well enough word games for now. Safety stock can be used to compensate for supply variability, quality problems, or inventory accuracy problems; but for the most part, we use safety stock to compensate for demand variability. More specifically, we use it to compensate for the amount of demand variability that may occur during the lead-time period. As you recall from the forecasting chapters, we use smoothing techniques to remove noise from the forecast. The reason we remove noise, is that noise is the element of demand that we are unable to accurately forecast using conventional period-based forecasting. Therefore, noise is the demand element that causes us to keep safety stock. You could even say that a safety stock calculation is a forecast for noise. But, unlike our other forecasting techniques, safety stock does not predict when noise will occur; instead, it just predicts the levels of noise that may occur and attempts to determine the likelihood (probability) that certain levels of noise will occur. In fact, safety stock calculations are so closely tied to forecasting that you could think of this chapter as another forecasting chapter. So I guess I lied when I said the previous chapter was the final forecasting chapter.

Another safety-stock-related item I'd like to clear up is confusion over the physical state of safety stock. Though I'm not going to go so far as to say this is never appropriate, for the most part, safety stock does not need to exist as specific physical units. In other words, there is generally not a need to physically keep a separate stash of inventory to be used as safety stock. Instead, safety stock is just a quantity that exists in your inventory system to be used in your ordering calculations. Your ordering system will take into account the expected demand during the lead time of an item and then add to that the safety stock quantity in order to determine at which point (inventory level) you need to reorder. Therefore, if your lead-time demand is 10 units, and your safety stock is 4 units, your system should recommend reordering when your inventory drops below 14 units. So the safety stock quantity just results in reordering earlier than you would without safety stock. We'll cover ordering systems in greater detail later in this book.

That being said, there may be isolated situations where a company may feel it necessary to keep an emergency stash of inventory physically separate from their main inventory. In theory, I'd like to say that this is never necessary, but in practice, I have to admit that this may occasionally be a workable solution. The most likely scenario that comes to mind would be a manufacturing operation that has a component (or a small group of components) that are absolutely critical to their manufacturing operation, and they have determined they simply cannot afford to ever run out of these items.

For a more specific example, let's say that there is a specific little connector that goes into just about everything you make. This little connector is rather inexpensive relative to the product you manufacture, but is made specifically for you and subsequently has a minimum lead time of several weeks. Therefore, running out of this little inexpensive connector would shut your entire manufacturing operation down for several weeks. I'll admit that even if I were running that operation and had confidence in my inventory system, the accuracy of my processes, and my quality systems, I still may consider stashing some of these just to be safe. I would make them physically unavailable (possibly have them locked up somewhere) but I would not take them off the inventory system. Instead, I would find a way within the system to show the quantity and location of the stash but make it unavailable (put it on hold, or create a special location). I want to make clear that this is the exception to the rule. Most companies should not need to do this, and those that do, should only do it under very specific circumstances.

How do we go about calculating safety stock?

I break safety stock calculations down into three groups.

- Keep-it-simple methods?
- Oversimplified use of statistical methods.
- Appropriate use of statistical methods.

It will quickly become obvious that I am not going to recommend using methods that fall into the first two groups. Unfortunately, those are the methods used by the vast majority of businesses, and I want to dedicate just enough time to them to help explain why they are likely not your best choice for calculating safety stock.

Keep-it-simple methods?

Based on my experience, these are the most widely used methods for calculating (I'm using that term loosely here) safety stock. Probably the most common is that of using the demand during a set period of time. For example, you decide to calculate your safety stock as the equivalent of two weeks' demand. If your demand is 20 units per week, your safety stock would be 40 units. If your lead time for this item is 10 weeks, you would then have a reorder point of 240 units (lead-time demand of 10 weeks times 20 units, plus safety stock of 2 weeks times 20 units). Beyond the fact that this set period of time is often arrived at somewhat arbitrarily, there are numerous problems with this method. Primarily, it does not consider the key variable that creates the need for safety stock. As already mentioned, we use safety stock to compensate for the amount of demand variability that may occur during the lead-time period. This simple calculation neither takes into account the lead time, nor the variability patterns of the item. As an extreme example, if you had two items with the same demand patterns and one had a lead time of one week and the other had a lead time of one year, would it really make sense to keep the same amount of safety stock for both items?

Another popular method of calculating safety stock is to use a fixed percentage of lead-time demand. For example, you decide to calculate your safety stock as the equivalent of one-half your lead-time demand. Therefore, given the previous example of an item with a 10-week lead time and demand of 20 units per week, your safety stock would be 100 units (one-half of 10 times 20). Your reorder point would then be 300 units (lead-time demand of 10 times 20, plus safety stock of one-half of 10 times 20). Once again, beyond the fact that this fixed percentage of lead time is often arrived at somewhat arbitrarily, there are numerous problems with this method. Though it does take into account lead time, it does not take into account the variability patterns of the item. This is most notable when comparing fast movers with slow movers—since we can usually assume that relative variability is lower with fast movers than with slow movers.

For example, if my average demand for a particular slow mover was 2 units per week, I would not be surprised to see some weeks of zero demand and some weeks with demand of 4 or even more units. Therefore, my demand could be 2 or more times as much as my average demand. Now if I look at a fast mover that has an average demand of 5,000 units per week, it would likely be unusual to see demand for a specific week drop below 3,500 units or exceed 6,500 units. This is just a natural characteristic of demand of slow movers versus fast movers (we'll discuss this further later). But, if I were to use the one-half lead-time demand calculation on both of these items, assuming a lead time of one week, I would end up with safety stocks of 1 unit for the slow mover and 2,500 for the fast mover. This would very likely result in frequent stockouts of the slow mover and more safety stock than I really need for the fast mover.

In addition, even though this method does use lead time in the calculation, different lead times for the same item with the same demand pattern will actually result in different relative demand patterns during the different lead times. Once again, this comes back to the demand characteristic of greater demand having less relative variability than lesser demand. So as an example, let's take an item with demand of 10 units per week and compare a one-week lead time with a one-year lead time. Using the one-half-lead-time-demand safety stock calculation, we would have safety stocks of 5 units and 260 units respectively. If your week-to-week variability was such that 5 units were adequate to meet your needs, it's highly unlikely that your variability over a period of one year would be great enough to justify having 260 units of safety stock.

Now I realize these examples are a bit extreme, but that is an easy way to demonstrate or test these types of calculations. Though your inventory may not be subject to these extreme differences, you should be able to assume that the characteristics of these calculations still exist, just at a less obvious level.

So if these calculations are so flawed, why do so many businesses use them? The answer is, simple. That's really the complete answer; it's all about "simple". People like things to be simple, and you don't get much simpler than these methods. Quite a few years back there was a very popular inventory management book that—to the best of my recollection—said to set your safety stock to one-half of your lead-time demand, and if that isn't enough, set it higher. And people absolutely loved it. I still regularly get into arguments with folks over this one. Apparently, it's not just that people like things simple, but that they really like simple stuff if it comes from a book. I'm theorizing that they think that since it was in a book, it must be legitimate. Therefore, they look for books that keep things as simple as possible, and if they follow the instructions in these books, they are able to feel like they are doing a good job without really trying all that hard. And if their boss were to ever question their simplistic methodology, they just submit the ol' book as undeniable proof of the legitimacy of their "system".

I mean it's not like anybody can put just any old thing in a book. Or can they? Here, let me try something. It's well known that since safety stock is essentially compensating for the randomness of demand, the best way to calculate safety stock would be to randomly generate numbers to use as safety stock. Therefore, you should integrate one of those bingo/lottery ping-pong-ball machines into your inventory system and let it select your safety stock levels.

Did that get in the book? Hmmm.

Some companies will attempt to get more out of these simple calculations by creating variations based upon item categories. For example, they may set different time periods or different percentages of lead-time demand for "A" items versus "B" items. While I agree it often makes sense to have different policies for different item categories, these policies are still based on very flawed calculations. And, while adding these parameters seems to add some logic to the calculations, and may even provide better results than the base calculations, they are also fooling you into thinking you have a logical safety stock calculation. Also, as you will find later in this chapter, there are additional variables not mentioned here that you may need to consider when calculating safety stock.

Oversimplified use of statistical methods.

There are a couple of very similar statistically-based safety stock calculations that you will likely encounter in many inventory books or courses. The basic logic behind these calculations is sound (sort of), however, these calculations and the associated logic is generally communicated in an oversimplified manner and therefore doesn't provide enough information to properly use them.

The two statistical safety stock methods you encounter most often are actually variations of the same basic statistical model. That is, they apply the Normal Distribution statistical model to safety stock. The inputs to the calculations include a calculation of the Standard Deviation or the Mean Absolute Deviation (MAD) of historical demand, a desired service level, and a table that associates a service level with a multiplier. You just calculate either the standard deviation or the MAD, then multiply the result by the multiplier from the table that corresponds with your desired service level (each model has its own table). The result of this calculation is a safety stock level that should meet your desired service level. Or is it?

The answer to this question will become obvious as we progress through this chapter. In fact, the remainder of this chapter is based entirely on this single model, but rather than taking the mucho popular keep-it-simple approach, I'm actually going to try to explain the logic of the model and how that logic can be adapted to inventory management. In addition I will provide some of my own little adjustments (mostly cheats) and try to explain the logic behind them, and in the process hopefully get you to the point where you can put together a safety stock calculation that works for you. Be forewarned though, things are going to get really complicated here.

Appropriate use of statistical methods.

I guess it makes sense to start out by addressing the question of why we would use a statistical model to calculate safety stock. To risk oversimplifying things a bit myself, statistics are used to interpret and explain data, but more importantly for our purposes, statistics can be used to assign probability based on a sampling of data. Since what we want to do is use our historical demand (a sampling of data) to help us determine how much inventory it would take to compensate for demand variability (the probability that a certain quantity of safety stock will cover our needs), it would seem that the use of statistics would be a perfect fit.

Let me just throw in a disclaimer here. My knowledge of statistics is rather limited (I am in no way an expert), and what I am trying to do here is share with you what I think I know about statistics. And more specifically, what I think I know about the statistical model we will be using to calculate safety stock. It's possible that my understanding and explanations of statistical terminology and theory are not entirely accurate. However, my understanding of statistics and how they can be applied to safety stock has worked for me rather well to date, and in that respect, even if not technically accurate (from a statistics standpoint), I feel it is useful information to share within the context of inventory management. Also keep in mind that several of the adjustments to the calculation that I will cover here are adjustments I put together based on my understanding of this statistical model and how it can be applied to calculating safety stock. It is quite possible that some of my logic may be flawed, but since I am about to go through excruciating detail (you'll see) in explaining "my logic", you should have everything you need to make your own logical decisions. Now you may be wondering why I can't just compare my logic to the logic used by other "experts" out there, to see if I'm on the right track. The truth is, I have yet to encounter anyone who has ripped the guts out of the application of statistics to safety stock the way I'm about to. So buckle up, because this is going to be one helluva ride.

And if it makes you feel better, this stuff gives me a headache too. In fact, one of the benefits I get out of writing these books, is that I now have an organized reference I can go back to when I work on these same issues. Yes, I read my own books—actually quite regularly. I'm pretty good at figuring stuff out, but there are limits to just how much I can retain (especially the level of complexity we are covering in this chapter). Historically, this meant that occasionally I would have to "figure out" the same thing over and over again (although I would sometimes have notes to fall back on). Now, I can just go back to my books, read the appropriate chapter, then crack a smile and say something to myself like "dude, you rock". Yeah, I've really done that, but enough about me.

To apply statistics to our problem, we will use a probability distribution (also known as frequency distributions or cumulative distributions). Probability distributions are used to describe the probability that a certain value, or set of values, will occur within a set of data. These are sometimes called frequency distributions because the frequency of a value or set of values occurring is directly related to the probability of those values occurring. Now you may also run into the term cumulative distribution (or cumulative distribution function) which is just the functionality of a probability distribution to assign cumulative probability of a range of values. To put this in the context of safety stock, we will be looking at demand variability, and therefore will look at the frequency of certain levels of demand occurring (based on history). From that, we can calculate the probability of a certain level of demand occurring, and more importantly, the probability that a specific quantity of inventory will meet demand.

In statistics, the individual values or groupings of values associated with the data that makes up the pattern are known as events. Since we will be using statistics to quantify demand variability, an "event" would be the demand that occurred in a specific time period (such as the demand during a specific forecast period or the demand during the lead time). Therefore, when we use a probability distribution to determine the probability that a certain event would occur, we are actually determining the probability that a certain level of demand would occur during a specific period of time. I want to clarify here how this is different from a forecast. In a forecast, you would be trying to determine a level of demand that is "most likely" to occur. What we are doing here, is determining the probability that certain levels of demand "may" occur.

There are various probability distributions used in statistics; each one is essentially a mathematical model designed to describe a certain pattern of event frequency (probabilities). We will be using the Normal Distribution Model for our safety stock calculations. As its name implies, the normal distribution is used for data that is "normally distributed". So what does "normally distributed" mean? Normally distributed data describes a set of data where most values (events) are close to the mean (average) value, fewer values exist at extreme distances from the mean value, and the total number of values occurring above the average value is close to the total number of values occurring below the average value. When normally distributed data is charted in a histogram (a type of bar chart used to visualize the shape of the frequency of specific values occurring), the histogram will take the form of a bell-shaped curve. Many of you may have experienced the anxiety of being graded based on a bell-shaped curve (a system that guarantees a certain portion of the group will fail). It just so happens that bell-curve grading is also based on the normal distribution model.

The normal distribution model is used frequently in statistics because normally distributed data is very common in science and many other applications of statistics. So why is normally distributed data so common?

Well, because normal is . . . well . . . normal.

We will use it because it does a good job of modeling the normal variation in demand we call noise. Now before you dismiss the suggestion that the demand variability in your business that seems to be so random and unpredictable, and can vary significantly from one item to another, is actually "normal variation". Let me explain a little more. Normal variation is not meant to describe a specific amount (quantity) of variation, but rather a pattern of variation. So if I took two different businesses and found an item sold by each business with an average weekly demand of 100 units, I am not saying that the variability (in quantity) for each item will be the same. One may have week-to-week demand numbers that range from 80 to 120 units, while the other could have week-to-week demand numbers that range from 25 to 175 units, yet they both may be considered to have normal variability. Therefore, even though it's obvious that the spread of the variability for these two items is very different, they both can fit into the normal distribution model because the normal distribution model has an element that measures the spread of the variability and incorporates that into the model. This measure of the spread is known as the Standard Deviation. The standard deviation is calculated as the square root of the average of the squared variances relative to the mean.

Any questions?

Here's a step-by-step for calculating the **standard deviation of a population**:

1. Calculate the mean (average) of the series of numbers (events).
2. Calculate the difference of each number and the mean (subtract the mean from the number).
3. Square each difference (multiply each difference by itself).
4. Calculate the mean of the squared differences.
5. Calculate the square root of the mean of the squared differences.

Note that this is the calculation of the standard deviation for a population. When calculating the standard deviation of a sample (instead of a population), rather than calculating the average of the squared differences (step 4), you would sum the squared differences, then, instead of dividing the sum by the number of values (to calculate the average), you would divide the sum by the number of values minus 1. What this does, is artificially inflate the standard deviation relative to the size of the sample. The reason for this (my guess) is that since you are calculating against a sample, it is assumed that the entire population may contain some more variability than was represented in the sample, and therefore you want to try to account for this. Does this sound like a cheat? Oh yeah. But since you'll find it in most statistics texts and there is even an Excel function to calculate it, it almost seems legit. Well get used to it because just about everything we're going to do in this chapter is some form of a cheat.

Here's a step-by-step for calculating the **standard deviation of a sample**:

1. Calculate the mean (average) of the series of numbers (events).
2. Calculate the difference of each number and the mean (subtract the mean from the number).
3. Square each difference (multiply each difference by itself).
4. Calculate the sum of the squared differences.
5. Divide the sum of the squared differences by the number of values minus one.
6. Calculate the square root of the result of #5.

Standard deviation of a sample

Period		1	2	3	4	5	6	7
Demand		5	8	7	8	10	2	3
Squared variance		1.31	3.45	0.73	3.45	14.88	17.16	9.88
Standard deviation (sample)								2.91

Figure 6A. Here is an example of calculating the standard deviation of a sample. In Excel, if the period #1 demand of 5 was in cell B3, the formula for cell B4 would be =(B3-AVERAGE($B3:$H3))^2 and the formula for cell H5 would be =SQRT(SUM(B4:H4)/(COUNT(B4:H4)-1)) .

You can also use Excel function STDEV to calculate the standard deviation of a sample, or STDEVP to calculate the standard deviation of a population.

Just to clarify the difference between a population and a sample, a population is the entire set of data, and a sample would be a portion of a population used to try to draw conclusions about the population. When we use historical demand variability to predict future demand variability, we are in fact using a sample, and therefore technically should use the second formula. However, since we will be implementing this by using the output to help define a key input (this will be explained later), either calculation can be made to work (though we will stick with the proper one).

Now let's get back to the standard deviation. As already mentioned, the standard deviation is used to measure the spread of event frequencies for a population or sample. More importantly, the standard deviation is used as a unit-of-measure in the normal distribution model. What this means is, we will assign probability based on the number of standard deviations a value is from the mean. We can do this because the normal distribution model is based on the theory that approximately 68% of the values are within one standard deviation of the mean, approximately 95% of the values are within two standard deviations of the mean, and approximately 99.7 are within 3 standard deviations of the mean. So, as a simplified example, if based on historical demand we had a mean (average) demand of 100 units per forecast period, and calculated a standard deviation of 20 units, we should be able to assume that 68% of forecast periods should have demand between 80 and 120 units (within one standard deviation of the mean), 95% of periods should have demand between 60 and 140 units (within two standard deviations of the mean), and 99.7% of periods should have demand between 40 and 160 units (within three standard deviations of the mean). I hope this is starting to make sense to you now, because this is the basis for everything else we are going to do in this chapter.

I just can't help but mention that this is all an elaborate cheat. Once again, I don't mean this in a bad way, but what we have here is a model developed to approximate probability when you don't have enough data to precisely calculate probability. And fortunately for us, this cheat is exactly what we need. Well, sort of.

But what we want to do is a little different. In the previous example, 95% of periods should have demand between 60 and 140 units, but is that the same as saying that 140 units will be needed to meet demand 95% of the time? Not exactly. Theoretically, 140 units should meet demand more than 95% of the time because it will also meet the demand for periods that have demand of less than 60 units. Remember, the theory states that 95% of values will lie within two standard deviations of the mean, so if we have 140 units, we are actually covering demand of 60 to 140 units (95%) plus demand of 0 to 59 units. So we are in effect covering more than 95% of the values. Therefore what we really want to do is be able to input a probability (percentage) that represents the percentage of values that are less than or equal to a specific value. And guess what? The statistics folks have already done this for us too. Even better yet, many spreadsheet programs have this function built into them (in Excel we will use the NORMSINV function). Below is a table created using the NORMSINV function in Excel. You may recognize this table since it is similar—if not identical—to tables you may have previously encountered in books discussing safety stock calculations.

Service level to service factor conversion	
Service Level	Service Factor
99.9%	3.090232306
99.5%	2.575829304
99.0%	2.326347874
98.0%	2.053748911
97.0%	1.880793608
96.0%	1.750686071
95.0%	1.644853627
90.0%	1.281551566
85.0%	1.036433389
80.0%	0.841621234
75.0%	0.67448975
70.0%	0.524400513
65.0%	0.385320466
60.0%	0.253347103
55.0%	0.125661347
50.0%	0.000000000

Figure 6B. To convert our desired service level (expressed as a percentage) into a factor that represents the number of standard deviations required to meet our service level, we can use the Excel function NORMSINV. So if our service level is in cell A3, the formula in cell B3 would be =NORMSINV(A3) .

This brings up a couple of new terms—service level, and service factor. Let me forewarn you that "service level" is a very misleading term in this context, and I would prefer to not use it. But since the term has been used with such consistency over the years to describe this element of the safety stock calculation, it would probably be more confusing if I were to introduce another term. I think you'll put together a good understanding of service level as we progress through this chapter, but for now, think of it as a key controlling input to the safety stock calculation.

The other term, service factor, is the multiplier that represents the number of standard deviations you will use to calculate your safety stock. To go back to the "overly simplified use of statistical methods" topic, you would take your demand history by forecast period and calculate the standard deviation (preferably using the sample calculation). You would then choose a service level from the table, and multiply the corresponding service factor by the standard deviation to calculate your safety stock. And then you pat yourself on the back because you have just implemented a statistical safety stock calculation.

So what's wrong with this calculation? Unfortunately it's just not that simple. Let's start with the service level. When you talk about service level in relationship to inventory, most people think of it as a "fill rate". The first question those of you familiar with fill rates may think to ask is, does service level represent "line fill" or "order fill"? Well, many people don't ask this, and instead, just assume that service level represents whatever fill-rate calculation they happen to use. Yes, I know, when I put it that way it makes these people sound like idiots, but herein lies the problem with just taking a table and a simple calculation out of a book and implementing it without having even a basic understanding of the logic behind the calculation. But since we took the time to go through the logic of the calculation, you should already know the correct answer. Well do you?

The correct answer is, neither. That's right, the "service level" element of the safety stock calculation does not represent any of the conventional fill-rate calculations people are familiar with. Where people generally calculate service level as the percentage of order line items filled complete or the percentage of entire orders filled complete, the "service level" element in the table actually represents the percentage of periods in which you can expect to meet all demand. Oh wait, that's not exactly correct either; the "service level" element in the table represents the percentage of periods in which you can expect to meet all demand, IF, at the beginning of each period you have a quantity on hand equal to exactly the mean demand plus the result of the service factor multiplied by the standard deviation. So when I choose a 95% service level, the result should be that if I stocked the exact amount at the beginning of each period, then in 95% of time periods I should have 100% fill rate, and in 5% of time periods I should have something less than 100% fill rate. How much less will the fill rate be during those 5% of time periods? I don't know because this calculation does not work that way.

Now that we all understand the service level element, and our understanding of it means that it does not correspond with any conventional service level measurement, how should we go about using it? Well basically we are going to use it the same way you would use a volume control on your stereo. A volume control generally has some type of measurement (such as numbers 1 through 10—or 1 through 11 for the Nigel Tufnel version) associated with it, yet these numbers do not by themselves tell you how loud your stereo will be. That's because different stereos have different power outputs and you also have to take into account other variables such as the speakers being used, the sound level of the input device, and the characteristics of the room where the speakers are located. So ultimately, you have to try out the various volume settings on your stereo, and listen to find out the sound level produced by each. The same concept applies to the service level in this calculation. You need to use a combination of educated guess and trial-and-error to see which service level from the table produces your actual desired service level. We'll cover this again a little later.

> *The "service level" element of the basic safety stock calculation does not represent any of the conventional fill-rate calculations people are familiar with. Instead, it represents the percentage of periods in which you can expect to meet all demand, IF, at the beginning of each period you have a quantity on hand equal to exactly the mean demand plus the result of the service factor multiplied by the standard deviation.*

But understanding service level is only part of the solution. The reality is, there are numerous other factors at play here, and we have a lot more work to do. I previously mentioned that the model assumed we had the exact quantity on hand at the beginning of each period? Well that's not exactly how things work in the real world. In addition, forecasts, lead time, order cycles, seasonality, and trend can all impact your safety stock requirements. So in order to take these other factors into consideration, we need to make some adjustments to the calculation. Many of these adjustments will in fact be cheats, and will—to varying degrees—compromise the integrity of the statistical model we are trying to use. But hey, that's the nature of the beast. We really have no choice here because the pristine normal distribution model just doesn't quite match our specific requirements for a safety stock calculation.

Incorporating the forecast.

When we use the standard deviation calculation(s) previously discussed, we are calculating the overall demand variability. However, since there are likely some trend, seasonality, and/or other forecastable factors present in the demand, we don't want to treat these as variability for the sake of the safety stock calculation since we will forecast these (treating these as variability in the safety stock calculation would result in excessive safety stock). We can either remove these elements from the demand history (normalize demand) before calculating the standard deviation, or we can just replace the mean in the standard deviation calculation with the forecast. Since removing trend from demand history can get kind of tricky, it's generally easier to just use the forecast instead of the mean in the standard deviation calculation. Be aware that this can create some additional problems (discussed later).

Standard deviation using forecast in place of mean									
Period	I	2	3	7	8	9	10	11	12
Forecast	123	141	162	164	159	153	158	150	145
Demand	120	149	173	158	147	173	148	144	138
Squared Variance	9	64	121	36	144	400	100	36	49
Standard deviation									10.95

Figure 6C. To calculate the standard deviation using our forecast, we simply replace the mean demand in the calculation with our forecast. This actually makes the calculation a little easier. In Excel, if the period #1 demand of 120 was in cell B4, the formula for cell B5 would be =(B4-B3)^2 and the formula for cell J6 would be =SQRT(SUM(B5:J5)/(COUNT(B5:J5)-1)) .

Incorporating lead time.

At the beginning of the chapter, I mentioned that we use safety stock to compensate for the amount of demand variability that may occur during the lead-time period. The reason for this is that the lead time defines the primary window of opportunity for stockouts. Yet up to this point, we've focused on calculating against the variability that occurs during forecast periods. The reason we usually start by calculating against forecast periods is because that's the data that is usually readily available. Ideally, it would be best to calculate demand during the lead-time periods and then use that as the input to the safety stock calculation, but that's more difficult than it sounds. First off, you generally have different lead times for different products, and would therefore need to create custom time buckets for each item, and then be able to change the time buckets whenever the lead time changes. In addition, if trend or seasonality were present, you would also need to create a forecast based on lead-time periods in order to properly apply our forecast-based safety stock calculation.

I guess to complicate this further I should mention that lead-time periods are not exactly static—in that you don't really know on what date to start the lead-time period. For example, if my lead time is two weeks, do I calculate the variability that occurs between today and two weeks from today, or tomorrow and two weeks from tomorrow, or the next day and two weeks from that? That being said, it is possible to do this to some extent, and good for you if you want to try giving it a shot, but we're going to move on to a way of dealing with lead time given the assumption that you will calculate your standard deviation against your forecast periods.

What we need to do here is take the variability and subsequent safety stock recommendations that we've calculated based on forecast periods, and figure out how to adjust this to our lead-time period. A simplistic approach would be to adjust the safety stock by the ratio of lead-time period to the forecast period. For example, if the forecast was based on one-week periods, and our lead time for a particular item was four weeks, we could just multiply the safety stock calculated for a forecast period (one week) by four to get our lead-time period safety stock level. The problem with this logic is the assumption that relative variability doesn't change based on the length of the time period, when in reality relative variability will generally be reduced as you increase the time period. Conversely, relative variability will generally be increased as you decrease the time period. When I use the term "relative variability" I'm talking about the amount of variability relative to the average (or forecasted) demand during that period.

If I had a relatively stable product that had forecasted demand of 5 units per period (weekly periods), and had actual demand that ranged between 0 and 15 units, I could represent my relative variability by saying demand could be as much as three times the forecasted demand (Note: the way I am calculating variability for this example is purely for demonstration purposes. In the actual safety stock calculation we will be using the standard deviation to represent variability). Now if I were to assume that relative variability does not change if I change the length of the time period, I would assume that no matter what time period I used, my actual demand could be as much as three times my forecasted demand. To prove this assumption wrong, let's go a little extreme here and change our forecast interval to one-year periods. Now, my forecasted demand for the year would be 260 units (5 units per week times 52 weeks), so am I to assume that for this relatively stable product I should still plan for potentially having demand of three times this quantity for the year? On the other hand, since we had never had demand of more than 15 units per week, given a five-day workweek, should I be able to assume that we won't have demand greater than 3 units for a single day? In reality, it is extremely doubtful that we would have annual variability that great, or daily variability that small.

This brings us to the "Law of Large Numbers", which sounds a bit weighty but really is just a simple observation that with larger numbers you can generally expect lower variability. As you may recall from the forecasting chapters, we discussed how forecasts tended to be more accurate at the aggregate level, and therefore used groups wherever possible to help reduce noise. This was just another way of applying the law of large numbers. Here's an example of the law of large numbers I hope you all can relate to. According to Wikipedia (so it must be true), the marshmallow charms in Lucky Charms cereal make up 25% of the volume, and the toasted oat thingies make up 75% of the volume. But as you're scooping spoonfuls out of your bowl in the morning, you observe that sometimes you get no charms in a spoon, sometimes you get all charms, and mostly you get a whole lot of variety of mix of charms and oat thingies, but rarely is it exactly 25%. In other words, you have significant variability from the 25% figure when comparing one spoonful to the next. Now if you were to compare how many charms you had in the entire bowl you had yesterday to the bowl you had today, you would still likely have some variability, but not as great as the spoon-to-spoon variability. To take it further, if you had way too much time on your hands and decided to separate the charms from the oat thingies in multiple boxes of Lucky Charms and compare the results, you would likely still not find exact matches among the boxes or to the 25% figure, but the variability would be less than the variability between bowls and significantly less than the variability between spoonfuls. And that my friends, is the law of large numbers.

Back to our safety stock calculation; we need to figure out how to take the results of our safety stock calculation based on one length of time and apply it to a longer or shorter length of time. So where, in the previous example (not the Lucky Charms example), we sort of came to the conclusion that the variability over a year would probably be less than 52 times the variability for a week, and that the variability for a day would probably be more than one-fifth the variability for a week, we don't really have a way of calculating this. What we do have here are two ratios based on comparing the time periods (52:1, and 1:5). These ratios can also be represented by fractions (52/1, and 1/5), or by decimals (52.0, and 0.20), and what we want to do is find a way to "soften" these ratios so a ratio greater than 1:1 is adjusted downward and a ratio less than 1:1 is adjusted upward. And the further the ratio is from 1:1, the larger the adjustment needs to be.

We can achieve this "softening" by calculating the square root of the ratio. By taking the square roots of 52.0 and 0.20 from the previous example, we get 7.21 and 0.45 respectively. Which means, by using the square root to adjust our ratio, we are saying that rather than the variability for a 52-week period being 52 times the variability for a one-week period, we are saying that it will be approximately 7 times the variability for a one-week period. And, that rather than the variability for a one-day period being one-fifth the variability for a one-week period, we are saying that it will be a little less than one-half the variability for a one-week period. To take this further and apply this to the example where for weekly demand of 5 units we experienced demand as high as 15 units (variability of 10 units), we would extend this to annual demand of 260 units with variability up to 72 units (7.21 times 10); otherwise stated as potential annual demand of up to 332 units (260 plus 72). Or daily demand of 1 unit with variability of up to 5 units (one-half of 10), otherwise stated as potential daily demand of up to 6 units (1 plus 5). Now I think most people who have experience with demand patterns would agree that those results look more reasonable than the direct ratio results.

Calculating a lead-time factor using the square root trick					
Examples	Ex. 1	Ex. 2	Ex. 3	Ex. 4	Ex. 5
Forecast interval (in days)	7	7	7	7	7
Lead time (in days)	3	14	30	60	120
Lead-time factor	**0.65**	**1.41**	**2.07**	**2.93**	**4.14**

Figure 6D. Here are some examples of using the square root trick to calculate a lead-time factor. The forecast interval in each example is 7 days, but each example has a different lead time. Assuming our lead time of 3 is in cell B4, our formula in cell B5 would be =SQRT(B4/B3) .

And here comes the warning. This little square root trick is a BIG CHEAT, and while it is very useful (and I've found it to be surprisingly accurate), you need to be very careful about getting too comfortable with it. It doesn't hurt to take some of your own raw data and test this calculation against the actual demand variation that would occur given different time periods in your specific environment. This is a little tedious to do, but you would only be doing it for a handful of items to test the calculation against your specific demand patterns. You would just summarize your raw data (usually order history) by different time periods (days, weeks, months, years) and then calculate the standard deviation based on these different periods. Then use the square root trick to convert between the various time periods, and compare your converted results to the actual results for the various time periods. Based on the results of this test, you may choose to tweak this adjustment to more accurately reflect your actual demand variability, or you may find that the results are adequate for your needs.

I have tested this many times in the past against different datasets, and have been extremely impressed at how accurate the results were given the simplicity of this cheat. I expected it to do all right with minor to moderate differences between time periods (which would cover most of our safety stock calculation needs), but figured it would be way off when trying to convert significantly different periods. So when I converted daily variability to yearly variability and vice versa, and then compared the results to actual variability during those time periods and found them to be within about 15% of each other, I was simply amazed. But again, be careful with this one. It's nice that it frequently provides useful results, but there's no magic here.

Actual standard deviation adjusted to different periods						
Period	Days in period	Actual Standard Deviation by Period	Adj. to Day	Adj. to Week	Adj. to Month	Adj. to Year
Weekdays	1	1.65		3.69	7.67	26.55
Weeks	5	3.66	1.64		7.61	26.34
Months	21.6	8.72	1.88	4.20		30.20
Years	259	31.08	1.93	4.32	8.98	

Figure 6E. This table shows the results I received when testing the square root trick against actual demand history of a real item. I took the actual demand history of the item over a three-year period and broke it down into weekdays, weeks, months, and years (based on that specific business). I then calculated the actual standard deviation of each group. I then used the square root trick to convert the standard deviation of each group into the time periods of the other groups. For example, my actual standard deviation for a day was 1.65, and I converted that to a yearly standard deviation of 26.55. My actual yearly standard deviation was 31.06. Given the extreme differences in the length of time of these periods, that's pretty impressive accuracy for cheat. But as I said before, you need to test it with your own data.

Implementing this calculation is rather easy, as it can be treated as a simple add-on adjustment to the base safety stock calculation. What we're going to do is multiply this factor by the standard deviation to get a "lead-time-adjusted standard deviation". We could then multiply the lead-time adjusted standard deviation by our service factor to get our safety stock adjusted for lead time.

Incorporating order cycle.

Order cycle is the length of time between receipts of an item. You can also think of it as the length of time an ordered quantity should last. Therefore, if my order quantity is 500 and my annual demand is 1000, I have an order cycle of six months because it should take me approximately six months to consume 500 units. And what does order cycle have to do with safety stock? Based upon the numerous questions I have received over the years on this issue, this is not an easy concept for many people to grasp. It basically comes down to order cycles having a direct relationship to service levels. Or more simply put, shorter order cycles inherently put you at greater risk for stockouts than longer order cycles.

Once again, this is best demonstrated by using an extreme example. Let's say we have two items that have the exact same demand pattern and a forecasted weekly demand of 10 units. To make this even simpler, imagine these items are related and every time someone buys a quantity of one item they must also buy an equal quantity of the other item. Now assume these items both have the same lead time (one week), but due to a large minimum buy quantity on one of the items, you must order an entire year's supply at one time for that item, whereas, you only order one week's supply at a time for the other item. In order to show the "inherent" service level associated with each order cycle, we'll assume that we are not carrying any safety stock on either item. At the beginning of the first week, one item has 10 units in stock and the other item has 520 units in stock. Without any safety stock, there's a 50/50 chance that we will have demand greater than 10 units for the week, and therefore would have a 50/50 chance of running out of the first item, but there isn't a chance in hell we will have demand of greater than 520 units, so there is absolutely no way we will run out of the second item. As you progress through the year, you will continue to be at risk of stockout for the first item during every week, but the second item will continue to have so much extra inventory in stock due to the large order quantity (and subsequently long order cycle) that it is extremely unlikely we would be at risk of stockout until the last few weeks of the year.

Since the first item had an order cycle and lead time equal to the forecast period (one week), we can assume that the one-week order cycle has an inherent period service level of 50%. Again, this is not service level as many people think of it, but rather that 50% of the weeks will have demand greater than forecasted demand, therefore we will be unable to meet all demand during 26 weeks out of the year. Where did the 50% come from? Assuming normal random variability (which is what we are planning for), during 50% of the weeks we would expect to have demand less than the forecast and during 50% of the weeks we would expect to have demand greater than the forecast (this assumes an unbiased forecast).

I hope you are understanding this so far because it is about to get a lot more confusing. Every time I've revisited this over the years, I go through a phase of "yeah, I understand this", which after a little more thought goes into a phase of "wait a minute, I think my logic is all wrong", followed by eventually thinking I understand it again but with some reservations that I may be wrong. The reason is, we are dealing with a base calculation (the normal distribution model) that would directly apply if our lead time, forecast period, and order cycle were all the same. Since this ain't happening in the real world, we need to adjust for these differences. Understanding that an adjustment is needed is one thing (and an important one), but figuring out how to make these adjustments while maintaining some level of integrity to the original statistical model is a whole different story.

We already adjusted the standard deviation with a lead-time factor, so if we were to apply our service factor at this point we would in essence be saying that our service level represents the percentage of lead-time periods (not forecast periods) where we would expect to be able to meet all demand. So now as we look to find a way to apply the inherent service level associated with order cycles to this, we need to remember that our standard deviation is now expressed relative to the lead-time period. We could try using our little square root trick again by calculating the square root of the ratio. Since we already adjusted our formula to represent lead-time periods, we would divide our lead time by our order cycle and calculate the square root of the result. We could then multiply this by our service factor to get an adjusted service factor. The main problem with this is that the logic itself is seriously flawed. When we applied this trick to our lead-time adjustment, we used it to soften a ratio to better simulate the impact of the law of large numbers. That is NOT what we are trying to do here. Here we have two separate service levels (the inherent service level associated with order cycle and the service level associated with the normal distribution model) that need to somehow be combined. Surprisingly, the square root trick does actually provide some usable results under certain circumstances (primarily when the difference between lead time and order cycle is not all that significant), but under other circumstances, it can provide very poor results.

So here's what I've come up with. I used the logic that we are looking at an overlap of service levels and therefore we should be able to use some statistical rules to resolve this. It's easier to follow my logic if we first convert service level (success rate) into stockout risk (failure rate). So if we were to select a service level of 95%, we are actually selecting a stockout risk of 5% (100% minus 95%). This translates to 5% of lead-time periods being at risk for stockout. When I refer to "lead-time periods" here, I am referring to sequential periods of time equal to the lead time. So now, when we look at stockout risk associated with order cycles, my logic assumes we are at risk of stockout for one lead-time period for every order cycle. Therefore, we can calculate our order cycle stockout risk by dividing the lead time by the order cycle. If we had a lead time of one week and an order cycle of ten weeks, we would have an inherent stockout risk of 10% (would be at risk of stockout during 10% of lead-time periods). So what we now have are two independent events (probability of stockout associated with order cycle, and probability of stockout associated with demand during lead time), that would have to occur simultaneously in order to result in an actual stockout. We therefore should be able to take the product of these two probabilities to determine the probability of a stockout due to demand during lead time that occurred at the same time we are exposed to stockout due to order cycles. So if we multiply 5% by 10%, we get 0.5%, which represents the probability of stockout due to both these events occurring at the same time. Which means that if we chose a service level of 95% for an item that already had an inherent service level of 90% due to order cycle, we should actually be getting a service level of 99.5% (100% minus our stockout probability of 0.5%).

This calculation didn't give us exactly what we were looking for, since we weren't looking to determine what our actual service level will be given our selected desired service level combined with our inherent service level associated with order cycle. Instead, what we wanted to calculate is the service level we would need to input into the safety stock calculation that takes into account the inherent service level associated with order cycle, and results in our desired service level. Well it's just a matter of some basic algebra to convert this calculation into the one we desire. So the final calculation looks something like this:

Adjusted Service Level =1-((1-Desired Service Level)/(Lead time/Order Cycle))

If we input into this calculation a requirement for a 95% service level, and use the item with a lead time of one week and order cycle of ten weeks, we will find that the adjusted service level only needs to be 50%. A 50% service level equates to a service factor of zero, which basically means we don't need any safety stock in order to get a 95% service level for this item. This brings up a couple of issues. In some cases, the adjusted service level may come out to be less than 50%, which results in a negative service factor and subsequently a negative safety stock quantity. This happens when the inherent service level associated with order cycle is so high, that even with zero safety stock, your service level would be higher than your requirement; therefore the calculation looks to reduce your inventory requirements to bring you down to your requested service level. Though this makes sense logically, I don't think too many people will be willing to accept negative safety stock, and to be honest, I'm not sure how most systems would react to a negative quantity in the safety stock field. So what you will probably need to do here is put in an override whereby if the adjusted service level is less than 50%, you use 50% as the service level. The other issue is really just a variation of the previously stated one and is somewhat of a psychological issue. That is, some people may have a hard time accepting that with some items they will not keep any safety stock, and therefore when these items come up for reorder (based on lead time), they would be running a 50/50 chance of stockout before the replenishment order is received. Because of this, you may choose to have a minimum adjusted service level that overrides anything below it. Again, this is more of a "peace-of-mind" adjustment than a logical one, but would be a simple matter of putting in an override whereby, if the adjusted service level is less than a predetermined level, you override it with the predetermined level.

So what we have so far is a safety stock calculation based on the normal distribution model that starts with a desired service level and a calculation of the standard deviation based on the forecast and forecast periods, then adjusts the standard deviation to the lead-time period, and adjusts the service level to account for the order cycle. Let's see how that could work in a spreadsheet:

Safety stock adjusted for lead time and order cycle		
Service level/ service factor	95.0%	1.645
Forecast interval (days)	7	
Lead time (days)	21	
Order cycle (days)	30	
Standard deviation based on forecast periods	3.07	
Unadjusted safety stock		**5.05**
Adjustments		
Adjusted standard deviation (adj. for lead time)	5.32	
Adjusted service level / service factor (adj. for order cycle)	92.9%	1.465
Adjusted safety stock		**7.79**

Figure 6F. Here you see how we can apply our lead-time and order-cycle adjustments. To set this up in Excel, fill in the values for Service level, Forecast interval, Lead time, Order cycle, and Standard deviation. Assuming the service level of 95.0% is in cell B2, enter the following formulas.

In cell C2 enter =NORMSINV(B2)

In cell C7 enter =B6*C2

In cell B9 enter =(SQRT(B4/B3))*B6

In cell B10 enter =1-((1-B2)/(B4/B5))

In cell C10 enter =IF(B10>0.5,NORMSINV(B10),0)

In cell C11 enter =B9*C10

The "unadjusted safety stock" quantity is there just for informational purposes. It basically represents the "oversimplified use of statistical methods" previously discussed.

You can see how we used our square root trick in cell B9 to adjust our standard deviation, then used our order cycle adjustment in cell B10 to adjust our service level. The "IF" statement in cell C10 is there to make sure we don't end up with a negative service factor. You can play with this worksheet by entering various forecast intervals, lead times, order cycles to see how our adjusted safety stock changes.

Relative history, seasonality, and trend.

There's a bit of a catch-22 with using this type of safety stock calculation. Your measure of variability (standard deviation) is more accurate if you input more data (more forecast periods), but, inputting more data means inputting older data, and subsequently you run the risk that the data is no longer as relevant as you would like it to be. Seasonality, trend, and changes in forecasting techniques can affect how relative the history you are using is to the upcoming time periods (where safety stock is used). We can try to make adjustments for some of this, but let me first say that if you have rather minor seasonality or trend, you may not find it necessary to go through the hassle of trying to adjust your safety stock to accommodate these factors. But, in operations with dramatic seasonal or trend changes, you should consider incorporating them into your safety stock calculation.

Let's start with seasonality. One way to deal with seasonality in safety stock calculations would be to base your safety stock calculation on the same relative periods from prior years. For example, if you have significant seasonality due to having a "busy season" and a "slow season" each year, you can calculate your safety stock for this year's busy season based on your demand variability from last year's busy season, and then do the same for the slow season. This is probably the simplest approach, and, depending on other variables, may be the most accurate way of doing it. However, it becomes more difficult if you have more complex seasonality (which is more likely).

So here's what I've come up with as one example of a neat little seasonality adjustment for your safety stock calculation that works a little better with more complex seasonality (Note: I will later cover an adjustment that takes both seasonality and trend into account). We're going to use our existing seasonality index here, but combine it with our square-root trick used to accommodate the "law of large numbers". What we want to do here is take the seasonal patterns that occurred during the time periods over which the safety stock calculation was based, and relate them to the seasonal patterns that are expected to occur during the upcoming lead-time period. To do this, we can average the seasonality indexes over the periods used for the safety stock calculation, then average the seasonality indexes that exist for the upcoming period of time equal to the lead time for that specific item. Then we divide the lead-time seasonality index by the history seasonality index, and calculate the square root of the result. This is now our seasonality index for our safety stock for the upcoming lead-time period. So once we have our lead-time-adjusted, order-cycle-adjusted safety stock quantity, we will multiply it by our lead-time seasonality index to get our lead-time-adjusted, order-cycle-adjusted, seasonality-adjusted safety stock quantity. Obviously this means you are frequently recalculating your safety stock (probably at least once a week). Also, this is not as simple as it sounds, given that lead-time periods and forecast periods are not always equally divisible. Therefore, you need to set up your calculation (program) to react appropriately when encountering these portions of time periods.

The previous calculation is based on the assumption that you calculated your demand variability (standard deviation) by comparing the actual demand to the forecast. However, you could optionally first de-seasonalize your demand and forecast, and then calculate your variability against this. Now you would not need to look at the historical seasonality index, but instead just calculate the average seasonality index over the upcoming lead time and take the square root of that to be used as your safety stock seasonality index.

Trend can be dealt with in a similar way by comparing the trend in the upcoming lead-time period to the trend that occurred in the historical periods. But I have an easier way to adjust for both trend and seasonality with a single not-too-difficult calculation. This uses the same "law of large numbers" logic, but simply uses the historical demand and the future forecast as inputs. All you need to do here is calculate the average demand per forecast period for the historical periods used for the safety stock calculation, then calculate the average forecasted demand per forecast period for the upcoming lead-time period. Then divide the average forecasted demand by the average historical demand and calculate the square root of the result. This is now your safety stock trend and seasonality multiplier.

If you're not grasping the logic behind this, let me explain it a little further. We're calculating the average demand that occurred per forecast period for the length of time upon which the safety stock calculation was based. So, if we based the safety stock calculation on the ten previous forecast periods (we'll say weeks), we would take the average demand per week that occurred during the previous ten weeks. Then, if my lead time is three weeks, we would calculate the average forecasted demand per week for the next three weeks. This allows us to compare (through a ratio) the future demand to the historic demand to see what overall demand changes (due to seasonality and trend) are expected. Now we can apply our square-root trick to this ratio to adjust it to account for variability changes that would be expected within the scope of the law of large numbers.

Just a reminder that this last calculation takes into account both trend and seasonality, therefore you do not need to do the previously detailed seasonality adjustments (pretty much making them obsolete). I decided to include the seasonality-index-based calculation to help explain the logic, but also to show various ways of accomplishing similar results. Once again, all of these are cheats, and the results will vary somewhat depending on the method chosen even though they all roughly use the same logic.

The output of this calculation is a multiplier that you would multiply by your "lead-time-adjusted, order-cycle-adjusted safety stock quantity" output from the earlier safety stock calculation to adjust it for seasonality and trend. I again want to point out that my example here is used to demonstrate the base calculation. Any actual implementation of this would need to get a little more complicated in order to deal with varying lead times and lead times that equate to partial forecast periods. This doesn't require changing the base calculation, only the method for calculating the average forecasted demand per forecast period during the lead-time period.

Trend and seasonality adjustment

Period	#1	#2	#3	#4	#5	#6	#7	#8	#9	#10	#11	#12	#13	#14	#15
Forecast	50	50	45	40	40	35	40	40	45	50	50	55	60	65	65
Demand	47	56	50	43	36	32	37	42	44	47	53	57			

Adjustment		
Average period demand during previous 12 periods	45.33	
Average forecast-ed demand per forecast period during lead time (LT = 3 periods)	63.33	
Lead-time/trend adjustment (multiplier)	1.18	

Figure 6G. Here we have an example of calculating our trend and seasonality multiplier. Assuming our period #1 forecast of 50 is in cell B3, the formula in cell B6 would be =AVERAGE(B4:M4) , the formula in cell B7 would be =AVERAGE(N3:P3) , and the formula for cell B8 would be =SQRT(B7/B6). This assumes our original standard deviation was calculated against the demand and forecast for the 12 previous periods, and we have a lead time equal to 3 periods. We would now multiply the output of our safety stock calculation by 1.18 to adjust it for trend and seasonality.

I also want to note that even though it's advisable to calculate your standard deviation against the most recent history, it's not absolutely necessary with this calculation. So, if you calculated your standard deviation over your demand for the entire year of 2008 and we are now in the middle of 2009, we can still use this calculation by inputting the average demand per period in 2008 (the period over which our standard deviation was based). The remainder of the calculation works exactly the same.

Biased forecasts and negative variability.

The normal distribution model is based on using the mean (average) to calculate the standard deviation. When applying this to our safety stock calculation, we generally replace the mean with the forecast because we don't want forecastable seasonality and trend to be treated as demand variability. And this works very well provided you have an unbiased forecast. However, if you have a biased forecast (intentionally or otherwise), it creates some real problems with the calculation. Once again, I will use an extreme example to demonstrate this. Let's say management is paranoid about running out of stock, so they intentionally bias the forecast so the forecast quantities represent the "most they could possibly expect to sell during each period". Subsequently, what they actually sell during each period is less than (sometimes substantially less than) the forecast amount.

When you look at the normal distribution model, you will notice that it treats demand that is less than the forecast, as variability. In fact, it really doesn't care at all whether the variability is negative (less than forecast) or positive (greater than forecast). Therefore, if you take our intentionally biased forecast, where we never actually had demand greater than the forecast, our safety stock calculation would produce a larger safety stock recommendation than we would get with an unbiased forecast. Common sense would say we would actually need little to no safety stock since our forecast is set up as the most we can possibly sell.

Even without a biased forecast, you may occasionally run into a situation where you have an unpredicted (and therefore not forecasted) very slow sales period. Again, as an extreme example, let's say you have an item that has had stable sales averaging 1,000 units per period (we'll call this our forecast) with actual sales ranging between 700 and 1,300 units per period. Suddenly you have a sales period that only produces sales of 100 units. Your safety stock calculation will treat the low demand of 900 units below forecast, the same as it would treat unusually high demand of 900 units above forecast, and therefore recommend a safety stock level that assumes this high level of variability even though you have never had a sales peak like that.

Is this a flaw with the normal distribution model? No. Is this a flaw with applying the normal distribution model to safety stock? Maybe. Both the examples used here represent data that is not "normally distributed" and therefore does not readily fit into the normal distribution model. In the case of the biased forecast, the demand data itself may be normally distributed but the biased forecast used in place of the mean compromises the calculation. In the case of the unusually low demand, we have demand (or at least a single event) that is not normally distributed because the normal distribution model expects the spread of variability to be near equal below the mean and above the mean.

The real question here is what can you do about this? In the case of biased forecasts, the simple answer is, don't have biased forecasts. For those thinking of intentionally biasing your forecast, realize that you can probably get the same or better results by just bumping up your service level in your safety stock calculation. You may even choose to bump up your service level during times of positive trend, then bring it down during times of negative trend.

Also realize that minor forecast bias (which will occasionally occur with normal forecasting practices) will probably not create any serious safety stock complications. Nor will minor instances of low demand. So don't sweat the small stuff.

Now I'm sure some of you are thinking "why not just ignore all periods with demand below forecast?" It would certainly seem logical to think that since we don't use safety stock for demand below forecast, we shouldn't even use those numbers in our safety stock calculation. And good for you for thinking that. Unfortunately, this would also compromise the normal distribution model to some extent. Another variation would be to treat all periods with demand below forecast as though the demand for those periods matched the forecast exactly (no variance). Again, this too compromises the normal distribution model. It's not that you can't try these options, or that you absolutely shouldn't use these options, but be aware that they do not work quite as cleanly as you might assume. And anytime you change the calculation, you need to go back and look at our other adjustments to see if they also need to be changed.

What it comes down to is this, you should monitor your forecasts for bias and also for unusual demand (something you should be doing anyway). When you see bias, you should first look at your forecasting configuration to see what is causing the bias and find a way to avoid it. In the case of unusual demand, I think it does make sense to provide the ability to use overrides to help reduce the impact. And this can also be useful for a single instance of unusually high demand as well as an instance of unusually low demand. In most cases you do want your safety stock calculation to take into account unusually high demand—that's kind of the point of safety stock—but you may have a case of unusually high demand that was not predicted, but once it occurred, you were able to determine why it occurred and—more importantly—that it was an isolated event that is extremely unlikely to occur again and therefore you don't want to be carrying safety stock for it. An override could be as simple as creating a way to flag these periods so that your safety stock calculation either ignores them or treats them as matching forecast. Yes, this too compromises the calculation, but on a much smaller scale. Another option would be to just have the ability to maintain an adjusted demand history—as was previously discussed in the forecasting chapters.

If bias continues to be a problem you can't resolve, you can attempt to make some adjustments for forecast bias, but be aware this is not an easy undertaking. I haven't spent a lot of time on this because I think that in most cases you should work to eliminate the bias and therefore don't need an adjustment, but here are some notes of what I've put together in the past.

Let's start with the example of an intentionally biased forecast (which I don't particularly recommend). If you recall from the forecasting chapter, I measured forecast error (and bias) using a percentage based on the following calculation:

([Forecasted Sales]-[Actual Sales]) / [Actual Sales]

But to adjust safety stock based on a continuous biased forecast, you would probably want to measure forecast bias as "average forecast error in units". So you would calculate [Forecasted Sales]-[Actual Sales] for each period the safety stock calculation is based, then calculate the mean (average). You could then subtract the bias quantity from the standard deviation calculated against the biased forecast. So if you had a bias of 5 units, you would subtract that from the standard deviation. Therefore, a positive bias would reduce the standard deviation, while a negative bias would increase the standard deviation. Remember, you would only want to do this if you expected your forecast to remain similarly biased in the future.

However, if you wanted to adjust your biased standard deviation to be used in a future unbiased forecast, you could try taking the bias as a percentage and adjusting your safety stock down by that same percentage (regardless of negative or positive bias). Therefore, if your forecast was positively or negatively biased by 5%, you would reduce your standard deviation by 5%. The logic here is that any biased forecast (positive or negative) will result in an inflated standard deviation, therefore you want to reduce the standard deviation to eliminate the impact of the forecast bias.

So does it sound confusing that you would calculate your bias in units and then subtract it (or add if it is negative) from your standard deviation for a continuous biased forecast, but then you would calculate your bias as a percentage and reduce your standard deviation by this percentage disregarding positive or negative if you expected to eliminate bias from the forecast? I agree. But that's what I came up with when I looked into this issue. If you plan on implementing something like this, I strongly suggest some serious testing to make sure you are actually accomplishing what it is you want to accomplish.

Are we there yet?

As much as I would like to say this calculation is now complete, we still need to talk about the relationship of service level to fill rates. As previously mentioned, most companies use fill rates as a measure of inventory performance, but our safety stock calculation has an input called service level, which is not equivalent to any standard measure of fill rates. After all our adjustments, our service level roughly represents the percentage of lead-time periods in which we should expect to be able to fill all orders if we use the safety stock level associated with that service level. I also mentioned that we would use the service level as an adjustable variable (your volume knob) to tune our safety stock formula until we receive an output that represents our target fill rates. So what I'm saying here is that even though we don't know what fill rate we will get if we set our service level to a specific value, we do know that if we increase the service level we should expect our fill rates to also increase, and if we decrease our service level input we should expect to see our fill rates decrease (within some limitations). I also want to note that there are some variables beyond demand variability that impact fill rates. These would include supply variability, inventory accuracy, defects, etc. And even though we didn't focus on these, our safety stock will provide some buffer against these, and as we tweak our service level input, we are sort of accounting for some of these.

What we need to do here is find a starting point for our service level input that hopefully comes close to meeting our requirements. There is no magical way to do this, and though I hate to say this, it will require some educated guessing on your part. A good starting point is to first take a group of products (best to start with a smaller group) and analyze your current safety stock levels for these items. I suggest calculating the total inventory value for all safety stock within this group, then run various service level inputs in your safety stock calculation against this same group and try to find the service level input that results in the same overall inventory investment. Remember, this is for the entire group, not the individual items within the group (you will run the safety stock calculation against the individual items, but you are looking to match the summarized inventory investment for the group). Some of you may be thinking that we have just spent a whole lot of time developing a complicated calculation and are now going to use this complicated calculation to replicate the results of our previous simple calculation, but that is not the case. The idea here is that by using the same overall inventory investment as the output of our more sophisticated safety stock calculation, we should see better fill rates on an item-by-item basis given the same overall inventory investment. That's because our safety stock calculation will more logically distribute the safety stock among the items based on all the variables we previously covered.

You should then look at the individual safety stock recommendations (the output of the calculation) of each item to see if they at least look right (your judgment is required here) based on the demand history, lead time, order cycle, forecast bias, etc. If everything looks right, implement the safety stock calculation with this service level for just this group of items. You then need to monitor fill rates on these items and gradually adjust your service level input until you get the overall fill rates required. If you had previously been meeting your fill-rate targets, you will probably end up decreasing your service level (and subsequently your inventory investment) because you should be getting greater performance from the same inventory investment.

It's important to note that this evaluation period (the time you are monitoring your fill rates and adjusting your service level) can be rather long. You will want most of your items within the group to run through at least one complete order cycle; in some industries this can be many months between each adjustment of your service level. Plus, you need to realize that initially your inventory investment will likely increase a little, and you will probably see some inflated fill rates just due to the transition from your old safety stock calculation to your new one. That's because initially you will increase your safety stock for items that had insufficient safety stock in your old system, but you will still have your excessive safety stock from your old system until the next order cycle.

After you are comfortable with the results for this group, you can start to expand your new safety stock calculation to cover other items. It's very important to be patient here and make sure your calculation and your service factor input is performing adequately before you expand it to other groups.

And now for more bad news. Even though this calculation can provide some respectable results, it is still logically flawed, not so much related to the base logic, but more related to the need to use a service level based on time periods to achieve a fill rate based on orders/lines. The problem here is you will not get the same performance from all items within the group because there still are some item-specific variables that impact the conversion from service level to fill rate. These include the order frequency and the level of variability during the lead time.

For example, consider very slow movers that have zero demand during many time periods. Because the service level is based on meeting demand in time periods, if many or most of your time periods have no demand, then the safety stock calculation can get a high service level from little to no inventory since you can meet demand in those periods without any inventory. But that doesn't translate to a high fill rate, therefore a selected service level may result in a substantially lower fill rate for items that have many periods with zero demand. However, if you have demand in all periods, and more specifically, if you have multiple orders in all periods, you would expect that your actual fill rate will be greater than your service level input. For example, if you chose a service level of 95%, you should fill all orders in 95% of your time periods (lead times). But in the 5% of time periods where you won't be able to fill all orders, you probably will be able to fill some orders; which means you will probably get a fill rate greater than 95%. The question here is how many of those orders during that 5% of periods can you fill? You can sort of estimate this based upon the number of orders and your historic demand variability relative to your expected inventory during your lead-time period, but implementing a calculation based on this can get very complicated (at least the ways I've experimented with have been very complicated). And unfortunately (or maybe fortunately) this level of complexity is getting beyond the scope of this book (I gotta stop somewhere). And to be honest, I don't have a solution to this one with which I feel comfortable enough to recommend—though I will say I have used a cheat where I create a table that represents the number of orders during the lead-time period and associate an estimated service-level adjustment with each. So what I'm saying here is the safety stock calculation I've put together for this chapter is incomplete.

In reality, I treat all calculations as being incomplete. That's because whenever I spend a little more time looking at a calculation—or looking at a specific environment in which a calculation is being used—I find more issues. For example, you may recall from the forecasting portion of this book that we discussed the possibility of using forecast consumption rules to allow excess demand or forecasts to roll over into other periods. What this does is allow the forecast to compensate for some variability (noise) that would otherwise require safety stock. Unfortunately, our safety stock calculation doesn't know that our forecast is doing this, so it's still going to plan safety stock for this variability. Once again, we would need to look at what kind of impact this is having in our specific environment to see if we need to look for a way to compensate for this.

So I'll repeat, this safety stock calculation is incomplete. But, in its incomplete form, it can still provide some very effective results for you. Based on your demand patterns and other business characteristics, you may be able to use it as is, or you may find that you need to tweak it a bit. But that's what you should be doing with any method used to run your business anyway.

> *This safety stock calculation is incomplete. But, in its incomplete form, it can still provide some very effective results.*

Where do I get my fill rate targets?

As previously mentioned, the service level input in the safety stock calculation is not the same as a fill rate. But, fill rates are the goal of safety stock, therefore we need to discuss them a little. Fill rates are generally expressed as line-fill rates, order-fill rates, or unit-fill rates. A "line" is a line item on an order, so if someone places an order for 5 units of Item A and 2 units of Item B, they have placed an order with two line items. A line-fill rate is the percentage of line items that were filled complete by the requested date. This is probably the most widely used fill rate in inventory management. Order-fill rate is the percentage of orders filled complete by the requested date. In almost all cases, your line-fill rate will be higher than your order-fill rate. Unit-fill rates are calculated as the percentage of units filled by the requested date. So if a customer ordered 100 units of item A, but you could only ship 90 units, that would be a unit-fill of 90%, but would represent an incomplete line in your line-fill rate and an incomplete order in your order-rate.

Choosing fill rate targets are important because they drive your decisions related to safety stock. Though people new to inventory management, or business in general, are sometimes surprised to learn they should not be trying for 100% fill-rates, they have to realize there is a cost associated with trying to stock enough inventory to fill every line on every order, and in most cases that cost is beyond what companies are willing to invest. Therefore, businesses need to make decisions as to just how far they will go to fill orders on time.

Since the constraint to high fill rates is the cost of inventory, it would make sense that this is therefore a basic cost calculation. You just need to compare the cost of inventory (carrying costs) required to fill orders to the costs associated with not being able to fill orders. And to some extent, this can be calculated. Carrying cost will be discussed in great detail in the next chapter so I won't duplicate it here. The costs associated with not being able to fill orders is known as stockout cost or backorder cost, and you can attempt to calculate this by putting together all costs associated with your inability to fill a line on an order. These costs can vary dramatically from one business to another. For example, in some businesses a stockout represents a lost sale, while in other businesses a stockout may just represent a backorder (a delayed sale). Sometimes a stockout may just result in a sale of a similar item (someone buys a green jacket because you were all out of blue jackets), and sometimes a stockout can result in any of the above. A stockout cost that results in a lost sale can be calculated as the net margin you would expect to receive had you been able to make the sale. Stockout costs associated with backorders may include operational costs from multiple handling of the order (multiple shipments against the same order) and additional freight costs associated with shipping the backordered items separately.

A big issue with trying to determine fill rates based on basic cost models comes when a stockout may result in a variety of outcomes (some result in lost sales, some in backorders, some in substitutions). You first need to determine what resulted from the stockout before you can apply costs to it. Though this is possible (and may be necessary in some businesses) to some extent, it can be very difficult and the results tend to be imprecise.

An even bigger issue involves trying to quantify the cost of customer dissatisfaction associated with stockouts. This can be the largest driving factor in fill rates for many businesses, yet is near impossible to calculate. I've witnessed enough arguments over this to realize that in many businesses, your fill-rate targets will come down to executive decisions based as much on gut feel as anything else. And to be honest, that's what executives are supposed to be doing. They need to use their business knowledge and their vision for the company to make these strategic decisions.

They will probably try to get fill rate info on their competitors, and depending upon their strategic goals, either try to match them, stay a little below them, or try to beat them. Hopefully they will consider the carrying costs associated with various fill rates in this decision, but the more tangible costs of stockout tend to fall by the wayside since, in many environments, they tend to pale in comparison to the perceived cost of customer dissatisfaction.

I'm not going to go into any more detail on this because in my experience, the people managing the inventory (those most likely to read this book), probably have little input on the fill rate targets other than possibly providing projected inventory investment amounts required to meet specified fill rates. For them, they just need to understand what the target fill rates mean, and then find a way to meet them (their safety stock calculation).

I will note though that you rarely have just a single fill-rate target. Instead, you will likely have target fill-rates broken down by some type of product grouping.

A quick note on safety stock and dependent demand items.

Conventional wisdoms says that since you are planning safety stock at the parent level (finished goods), there is no need to plan safety stock as the component level (dependent demand). And for the most part, this is good advice. There is simply no need to plan safety stock for demand variability of dependent demand items because it is already being accounted for at the finished goods level. However, there may be circumstances under which you feel you need to carry component safety stock to compensate for supply variability or other non-demand related issues. First of all, let me repeat that you should first look for other ways to resolve these issues. For example, if component scrap is an issue, you can build component scrap into the bill-of-materials (discussed later) to allow you to plan for it.

I'm not going to go into how you calculate safety stock for dependent demand items because that depends upon exactly what you are trying to compensate for. What I will say is, you need to thoroughly understand exactly why you need safety stock for these items, then try to find a way to logically quantify that requirement.

A final word on our safety stock calculation.

Of all the imperfect calculations we use in inventory management, our safety stock calculation is clearly among the most flawed and most confusing. Certainly some of you may be thinking that if the result of all this work is still a seriously flawed calculation, why go through all the trouble? Or, isn't there a cleaner option to calculating safety stock? The fact is any calculation you use to try to determine the probability that a certain level of safety stock will meet demand in real-world applications will have to take into account all these same factors, and subsequently will be just as messy. Therefore, even with all the flaws, it's still probably your best option for calculating safety stock.

Order Quantities / Lot Sizes

Answering the question: How much to make or order?

Since the terms order quantity and lot size pretty much mean the same thing, your choice of terms will most likely be the result of your place in the supply chain. If you manufacture something you are more likely to use the term lot size to describe the quantity you manufacturer in a single run of an item; while if you purchase something you are more likely to describe the quantity you order to be delivered on a specific date as an order quantity. I will try to jump around and use both terms randomly just to keep things interesting.

In many companies, order quantity will be the single most important factor in determining total inventory investment (the amount of money a company has invested in inventory). This isn't to say that safety stock doesn't also play an important role. In fact, in some businesses, you may find that safety stock affects your inventory investment more than lot sizes do, but this is not the norm. Therefore, given that order quantity has the greatest impact on inventory investment and that inventory investment is often the largest investment of a business, you would think that businesses would put a priority on determining the most appropriate order quantities for their businesses. Yeah, you would think.

Unfortunately, most businesses (in my experience) do a lousy job of determining order quantities. It's not that they don't care; I find most businesses are in fact very concerned about inventory investment and do understand that order quantity generally has the biggest impact on inventory investment. In addition, they probably have had numerous meetings over the years discussing order quantities and inventory investment. But . . .

Where do most companies go wrong in determining order quantities?

Oh where do I start on this one? Let's start with the keep-it-simple crowd—which I will now refer to as the simpletons. Not surprisingly, the simpletons like to stay away from complex mathematical calculations, data analysis, or basically anything that would force them to use that squishy thing between their ears. I already discussed this group a little in the previous chapter when I covered keep-it-simple methods for calculating safety stock, but I kind of held back on the name-calling until now. The simpletons generally set their order quantities as the demand that would occur during a fixed period of time. For example, "we always try to order a 30-day supply" or "we order enough to cover two week's worth of demand". So where did they get 30 days or two weeks from? Don't ask. OK, to be fair some of them may have done a little analysis to come up with the time period they use to determine order quantities. And many of them may have taken it a step further by grouping their products (usually by some ABC classification) and setting different time periods for different groups. For example, they may order a 2-week supply of their fastest movers, a 30-day supply of their medium movers, and a 60-day supply of their slow movers. While I'll give them some credit for effort here, their businesses likely deserve better.

And then there are the Just-in-time/inventory-reduction extremists—which coincidentally make up a subset of the simpletons. Let me clarify that I'm not saying that there is no value in the JIT philosophy or that a desire to run your business with less inventory is a bad thing. However, the extremists vehemently believe inventory is inherently evil; and based on this belief, will proceed to arbitrarily reduce or eliminate it.

One of the most amazing—and when I say amazing, I actually mean incredibly stupid—statements I've encountered in inventory management, is a recommendation made related to ways to reduce inventory. So prepare yourselves, it goes like this: "order half as much, twice as often". Oh, how the simpletons love this crap. I don't know where this originated but it's been repeated enough to make me feel ashamed to admit I'm in the inventory management business. It just doesn't get much more arbitrary than this, and I truly hope you understand how ridiculous this recommendation is. But for those who don't, let me explain. Certainly ordering half as much twice as often will reduce your inventory, but if ordering half as much twice as often works to reduce inventory, wouldn't ordering one quarter as much, four times as often, or ordering one tenth as much ten times as often, or ordering one one-hundredth as much one hundred times as often work even better? The problem is that by saying it's a good idea to order half as much, you are assuming—without any basis for this assumption—the current ordering policy is ordering twice as much as should be ordered.

Finally, we have businesses that try to determine optimal order quantities but just make mistakes in the calculations or the inputs to the calculations. I will not be ridiculing this group because they are at least trying and are on the right path. There are also varying degrees of mistakes made in this group—some are making significant errors in the calculations resulting in significantly flawed results, while others may be making more minor errors that are resulting in flawed but still useful results.

Though I use the terms optimal and optimize, the truth is, we are not really going to find the absolute perfect order quantity. There are just too many variables to be able to accurately account for all of them. Therefore, when I use the term "optimal", I'm referring to the "best practical result". And since it's nearly impossible to determine the absolute perfect order quantity, I can't definitively tell you that the difference between the perfect order quantity and the practical optimal order quantity you get as a result of what you will learn in this chapter, will be negligible. But I can say that based on my experience, once you incorporate the most significant variables into the calculation, incorporating additional less significant variables tends to change the output very little.

Before we continue, let me offer a word of encouragement to the simpletons out there. Being a simpleton is not a permanent condition. Some people are simpletons by nature, others by choice, and still others because they work in an environment that encourages simpletonism—they basically just followed the path of least resistance. But all—well maybe not all all, but most all—can choose to break their simpletonistic habits and join the ranks of people who actually attempt to understand what it is they are being paid to accomplish.

Based on my experience, the majority of businesses tend to go the simplistic route. And that's a shame because it is really not all that difficult to calculate more effective order quantities. On that note, you'll be happy to know that this chapter is nowhere near as complicated as the previous one.

Economic order quantity (EOQ).

If you've even minimally worked in inventory management, you have almost certainly run into the term economic order quantity or the acronym EOQ. In most cases, this refers to a specific calculation that was devised roughly a century ago to calculate the order quantity that would result in the lowest overall cost to the company. Why use costs to calculate order quantities? I can't believe this needs to be answered, but there are some claimed "experts" out there who denounce economic-based order quantity calculations (these are the Just-in-time/inventory-reduction extremists I discussed previously). We want to use costs to calculate order quantities because calculating order quantities is a business decision that has a significant impact on business expenses. And since the goal of a business is to be profitable, and profits are based on revenue minus expenses (costs), it would make a hell of a lot of sense to make your order quantity decisions based on how these decisions impact profits. More importantly, if you don't use costs as a basis for these types of decisions, what do you use?

The reason EOQ has gotten a bad reputation over the years is that there is a perception that economic order quantity calculations inherently mean large order quantities, and therefore a large inventory investment. This just isn't the case. However, I will acknowledge that the most significant error I see in order quantity calculations is an exaggeration of order costs, which will result in larger order quantities. Again, this isn't really a problem with cost-based order quantity calculations, but rather a problem with how people frequently implement these calculations.

A quick history lesson and the basic EOQ calculation.

I personally own a copy of a book that was published in 1931 (Purchasing and Storing, a textbook that was part of a "Modern Business Course" at the Alexander Hamilton Institute in New York) that covered "minimum cost quantity", which is essentially the same calculation we now call EOQ. According to Wikipedia, the EOQ model was originally developed by F. W. Harris in 1913. My cynical side tends to assume that the person who gets credit for a calculation was probably not really the first person to develop the calculation, so it may very well be that the calculation—or similar calculations—was in use well before that.

To think that about 100 years ago, there were people without computers or even reasonably functional desktop calculators, that were more effectively calculating their order quantities than many "inventory managers" do today. Yeah, but then again, they weren't distracted by today's essential technology-related activities, like placing smiley-face emoticons in all their text messages :-)

Despite its age, the basic EOQ calculation is still very useful today. In fact, I would argue it's actually more useful today than it was back then since we can now use computers to automate the calculation. The base calculation looks like this:

$$EOQ = \sqrt{\frac{2(OrderCost)(AnnualDemand)}{(AnnualCarryingCostperUnit)}}$$

Figure 7A. This is the basic EOQ formula. A more Excel-like representation would be =SQRT(((2(OrderCost)(AnnualDemand))/(AnnualCarryingCostperUnit))

Ooo scary, a square root sign. To just look at this calculation in its current form, there is no obvious way to understand how this produces the "optimal" order quantity. I mean, where does that 2 come from and why are we calculating square roots? If you are a responsible inventory manager, these questions should concern you. So let's try to make sense of it.

All cost-based order quantity calculations look to determine the order quantity that results in the least overall costs to the business. The costs are broken up into two groups: carrying costs (also called holding costs), and order costs (also called purchase costs or setup costs). Carrying costs are the costs associated with having inventory; they primarily include the cost of the inventory investment and the costs associated with storing the inventory. The larger your order quantity, the greater the associated carrying costs will be since you will be carrying more inventory. Order costs, on the other hand, are the costs associated with processing an individual order. The larger your order quantity, the smaller your order costs are (over time) since you will be placing fewer orders.

In other words, as your order quantities go up, your carrying costs go up and your order costs go down. Conversely, as your order quantities go down, your carrying costs go down and your order costs go up. If you plot these costs (as annual costs) on a graph, you should see a gradually curving line going down that represents order costs as the quantity increases, and an angled line going up that represents carrying costs as the quantity increases (see Figure 7B). What we want to do is find the order quantity with the lowest overall cost (sum of total order costs and carrying costs over a period of time) and it just so happens that the quantity with the lowest overall cost is the point where the two lines intersect on the graph. In other words, it's the quantity at which order costs and carrying costs are the same. So how do I know that the lowest overall cost is at the point where order costs and carrying costs are the same? Well, many years ago I read about this in a book on inventory management, but being someone who doesn't necessarily believe everything he reads in books, I tested the hell out of this little gem of wisdom to see if I could make it fail. I'm pleased to say I couldn't. I'm sure there is some mathematical theorem that explains this phenomenon, but even if I knew what that theorem was—which I obviously don't—I would still have tested the hell out of it anyway because that's just how I roll.

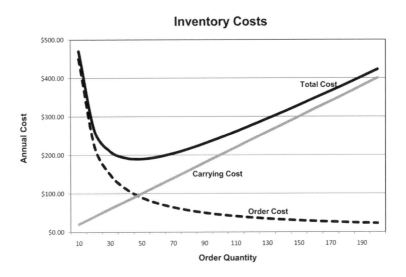

Figure 7B. This chart shows an example of the relationship between order costs, carrying costs, and total costs as the order quantity changes.

Now that we are comfortable with the assumption that the lowest overall cost will occur with the quantity where the order costs and carrying costs are equal, we can start to put together a little algebraic calculation that represents this. We first need to find a way to express order cost and carrying costs in the same terms (period of time). We can do this by basing our calculation on costs that occur during a period of one year. Carrying cost is generally represented as a percentage of your average inventory value. Therefore, if we determine our annual carrying cost to be 12% of our average inventory value, we can express our annual inventory carrying cost as 0.12 multiplied by our average inventory investment. Assuming that our demand is relatively consistent (we'll talk more about this later) we can calculate our average inventory as one-half of our order quantity. Since our order quantity is the unknown here, we will represent that as "x". So our average inventory value for an item would be one-half of x times the unit cost of the item. Therefore, our annual inventory carrying cost for the item would be calculated as the carrying cost percentage times one-half of x times the unit cost. Or, in algebraic terms, where carrying cost percentage is represented as "c" and unit cost is represented as "u", we would have c*1/2x*u.

Now on to annual order costs. Order cost is generally represented as a dollar amount per instance of a purchase. To determine how many times a year we would purchase something, we can divide the annual demand by the order quantity. Therefore, our annual order cost can be expressed as order cost times our annual demand divided by our order quantity (x).

In algebraic terms, where order cost is represented as "p" and annual demand is represented as "a", we have p*a / x.

Since the lowest cost occurs where the annual order cost and annual carrying costs are the same, we can put together the following equation:

c*1/2x*u = p*a / x

Now all we have to do is solve for x. Can you believe it? There actually are times in real life where you will need to solve for x. Now for those of you who have completely forgotten how this works, you basically perform a series of mathematical operations equally against both sides of the calculation in order to eventually isolate x to one side of the calculation. There are a few decades between me and my last algebra class, so I rather doubt that I have the steps in the "proper" order, but this is pretty much what I did:

1. Multiplied both sides by x to remove x from the right side.
2. Multiplied both sides by 2 to get rid of 1/2 from the left side.
3. Rearranged things a little bit to make the next step make more sense.
4. Divided each side by cu to remove cu from the left side.
5. Took the square root of each side to turn x squared to x.

Figure 7C shows the equation as it progresses through these steps.

Holy elementary algebra Batman, that's it! Now we can look at the EOQ formula and understand that the 2 in it comes from the 1/2 order quantity that represented our average inventory level, and that the reason we have to take the square root is because in the process of isolating x, we had x squared on one side of the equation and therefore needed to take the square root of everything on the other side of the equation. I'll admit I was rather pleased with myself when I worked this out many years ago. It's not that I think I absolutely need to understand all the details of every tool I use, but I like to at least give it a shot. But always remember, in the absence of completely understanding something, you can at least fall back on testing the hell out of it to verify the output.

$$c \cdot \tfrac{1}{2} x \cdot u = p \cdot a \div x$$

$$x \cdot c \cdot \tfrac{1}{2} x \cdot u = p \cdot a$$

$$x \cdot c \cdot x \cdot u = 2 \cdot p \cdot a$$

$$x^2 \cdot cu = 2\, pa$$

$$x^2 = \frac{2\, pa}{cu}$$

$$x = \sqrt{\frac{2\, pa}{cu}}$$

Figure 7C. Here we see the progression from our original equation to the final EOQ formula where x (our order quantity) is isolated to one side of the equation.

But getting EOQ (or other cost-based order quantity calculations) to work, requires more than just understanding the math.

Order costs and carrying costs. Getting them right.

This is where many order quantity calculations go wrong. You have to get your inputs right; and in the case of order quantity calculations, we're talking about getting your order costs and your carrying costs right. The biggest mistake you can do here is to take some "benchmark" or "rule of thumb" number you come across in a magazine or book, and think you can just use that. No matter how much you want it to be that easy, it just doesn't work that way. The only way to get the right carrying costs and order costs for your operation is to do it the old fashion way, by calculating them yourself based on your own costs. And it's not just a matter of gathering costs, you really need to make sure you are getting the right costs in the right bucket—which is not always as obvious as you might initially think.

Order cost.

Let's start with order costs. Order cost is the sum of the fixed costs that are incurred each time an item is ordered or produced. You need to think of this as costs associated with the instance of an order, which is not the same as all costs associated with ordering and receiving inventory. I know this sounds a little confusing, but we will go through some examples. It's important to note here that when we calculate order cost, we are really calculating the costs associated with a single line item on an order, not the cost to process an entire order (that may have multiple line items on it). Therefore, when I refer to order costs or orders processed, I am referring to cost per line item or the number or line items processed.

Order processing. Order cost would include the costs associated with determining the need to order (reviewing items at their reorder point); creating the purchase order, requisition, or manufacturing order; any approval steps; monitoring open orders; and expediting or de-expediting open orders. It would also include costs associated with phoning, faxing, or mailing orders to suppliers. This would not include costs associated with maintaining and reviewing forecasts, reorder points, safety stock, or general system, item setup, and maintenance tasks.

Depending on your specific processes, it may or may not include costs related to sourcing and getting quotes. For example, if you re-source and/or require new quotes every time you order, these costs would be included, otherwise they would not.

If you're still having difficulty grasping why some of these costs are included and others are not, remember that the cost must be associated with the instance of the ordering transaction. Therefore, tasks like maintaining and reviewing the forecast and safety stock quantities would generally not be included because you would (should) be doing these tasks regardless of the order frequency.

Third-party logistics costs. Transactional costs associated with freight forwarders or other third-party logistics activities would be included, as would costs associated with communications with them regarding specific shipments. But not all costs associated with these services would be included.

Receipts processing. At the point of receipt, order costs would include costs related to processing the receipt, but not costs related to the quantity being received. Time spent entering the receipt into your system, checking to make sure the items match the packing list, and handling bills of lading, would be included. Time spent unpacking shipping cartons would be included under most circumstances provided it's not due to quantities being processed. This is where things get tricky. If I generally receive multiple items in the same shipping carton, or if I receive single items that come in only one carton, I would generally include these costs because they are related to the "instance" of the order. But, let's say I have receipts of items where I get multiple separate cartons or containers of the same item. In this case you would generally not include this because regardless of whether I get 5 cartons 10 times a year or 25 cartons twice a year, I still need to handle 50 cartons, therefore there are no incremental costs associated with more frequent receipts. The same holds true of unloading trailers. Time spent unloading full pallets from trailers would almost certainly not be included since this is more related to quantity than to the instance of the receipts. However, if you are receiving rather small parts from a parcel carrier, you probably would include any time you spent handling those parcels. Why? Well think of it this way. Let's say I'm ordering little rubber o-rings. If I ordered an entire year's supply at once, it would probably come in a single box from a parcel carrier, but if I order smaller quantities every two weeks, I would end up handling 26 cartons over the period of a year instead of one carton. Therefore, the additional costs associated with handling all those parcels are due to the instance of an order and not to the quantity.

If you count the inventory as part of the receipt process, you may include the setup time associated with counting the product but not the actual time spent counting. For example, if you use counting scales for small parts, you could include the time spent creating and checking your sample quantity because that is due to the instance of the receipt.

Inbound inspection costs. If you require quality inspections of inbound goods, part or all of that time may be included depending on your inspection process. Any setup and processing times associated with determining the specs (getting drawings or bringing up specs on a computer) and entering inspection information into the system during the inspection process would be included. Time spent inspecting individual units would be included if you inspect a fixed number of units per receipt, but not if you inspect a fixed percentage of units. Once again, you need to determine if the cost is associated with the instance of the receipt or with the quantity.

Putaway. Time spent stocking the receipts (putaway) would need to be assessed using similar logic. If the putaway time is mainly due to the instance of the receipt, you would include it; if it is mainly due to the quantity of the receipt, you would not.

Accounting. In the accounting department, you would apply costs associated with matching invoices to receipts and paying vendors.

Manufacturing. In manufacturing operations, order cost would include the labor associated with setting up a production run and may even include cost of scrap if scrap is related to setup. For example, in a printing operation there is usually some scrap associated with setting up the print run; this would be included in order cost. Normal scrap that occurs during the running of a process would not be included. Some tooling may even be included if that tooling cannot be reused in subsequent production runs due to the setup characteristics of that operation, but you would not include tooling that gets worn out during the production process itself (related to quantity, not instance). You would also include costs associated with picking and issuing components for production, but not the time spent counting these components as they are picked.

Up to this point, much of what we've covered is labor costs. We've figured out which tasks can be applied to order cost; now we must try to assign costs to these tasks. The classic way to do this would be to go out and time each specific step of each specific task associated with processing an order, and then assign labor costs accordingly. If you've been trained in how to accurately conduct time studies, you might be able to go this way, but most people will probably make a mess of this (it's harder than it seems). What I find works better, still involves some time-study work, but does it in a way that reduces the likelihood of major mistakes. You will still measure the time it takes to perform tasks, but rather than trying to measure these one order at a time, you will look at the various tasks and see which ones can be isolated to get more accurate measurements. For example, in accounting, the person who handles matching invoices to receipts will generally do these in groups. It's easier to measure as a whole how much time this person spends on this task, and then divide this time by the number of receipts matched. In other departments as well, it's generally more accurate to try to determine what percentage of the worker's time is dedicated to the tasks that would be considered part of order cost, and then multiply this percentage by the total labor cost for this worker, and divide the output by the number of orders processed during a given period of time. Or, if most of their time is dedicated to these tasks, just measure the tasks that are not part of order cost and deduct this time from the overall time. You may also be able to do this on a department-wide basis if you can determine what percentage of the overall labor in the department is dedicated to the tasks that would be part of order cost, then multiply this percentage by the total labor in the department over a period of time, and divide this by the number of orders processed. Just another reminder: when I say "orders processed", I mean line items processed.

Though it can get very complicated trying to isolate all the varied tasks that either do or don't affect order cost, in most cases it's not all that difficult. For example, if you deal primarily with small quantities of small parts, you will find that al-most all your receiving and putaway time is related to the instance of the receipt. Conversely, if you are in a full-pallet environment you will find that most of your receiving labor is related to quantity and therefore you only need to isolate those tasks related to the instance of the receipt (primarily clerical tasks in this example).

You may very well find that you have some products that have significantly differ-ent order costs than others. An example of this would be the differences between items that are purchased domestically versus items that are purchased overseas. The items purchased overseas can have significantly higher order costs due to ad-ditional tasks such as more complicated communications, freight forwarder trans-action fees, and additional costs associated with prepayments and international payments. It's also not unusual for overseas receipts to take more time to check-in and process through receiving due to the way imports are often packed, marked, and shipped. You may also have a vendor certification program that allows more streamlined processing of orders from certain vendors, therefore reducing order costs associated with orders from these vendors. Though you don't want to over-complicate things here, it does make sense to create "order groups" for items that have similar order costs if you have a diverse supplier base.

Inbound freight costs? This is another area that can be rather tricky. This once again comes down to the nature of your inbound shipments. Freight costs related to the weight of a shipment should generally not be included, however, freight costs related to the instance of the shipment can. At one end of the spectrum would be full-truckload shipments, where there is virtually no additional freight costs related to the instance of an order. At the other end of the spectrum would be something like that o-ring scenario I previously described. In the case of the o-rings, if the individual shipments weigh less than one pound, you can almost assume that you can include most— if not all— of the freight cost in your order cost. In between these two scenarios, things get more complicated. For example, if I receive five three-pound packages a year, my cost per pound is higher than if I received one nine-pound package per year. Therefore the difference should go into order cost. If you have vendors that charge you handling fees or minimum order fees, these may also be included in order cost provided you can be reasonably accurate about applying them.

As you can see, applying freight costs can get very complicated and in most operations you're going to have to compromise here. It's generally not practical to try to get the correct incremental freight costs associated with each order. You need to start by doing some sample analysis of your inbound shipments to see how much your freight costs are affected by order frequency. If you have a diverse product mix, you may want to consider setting up "inbound freight groups" to categorize items that share similar freight characteristics. Be aware that this goes beyond just the physical characteristics of the items themselves. Depending on the supplier, some items may end up being shipped in the same carton with other items; this would significantly change their incremental inbound freight costs. And, of course, you need to determine if you are even paying inbound freight—there's no need to go through all this if your supplier pays the inbound freight. Though this seems like a daunting task, you will likely find that you can create a handful of freight groups that you can apply some ballpark freight costs to that can be "good enough" for your order quantity calculation.

Carrying cost.

And now on to carrying cost. Carrying cost (also known as holding cost) includes the costs associated with having inventory, or more specifically, the costs associated with having specific quantities of inventory. If the cost doesn't change when inventory levels change, then it should not be included in carrying cost. As you can see, this is pretty much (though not exactly) the flipside of the logic we use to determine order cost. Carrying cost is generally expressed as a percentage of inventory value. Since we are basing our EOQ calculation on an annual time frame, carrying costs would be the total annual costs associated with having inventory, divided by the average inventory investment. As with order costs, carrying costs are not always as obvious as they seem. Let's start with the easy ones.

Cost of capital. There is a cost associated with having capital tied up in inventory. In other words, money costs money. Most businesses have debt associated with inventory, therefore the easiest way to apply capital costs associated with having inventory, is to use the interest rate paid on your debt. I think this is the best way to go for most business. Unfortunately there are always potential complications.

For example, there are limits on the capital to which a business has access. Therefore, theoretically, if it can reasonably be assumed that if the money invested in inventory could be invested elsewhere for a greater return, then the actual cost of capital would be the return-on-investment you could expect if you did not have that money tied up in inventory. You really need to leave this decision to the execs and accountants, but you should question them if they seem to be unreasonable in their expectations of their potential return on investment.

Insurance. This one is pretty straightforward. You almost certainly have your inventory insured, and this insurance is based on your total inventory investment, therefore your insurance costs as a percentage of your average inventory investment would be part of carrying cost. It is possible though that some of your inventory is insured at a higher rate, so you should look into this to see if you need to apply multiple insurance rates.

Taxes. In some places (certain states/localities), inventory is taxed (I'm assuming it's a form of property tax). I personally have not worked anywhere where inventory was taxed—or I was unaware of it if I did—but if your inventory is taxed, you can include that in the carrying cost. Once again, you would just divide this tax amount by your average inventory investment to determine a percentage that would be applied to your carrying cost.

Storage costs. Certainly, storage costs work into the carrying cost calculation, but it's not as simple as just determining the annual cost of your warehouse and dividing that by your average inventory investment. Many areas of a warehouse are related more towards processing activities than to storage. Areas set up for shipping and receiving operations, order picking and order consolidation, packaging, assembly, quality control, trash, and other processing activities can account for a significant percentage of your total warehouse. In addition, some areas that appear to be storage areas may not necessarily be included in storage costs. For example, in small-parts picking operations it is common to set up fixed picking locations that hold a specific quantity of inventory to support an efficient picking operation, and then use reserve storage inventory areas for overflow storage of inventory that doesn't fit in the picking location. In this scenario, I would generally not include the picking locations as part of the storage cost because I consider them as more process-related than storage locations. If these locations are sized primarily for picking efficiency, they do not change based on order quantities, therefore the costs associated with them do not change based on order quantities. If, however, these locations are sized according to inbound order quantities, I probably would include this in storage costs. In either case, the overflow storage would certainly be included in storage costs. Also, the aisles in storage areas would be included as part of storage costs because they are there to support the storage of inventory.

Some of you may be thinking that your warehouse space is essentially fixed, therefore the cost doesn't really change if inventory levels change. Well good for you. This is another one of those tricky areas because to some extent this is true.

However, you also need to consider that you are paying for that warehouse space because you had the expectation that you needed it to support your inventory levels that are a result of your order quantities. We'll come back to this a little later.

Not all your inventory has the same storage costs. In the classic EOQ calculation, we incorporate storage costs as part of carrying cost, and therefore represent it as a percentage of average inventory value. In other words, we use the cost of the item to calculate the storage cost for EOQ. Therefore, if you apply a single storage cost percentage to your entire inventory, you are assuming that all your inventory shares similar cost-to-storage-cost characteristics. In some businesses this may be a reasonable assumption, but in many businesses you will find you have a product mix that has varying cost-to-storage-cost characteristics. If you look at the product mix at any of the big retailers these days, you will find dramatically different products. For example, my local home center sells a little bit of everything now; they even opened up some grocery aisles recently. I mean come on, groceries at the lumber yard? It used to be that a Saturday morning trip to the lumber yard meant you were going to be spending your weekend doing man-stuff; now it just means you're catching a sale on toilet paper and canned yams. OK, back on topic. If I looked at the inventory of my local home center, I could pick out some nice examples to show the differences in storage costs within that facility. They sell some small items such as watch batteries or bits for rotary tools that are very expensive relative to the physical size of the item. Then there are larger items such as bags of sand or landscaping timbers that are very inexpensive relative to their physical size. So if you compared the physical storage space that $500 worth of rotary tool bits or watch batteries would take, to the space $500 of sand or landscape timbers would take, it would be obvious that there are very different storage costs that should be associated with these items. In addition, you may also have items that require a more costly storage environment. Cold storage is obviously more costly than typical dry storage, and storage of some hazardous materials may require a storage environment that is more costly.

Once again, you are probably not going to try to calculate exact storage costs for each item, but instead would likely just create a handful of storage groups to use to apply storage costs. Although, if you are using a warehouse management system and have set up extensive dimensional and storage characteristics for your inventory, you may be able to use this existing data to automatically calculate more accurate item-by-item storage costs.

Risk of damage, theft, spoilage, or obsolescence. This is an important part of carrying cost that is frequently missed. The more inventory you have, the greater your exposure to damage, theft, spoilage, or obsolescence. Once again, not all items are created equal, so you need to apply these costs according to the characteristics of the item. If we go back to our home center example, those little expensive items are going to have a high risk of theft. In addition, something like windows or fluorescent light bulbs would have a higher risk of damage, the new food items they've added would have a greater risk of spoilage, and I spotted some cool new electronic gadgets in the tool department that would have a greater risk of obsolescence. These would all be contrasted against many products that have much lower risk of any of these factors. So I guess we need yet another storage group data element to use to apply categories for these risk factors.

This is another one of those areas where you generally start with your knowledge of your inventory to begin to put together risk groups, and then work from there to validate your assumptions and apply appropriate costs. Ideally, you would have already been tracking actual item-level costs associated with these types of transactions, so you should be able to use this existing data to build your cost model. For example, if you have a specific transaction type used for deducting obsolete goods from inventory, you can use your transaction history to determine the actual value of obsolete goods within a specific product group during a period of a year. Then you can divide that by the average inventory level of that product group to determine your obsolescence carrying cost percentage for that group. This does get a little trickier when you get into damage and theft though. While having more inventory certainly exposes you to greater risk of damage and theft, it's not the only factor that contributes to these risks, and probably isn't even the most predominant factor. Therefore, you'll need to adjust your damage and theft amounts based on how much is due to "more" inventory being there, versus how much is due to just "some" inventory being there. Well good luck with that one. It's probably impractical to scientifically arrive at an accurate figure here, so you're likely stuck with combining a little analysis with some judgment (educated guessing) to determine how much to factor the actual amount down in order to arrive at an amount that is more likely due to the actual quantity stored than it is to just the existence of any quantity stored.

Labor costs. There are also some labor costs that should be included in carrying cost, for example, the labor costs associated with the physical counting of inventory for a cycle count program or a physical inventory. There is no doubt that more inventory means more labor costs associated with these activities. In addition, you may need to include some handling costs where inventory is handled multiple times due to the quantity stored. For example, if ordering a larger quantity results in some inventory having to be temporarily stored in reserve storage areas and then later moved into the main storage area, one of those movements is the result of the order quantity and therefore could be included in carrying cost. Even if the additional inventory doesn't result in multiple handling, it may result in more travel time. This is especially true in full-pallet environments where more inventory can result in a much larger storage area and therefore longer distances being traveled to put away and pick inventory. Don't overdo it with these types of labor costs because they are generally a very small portion of your total warehouse labor and can be tricky to accurately apply.

Gray areas: when is a cost, not a cost?

I touched on this briefly with storage costs, and whether a smaller order quantity saves money in storage costs since your warehouse space may be fixed. My recommendation here is to start with the "theoretical storage cost", which is essentially the storage cost we previously discussed that assumes changes to inventory levels will have an immediate impact on storage costs. However, there are situations where I feel it is appropriate to adjust this cost to account for actual storage conditions. For example, if you are underutilizing your warehouse space and are not in a position to be able to recoup the costs of these empty areas, it may make sense to artificially reduce the storage portion of your carrying cost to allow you to therefore utilize your space better and reduce the labor associated with more frequent receipts. On the flipside, if your warehouse is getting maxed out, it makes a lot of sense to artificially inflate your storage portion of carrying cost to be able to continue to work within your current space limitations under certain circumstances.

You'll also find that operational costs tend to go up as a warehouse starts to get near or exceed capacity. The reasons for this include additional handling due to location consolidation, more time to just find room to stock product, and a greater risk of damage due to cramped conditions. Even though it may be difficult to calculate actual costs associated with a full warehouse, it will be obvious that these costs exist and therefore it would make sense to at least make an educated guess, and increase your storage costs accordingly. Obviously, this isn't the only solution to a "full warehouse" and it certainly has its limitations, but if moving to a bigger warehouse or even getting some additional off-site storage are impractical alternatives, this can provide some short-term relief and may even work as a longer-term solution. Just don't forget that you have artificially inflated the storage cost, because your long-term planning should take into account that you probably need more storage space.

Similarly, if it looks like there are going to be some cash-flow problems on the horizon, it may make sense to inflate the cost-of-capital portion of your carrying cost to reduce your inventory investment and free up some cash.

There may also be times when you want to artificially inflate or deflate order costs or set-up costs. In manufacturing, if you lack the capacity to meet the production schedule using the EOQ, you may want to artificially increase set-up costs to increase lot sizes and therefore reduce overall setup time. If you have excess capacity you may want to artificially decrease set up costs; this will increase overall set up time and reduce inventory investment. The idea is that if you are paying for the labor and machine overhead anyway it would make sense to take advantage of the savings in reduced inventories. To a lesser extent, you can apply this same logic to order costs in non-manufacturing environments, though I see this as less likely.

So what makes these seemingly arbitrary adjustments any different from the "order half as much, twice as often" recommendation that I previously ridiculed? Well for one, they really aren't arbitrary. These adjustments to order costs or carrying costs are made based on the knowledge that there are some less tangible factors at play here. In addition, these adjustments only change a portion of the equation. For example, even though I may be artificially adjusting my storage cost, the other costs associated with carrying inventory, as well as other factors such as unit cost and order costs are still in place and are appropriately affecting my order quantities. As a more specific example, if we go back to the home center example and increase our storage cost because we are out of storage space, we would see much smaller order quantities for bulky inexpensive items such as bags of sand , while our order quantities for smaller more expensive items would change minimally if at all. Conversely, if we increased the "cost of capital" portion of carrying cost because we were expecting some cash-flow problems, we would see a more dramatic reduction in the order quantities for small expensive items and a minimal reduction in the order quantities for lower-cost bulky items.

Alright, so I've talked about possibly setting up order groups to group items that share similar order costs, freight groups for items that share similar order-related freight costs, and a variety of storage groups based on size to cost, storage environment, or risk of damage, theft, spoilage, or obsolescence. That may seem like a whole lot of work just to calculate your order quantity. And for initial system setup in many environments, it is a hell of a lot of work. However, group logic does make it much easier to set up and maintain this data long term. And it should be obvious by now that just using a single order cost and carrying cost for all items is probably not going to be as effective as you would like. However, you also need to realize there is no need to create different groups unless there is a fairly significant difference in order costs or carrying costs associated with different groups of items. So how much is a "fairly significant difference"? I'll let you judge that for yourselves. Once you get your calculation set up (which we'll be doing next), you can play with it and make changes to your order cost and carrying cost to see how much it changes your recommended order quantity. You will find that small changes to these costs don't dramatically change the order quantity.

Order cost recap.

If the total annual cost does not change as order frequency changes, the cost should not be included in order cost. In other words, if the specific cost (annualized) doesn't increase if I were to switch from placing a single order once a year, to placing orders every week, then it is not an order cost for the purposes of our lot-sizing calculations. Order costs are the result of the instance of an order, not the quantity.

Carrying cost recap.

If the total annual cost does not change as inventory levels change, the cost should not be included in carrying cost. In other words, if the specific cost (annualized) doesn't increase if I were to switch from carrying a one-week supply to carrying a one-month supply, then it is not a carrying cost for the purposes of our lot-sizing calculations. Carrying costs are the result of carrying a specific quantity of inventory.

Back to the calculations.

Let's go step-by-step setting up some order quantity calculations in a spreadsheet.

The basic EOQ calculation is really simple.

B7	▼	f_x	=SQRT((2*B2*B5)/(B3*B4))	

	A	B
1	**Basic EOQ**	
2	Order Cost	$13.00
3	Carrying Cost	20%
4	Unit Cost	$5.25
5	Annual Demand	300
6		
7	**Order Quantity**	**86**
8		

Figure 7D. The basic EOQ calculation

In cell B2 enter your order cost. For this example, we will use $13.00.

In cell B3 enter your carrying cost. For this example, we will use 20%.

In cell B4 enter your unit cost. For this example, we will use $5.25.

In cell B5 enter your annual demand. For this example, we will use 300

In cell B7 enter   =SQRT((2*B2*B5)/(B3*B4))

The result is an EOQ of 86 units. That's all there is to it. You now have a working EOQ calculation and can change the values in cells B2 through B5 to reflect your own examples.

Now let's try testing our output a little using another calculation.

In cell B9 enter 86 (the result of our EOQ calculation)

In cell B10 enter   =(B3*0.5*B9*B4)+(B2*B5/B9)

What you've just entered in cell B10 is the calculation of the expected total annual cost given the order quantity in cell B9. If you recall when we first started solving the EOQ formula, we had the following calculation that represented annual carrying cost on the left side as being equal to annual order cost on the right side.

$c * 1/2x * u = p * a / x$

We can simply move things around a little to get a calculation for total annual cost. So instead of having annual carrying cost equal to annual order cost, we have a calculation that represents total annual cost as being equal to annual carrying cost plus annual order cost.

Total annual cost $=(c * 1/2x * u)+(p * a / x)$

So what can we do with this? We can start by manually changing the value in cell B9 to see if we can find an order quantity that provides a lower total annual cost than our EOQ output. You can also use it to see just how much your total annual cost changes with different order quantities. This is helpful to show that a small change up or down from your EOQ tends to not usually have a significant impact on total annual cost. So rather than having a single "optimal" quantity, we really have a "sweet spot" that includes a range of quantities. You can also go back to the original EOQ calculation and make small changes to the order cost and carrying cost to see that the "sweet spot" does not change much with minor cost changes.

	B10		f_x	=(B3*0.5*B9*B4)+(B2*B5/B9)
	A			B
1	**Basic EOQ**			
2	Order Cost			$13.00
3	Carrying Cost			20%
4	Unit Cost			$5.25
5	Annual Demand			300
6				
7	**Order Quantity**			**86**
8				
9	Order Quantity Test			86
10	Total Annual Cost of Test Quantity			$90.50

Figure 7E. By adding a test quantity and a total annual cost calculation, we can manually change our order quantity (the test quantity) and see how it impacts our total annual cost.

We can also use our total cost calculation as a basis for playing around with the Solver add-in for Excel to set up an alternate means of calculating our order quantity.

To see if the add-in is already installed and loaded click Tools>Add-Ins in Excel 2003 or earlier, or Office Button>Excel Options>Add-Ins>Manage Excel Add-Ins>Go in Excel 2007 or later. If you don't see it on the list, check the Microsoft documentation on installing and loading the Solver add-in.

First change the test quantity in cell B9 to 1, then, in Excel 2003: Click Tools>Solver, or in Excel 2007: Click Data>Solver

The Solver Parameters window should appear.

In "Set Target Cell", enter $B$10

In "Equal To", click the Min selection

In "By Changing Cells", enter $B$9

In "Subject to Constraints", click "Add"

In "Cell Reference" enter $B$9

Select >=

In "Constraint" enter 1

Click OK

Click Solve

What you should see now, is that solver has changed Cell B9 to 86 (actually 86.1891607384104). What we've just done is tell Solver that we want to minimize the value in cell B10 (total annual cost) by changing

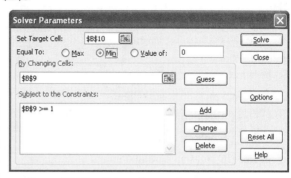

Figure 7F. The Solver Parameters window.

the value in cell B9 (order quantity). In other words, we told solver to find the order quantity that results in the least total annual cost. Pretty cool huh. It's important to realize that optimization algorithms (such as solver) have their limitations. We will see an example of this later.

Now that we've calculated an order quantity using EOQ (and a similar calculation using Solver), we need to examine the potential shortcomings of these relatively simple calculations. The most commonly cited issue with EOQ is that it is based on a model that assumes constant demand over an extended period of time. Well that works great if you have no seasonality or trend, but as I have said before, it's very rare to have demand that does not have some level of seasonality or trend. So how big of an issue is this? Well that primarily depends on just how much seasonality or trend you have. I've found EOQ to still perform reasonably well with minor to moderate levels of seasonality or trend. In addition, there are some tricks you can use to try to compensate for seasonality and trend. We'll discuss seasonality and trend more a little later.

The other issue relates to EOQ being based on a single cost. In other words, EOQ does not understand quantity discounts. Well, this is a rather important issue if you purchase items that are subject to quantity discounts. The good news here is you can combine some basic spreadsheet functionality with our EOQ calculation and our total annual cost calculation, to calculate an order quantity within a quantity discount structure. Be aware this does get quite a bit more complicated than our simple EOQ calculation, but it's really based on fairly simple logic.

Incorporating quantity discounts.

What we are going to do is set up a spreadsheet with our EOQ inputs and a quantity discount structure. Then we will calculate total annual cost at each quantity break, and EOQ at the discounted cost at each quantity break; then compare these to determine the best order quantity. Note that we will be using a little different total-annual-cost calculation here. Instead of just adding the annual carrying cost to the annual order cost, we will also add in the cost of the inventory itself (inventory consumed during the year). We didn't need to do this in previous calculations because the cost of the inventory itself didn't change, given that the cost per unit didn't change.

So here goes.

Start with an empty worksheet.

In Cell C4 enter an order cost of $10.00

In Cell C5 enter a carrying cost of 15%

In Cell C6 enter an annual demand of 2000

Now we'll enter the quantity discounts

In B9 enter 1

In B10 enter 100

In B11 enter 250

In B12 enter 1000

In C9 enter $10.00

In C10 enter $9.50

In C11 enter $9.25

In C12 enter $9.10

And now for the formulas.

> **Formula tip:**
>
> In the formulas below, the characters "" are two sets of double quotes (not four single quotes).
>
> Go to InventoryExplained.com for more help with these formulas.

In D9 enter =IF(ISBLANK(C9),"",IF(E9>B9,(C$5*0.5*E9*C9)+(C$4*C$6/E9)+(C$6*C9),(C$5*0.5*B9*C9)+(C$4*C$6/B9)+(C$6*C9)))

Copy cell D9 and paste into cells D10 through D15

In E9 enter =IF(ISBLANK(C9),"",(SQRT(2*C$6*C$4/(C$5*C9))))

Copy cell E9 and paste into cells E10 through E15

In F9 enter =IF(D9=D$16,(B9),"")

Copy cell F9 and paste into cells F10 through F15

In G9 enter =IF(ISBLANK(F9),"",IF(E9>F9,(E9),F9))

Copy cell G9 and paste this into cells G10 through G15

In D16 enter =MIN(D9:D15)

In C17 enter =MIN(G9:G15)

Now you can add the labels per example in Figure 7G and add formatting if you like.

	A	B	C	D	E	F	G
1							
2		**EOQ with Quantity Discounts**					
3							
4		Order Cost	$10.00				
5		Carrying Cost	15%				
6		Annual Demand	2,000				
7							
8		**Price Break Qty**	**Unit Cost**	Annual cost	EOQ at discount	Best Price Break	Buy Quantity
9		1	$10.00	$20,244.95	163		
10		100	$9.50	$19,238.75	168		
11		250	$9.25	$18,753.44	170	250	250
12		1000	$9.10	$18,902.50	171		
13							
14							
15							
16				$18,753.44			
17		**Order Qty**	**250**				

Figure 7G. This is our EOQ with Quantity Discount worksheet with the added labels and formatting.

Then to make it a little slicker, you can hide columns D, E, F, and G (select columns, then Format>Column>Hide). And to automate things a little better, I created a button with a macro to clear cells B10 through C15 before I start inputting data for another item. I'm not going to explain how to create a macro here, and you don't need this to test the calculation. See Figure 7H.

In case you're wondering what all that "IF" stuff is, some of it is to just make sure there is a quantity discount in the cells to the left (since different items may have different numbers of quantity breaks). The rest is just my way of isolating the quantity break with the lowest overall cost, and also verifying if an EOQ calculated at that quantity discount is greater than the quantity break (usually the order quantity ends up being the quantity discount break quantity, but sometimes the EOQ at that quantity discount is actually larger than the break quantity).

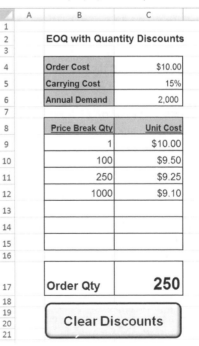

Figure 7H.

Realize there are many ways to accomplish this same thing in Excel and this is just how I chose to do it.

Well, now you have a working (hopefully) EOQ with quantity discounts calculation you can use on your desktop. Though I think you'll find this is quite useful, this really isn't how you want to deal with large numbers of items. Fortunately, the logic used to accomplish this on your desktop is not all that different from what a programmer would use to create a more automated program.

Seasonality and trend.

So let's get back to our seasonality and trend issues. The greatest variability would most likely be related to seasonality, so I will start by focusing on that. I want to once again mention that the basic order quantity calculations we covered previously are probably fine for most companies with mild seasonality and even some with moderate seasonality. But, if you have significant seasonality or suspect that your seasonality, combined with the size of your inventory is substantial enough to justify accounting for it in your order quantities, you should consider doing so.

Let's start with some cheats. If you have a rather simple but dramatic seasonal pattern, such as having extremely high demand for a period of time (your busy season), and then having dramatically lower demand the remainder of the year, you can do something as simple as calculating two order quantities—one based on the demand of your busy season and another for the rest of the year. You can do this by taking the average demand during your busy season and then calculating what your annual demand would be if you had that same demand all year long. You would then use this annual demand in your order quantity calculation to calculate the order quantity you use during your busy season. Then do the same for your slow season. You may need to put in an override to make sure that your order quantity during your busy season does not exceed your total demand during your busy season. This option is a bit simplistic, but may be adequate for some businesses.

Using period order quantity (POQ).

Another cheat is to calculate your EOQ based on your annual demand, and then convert your order quantity into a period order quantity (POQ). Period order quantity simply states your order quantity in time rather than units. Therefore, what you would do is calculate your EOQ, then calculate your average daily demand (annual demand divided by 365 for most purchasing systems), and divide your EOQ by your average daily demand to determine your period order quantity in days. For example, if your annual demand is 300 and your EOQ is 86, then your POQ would be 105 days. By stating our order quantities in days, we will then use our near-term forecast to determine our actual order quantity when an item comes up for reorder. This will naturally give you larger order quantities during your periods of higher demand, and vice versa. And as luck would have it, many (if not most) inventory systems come with period order quantity functionality already installed.

B8	▾	fx	=B7/(B5/B6)

	A	B
1	**Basic EOQ & POQ**	
2	Order Cost	$9.00
3	Carrying Cost	13%
4	Unit Cost	$175.00
5	Annual Demand	250
6	Ordering Days in Year	365
7	**EOQ**	**14**
8	**POQ (in days)**	**21**

Figure 7I. Here we took our basic EOQ calculation and added a value for the ordering days in the year in Cell B6. To convert our EOQ to POQ (stated in days), in Cell B8 we enter =B7/(B5/B6)

Example of quantities resulting from POQ

Week#	1	2	3	4	5	6	7	8	9	10	11	12	13	14	15
Forecast	3	3	3	3	5	8	12	15	20	15	10	5	3	3	3
Order quantity based on POQ of 21 days	9			16			47			30			9		

Figure 7J. Here we took our POQ of 21 days from the previous example and showed what our order quantities might look like over a 15-week period given a forecast with some significant seasonality and/or trend.

As clever as this sounds, this solution is far from perfect. Though you can logically expect your order quantities should be higher during periods of higher demand, this conversion from an order quantity based on annual demand, to a period order quantity, and then back to an order quantity based on the near-term forecast, does not necessarily accurately reflect the correct proportional change you would see if you used a more sophisticated calculation. I'm not saying that a straight conversion from EOQ to POQ to compensate for mild to moderate seasonality does not work. In fact, I think many companies will find this is adequate for their needs. But, for those needing a higher level of accuracy, let's explore some more options.

As with any cheat, you can tweak this calculation to provide better results for your specific demand patterns and your order quantity calculation profile (your order costs and carrying costs). In my experience, this POQ cheat tends to change the order quantity a little more than it should. In other words, during busy times, even though you should be ordering more, it tends to order a bit too much more, and during slow times it tends to order a bit too little. So one tweak could be to compare the output of the POQ calculation (after it has been converted back to units using your forecast) to your original EOQ, and take an average or weighted average of the two values. Another option would be to calculate a ratio of the output of the POQ calculation (after it has been converted back to units using your forecast) to your original EOQ, then use our square-root trick (calculate the square root of the ratio) and multiply that by your original EOQ to get your adjusted order quantity. Obviously there are numerous other little adjustments you could include here to get the output to more accurately reflect the cost impact of seasonality. Let me again mention that we are doing some serious cheating here, but these cheats can prove to be effective in many environments.

Using optimization.

But what about more sophisticated solutions? We had previously used an optimization algorithm (the Solver add-in) to determine the order quantity that resulted in the lowest annual cost. But, in the case of seasonal demand and trends, we don't want to calculate a single order quantity that results in the lowest annual cost. Instead, we want to calculate one or more potentially different order quantities based on the demand forecasted to occur during specific periods. Can we use an optimization algorithm to do this? Maybe. Can we use the free Solver add-in that came with Excel to do this? Well, let's see.

When you use an optimization plug-in in a spreadsheet, you need to start with a model that describes the relationships of the variables. Though this sounds complicated—and can get complicated in practice—the basic idea here is rather simple. You just need to start by putting all inputs onto your spreadsheet, and then start building the mathematical relationships between your inputs and your output(s). We did this earlier in this chapter when we built a simple total cost model, and then used Solver to determine the best order quantity to use to get the lowest annual cost. Now we'll build a little more complex model to demonstrate how we can model the impact on total cost when we use different order quantities in specific time periods in an operation where demand changes from period to period (seasonality or trend).

	A	B	C	D	E	F	G	H	I	J	K	L	M
1	Period-based order quantity cost model												
2	Order Cost	$30.00											
3	Carrying Cost %	20%											
4	Unit Cost	$15.00											
5	Beginning Inventory	0											
6													
7	Month	1	2	3	4	5	6	7	8	9	10	11	12
8	Demand	50	50	75	75	100	75	50	50	75	100	150	150
9	Beginning Inventory												
10	Order												
11	Ending Inventory												
12	Average Inventory												
13	Carrying Cost $												
14													
15	Simple EOQ												
16	Total Orders												
17	Annual Order Cost												
18	Annual Carrying Cost												
19	Total Annual Cost												

Figure 7K. Start by creating a spreadsheet as shown here.

Start by creating a spreadsheet and filling in the cells as shown in Figure 7K, then move on to the following instructions.

In Cell B9 enter =B5

In Cell C9 enter =B11

    Copy Cell C9 and paste it into cells D9 through M9

Enter 0 in cells B10 through M10

In Cell B11 enter =B9+B10-B8

    Copy Cell B11 and paste it into cells C11 though M11

In Cell B12 enter =B9+B10-(0.5*B8)

    Copy cell B12 and paste it into cells C12 through M12

In Cell B13 enter =($B3/12)*B12*$B4

    Copy Cell B13 and paste it into cells C13 through M13

In Cell B15 enter =SQRT((2*B2*(SUM(B8:M8))/(B3*B4)))

In Cell B16 enter =COUNTIF(B10:M10,">0")

In Cell B17 enter =B16*B2

In Cell B18 enter =SUM(B13:M13)

In Cell B19 enter =SUM(B17:B18)

That completes our model. This is essentially the same way we would set up a model to use manually. For example, you could now manually start putting in order quantities in cells B10 through M10 and see how they affect the total cost in cell B19. You don't need an order quantity in each period (you can leave zero in some), but you do need to monitor the "Ending Inventory" quantities (cells B11 through M11) to make sure your ending inventory for each period is not a negative number (that would mean you could not meet your demand for that period). For now, let's start by using our simple EOQ quantity of 141 to create our order quantities based on demand (to eliminate the negative ending inventory balances). Note that for the last two periods we will need to bump up our quantity just a little to meet demand. Your spreadsheet should now look like Figure 7L.

Here is a quick explanation of some of the other formulas I used here. I calculated average inventory as the beginning inventory plus the order quantity, minus one-half of the demand (our forecast). This assumes the order quantity arrives right at the beginning of the period and our demand is stable during the period. To calculate carrying cost per period, I divided our annual carrying cost percentage by 12 (the number of months in a year), and then multiplied that by our average inventory for each period, and by the unit cost. The "Simple EOQ" calculation is purely informational. It shows what our order quantity would be if we only considered annual demand as we did in previous calculations. The total orders calculation simply counts the number of periods that show an order quantity greater than zero. The annual order cost calculation then multiplies the number of orders by the cost per order. The annual carrying cost is just the sum of all period carrying costs.

	A	B	C	D	E	F	G	H	I	J	K	L	M
1	**Period-based order quantity cost model**												
2	Order Cost	$30.00											
3	Carrying Cost %	20%											
4	Unit Cost	$15.00											
5	Beginning Inventory	0											
6													
7	Month	1	2	3	4	5	6	7	8	9	10	11	12
8	Demand	50	50	75	75	100	75	50	50	75	100	150	150
9	Beginning Inventory	0	91	41	107	32	73	139	89	39	105	5	0
10	**Order**	141	0	141	0	141	141	0	0	141	0	145	150
11	Ending Inventory	91	41	107	32	73	139	89	39	105	5	0	0
12	Average Inventory	116	66	144.5	69.5	123	176.5	114	64	142.5	55	75	75
13	Carrying Cost $	$29.00	$16.50	$36.13	$17.38	$30.75	$44.13	$28.50	$16.00	$35.63	$13.75	$18.75	$18.75
14													
15	Simple EOQ	141											
16	Total Orders	7											
17	Annual Order Cost	$210.00											
18	Annual Carrying Cost	$305.25											
19	Total Annual Cost	$515.25											

Figure 7L. Here we have a working model that we can use to experiment with different order quantities in different periods to see how they affect our total annual cost.

Now let's try using the free Solver add-in to optimize our order quantities. First, make sure you reset cells B10 through M10 back to zero. Then do the following:

Select cell B19

in Excel 2003: Click Tools>Solver, or in Excel 2007: Click Data>Solver

The Solver Parameter window will open.

In "Set Target Cell", enter $B$19 if it is not already populated.

In "Equal To", click the Min selection.

In "By Changing Cells", enter $B$10:$M$10 (or you can select cells B10 through M10 and it will automatically populate the field).

In "Subject to Constraints", click "Add"

In "Cell Reference" enter $B$10:$M$10 (or you can select cells B10 through M10 and it will automatically populate the field).

Select >=

In "Constraint" enter 0

Click "Add"

In "Cell Reference" enter $B$11:$M$11 (or you can select cells B11 through M11 and it will automatically populate the field).

Select >=

In "Constraint" enter 0

Click OK

The "Solver Parameter" window should now look like Figure 7M.

Click "Solve"

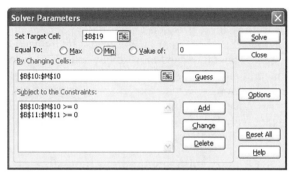

Figure 7M. The Solver Parameters window should look like this before you click solve.

Solver should now populate your order quantities.

If you look at the order quantities, you should see that solver populated them with quantities equal to the demand for each period (though you may get different results). This resulted in a total annual cost of $485.00. Though having the order quantity for each period equal to the demand is possible, it looks a little suspicious here, so let's look at the result of our simple EOQ calculation. Our simple EOQ of 141 represents the EOQ if the annual demand was spread equally across all 12 months. Logically we should expect that the order quantities that resulted from the optimization should roughly average approximately 141 (some higher, some lower), but it is obvious that they do not. This is a pretty clear clue that something may be wrong. So let's try changing a couple of order quantities and see if we can do better. Since our EOQ was 141 and our seasonality was not enormous, it seems unlikely that we would end up with an order quantity of 50 for the first month, so let's put 100 in month 1, and 0 in month 2. Now we still have enough inventory to meet demand, but our total annual cost has gone down to $467.50. Obviously, something went wrong with our optimization using the free version of the Solver add-in. There is a very important lesson to be learned here. Not just that we got bad results, but also, that the optimization program produced the bad results without giving us an error.

The problem here is not that the free Solver add-in doesn't work, or that our model was not set up correctly. The problem is that the optimization algorithm(s) used by the free Solver add-in are not appropriate for our optimization model (I covered this briefly in Chapter 2). What we need to do now is try another optimization algorithm, or consider changing our model to fit the current optimization algorithm. We'll try the former. Frontline Systems Inc. (the makers of the Solver add-in) sells a premium version of Solver, and there is also a product called Evolver sold by Palisade Corporation that is also an Excel add-in for optimization. As of the writing of this book, I believe both companies offer trial versions of their products.

I'm not going into detailed instructions on how to use these products because I'm not proficient enough in their use to feel comfortable instructing others on them. The truth is, these products are far more complex than the free add-in, and if you plan to use them for your business, you really need to invest some time in learning more about them and more about optimization in general. In fact, if you want to incorporate their use in your business, you probably need to get some outside help from someone with expertise in optimization and the product you intend to use. What I will do here is give a quick description of my limited experience playing with these products, and some tips that may help you should you choose to experiment with them.

My experience with advanced optimization programs.

The good news is, the basic interface of these advanced products is very similar to that of the add-in we just used. You start by setting up the cell you want to optimize, the cells that can be changed, and any constraints, just as you would in the free add-in. The bad news is, there are now a whole bunch of additional parameters that can/should be set up on these advanced products. And, for those unfamiliar with optimization, the additional parameters are not exactly intuitive.

My initial plan was to go straight to the genetic/evolutionary algorithms because—based on my limited understanding of optimization—I figured they could solve just about any model I could build in Excel (including models using conditional statements). And in theory, I think I'm right on this point, but in practice, I quickly ran into some practical limitations. Well, actually, one big practical limitation. That is, when I tried solving the problem using either the genetic algorithm in Palisade's Evolver or the evolutionary algorithm in Frontline System's Premium Solver, it took forever to get a solution. Wait a minute, that's not exactly true because I never actually let either program finish. After several hours running my CPU at 100%, I opted to stop the programs. And this was after I had added constraints, including setting the order quantities to be integer values and setting an upper limit to the order quantities. I did this in an effort to reduce the number of possible solutions, assuming (rightly or wrongly) that this would allow the program to solve the problem quicker.

I should note that I also had to change other parameters just to get the programs to run. There are various limits built into these programs that automatically stop them after a certain amount of time, certain number of iterations, or a variety of other parameters. The default values may result in stopping the program long before it finds an optimal solution, so you need to go through and turn some of these things up. Again, I'm getting out of my comfort zone here, so you'll need to do some of your own experimenting to find which ones you need to adjust.

OK, so I'm a bit discouraged at this point. I still believe these programs will solve the problem eventually, but having to wait hours or days to get a solution for an order quantity for a single item is not even close to being practical for my intended purpose, but I wasn't ready to throw in the towel. In reading through the documentation on the Premium Solver product, I ran into a cool feature (that's a technical term) that can potentially transform models containing some conditional statements (IF statements), into a model that can be solved using more conventional (not the evolutionary) algorithms.

So I gave it a shot. If you have the Premium Solver product, go to the solver parameters window, and then click [Model] to bring up the Solver Model Window. At the bottom of this window, check the Transform: Non-Smooth Model box, then click [Check Model]. Our model (shown in the upper left of window) now shows as NSP, which stands for Non Smooth Problem—which basically means we still can't use a conventional algorithm to solve it. But we're not done yet. In the model I built, I used the conditional COUNTIF function to determine the total numbers of orders. Well, apparently the cool feature I found in Solver can't transform my COUNTIF function, but it claims it can work with simple IF functions.

Well, if I can change my model to use IF instead of COUNTIF, this still may work. So, I inserted a row titled Order Cost $ (into row 14), and in cell B14 entered =IF(B10>0,$B$2,0). I then copied B14 and pasted it into cells C14 through M14. I then deleted the Total Orders calculation and replaced the annual order cost calculation with =SUM(B14:M14). What I did here was calculated a separate order cost for each period using my IF statement, and then just summed them for the annual order cost, thereby allowing me to get rid of my COUNTIF function.

Now, if I go back and use the transform non-smooth model feature, when I click [Check Model], it shows that my model is now "LP Convex". Sweet! I can now go back to the Solver Parameters window and change the optimization method from "Standard Evolutionary" to "Standard GRG Nonlinear" and try to solve my problem again. Well, it still takes a little while, but within about 20 minutes I have a solution that looks pretty good to me.

So what happened? Well, apparently there are alternate means of achieving the same results of an IF statement without using the IF statement, and some of these techniques are friendlier to optimization programs. Experts in optimization are familiar with these techniques, and Frontline Solutions built some of this into their program so we lazy non-experts can continue to use our IF statements. This allows us to use a more conventional—and faster—method to solve our problem.

While I'm a bit disappointed in the impracticality of using an evolutionary algorithm, I'm happy to find out that I don't need to use it for this particular problem. This isn't to say that I'm thrilled with it still taking 20 minutes to solve my problem using a more conventional algorithm, but at least that brings me closer to the realm of practicality.

Actually, the solution it gave matches exactly a solution I came up with manually using my simple EOQ as a reference and then just manually adjusting the periods to reflect my educated guess to what I felt would likely be an optimized order quantity given the demand for those periods. I don't mean to show off, but I manually solved this one in about a minute; but then again, I knew some stuff the optimization program didn't know. For example, I knew what the simple EOQ was, and I could then estimate a smaller range for each period based on the simple EOQ. I also knew that the order quantity would either be zero or would exactly match the sum of the demand for one or more consecutive periods. These two little tidbits of information made it much easier to figure out the likely optimized order quantities.

Which brings me to my next point. You could potentially build your own optimization model using this additional information, or possibly (I'm guessing here) find a way to input this into one of these packaged products to more quickly find a solution. In addition, I suspect an expert in optimization would be able to get a lot better performance out of this than I did. Plus, there are always faster computers.

On the down side, you may have to build a more complex model for your specific application. This model only has twelve periods (variables), but you may need more. Each additional variable will add to the processing time required to find an optimal solution. In addition, the optimal solution provided here might not really be the optimal solution. This is partially because the optimization algorithm doesn't necessarily find the best solution (although I think it does in this situation), but also because our model itself is a compromise. The optimal order quantities provided by our model will always be the exact sum of the demand of one or more consecutive periods. That's just the inherent result of building a model like this using forecast periods. This means that we would very likely get different results if our model used weeks instead of months, or days instead of weeks.

Where does this leave us? My feeling is, in most operations, I can get close-enough-to-optimal results using variations of EOQ along with a little cheat here and there. Therefore, I don't see a significant enough benefit to justify the expense, complexity, and potential practical limitations of implementing this level of optimization for this specific purpose. However, I think it's very practical to use this type of optimization on your desktop to help validate or invalidate your lot-sizing calculations. In addition, when I compare the capabilities of computers and software today (2008) to that of just ten or fifteen years ago, it's pretty easy to imagine a point in the very near future when these programs become practical for a much broader range of applications. So now is probably not a bad time to at least start playing around with them a bit.

I also wanted to mention that these optimization programs are not limited to spreadsheets. The companies that sell these Excel add-ins also provide developer kits that allow you to use the optimization algorithms with programs outside of Excel. In other words, if you like the results you get in Excel using these algorithms, you can add this same functionality to your inventory system.

And I wish to add just one final warning on the potential dangers of these programs. As we saw with the earlier example where we tried to use the free solver product to optimize our model, these programs will spit out a solution even if it is not the best solution. Let me rephrase that, these programs will calculate the best solution based upon the capabilities of the specific algorithm used; but, the best solution provided by the algorithm is not necessarily the optimal solution you were looking for. Even using the correct algorithm for your specific problem can provide some very bad results if you have one or more parameters set incorrectly—as you will likely experience when you first start playing with them. So be careful out there.

More lot-sizing stuff.

Lot-for-lot lot sizing?

You may run into this term if you are setting up an MRP (discussed later) or similar ordering system. Lot-for-lot lot sizing is a very basic method that just uses demand during the specified planning time period (time bucket) as the lot size. In most cases the planning periods would be your forecast periods, therefore your lot would be equal to the net demand in the forecast period in which the order is planned on being received. In other words, lot-for-lot lot sizing would result in one order for each forecast period, and the order quantity in a forecast period would match the net demand for that forecast period.

To describe lot-for-lot lot sizing as a technique would be extremely generous. It's essentially an order quantity based on the demand that is expected to occur in a fixed period of time. If you recall, I already provided my thoughts on this in the "simpleton" section earlier.

You may also run into a variation in which orders for components are created as a direct result of individual orders of higher-level items. In other words, each order for a higher-level item would trigger individual orders of all components for the exact requirement of the order for the higher-level item.

Fair-share distribution.

This is a lot sizing method (sort of) sometimes used in a multi-location distribution network. I'll cover this in more detail in the DRP chapter.

Overrides.

It's not uncommon to incorporate some overrides into your order quantity calculation. For example, with perishable items or items highly prone to obsolescence, you may want to incorporate a fixed maximum order quantity (probably stated as a period of time, similar to period order quantity). If you've already incorporated these risks in your carrying costs, you may need to adjust that (down) to compensate for the fact that you also are using a max order quantity for these items.

Case quantities.

Failing to consider case quantities in ordering decisions is a minor pet peeve of mine. There are numerous benefits to ordering in case quantities, and though none of them jump out as being dramatic improvements that provide easily measureable results, they are still very real improvements that can ultimately add to the bottom line of your business.

What are these benefits?

- Reduces picking time and picking errors. Sure, this is your supplier's responsibility, but why not be a good customer and make things easier on your supplier. Plus, those picking errors will end up on your dock, and if you don't catch them, they end up being your inventory problem. Even if you do catch them, it will cost you money to resolve them.

- Better protection during transportation. Though this isn't an absolute, in many instances the product is better protected in full-case form than it is in partial-case form.

- Easier to check-in and process through receiving and putaway. This depends a little on the nature of the product and your processes, but having spent a fair amount of time running warehouses, I can say with confidence there are some very real opportunities for savings here.

- Makes cycle counting and physical inventories easier and more accurate. It's reasonable to expect that you can accept the case quantity as being accurate for sealed full cases, therefore you generally don't need to open them and count the individual contents during a cycle count or physical inventories. On the other hand, partial cases generally do need to be opened and counted. In addition, if you have locations that are full of combinations of full cases and partial cases, it either requires a lot of labor to verify (sort out) the partials, or you risk counting errors if your counters don't realize there are partial cases mixed in with the full cases.

So what's the downside? There really isn't a significant downside here. I'm not suggesting that you force your system to always order in case quantities, but rather that, if the case quantity (or a multiple of the case quantity) is close to your calculated "optimal" order quantity, you go with the case quantity. As I said before, the output of our order quantity calculations identifies a "sweet spot", so you in effect have a range of quantities near this sweet spot that you can order without significantly changing your total annual cost. For example, if my calculated order quantity is 260 units, and the product I'm ordering comes in cases of 50 units, I would feel pretty comfortable adjusting my order quantity to 250 units.

I first recommend you do a quick review of your inventory just to get some idea of where case quantities may apply. You will likely find this only affects certain product groups.

Next, you need to figure out how to implement this. Many (not all) inventory systems come with the ability to use "multiples" when recommending purchase quantities. What this normally means is that you would set up the multiple (case) quantity for the item and then set a parameter that tells the system to use the case quantity when creating recommended order quantities.

The problem with this type of setup is it is essentially either on or off. If you tell it to use case quantities, it will use case quantities regardless of how close your economic order quantity is to the case quantity. In other words, if you had an item with an EOQ of 5 units, and it came in cases of 500 units, it may bump the order quantity up to 500 units if you set the item to use case quantities. Obviously, this is not what you want to happen.

You could manually review each item, and only set the case quantity switch for those that meet your criteria. This may be a workable solution in some business-es, but is potentially problematic since the economic order quantity will change periodically, and if you don't continue to monitor these changes and how they affect your original decision to set (or not set) the case quantity switch for the item, you could eventually end up with problems. A better solution would be to quantify your decision-making process related to case quantities, and then have a little program written that can turn the case quantity switch on or off as frequently as you recalculate your economic order quantities.

To complicate things further.

Yeah, I just hate to let you go thinking you have a handle on this lot-sizing thing. As with just about everything else I'm covering in this book, the closer you look, the more issues you find. Let's briefly cover a few of them.

Payment terms? The calculations in this chapter assume that you pay for inventory as soon as it is received. The reality is almost no one pays for inventory as soon as it is received. In most cases, you will have a period of time after being invoiced to pay for the goods. In other cases—such as some international orders—you may even have to pay in advance of shipment. Therefore, once again, we are working with a flawed calculation. I'll be honest with you, I've convinced myself—rightfully so or not—that for most businesses it is just not worth the effort to try to tackle this one. While on the surface it sounds pretty straightforward, whenever I've attempted to do this I've found it to be far more complicated than it seems, and the results I received were just not all that different from the results without considering payment terms. Keep in mind that I never quite got to a calculation I was happy with, so I may change my opinion on this one some day.

Safety stock? Our calculations so far have calculated carrying cost based on average inventory levels that did not include safety stock. This would be perfectly fine for our order quantity calculations if the resulting order quantities did not have any affect on our safety stock levels. But, if you recall from the safety stock chapter, we did take order quantities into account in our safety stock calculation. So it goes something like this: if my order quantity changes, then my safety stock changes, but then if my safety stock changes, my order quantity changes, but then if my order quantity changes, my safety stock changes again, but then if my ...

oh my god, my head's exploding! If you decided to go the route of using an optimization algorithm, you can theoretically build your model in a way that includes the safety stock calculation. But, once again, I think it's unlikely that this will change the output enough to make it worth the effort—or the headache.

Global optimization? There's no getting around the fact that the order quantity calculations discussed in this chapter are an example of local optimization. That is, they seek to optimize the order quantities at one point in the supply chain with no regard for how that affects the rest of the supply chain. The reality is, when you take practicality into consideration, that's about all many businesses can expect to accomplish; and to be honest, it's almost certainly a big improvement over what most of them are currently doing. However, if you want to explore true supply-chain optimization, you need to be prepared for some far more complex modeling (well beyond the scope of this book). Therefore, in addition to your order quantity affecting your own order costs and carrying cost, you need to determine how your order quantity affects the costs at your supplier and your supplier's supplier. For example, larger order quantities should result in lower outbound order costs for your supplier since he will be shipping less frequently to you, but larger order quantities may lead to greater demand variability at your supplier, therefore possibly resulting in more safety stock and subsequently more carrying costs.

And that's only part of supply chain optimization. In reality, you should be considering using supply chain visibility (information sharing between various levels in the supply chain) to help manage inventory levels (see DRP chapter for more information on the advantages of supply chain visibility). Costs related to transportation will also likely play a larger role when you start analyzing entire supply chains. How you utilize this shared data will have an impact on your model.

As I implied before, supply chain optimization is not only beyond the scope of this book, but also is beyond the practical limitations of many businesses. This doesn't mean you shouldn't consider some of these global factors, but it's unlikely you will effectively build a true global optimization model.

Additional factors related to your specific business. When you get down to the nitty gritty of implementing a lot sizing calculation for your business, you very likely will find some additional business conditions that you need to account for. The model I used for the optimization example was a rather simple model, and while it served the purpose of demonstrating the use of an optimization program, it will likely not be adequate to meet the needs of your business. For example, what if you knew about price changes from a supplier well in advance of the price change going into effect? This could be the result of regularly scheduled price increases, discounts, or even seasonal pricing. Would you want to incorporate this into your order quantity calculation? Possibly. And actually, if you are already building a model to use with an advanced optimization algorithm, it isn't all that hard. You would just build your model to reflect the cost at each time period. For another example, what if you wanted to incorporate quantity discounts and a period-based model? Once again, this is doable using an advanced optimization program. It just means that you need to build your model to reflect quantity discounts (you would combine the quantity discount calculation we discussed, with your period-based order quantity model). Not to imply that this is easy. These models can get very complex, so it's even more important that you think through your calculation and test extensively to make sure that not only is your model accurate, but also that your model is playing nice with the optimization program you use.

However, given that many of us will not be using an optimization algorithm for our calculation, we will need to find ways to tweak our calculations to try to account for these various additional issues that may arise.

Inventory reduction strategies.

I always cringe when I hear a company is embarking on an "inventory reduction initiative", not because I have a problem with a company wanting to run on less inventory, but because I suspect they are about to do something really stupid—like follow the advice of one of those order-half-as-much-twice-as-often geniuses. The problem here is that these initiatives tend to be far too simplistic. Upper management feels the company has too much inventory and therefore decides that an inventory reduction initiative is in order. Obviously, the best measure of success of this initiative would be the inventory levels themselves. So what happens? The inventory planners simply start slashing their order quantities (ordering less, more often).

Yeah, inventory reduction is just that easy. What's missed in all this is the fact that you now may be missing quantity discounts, paying more inbound freight costs, and increasing operational costs to manage the increased number of orders being placed. But hey, ignorance is bliss, right?

The smart way to reduce your inventory is to look at the factors that cause you to have inventory, and work on controlling those. For example, streamline your ordering process and your receiving and putaway processes to reduce your order costs. Reduce manufacturing setup times and setup scrap. Work with your suppliers to get quantity breaks or minimum purchases lowered. Consider resourcing to suppliers that offer lower quantity breaks or shorter lead times. Work on improving the accuracy of your forecasting and safety stock calculations. Monitor product life cycles to prevent being stuck with obsolete inventory. See what you can do about reducing demand variability. What I'm really saying here is that you should be focused on managing your inventory, not just reducing it. A big part of inventory management is essentially looking at ways to effectively operate the business with less.

In other words, it's OK to want to run your business on less inventory, but it's not OK to just arbitrarily order less because you want less inventory. What you should be doing, is making business decisions and process changes that result in it being economically advantageous to run your business with less inventory.

Now just to mess with you a little bit, you also have to realize that some business improvements can actually result in more inventory. For example, if you're able to negotiate a better interest rate on your business loan, or redesign your warehouse to improve space utilization and therefore reduce your storage costs, or relocate to a place that doesn't tax your inventory, it will now make sense to carry more inventory. I can see it now, an article in a trade magazine that states, "as part of their cost-reduction strategy, company Z increased their inventory by 20%". Yeah, like that's going to happen.

My closing argument.

I've been an advocate of EOQ for many years despite the industry trend of indifference or even disdain towards it. In fact, my first published work was an article on EOQ. Had it not been for my interest in EOQ—and that article—I may not have ever started writing books. Wow, I need to absorb that one for a minute . . . . . then again . . . had I not started writing books maybe I would have become a pro skateboarder . . . .or an astronaut . . . . or a stuntman . . . . or a superhero . . . . or a bikini inspector . . . yeah, that's the ticket.

As I was saying, I have shown a special interest in EOQ over the years, not because it's an amazing revolutionary inventory management technique—it's not—but instead, because it is a simple yet effective technique that tends to be overlooked by the inventory management community. I'm not saying the inventory management community isn't aware of EOQ. In fact, EOQ is "taught" in virtually every introductory inventory management course I've ever encountered. Unfortunately, far too few businesses actually implement EOQ, and of those that do, many make serious mistakes in the implementation.

When properly implemented, EOQ works. Yes, it has limitations, but you can easily adapt it to provide effective results in most environments. While optimization is an option, I don't think it is yet practical for many businesses. I do, however, encourage all of you to experiment with optimization because I feel it has a place in inventory management, and believe it will become more practical as computer processing power and software capabilities continue to advance.

And when you run into those boneheads that argue against economic-based lot sizing, don't let them con you into blindly accepting their theories. Instead, consider investing some time into analyzing exactly how they determine lot sizes —assuming they can communicate their "logic". I think you'll be surprised at just how illogical their methods are.

8

Ordering Systems

Ordering systems take the output data from the calculations we've covered up to this point and turn it into actions (orders). There are numerous order/reorder methods available with varying levels of sophistication, and we'll cover them in these next two chapters by starting with the most basic and moving to calculations that are more complex. The good thing about ordering systems is they are very mechanical in nature. So unlike some of the topics we've covered previously, there's not a lot of theory or gray areas here, it's just simple addition and subtraction (maybe a little multiplication and division).

But before we get into ordering systems, we need to cover a few more inputs in greater detail.

Knowing how much you have.

One of the key inputs into any ordering system is the current on-hand inventory level. Most (not all) of the ordering systems covered in this chapter are based on a perpetual inventory system. I introduced perpetual inventory systems briefly in Chapter 1, but I want to expand on this a bit here. Though the term perpetual inventory system sounds rather dramatic, it just comes down to a system that tracks changes to inventory levels as they occur. So when you process a receipt, it adds that quantity to your on-hand inventory, and when you process a shipment, it reduces your on-hand inventory. It's really just some very basic accounting.

I do need to note that a perpetual inventory system is not necessarily a "real-time" inventory system, meaning, there are sometimes delays between the physical addition or removal of inventory, and the updates to your inventory system. This is probably most notable in sales-order processing where many systems do not reduce the on-hand inventory until the invoice is processed (created). This is often done in a batch process sometime after the day's activities have been completed, therefore there could be several hours between an item being picked and shipped, and the on-hand balance being updated. Some manufacturing systems follow a similar delay in processing quantities associated with production orders.

And even if the system updates inventory levels right away, there are often delays between the physical activities that change inventory levels (order picking, shipping, receiving, putaway, manufacturing) and data entry tasks that tell the system these activities have occurred. For example, a production worker may just document his production on a form, then hand if off to someone else for data entry; or a warehouse worker may complete a number of tasks over a period of time, then enter them all in the system at once.

There's no doubt that there are some distinct advantages to having real-time data. And if you spend any time reading the trade magazines, you will undoubtedly see numerous articles and advertisements telling you that if you don't have real-time data, you cannot possibly compete with the world class, best-practices using, technology leveraging, paradigm changing, lean, agile, real-time centric, businesses of the new millennium. Well let me share a little secret with you—real-time data is overrated. Being a bit of a data freak, I personally have a great appreciation for real-time data. I mean, I've spent time sitting in front of a computer monitoring records being added to transactional database files, and used that as a way of monitoring what was going on in the plant. I'm not talking about watching some cute little graphical desktop "dashboard", I'm actually admitting to spending time watching the raw data in the database change. But hey, that's me. The reality is most business processes get very little benefit from absolute real-time data, and you may be surprised to find out that most key inventory management processes fall into this category. Most MRP and DRP generations (we'll discuss these later) along with other key inventory planning programs, are run (at most) once a day, usually at night. So whether you have a fancy RF real-time data-collection system running in your warehouse and manufacturing plant, or just have a paper-based system and make sure all transactions are completed before the night-run starts, makes absolutely no difference in the effectiveness of your planning process if you are using these night-run-based systems.

Obviously, the argument can be made that if you get away from these night-run-based systems, you could then take advantage of your real-time data and do some "re-planning" during the day. I do agree there is value in doing some re-planning during the day in many environments, but, you probably don't need absolute real-time data to do this either. The combination of allocation systems (discussed next) and a policy of having inventory transactions processed within a reasonable time frame (not real-time, but on a regular basis throughout the day), will likely get you most or all of the benefits of a real-time system. Once again, let me make it clear that I am not saying that real-time is bad, only that it may not be as necessary or as beneficial as you are led to believe.

Understanding allocations.

So let's move on to allocations. Allocations refer to actual demand created by sales orders or production orders against a specific item. The terminology and the actual processing that controls allocations will vary from one software system to another. A standard allocation is an aggregate quantity of demand against a specific item in a specific facility. I have heard standard allocations referred to as normal allocations, soft allocations, soft commitments, or regular allocations. Standard allocations do not specify that specific units will go to specific orders.

A firm allocation is an allocation against specific units within a facility, such as an allocation against a specific location, lot, or serial number. Firm allocations are also referred to as specific allocations, frozen allocations, hard allocations, hard commitments, holds, or reserved inventory. Standard allocations simply show that there is actual demand, while firm allocations reserve or hold the inventory for the specific order designated. Though, depending upon just how your system works, standard allocations may actually prevent some orders from becoming firm allocations, therefore, you could say that standard allocations also hold inventory (make it unavailable for other orders).

Allocations can also be thought of as outbound quantities since they are quantities that are associated with outbound orders (or internal manufacturing orders). One of the trickier areas related to allocations in inventory management concerns future orders. Many inventory systems have a user-defined designation for what makes up a future order. It usually comes down to the requested date for an order relative to today's date. Generally, orders designated as future orders are excluded from the allocation system. Let me explain why you would want to do this. Let's assume I currently have 50 units in stock and have a sales order on my system for 100 units scheduled to ship in 30 days. I also have an inbound quantity (a purchase order) for 200 units scheduled to arrive in 15 days. In many allocation systems, the sales order for 100 units would allocate against current inventory if the order is not designated as a future order. Therefore, if another customer placed an order today for 10 units, the system would likely automatically backorder it, even though you have 50 units in stock and should have more in stock in time to ship the order for 100 units. The need for a "future order" designation is the result of an allocation system that is not sophisticated enough to properly allocate inbound and outbound quantities based on date. Unfortunately, many allocation systems fall into this category.

Allocation systems must also account for inventory intended to be used in manufacturing orders. This is another area where it can get confusing when you have a combination of production orders and sales orders all vying for the same inventory.

In addition to outbound quantities, inventory systems also have inbound quantities. An inbound quantity would be an open quantity on a purchase order, manufacturing order, or transfer order. In other words, these are quantities associated with orders that are expected to be received into inventory at some point in the future.

And then you may even have something called an in-transit quantity. Quantity in transit is most likely used in a multi-plant environment, and represents a quantity that has been shipped from one facility and has not yet been received into another facility. We'll cover this more in the section on DRP.

Inventory quantities		
On hand		
	Quantity on hand	158
	Quantity on hold	10
Total quantity on hand	**168**	
Outbound quantities		
	Standard allocations	15
	Firm allocations	4
	Future orders	45
	Transfer orders (outbound)	20
Total outbound quantity	**84**	
Inbound quantities		
	Open purchase orders	50
	Open manufacturing orders	100
	Open transfer orders (inbound)	50
Total inbound quantity	**200**	
In-transit quantities		
Quantity in-transit	**25**	

Figure 8A. Here is an example of the quantities you may see in your inventory system. Keep in mind that a single item would generally not have quantities in every category (as in this example). Also note that calculations based on these quantities will vary based upon the intended use of the calculation. For example, the calculation that determines availability for your sales-order process may be different than the calculation that is used by your ordering system.

Unfortunately, there are many inventory planners out there who have no clue how their allocation system works. These systems can be a bit confusing and each one tends to have its own set of peculiarities related to how it allocates inventory. But, they are a key part of your inventory system and it is therefore very important you understand how yours works. So take the previous paragraphs as a general intro to allocations, but also make sure you read the documentation for your system and test the hell out of it to make sure you have a thorough understanding of exactly how your allocation system works.

Understanding lead time.

As stated in Chapter 1, lead time is the period of time that occurs between the time an order is placed and the time the goods or services are received. In your inventory system, lead time is almost certainly stated in days, and for purchased items, lead time is generally stated in calendar days. However, in manufacturing systems, lead time is frequently stated in work days (requires setup of a work-day calendar).

So before you do anything else with lead time in your system, you need to make sure you understand how your system handles lead time. Checking your system's documentation is a good place to start, but ultimately you should conduct some tests on your system to make sure it treats lead time the way you think it treats lead time. So which system is best? Well for manufactured items in a manufacturing operation, using work days is the way to go. But, when it comes to purchased items within a manufacturing system, or purchased items in general, there really is no perfect way to deal with lead times. Using work days assumes your work-day schedule is the same as your vendor's work-day schedule, but using calendar days can create imprecise planning calculations when weekends or holidays are involved.

In addition to understanding how your system interprets lead times, you need to verify how your system interprets your forecast. Remember, we are stating our lead time in days here, but we probably are not stating our forecast in days. In order to figure out when to place an order we must calculate the demand that is expected to occur during the lead-time period. Therefore, if you state your lead time in days and your forecast in weeks or months, you need to know how your system uses this to calculate your lead-time demand.

And for purchased items, you also need to verify how your supplier states his lead time. If your supplier says the lead time for an item is 10 days, does he mean 10 calendar days or 10 work days? And is transportation time included in this lead time (it probably is not)? You then need to compare all this to how your business operates to determine what exactly you should be entering as lead time into your system. Keep in mind that translating how your supplier calculates lead time to how your system uses lead time and forecasts, all within the context of how your business operates, is not always going to be clean. That's right, we have yet another flaw in our inventory system.

Safety lead time.

And while we're on the topic of lead time, I want to mention a neat little feature called safety lead time. In addition to safety stock, many inventory systems have the functionality to utilize safety lead time in their ordering systems. What safety lead time does (or should do), is add some time to your lead time as part of your ordering calculations. But it's not quite as simple as that. Though safety lead time is used in the ordering calculation to determine when you need to order something, it is excluded from the calculation that then determines the "requested date" for the order. This can be a real handy way of dealing with internal processing time for receipts and certain other issues. For example, if it generally takes 24 hours to get a receipt from the dock, through your receiving and incoming inspection process, and into stock and available for sale, you could consider entering a safety lead time of 1 day into your system to account for this.

How is this different from just adding a day to the lead time? Here's an example; if you have a lead time of 3 days and just changed it to 4 days to account for internal processing, your system would properly calculate the demand during the 4-day period and you would therefore order the inventory on time, but, your system would almost certainly calculate a requested date of 4 days from today and print that on the purchase order. This would lead your supplier to believe that you want the shipment in 4 days instead of 3. However, if you set your system lead time to 3 days and your safety lead time to 1 day, it would still order the inventory at the same time, but the purchase order requested date would be calculated as 3 days from today. Don't underestimate how useful this little feature can be.

While we're on the topic of requested dates, this is another area where you need to make sure there is no miscommunication between you and your suppliers. Generally, requested date on a purchase order is the date you expect the shipment to arrive at your dock, not the date your supplier is expected to ship the order. So your supplier should be (don't assume this) adjusting your requested date by the expected shipping time to determine the proper shipping date to enter on his sales order. The confusing thing here is that most sales-order systems use a date known as a requested date on the order, but most implementations of these systems treat the requested date as the requested ship date. Therefore, the requested date on the purchase order you provide to your supplier should not be the same as the requested date he enters on the sales order associated with the purchase order. Ideally, your ordering system would also allow you to enter a transit time (shipping time) and then use this to calculate a requested shipping date for your purchase orders in addition to the requested date (which you would call a requested arrival date). Unfortunately, most ordering systems don't have this functionality, and even if they did, you would still need to make sure your supplier understands how to use these dates.

In addition, you need to know if your supplier even looks at requested date. In many industries, the norm is that you place an order with a supplier and they ship it as quickly as they can. Most of our ordering methods follow this expectation (you place an order at the last moment possible in order to get it in stock in time to meet demand). But some businesses find it useful to plan a little further in advance and place purchase orders for future shipments. If you do this, you need to make sure your supplier knows you don't want the order shipped immediately. Their order system is probably fully capable of handling this, but you need to make sure that when they enter your order they pay attention to your requested date.

Ordering systems.

Now, let's get back to ordering systems. The following sections cover the most common methods used to determine when you need to place an order.

Periodic review.

Periodic review is the most basic of ordering systems. In its purest form, periodic review consists of having a person physically go to where the inventory is stored to see how much is there, then decide if more is needed, and if so, place an order for more. This is basically the same way most people handle their grocery shopping. The "periodic" part of this comes from the fact that this is most likely done on a fixed schedule (once a week, once a month, etc.). Periodic review is most likely used in very small businesses where you have suppliers that supply multiple products with short lead times on a regular delivery schedule. For example, let's say I run a restaurant and the "meat guy" delivers once a week (we'll say it's all frozen meat) on Thursday, and I need to get him an order each Monday for the Thursday delivery. So each Monday I need to look at what I have (pretty much go out and count it), and then figure out how much I will need until my next delivery opportunity (one week from Thursday, or roughly 10 days from today). So anything with less than a 10-day supply plus safety stock will need to be ordered.

Realistically, the inputs to a periodic review system are likely going to be far more simplistic than what we've been covering. The people doing the ordering will likely use a simple average demand number and a simple time-based safety stock number (like 2-day's supply), and then factor in any specials or seasonality that is expected in the next 10 days (they will probably do this in their head as they are doing the ordering). This isn't to say that you can't or shouldn't be using more advanced calculations for the inputs to periodic review, only that in the environments that periodic review is used, they probably aren't going to great lengths to manage their inventory.

The pure periodic review system assumes you do not systematically keep track of inventory levels (no perpetual inventory system). There is also a variation on periodic review we will cover later that works within a perpetual inventory system and takes a more sophisticated approach to these requirements.

Fixed reorder point.

Fixed reorder point (also called fixed order point) is the most basic method used within perpetual inventory systems for ordering inventory. As the name implies, it's a fixed point (quantity) that triggers the need for a new order being placed. Reorder point (fixed or otherwise) is calculated as the demand that is expected to occur during the lead time, plus safety stock. Since this is a "fixed" reorder point, it can't take into account demand variability related to seasonality or trend, other than to just set it for the period of time where demand would be greatest or to adjust it periodically. Because of this, fixed reorder point is not a very effective means of triggering orders in a business that is subject to even low to moderate levels of seasonality or trend.

Surprisingly, fixed reorder point may very well be the most common ordering system in use today by businesses that claim to have "inventory systems". And while fixed reorder point may be appropriate for some businesses (or some product groups within a business), many businesses using fixed reorder point would be far better off stepping up to a more sophisticated ordering system. Despite the term "fixed", fixed reorder point does need to be occasionally recalculated. The more frequently you recalculate it, the more it can compensate for trend and maybe some level of seasonality.

Even the most basic of inventory systems will have the ability to utilize a fixed reorder point. In its most basic form, all it consists of is a place to enter and store the reorder point for each item, and a simple report that shows any items that are at or below reorder point. As always, make sure you test your system to see how it determines the items to print on the reorder report. First, you want to determine whether it triggers reorder when an item is at reorder point, or when it is below reorder point. The difference here may not seem significant, but it can be, especially with slower movers. The term "reorder point" would imply that reorder would be triggered when an item reaches this point (at reorder point), however many reorder systems don't trigger reorder until an item's inventory falls below reorder point. There are arguments that can be made for either method, and for most medium to fast moving items it probably doesn't make much of a difference since you rarely would have in item at exactly reorder point (they will usually go from a level above reorder point to a level somewhere below reorder point). But, as I mentioned previously, it can make a difference with slow movers. For example, if you have an item with a reorder point set to one, did you intend that you would reorder when you have one in stock (at reorder point), or when you are out of stock (below reorder point)?

In addition, you need to determine whether your reorder report is taking inbound quantities and allocations into account. As a bare minimum, the reorder calculation should add any inbound quantities to the current on-hand quantity, and then compare that to the reorder point. Optionally, they may provide the ability to deduct current allocations, but you may or may not want this to happen depending upon how you process orders.

As already mentioned, reorder point (fixed or otherwise) is calculated as lead-time demand plus safety stock. Therefore, if your lead time is 5 days and your expected demand is 10 units per day, and your safety stock is 15 units, your reorder point would be 65 units. This basic reorder point calculation is actually part of almost all reordering methods. In the case of a fixed reorder point, it simply means that once the reorder point is calculated, it remains the same for an extended period of time (months, years, forever). In some systems, fixed reorder point is calculated manually and entered manually into the system, in others, there may be some automation to this process. If your system automatically calculates a reorder point for you, you need to figure out how it does this.

If your system allows you to enter a safety stock quantity separately, you need to test to determine how it uses this quantity relative to your reorder point. Generally, a fixed reorder point already includes the safety stock, so you don't want your system to add it in again to determine your ordering needs.

Fixed reorder point systems tend to also incorporate fixed replenishment quantities (order quantities) in them. Therefore, whenever your inventory drops to a point at or below the fixed reorder point, you would order a quantity equal to your fixed replenishment quantity. Hopefully, this fixed replenishment quantity is the output of one of the cost-based order quantity calculations we covered in the previous chapter.

Given demand patterns with little to no seasonality or trend, a fixed-reorder-point/fixed-replenishment-quantity system should perform about as well as some of the more sophisticated systems we will cover here. Unfortunately, most businesses will have more complex demand patterns.

Min-Max.

A min-max system is just a slight variation on a fixed-reorder-point/fixed-replenishment-quantity system. The "min" part of min-max is essentially your fixed reorder point. The "max" part represents a quantity you want to order "up to". In other words, when inventory drops at or below your min, you order enough to bring you to your max. So assuming that I don't already have some inventory on order, if my min is set at 10 units, and my max is set at 50 units, and my current on-hand inventory is 8 units, I would place an order for 42 units because I am below my min, and 42 units in addition to the 8 units I currently have in stock would bring me to my max of 50 units.

To calculate a min-max, your min would be calculated the same way you would calculate your reorder point. When it comes to calculating your max, you need to realize that the max quantity controls the quantity you will order, therefore, hopefully you will use the output of a cost-based order quantity calculation as an input to your max calculation. Since the quantity you will order will be calculated by subtracting your current on-hand from your max level, and since the point at which you do this will be when your current on-hand is at or below your min (reorder point), it would make sense to set your max to the equivalent of your min (your reorder point) plus the output of your cost-based order quantity calculation.

So what we essentially did here is go through some extra work to try to get a min-max system to work like a fixed-reorder-point/fixed-replenishment-quantity system. So why not just use a fixed-reorder-point/fixed-replenishment-quantity system? Exactly.

The truth is, companies that have historically used min-max probably did not use a cost-based order quantity calculation. Instead, they used a max because it represented the physical amount of shelf space they had for that item, or because it represented some arbitrary quantity they felt was the most they wanted to have, or it represented a quantity that was equal to the demand for a fixed period of time. If we go back to the "meat guy" example from the section on periodic review (earlier in this chapter), where we had a fixed delivery schedule (once a week) and placed an order each Monday for a Thursday delivery, I may set my max to represent a 10-day supply plus safety stock (the quantity I would need to get me to my next delivery). This way, I would be planning on ordering this item each week, and planning on ordering just enough to get me through until my next opportunity for ordering. Oddly enough, this scenario would result in a min-max where the min and max are the same quantity.

I think the meat example is a good example of where min-max is applicable. You've got a group of short-lead-time items with a regular delivery schedule, where it doesn't make a lot of sense to order more than the quantity to get you through to the next delivery (order costs in a scenario like this are generally very low, so a small lot size makes sense).

Kanban, Two-bin, and that whole Push-Pull thing.

If you've worked in manufacturing, and especially if you've been exposed to "Lean Manufacturing", "Just-In-Time", or the "Toyota Production System", you have probably encountered the term Kanban. Kanban is a Japanese term that means signal or card or signal card or sign or signboard or . . . hell, I don't know, it's not like I speak Japanese.

But before we get to Kanban, I want to briefly cover an ancient, but still used, reordering method known as the two-bin system. And the really nice thing about the two-bin system, is that the name pretty much says it all. Each item has two bins (or other type of container), and when one bin is emptied, it is sent somewhere to be refilled. This would most commonly be used for internal replenishment where the empty bin would be sent either to a production area where the needed item is manufactured, or to a reserve storage area where bulk quantities of the item are stored. In reality, we should call this a multi-bin system since you can just as easily use more than two bins if you want.

And now back to Kanban. The reason I briefly covered the two-bin (multi-bin) system first, is that Kanban is essentially the same thing as a multi-bin system. The only difference is that sometimes, instead of sending an empty bin somewhere for replenishment, Kanban systems may just use a card or other "signaling" device such as a light, colored plastic marker, golf ball, paper airplane, snowball, whatever. OK, I was kidding about the paper airplane and snowballs, but there have been a wide assortment of "signals" used in Kanban systems. Regardless of the signaling device used, Kanban still comes down to an empty bin (or other type of container) triggering the event. For example, when using "Kanban cards" with totes, each tote containing inventory would have a Kanban card attached to it. When a tote is emptied, the card is removed from the tote and sent back to the operation that creates the item that was in the tote. That operation will then produce the item, place it in another tote, put the card on that tote, and forward it back to the location where the item is used.

Whether you are returning an empty bin, tote, or other container as the signal to replenish, or just sending a card or using some other signaling device, is really just a matter of what is physically most effective in a given environment (a matter of the physical handling and physical flow characteristics of the specific environment), and doesn't change the basic mechanics of Kanban. So in order to avoid confusion, I'm just going to use a multiple bin system to further describe the process. We can refer to each bin in the multiple bin system as a Kanban.

So the big questions people have when they decide to start using Kanban are "how do I determine how many Kanbans to use for an item?" and "how do I determine what quantity to associate with each Kanban?". Now I've encountered a few "Kanban calculations" and have to say that I was less than impressed. So rather than me nitpicking these, why don't we just take a look at what Kanban is really doing?

Whenever I empty a Kanban, I send it somewhere and they then will send it back to me with the Kanban quantity. So essentially, this "Kanban quantity" is our order quantity or lot size. Well heck, we just went through a whole chapter on order quantities so I guess we've got that part covered.

Now let's look at the number of Kanbans we need. Whenever I empty a Kanban, I send it back for replenishment; so logic would say this is my reorder point. In other words, the quantity that triggers a reorder in a Kanban system is the total quantity in all Kanbans minus the quantity of one Kanban. As I had previously mentioned, the reorder point calculation is basically the same for just about every reordering method. It always comes down to the expected demand during the lead time plus safety stock. And we already know how to calculate these, don't we?

Since Kanbans are based on fixed quantities (the same quantity repeats for every Kanban for the item), what we really have here is a fixed reorder point system with a fixed replenishment quantity. So here's how you can have some fun with the Lean folks. Next time you encounter a Lean advocate pushing Kanban, just mention to him that your company uses a fixed reorder point with fixed replenishment quantity system. Watch as he rolls his eyes in acknowledgement of your existence in the dark ages of inventory management; then give him just a little time to dig the hole before you explain that "that's pretty much what Kanban is anyway". Yes, grasshopper, then you will have proven whose inventory-fu is better.

Back to the calculation. Since Kanban requires that each Kanban is set up for the same quantity, it does change the order-point calculation a little because the order point must end up being an exact multiple of the order quantity. In addition, the mechanics of a multi-bin system require that your order point is greater than or equal to your order quantity (it would be equal to in a two-bin system, and greater than in anything more than two bins). Once again, these are not added features of Kanban as much as they are added constraints of using a multi-bin system where each bin (Kanban) must carry the same quantity.

So if Kanban is really just fixed reorder point with fixed order quantity, plus some additional constraints that restrict your flexibility in setting order points and order quantities, why are the Lean folks so enthralled by it? Well let me start with their explanation, and then I'll provide my own opinion.

The Push/Pull argument.

Lean proponents like to make a big issue of using pull systems in place of push systems for inventory and production management. So what is the difference? In its purist form, a pull system is one that creates products to actual known demand. In other words, a pure pull system would be a make-to-order system where something is only manufactured after an actual customer order is placed. In addition, for it to be pure pull, you would not procure or manufacture any components or subassemblies until you had actual demand for the finished item. On the other hand, the concept of "push" implies that you are pushing inventory into the system with the hopes that someone is going to buy it. At this level, it's pretty easy to differentiate the two strategies, and obviously if you are in an industry where make-to-order is feasible, there are some significant advantages when it comes to inventory management.

However, many businesses cannot operate a pure pull system; and within the Lean movement much of what they call "pull" could arguably be called "push". The Lean guys tend to demonize the whole idea of make-to-forecast as a push system, and therefore the cause of inventory problems (too much inventory, wrong inventory). Yet, if a business cannot truly operate on make-to-order, how can it use a pull strategy? I would argue that you can't, but the Lean folks will argue that you could be using Kanban; and since they claim Kanban is a pull system, you are now by default using a pull system. So how is Kanban a pull system? The claim is that since you cannot make any more of an item until some of that item is used (creating an empty Kanban), Kanban is pull because the creation of more is a direct result of actual demand. And if you don't think too hard about it, it seems to make sense.

But what if you actually do think about it a little? Let's review the mechanics of Kanban again. The quantity of all Kanbans minus one Kanban essentially represents a reorder point. The reason this inventory exists is to fill the expected demand during the lead-time period. Since the demand during the lead-time period is not known (not a make-to-order environment), this inventory represents an "estimate" of future demand. And no matter what funky little calculation you used to get this number, or what you call it, it is still essentially a forecast. So if the Lean folks claim using a forecast is a push system, then Kanban must also be a push system.

And what about that little you-can't-make-more-until-some-is-used argument for pull? Well, in a fixed reorder point system or a forecast-based system, the trigger for making more is also generally the result of actual demand reducing current on-hand inventory to a point below the expected demand during the lead-time. Once again, how is this any less pull than Kanban? Granted, it is possible that an increase in forecasted demand can trigger an order even without a change in current on-hand inventory, but you kind of want that to happen, don't you? And actually, this same scenario happens in Kanban as well since they sometimes need to adjust the number of Kanbans or the quantity per Kanban to account for changes in demand. Therefore, the whole Kanban-is-pull argument is really just a shell game. The point is to keep you focused on the empty bin and use that as the argument for why it is pull, while keeping you from thinking about the fact that there are a whole bunch of additional bins sitting around with inventory in them that in effect represent a forecast.

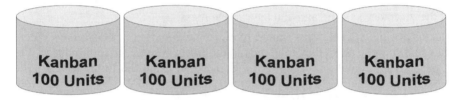

Figure 8B. This example shows a Kanban replenishment system that uses four Kanbans, with each Kanban set for 100 units. When the first Kanban is empty, it is sent back to the supplying operation signaling them to make 100 more units. In other words, whenever we are down to 300 units, we order 100 units.

So basically, the 300 units represent our forecasted demand during the lead time, plus safety stock. How this can be considered pull while our other ordering systems—that basically do the same thing—are considered push, is beyond me.

So why is it that the Japanese (Toyota Production System) and others swear by the operational improvements and reductions in inventory they received from switching to Kanban? Well, probably because they actually did see improvement to their operations as a direct result of using Kanban. Does this prove that Kanban is pull and that pull is better than push? Not at all, it only proves that Kanban worked better than what they were doing before.

And now it's time for my theory (I have absolutely no facts to support this, but I'm not going to let that stop me) on why the Japanese really started using Kanban and why others also see operational improvements after switching to Kanban. In the olden times (pre-computer), multi-bin systems were essentially very simple production-scheduling methods for continuous production environments (like the auto industry). At the time, a lack of sophisticated computer programs for scheduling made these systems an effective choice. Just imagine what it must have taken to try to coordinate (without computers) all the activities that go into manufacturing and purchasing the components for an automobile, and getting them all together to assemble the final product. And I'm sure that back in these times, an inability to effectively coordinate all these activities easily led to stockpiles of inventory. As time went on and computers became more readily available and software more sophisticated, manufacturers now had tools to more effectively plan these activities. But there was a catch, someone needed to know how to set up and run these planning systems. It was—and still is—common for these systems to be set up with exaggerated setup and queue times. That, combined with poorly calculated lot sizes based on overstated setup and order costs, frequently resulted in large inventories. Then you throw in some inferior forecasting techniques and an unwillingness to react to changes in demand, and you have even more inventory. On top of that, you often had different parts of the same organization on separate computer systems, and therefore had a disconnect between these activities. Add in some misguided accounting practices that focused too much on consuming overhead, and informal processes that developed because of a distrust of the inventory system, and you have a real mess.

Not surprisingly, some folks started reminiscing about the good ol' days before they had computers, so they took the old multi-bin system and reintroduced it as Kanban. They found that if they set their Kanban quantities to the lowest point possible that still allowed them to continue production, all these scheduling problems and excess inventory problems seemed to be solved.

So I guess what I'm saying here is the benefits companies get today from switching to Kanban are primarily related to the fact that they didn't know how to work their computerized inventory system. Though Kanban is often tied into your computer system for transactional and reporting purposes, it essentially operates independently of it. So regardless of inventory accuracy problems, planning mistakes, incorrect item setup, or even complete computer system failure, Kanban continues to operate. You will never build more inventory than the quantity dictated by the Kanbans, and you will always continue to build whenever a Kanban is physically emptied. Heck, when I say it like that, it does sound like the greatest thing since sliced bread.

I'm thinking that in the process of explaining how Kanban is not what it is often touted to be, I've convinced some of you that it is a lot better than you thought it was. Well I'm not finished yet. The simplistic nature of Kanban and its disconnect from your computer systems, also limits its flexibility. Sure, Kanban keeps chugging along maintaining the same inventory levels for your items regardless of what is happening in your computer, but is that what you really want? What if you want to change inventory levels for an item? I mean, we have all this stuff like trends, seasonality, items being discontinued, new items, engineering changes, sourcing changes, and so on. With Kanban, these changes require someone physically changing the Kanbans out on the shop floor. In addition, what if you don't want your reorder point to be an exact multiple of your order quantity? Or, what if you don't want your reorder point to be equal to or greater than your order quantity? Or—and this is a big one—what if you are not in a continuous production environment and therefore don't want to have Kanbans full of components sitting around even though you don't expect to be using them for quite some time? My argument here is not that Kanban cannot be effective in certain environments, but rather, I think you can do better in a lot of environments (including some of those where Kanban seems to work really well) by using a good planning system.

Now for a little more on calculating Kanban quantities.

My inclination is to treat Kanban for what it is (fixed reorder point with fixed replenishment quantities) and use the order quantity, safety stock, and forecast calculations we covered in the previous chapters as inputs to the Kanban quantities, then just adjust to meet the need to have the reorder point to be greater than or equal to and an exact multiple of, the reorder quantity. The Lean folks, however, tend to approach this more from a pure operational standpoint, in that they will try to get the smallest Kanban size and the fewest number of Kanbans that still allow you to meet demand. This is based on their belief that inventory is inherently wasteful and that having any more than you immediately need, regardless of calculated cost benefits, will damn your soul to inventory hell. I will concede that there may be times when you can receive some operational benefits by adjusting your lot sizes to help things flow better through your manufacturing operations, but I think you want to start by at least knowing what an economic-based lot size looks like. From there, you can make your own informed decision.

Ordering systems that directly utilize the forecast.

I didn't know what to call this section because there's not a single industry standard name for these types of systems. So you may run into them referred to as time-phased order point, time-dependent calculated order point, dynamic reorder point, automatic order point, calculated order point, and others. I'll stick with the term time-phased order point for the remainder of this book. Also be aware these same terms may be used to describe other types of functionality, so don't make any assumptions based on them.

I've already made the argument that all reorder systems use some type of a forecast. What is different with a time-phased order point system is the system directly uses a formal forecast and actual orders (optional) whenever it evaluates the need to order. In other words, there is no order point quantity (such as a fixed reorder point, or a min) in your system. Instead, your system calculates order point on the fly based on your forecast, orders, lead time, and safety stock.

As you can see, there is nothing all that unique about the calculation for this type of system other than that it recalculates your ordering information as often as you want (usually daily), and that it uses the immediate forecast and orders within the lead-time period to do this. For example, if it's Monday morning and I have a lead time of three days, my ordering system will use the forecast and orders for Monday, Tuesday, and Wednesday, plus my safety stock quantity to determine my order point for today. On Tuesday morning, it would use the forecast and orders for Tuesday, Wednesday, and Thursday, plus safety stock. This way, any trend, seasonality, or predictable demand changes that you've built into your forecast, will immediately be incorporated into your ordering calculations. This is kind of the whole point of all that work we did in the forecasting chapters.

Though the calculation seems simple, it can get complicated in that there may be a number of additional calculations that serve as inputs to this calculation. We had already covered some of these but I want to review them again here briefly to provide a better overall understanding of how an ordering system works. The forecast is obviously a key input here, but it isn't quite that simple. For example, we had already discussed how the forecast is probably stated in weeks or months yet the lead time is probably stated in days. Your system therefore needs to convert your forecast into days (or convert your lead time into forecast periods), and you're going to have to verify just how your system does this.

But, before it can convert the forecast to days, it first needs to determine what forecast quantity to use. This is pretty straightforward for future forecast periods, but what about the current forecast period? Remember, we will need to be able to make this calculation at various times during a forecast period. For example, if we have monthly forecast periods and we need to calculate our ordering needs in the middle of the month, what quantity do we use to represent the forecast for the remainder of the forecast period? Some systems may just divide the original forecast quantity for the month by the number of days in the month to get a daily forecast quantity that can then be applied to the portion of the lead-time period that will occur within the remaining portion of the month. However, more so-phisticated systems will likely use your forecast consumption rules (see forecast consumption in Chapter 5) to determine how much of the forecast remains (was not yet consumed) and then calculate that against the number of days remaining in the month.

Then there's the whole issue of current orders (allocations), and how they may or may not affect your order calculation. It may be that your system completely ignores current allocations and relies solely on your forecast. Or, it may be that your system incorporates some logic to use both your current allocations and your forecast to determine demand during the lead-time period. If it can or does use current allocations, you need to figure out exactly how it does this and what control you have over how it does this. It may be using your forecast consumption rules and reduce the forecast by these order quantities in the appropriate forecast period, or, it may have some rules you can set up specifically for current orders, or, it may just "do something" behind the scenes based on what the programmer thought made sense at the time.

Once your system has calculated your daily demand (forecast and orders), it then needs to calculate this relative to the lead-time period. As already discussed, you need to make sure you understand how your system uses lead time (calendar days? work days? something else?). If your system has the ability to incorporate safety lead times, you also need to make sure you understand how it handles this.

Now that your system has calculated your lead-time demand, it can add your safety stock to it to calculate the order point it will use to determine today's ordering needs. Your safety stock quantity will either exist in your system as a fixed quantity, or will be generated as the output of a calculation similar to those discussed in Chapter 6. In either case, it will just be added to your lead-time demand to get your order point.

Then it's just a matter of comparing your order point to your current on-hand inventory and your current inbound orders to determine if you need to order more inventory. As with a fixed reorder point system, this would involve adding inbound quantities to your on-hand quantity and then comparing this to your order point to see if you need to order more. In some of the more sophisticated systems it may take the dates associated with the inbound orders into account here, but that would more likely be used to expedite or de-expedite existing orders rather than to create a new order to come in before an existing one.

Time-phased order point

Period (weeks)	#1	#2	#3	#4	#5	#6	#7	#8	#9	#10	#11	#12	#13	#14	#15
Forecast	50	50	45	40	40	35	40	40	45	50	50	55	60	65	65
Lead time = 21 days															

Figure 8C. Here we see a forecast that obviously has some level of seasonality and/or trend present. Assuming we are using calendar days in our order system, at the beginning of week #1 our time-phased order point calculation would calculate the lead-time demand to be 145 units. At the beginning of week #6 it would calculate lead-time demand to be 115 units, and at the beginning of week #13 it would calculate lead-time demand to be 190 units. You can see how this would be far superior to a fixed order point calculation that would use the same order point at each of these points.

Now if you combine this with our safety stock calculation that also takes trend and seasonality into account (see Chapter 6), you really start to see the benefits of utilizing your immediate forecast for your ordering decisions, as well as the importance of developing a forecast that takes trend, seasonality, and events into account.

A quick intro to planned orders.

We'll be covering planned orders in the next chapter on MRP and DRP but I want to briefly mention it here because your non-MRP/DRP ordering system may also have the ability to use planned orders. We've covered how your system can utilize your forecast and current orders to determine your immediate ordering needs, but it can also use this same logic to estimate your future ordering needs. It can do this through the use of "planned orders", which are essentially a series of quantities and dates that represent an estimation of your future ordering needs (purchase orders or manufacturing orders) based on your current on-hand inventory, current orders, forecast, safety stock, and order quantities. For example, we've already covered how the system can determine if I need to place an order today to replenish inventory. Once it determines the need, it will look at our order quantity rules (See Chapter 7) to determine how much to order. Then it can use this order quantity and compare it to future forecast periods to see when we will likely need to place the next order, and the next order, and the next, and so on.

Outside of MRP and DRP, there is not as significant a need for planned orders. You'll learn more about planned orders in the next chapter, and even if you do not expect to be using an MRP or DRP system I suggest reading that chapter because you may find some of this standardized functionality exists in your non-MRP/DRP system.

More advanced periodic review.

Earlier in this chapter we discussed a "pure periodic review system" as a simplistic method commonly used by very small businesses that place orders on a fixed schedule. However, fixed-schedule ordering is not unique to small businesses; in fact, it is a very common requirement for at least a portion of the inventory in many larger businesses. The idea of fixed-schedule ordering comes down to having one or more items supplied by the same supplier where, either the supplier delivers on a fixed schedule (weekly, monthly, etc.) or, due to freight considerations (costs), you decide to group the products into regularly scheduled deliveries.

In the pure periodic review system previously discussed, the process was likely entirely manual. However, there are ways to automate this, and more importantly, there are ways to fit this into the same systems you may be using for your other ordering needs. When we compare the requirements of fixed-schedule ordering with the requirements of general ordering, the key difference is the fixed schedule. Duh! To put it in other words, a typical ordering system assumes that you have an opportunity to place orders every day, while a fixed-schedule ordering system restricts you to ordering only at specific times. This restriction forces you to rethink how you calculate your order point. For example, if I have an item with a lead time of 7 days, daily demand of 10 units, and safety stock of 30 units, my standard order point would calculate to 100 units (7 x 10 + 30). But, if I have 110 units in stock for that item on Monday and it is on fixed-schedule ordering where I can place orders only on Mondays, what would I do? Technically, I'm still above my order point of 110 units, but it will probably drop below the order point on Tuesday or Wednesday, yet I won't be able to place another order until the following Monday, in which case I will almost certainly run out before my replenishment order comes in. So despite the fact that my standard order point calculation says I have enough, I will need to place an order today or risk running out of inventory. What we need to figure out is how to quantify the logic that we must have just used to figure out that we really don't have enough.

When we think about this example, what we find we really need to do is determine the quantity of inventory that will not only cover our demand during the lead time, but also cover our demand until our next opportunity to order. So in the case of fixed-schedule ordering, our "effective lead time" is the lead time plus the time between ordering opportunities. Therefore, in this example, our effective lead time is 14 days.

Unfortunately, your inventory system probably doesn't have a place to enter "effective lead time" or a place to enter fixed-schedule information (though I'm hoping books like this one will help to change that). This means you will probably end up calculating your effective lead time and placing that into the lead-time field in your ordering system (or use that to calculate a fixed reorder point or a min if your are using those methods). Then you will need to find a way to "ignore" these items as they come up for reorder on days other than your fixed ordering days for those items. Since these items are generally grouped by vendor, you can usually use the vendor number as a means to exclude these items from your regular reorder reports (if you use reorder reports), and include them on special reorder reports set up specifically for these fixed-schedule order items. You can use similar criteria to handle this in more automated ordering systems, and it's also not too difficult to manage manually in some operations since inventory planners tend to quickly gain familiarity with the various suppliers and can simply ignore these suppliers until it comes to their regularly scheduled ordering day.

The problem with entering an effective lead time in your system in place of the actual lead time is that some calculations that use the lead time may not provide the results you want. For example, many systems will automatically calculate the requested date based on the lead time. So if we go back to the example we were using, the requested date generated by the system would end up being 14 days from today, however, you really want the shipment delivered 7 days from today (the actual lead time). Therefore, barring any system modifications to accommodate this, your planners would need to remember to change this to avoid confusion with the supplier. In addition, having an effective lead time entered in place of the actual lead time can lead to further confusion when it comes to vendor analysis and ongoing maintenance. For example, if you have someone reviewing lead times with suppliers (a good idea), they need to remember that the lead time in the system is not accurate. Also, if you want to change your order frequency (your fixed schedule), you would need to figure out what the actual lead time is and then recalculate your effective lead time. Not that these are insurmountable problems, but they can be annoyances and could potentially lead to errors.

Another option would be to keep your lead time accurate, but include the time between ordering opportunities in your safety lead time (assuming you have that functionality). You would still need to find a way to ignore these items as they come up for reorder on days other than your fixed ordering days for those items, but safety lead time does resolve some of the other issues.

Ideally, software vendors will eventually start including more functionality to accommodate these requirements. It's important to let your software vendor know if this is functionality you want so they will consider it in future versions. If this is critical to your business, it also may be worth some modifications to your system. In the meantime, the workarounds described here can be effective.

I also want to mention that the term "effective lead time" is not a standard industry term, and therefore could have a different meaning depending on the context of its use.

In addition, when calculating safety stock in a periodic review system, you would want to use the effective lead time (not the actual lead time) as an input to your safety stock calculation.

Optional reorder point.

Optional reorder point (also called optional replenishment point) is sometimes used in fixed reorder point or min-max systems, but can also be incorporated (a little trickier) in a time-dependent calculated order system. The idea is that you have a separate reorder point that is a little higher than your normal reorder point, and you would use this to avoid down-time on machines (I can hear the Lean guys cringing here) or meet minimum order amounts, discounts, or freight policies for purchased items. It's basically just a quick way of identifying items that are close to reorder point. For example, if I'm putting together a purchase order for a specific supplier and all the items currently below reorder point add up to a purchase order total of $900, but the supplier provides free freight for any orders over $1,000, it may make sense to either increase some order quantities to hit this amount or look for other items that may be close to reorder point to add to the order. Optional reorder point would be a means of achieving the latter.

A quick note on requisitions and approval processes.

Many ordering systems have functionality for using requisitions and/or approval processes. Requisitions are generally used to provide a way for people who don't have purchasing authority (authority to create purchase orders) to create purchase-order-like documents (within the purchasing system) that specify item, quantity, cost, terms, and vendor information for something they require. These requisitions would then be reviewed by someone who does have purchasing authority, and if approved, would be converted to an actual purchase order.

On the other hand, approval processes are a means of setting purchasing control measures for people who do have purchasing authority. A basic approval process would set limits for particular individuals and automatically forward purchase orders beyond these limits (amounts) to individuals with authority to approve purchases of that amount.

I'm not talking about paper being shuffled around here. These are system tools that provide an efficient means of accomplishing these tasks. For example, Bob in maintenance, may go to the system and enter a requisition for some maintenance supplies he needs. Fred in purchasing, will inquire on all open requisitions twice a day and review them. If a requisition looks good he will use an option in the system to convert the requisition into a purchase order (or create a purchase order based on the requisition). Then, if the amount of the purchase order is within Fred's authority, the purchase order is automatically released, but if it is above Fred's authority it will go into a queue awaiting approval. Fred's boss will now receive a system message notifying her that there is a purchase order awaiting her approval. If she approves it and the amount is within her authority, it is automatically released, but if it is beyond her authority, it moves to the next level in the approval process.

Depending on your needs and your system's capabilities, your approval processes can be much more complex than this example. They may incorporate spending limits based on periods of time, spending limits based on department, spending limits with specific suppliers, and pretty much anything else you can think up. I do want to mention that it's easy to get carried away with requisition and approval processes. The problem lies in setting up cumbersome processes or "rubber stamp" systems that just end up wasting time. For example, if I'm part of the approval process and over a period of time I find that I have "reviewed" and approved hundreds or thousands of purchases without ever rejecting one, it's very likely that the purchasing limits are set too low or I'm not really reviewing them (just going through the motions of approving them). In either case, nothing has been accomplished here other than delaying the processing of the purchases and wasting my time.

Quick summary.

In this chapter we reviewed the key inputs to ordering systems and covered the mechanics of basic ordering systems. It's important to remember that all order/reorder systems essentially use an order point, and the basic logic of calculating an order point (demand during lead time plus safety stock) is essentially the same for each method used. The differences among ordering systems are related to how frequently the order point is calculated, and the specific mechanics of executing the ordering process.

It should come as no surprise that I think most of you should be using an ordering system that directly utilizes the forecast. I didn't dedicate three chapters on developing detailed forecasts that take into account trends, seasonality, and events, only to have you implement a basic fixed reorder point or min-max system. This isn't to say these simpler methods don't have a place, only that most of you probably will benefit from a more sophisticated system.

In the following chapter we will be covering MRP and DRP. Even if you don't plan on using these systems, I strongly recommend reading this chapter because some of the functionality discussed may be of use to you in your non-MRP/DRP environment

9

MRP, Multi-plant MRP, and DRP

MRP is a great example of utilizing a computer to do tasks that are nearly impossible to accomplish without one. It's not that the logic or math behind MRP is beyond the capabilities of a human being, but rather the number of calculations that need to occur and the sequence they need to occur in to achieve the desired output can be so extensive that it is just impractical to try to do them manually.

Well before going any further, I guess I should explain a little about what MRP is. Originally, MRP referred to an inventory planning method used in manufacturing operations known as Material Requirements Planning. The basic idea of Material Requirements Planning is to take known or forecasted demand (or a production schedule) for top-level items (finished manufactured items), and use that demand or schedule to calculate demand for all the lower level components required to manufacture those items; to "time-phase" the demand to determine exactly when specific quantities of specific items will be needed; then to take this time-phased demand and "net" it against current and projected on-hand balances and order policies to determine how much needs to be ordered, and use lead times to determine when these orders need to be placed.

Eventually, labor and machine resources planning were incorporated into MRP, and it became known as Manufacturing Resource Planning or MRPII. MRPII is the consolidation of Material Requirements Planning (MRP), Capacity Requirements Planning (CRP), and Master Production Scheduling (MPS). We'll touch on this additional functionality a little bit, but the primary purpose of this chapter is to cover the "materials" aspects of MRP.

The basic MRP calculations.

I'll go through several examples here, starting with a very simple manufacturing operation and progressing to more complex ones. For my first example, we'll say I've opened up a small bicycle wheel-building business. I purchase all my components and then assemble them into finished wheels. Therefore, this is just a simple assembly operation.

To build a wheel, I need a rim, rim strip, spokes, nipples, and a hub. For this example, we'll assume our wheel has 32 spokes. We have a bill of materials that looks like this:

Bill of materials		
FW001 Front Wheel		
Item#	Desc.	Quantity Per
RM001	Rim	1
RS001	Rim Strip	1
HB001	Hub-front	1
NP001	Nipple	32
SP001	Spoke	32

Figure 9A. Bill of materials for a front wheel.

From this, it's easy to calculate—even without a computer—that if we wanted to make 10 wheels, we would need 10 rims, 10 rim strips, 10 hubs, 320 nipples, and 320 spokes (our gross requirement assuming no scrap). The next thing we need to look at is our manufacturing lead time to determine when we would need these items. Manufacturing lead time essentially consists of setup time (the time it takes to set up equipment), run time (the actual assembly or manufacturing time), queue time (a buffer that represents the time stuff just sits around waiting to be worked on) and move time. For now, we'll just say our total manufacturing lead time for 10 of these wheels is one week (7 days).

So now I know that if I needed to have these 10 wheels completed at the beginning of week #3, I would need all these materials available at the beginning of week #2.

Calculating demand of components				Week 1	Week 2	Week 3
FW001 Front Wheel (lead time = 1 week)						10
	Item#	Desc.	Quantity Per			
	RM001	Rim	1		10	
	RS001	Rim Strip	1		10	
	HB001	Hub-front	1		10	
	NP001	Nipple	32		320	
	SP001	Spoke	32		320	

Figure 9B. Here we show how through an MRP explosion with lead-time offsetting, our demand for 10 wheels in week #3 creates demand in week #2 for the components.

My next step is to see if I already have some of these materials in stock or on order. To keep things real simple for now, we'll assume these 10 wheels are the only things we are planning on manufacturing during this time period that use these specific components. So it's just a matter of looking at each component and adding the current on-hand quantity to any quantities on order (assuming they would be received before the beginning of week #2), and then comparing this to our requirements to determine if we need to order more (this is called netting).

If we do need to order more, we need to look at our order (lot sizing) policies to determine how much to order, and the lead time for each component to see when we would need to place the order. Again, we'll keep things real simple for now and say that all the components come from a regional distributor and have a lead time of one week. Therefore, any components needed would have to be ordered by the beginning of week #1 in order to be in stock by the beginning of week #2, so I can have the wheels completed by the beginning of week #3. Though a computer program would be useful for calculating our requirements in this example, it's hardly necessary. However, this is an extremely simple example.

So we'll now step up the complexity just a bit in our wheel building operation. Over the next three months, we have demand (either forecasted or actual orders) that totals 200 units (wheels) spread out among 20 different wheel configurations. Some of these wheel configurations share certain components with other wheel configurations. For example, one hub is used on several different wheels, but each of these wheels uses different rims and/or spokes, however, each of these rims and spokes is also used on other wheels with different hubs.

Vocabulary Note:

When I refer to "actual orders" when talking about demand, I am referring to real sales orders or other shipping orders (such as transfer orders). When I use the term when talking about supply, I am referring to real production orders, purchase orders, or transfer orders.

Due to the space required to show all 20 different wheel configurations, I'm only showing 5 different wheels in the following example. See Figure 9C.

The process still starts out the same, in that we need to start with the required quantity of each of the finished items, then use the bill of materials to determine the quantity required of each component. Then we use the manufacturing lead time of each finished item to determine when we need each component. In the example, I show five different wheels and the demand for those wheels over a six-week period. Since each wheel has a one-week manufacturing lead time, all component demand is shown in the week prior to the finished wheel's demand. But now we also need to accumulate the requirements for each component so when we evaluate the need to order a specific component we can see all the requirements for all the items this component is used to manufacture. Figure 9D represents the accumulation of demand for each component.

MRP Explosion - Multiple Items

FW001 Front Wheel (LT = 1 week)

Period (weeks)	1	2	3	4	5	6
			10			5

Item#	Desc	Qty Per	1	2	3	4	5	6
RM001	Rim	1		10			5	
RS001	Rim Strip	1		10			5	
HB001	Hub-front	1		10			5	
NP001	Nipple	32		320			160	
SP001	Spoke	32		320			160	

FW002 Front Wheel (LT = 1 week)

Period (weeks)	1	2	3	4	5	6
				3		

Item#	Desc	Qty Per	1	2	3	4	5	6
RM002	Rim	1			3			
RS001	Rim Strip	1			3			
HB001	Hub-front	1			3			
NP002	Nipple	32			96			
SP002	Spoke	32			96			

FW003 Front Wheel (LT = 1 week)

Period (weeks)	1	2	3	4	5	6
					20	

Item#	Desc	Qty Per	1	2	3	4	5	6
RM001	Rim	1				20		
RS001	Rim Strip	1				20		
HB002	Hub-front	1				20		
NP003	Nipple	32				640		
SP003	Spoke	32				640		

RW001 Rear Wheel (LT = 1 week)

Period (weeks)	1	2	3	4	5	6
			5			

Item#	Desc	Qty Per	1	2	3	4	5	6
RM001	Rim	1		5				
RS001	Rim Strip	1		5				
HB003	Hub-rear	1		5				
NP001	Nipple	32		160				
SP001	Spoke	32		160				

RW002 Rear Wheel (LT = 1 week)

Period (weeks)	1	2	3	4	5	6
				2		

Item#	Desc	Qty Per	1	2	3	4	5	6
RM002	Rim	1			2			
RS001	Rim Strip	1			2			
HB003	Hub-rear	1			2			
NP002	Nipple	32			64			
SP002	Spoke	32			64			

Figure 9C. Here we show an MRP explosion and lead-time offsetting for five items. I kept things simple here by giving each item a lead time of one week.

Total Gross Requirements by Component										
			Period (weeks)		1	2	3	4	5	6
	RM001	Rim				15		20	5	
	RM002	Rim					5			
	RS001	Rim Strip				15	5	20	5	
	HB001	Hub-front				10	3		5	
	HB002	Hub-front						20		
	HB003	Hub-rear				5	2			
	NP001	Nipple				480			160	
	NP002	Nipple					160			
	NP003	Nipple						640		
	SP001	Spoke				480			160	
	SP002	Spoke					160			
	SP003	Spoke						640		

Figure 9D. Here we show the accumulated gross requirements for each component from the previous MRP explosion (Figure 9C).

Let me just note here that these examples are purely to help visualize what needs to occur within MRP. In reality, you will not see anything that looks like this in your MRP system since the calculations are happening behind the scenes. I'm also not going to even attempt to show you how to build an MRP system in a spreadsheet, because it would be really really hard, and since MRP systems are so readily available, there is no need to build your own.

Now that we have the gross requirements for each component, we can begin planning orders for them. Figure 9E (on the following page) shows an example of how MRP would plan the first component (RM001 Rim). I extended demand for RM001 out to 11 weeks just to provide more data to use in the example. In the example, you can see that we have a beginning inventory balance of 10 units, and are using a lot size of 25 units for our reorder policy. We don't have any current scheduled receipts (open purchase orders) for this item, but if we did, we would add our scheduled receipts to the on-hand balance for that period before comparing it to our gross requirements to see if we have a net requirement. Also note that in these types of MRP examples it is always assumed the receipts will be available as of the beginning of the period they are scheduled, and the on-hand balances reflect the expected on-hand balance at the end of the period.

In week 1, we don't have any gross requirements, so the on-hand balance of 10 remains and there will not be any net requirement (just ignore the planned order release in week 1 for now).

In week 2, we have a gross requirement of 15 units. Since we show an on-hand balance of 10 units at the end of week 1, and no scheduled receipts for week 2, our net requirement for week 2 will be 5 units (gross requirement of 15 minus on-hand of 10). Since our order policy for this item is set to order lot sizes of 25 units, MRP will create a planned order receipt of 25 units for week 2. And since

Net Requirements and Plannned Orders

RM001   Rim   (beginning inventory = 10 units, lot size = 25, lead time = 1 week)

Period (weeks)		1	2	3	4	5	6	7	8	9	10	11
Gross requirements			15		20	5		10	30		5	15
On hand	10											
Scheduled receipts												
Net requirements			5		20	5		10	30		5	15
Planned order receipts			25			25			25			25
Planned order releases		25			25			25			25	
Planned on hand			20	20	0	20	20	10	5	5	0	10

Figure 9E. Here we show how we net the requirements and create planned orders for one of our components from the previous example. We start with 10 units on hand in week #1, therefore our gross requirement of 15 units in week #2 results in a net requirement of 5 units in week #2. Since the lead time for this component is one week, our planned order receipt in week #2 results in a planned order release in week #1. Our planned on hand at the end of week #2 will then be 20 units. This is the result of subtracting our net requirement from our planned order receipts for that period.

The planning process then continues through subsequent weeks using the same logic. We currently don't show any scheduled receipts for this item, but once we convert the first planned order to an actual order, the planned order release in week #1 and the planned order receipt in week #2 will disappear, and we will show a scheduled receipt in week #2. Scheduled receipts are then included in the calculation for net requirements.

our lead-time for RM001 is one week, MRP will create a planned order release in week 1.

Just to clarify this whole planned-order-release/planned-order-receipt issue, the quantity of 25 shown in periods 1 and 2 represents a single planned order that has a required date in week 2, and therefore must be released in week 1 due to the lead time of one week. If you were to inquire on this item in a typical MRP system, the planned order quantities would be associated with the planned receipt date, not the planned released date. The planned release date is purely used to signal to the planner (via an order report, ordering screen, or action messages) to place the order.

If you look at the last line of the example, we show a planned on-hand balance of 20 units at the end of week 2. This is calculated by subtracting our net requirement of 5 units from our planned order quantity of 25 units. As we go into week 3, we have no gross requirements, therefore no net requirements; and since we don't show any scheduled receipts, we will maintain our planned on-hand balance of 20 units through week 3. Week 4 shows a net requirement of 20 units, so since we have a planned on-hand balance of 20 units at the end of week 3, this will cover our net requirement for week 4 and result in a planned on-hand balance of 0 for the end of week 4.

Week 5 shows a net requirement of 5 units, so since we used the remainder of our planned inventory in week 4, MRP will create a new planned order receipt for 25 units in week 5, and a planned order release of 25 units in week 4.

If you continue through weeks 6 through 11, you just repeat the same calculations. If you were to then go ahead and do this for each of the 11 other components that showed gross requirements in Figure 9D, you would have completed the basic tasks that MRP would do to plan the component demand for those 5 wheels.

As you can see, the calculations here are rather simple, but you should also have realized that doing these simple calculations for just these 5 wheels and the 12 components used to assemble them, can end up being a lot of work. Now remember, our example was supposed to be for 20 different wheels but I cut it to 5 in the example to save space. Technically, 20 wheels could still be calculated manually, but in the real world it would likely get a lot more complicated than our example. For example, each of our finished items (wheels) only required 5 components and had a lead time of one-week. And each of our components, conveniently, also had a lead time of one week. Imagine how much more difficult it gets when each end item and component has a different lead time, and some end items have tens or hundreds of components.

You may have been wondering why our example calculated planned orders out 11 weeks even though our component had only a one-week lead time. The truth is that in this example, there really isn't a need to calculate planned orders out that far, but as I change our example a little bit, it will begin to make sense.

Multi-level BOMs.

Well our little wheel-building operation has grown and we've decided to expand and start manufacturing some of our own components. We're going to start by manufacturing some of our own hubs. This brings up the concept of multi-level bills of materials. So now my wheel has a bill of materials containing a rim, rim strip, spokes, nipples, and a hub. But the hub on that bill of materials also has its own bill of materials that contains the components required to manufacture the hub (axle, bearings, bearing races, housing, quick-release skewers, and various nuts, washers, and seals).

A common misconception among people new to MRP when they start reading about multi-level BOMs, is that you need to set up this massive thing called a multi-level bill. Well, you don't. All you're doing is setting up all the individual BOMs, and MRP will figure out the rest. For

Vocabulary Note.

Is it bill of material, bills of material, bill of materials, or bills of materials?

Who cares! It's not like someone is going to be confused if you choose to use one term over another. But feel free to waste your time arguing about it with your coworkers.

Multi-level BOM

Item #12345   Front Wheel

	Item#	Desc.	Quantity Per		
	RM001	Rim	1		
	RS001	Rim Strip	1		
	NP001	Nipple	32		
	SP001	Spoke	32		
	HB001	Hub-front	1		
L		Item#	Desc.		Quantity Per
		HH001	Hub Housing Front		1
		AX001	Axle- Front		1
		BR001	Bearings 3/16		20
		CN001	Bearing Cone		2
		SK001	Skewer Front		1
		SL001	Seals		2
		HD001	Hub Hardware Kit		1

Figure 9F. Here we see an "indented view" of a bill-of-materials structure. In this example, the hub used in the wheel assembly is a manufactured part and has its own BOM. Keep in mind that this is only a "view" created by a computer program. The BOM for the wheel and the BOM for the hub actually exist as separate bills.

example, it will calculate the gross and net requirements for all the components for the wheel and create planned orders. Then it will look at each component, and if there is a bill of materials attached to a component, it will go through the whole process for those components as well. And if any of those components have their own BOMs, it will keep going.

This is where planned orders are so important—in fact, they are the driving force in MRP. When MRP plans orders for the hub used in the wheel, it may be planning out several months of planned orders even if our manufacturing lead time for the hub is only one week. Why? Because MRP will use those planned orders to drive the planning of the components for the hub, or the components of the components of the components of the hub. Because of this, we need to make sure our planning horizon equals or exceeds our longest total cumulative lead time. What does all this mean? It means we need to understand the difference between concurrent lead times and consecutive lead times.

In our original wheel example we purchased all our components and assembled the wheel as a single assembly, therefore, we just had a single-level BOM. In this scenario, our minimum planning horizon (the distance into the future we need to plan the wheel in MRP) only needs to include the manufacturing lead time for the wheel plus the lead time for the component with the longest lead time. Since our manufacturing lead time for the wheel is one week, and all components had a lead time of one week, our planning horizon only needed to be two weeks into the future. This is because the lead times for each of the components occur concurrently. In other words, all components for the wheel only need to be available one week prior to the requirement for the wheel, and since they all have a lead time of one week, they can all be ordered two weeks prior to the requirement for the wheel.

However, if we also manufacture the hub, we now must add the manufacturing lead time for the hub plus the lead time for the component of the hub with the longest lead time. For example, if our manufacturing lead time for the hub is one week, and the hub housing (the component with the longest lead time) has a lead time of five weeks, we need to be able to place an order for the hub housing seven weeks before the requirement for the finished wheel in order to get everything in stock in time for the manufacturing operations. Therefore, these lead times occur concurrently.

To explain it another way, if we need the completed wheels in week 10, we need to have the hubs available in week 9 because it takes us a week to assemble the wheel. But it also takes us a week to manufacture the hub, so we need all the components for the hub available in week 8. And since the hub housing has a lead time of 5 weeks, we will need to order in week 3 in order to have them in stock in week 8. That's why our planning horizon for the wheels needs to be at least seven weeks, even though the manufacturing lead time for the wheel is only one week. We need the demand for the wheels to generate planned orders for the hubs far enough into the future that they can trigger planned orders for the hub housing.

This is the nature of planning "dependent demand". That is, the demand for the hub housing is dependent on the demand for the hub, and the demand for the hub is dependent on the demand for the wheel. Therefore, rather than trying to forecast demand for the hubs and hub components, we can use our forecast (or actual orders) for wheels to calculate the demand for these other items.

If we now decided to turn our wheel-building operation into a bicycle-manufacturing operation, we would start forecasting demand for bicycles and use that demand to calculate demand for the wheels, which will drive the demands for the hubs, which will drive the demand for the hub housing. We would also need to add the time to manufacture the bicycle to our planning horizon, and check the lead time for all the additional components we will be using to determine our total cumulative lead time for a bicycle.

As you can see, each time we added a level to our bill-of-materials structure, we also needed to extend our planning horizon. The extended planning horizon means that we are now using forecasts from more distant future periods. If you recall from the first forecasting chapter, forecasts tend to be less accurate the further they extend into the future. Therefore, our adding levels to our bill-of-material structure is likely resulting in using less-accurate forecasts as part of our planning.

This brings us to the concept of "flattening" your bill-of materials structure. While flattening your BOMs sounds like a clerical or systems activity, what it really implies is changing your manufacturing practices in a way that results in fewer levels in the BOM structure. In the case of our wheel, if we could incorporate the manufacturing of the hub as part of the wheel manufacturing process (rather than a completely separate manufacturing process) we could "potentially" reduce our planning horizon, and also reduce the planning and related activities associated with running these as separate processes. I use the term "potentially" because flattening your BOMs doesn't automatically result in reducing your planning horizon. You must also change your manufacturing processes in a way that reduces your overall manufacturing lead times.

Master Production Schedule (MPS).

Up to this point, I just referred to top-level demand as "demand" and used that to start the MRP process. I did that intentionally to avoid getting too confusing too soon. However, there is a more formal system for feeding demand into MRP, and that is known as the Master Production Schedule (MPS).

Think of the MPS as an additional layer that sits between your demand and your MRP system. For the most part, the need for this extra layer comes down to an annoying little piece of reality known as capacity. Due to seasonal demand variability or lumpy demand, many manufacturers simply don't have enough capacity to produce exactly what is needed in the period in which it is needed. If I had my forecast directly driving my MRP system, during my peak periods the MRP system may end up telling me to manufacture more than I am capable of manufacturing during that time (we'll cover finite and infinite scheduling shortly).

So essentially what MPS does is provide a way for a planner to move production from periods where capacity is exceeded into periods where excess capacity is available (preferably earlier periods), and allow this to drive MRP to make sure all components and subassemblies are aligned with these changes. It really is just that simple. I've been amazed over the years as I've read book after book that cover the process of MPS but fail to mention why someone would need to use an MPS. The reason I bring this up is that there is some confusion about MPS and MRP. This sometimes results in manufacturers being scared away from using MRP due to the complexities and requirements of MPS and related processes. The story goes something like this; someone from the company takes a course or gets their hands on an MRP book. They are soon working through this highly structured process of starting with a formal production plan that is checked against resource requirements planning (RRP), then starting a master production scheduling process and checking that against rough-cut capacity, and then running MRP and checking that against capacity requirements planning (CRP). They quickly realize that they simply don't have enough people available to do all this stuff, and subsequently write MRP off as something for bigger companies. Well the truth is you don't need to do all that stuff.

Don't get me wrong, there are companies that need to use MPS and CRP, but MRP doesn't require that you use it. And if you are fortunate enough to have either relatively stable demand and/or some flexibility in your manufacturing capacity, there is no reason to go through all that extra work. You can (in most systems) just use your forecast and actual orders to directly drive MRP. You may technically still have an MPS, but it is just automatically populated by your forecast and lot-sizing rules. And you may still occasionally run CRP, but unless you run into some very unusual capacity requirements, you probably won't be adjusting your schedule to it.

Example of MRP planning without MPS

	Jan	Feb	Mar	Apr	May	Jun	Jul	Aug	Sep	Oct	Nov	Dec	Totals
Item A (beginning inventory = 10 units, lot size = 100)													
Forecast	30	30	30	40	50	40	20	30	40	50	75	75	510
Planned order receipts	100	0	0	100	0	100	0	0	0	100	100	0	500
Projected on-hand	80	50	20	80	30	90	70	40	0	50	75	0	
Item B (beginning inventory = 30 units, lot size = 75)													
Forecast	20	20	25	30	35	35	15	20	25	35	50	60	370
Planned order receipts	0	75	0	0	75	0	0	75	0	75	0	75	375
Projected on-hand	10	65	40	10	50	15	0	55	30	70	20	35	
Item C (beginning inventory = 25 units, lot size = 150)													
Forecast	70	75	75	85	100	100	50	75	100	100	200	300	1330
Planned order receipts	150	0	150	0	150	150	0	150	0	150	150	300	1350
Projected on-hand	105	30	105	20	70	120	70	145	45	95	45	45	
Capacity checking													
Total production (units)	250	75	150	100	225	250	0	225	0	325	250	375	2225
Capacity (in units)	200	200	200	200	200	200	200	200	200	200	200	200	2400
Variance	-50	125	50	100	-25	-50	200	-25	200	-125	-50	-175	

Figure 9G. Here we have an example of how MRP would plan production for 3 items given the beginning inventory, lot sizes, and forecasts shown (note: I'm not using any safety stock in this example). For this example we will assume these are the only 3 items manufactured using a key piece of equipment, and this piece of equipment can only produce 200 units per month. If we look at the capacity comparison at the bottom of this example, we can see that in total (the full year) we have enough capacity to manufacture these items. But, on a month-by-month basis, we have some months that are scheduled well above capacity and others that are scheduled well below capacity.

Some of these conflicts are caused by our lot sizes, but the last three months of the year clearly have demand well beyond our capacity. This is a classic example of where MPS can be used to produce a schedule that meets both our demand and our capacity constraints.

Since I just threw around a whole bunch of new terms here, I should probably explain a little more what they mean. Thanks to a very close relationship between the early adopters (and creators) of MRP and the American Production and Inventory Control Society (APICS), a standardized language as well as some standardized processes were developed. Part of this is a formalized process for production planning. This formalized process starts with what is called a Production Plan. A production plan is a very high-level long-term plan of what will be produced. It is generally stated in terms of families of products rather than specific products, and in large time periods such as months, quarters, or even years. For example, a production plan in our bicycle company would likely categorize groups of bicycles. It may have a category for entry-level road bikes, another for mid-level road bikes, and another for high-end road bikes, as well as various categories of mountain bikes, hybrids, kid's bikes etc. It then may simply show the number of units of each category we plan on producing during each quarter (three-month period) over the next two or three years. Production plans generally cover a period of anywhere from one to ten years into the future (though ten years would be very unusual these days).

The purpose of the production plan is for planning for longer-term requirements such as facilities and equipment. Therefore, the production plan is checked by a process known as Resources Requirements Planning (RRP), which translates the production plan into capacity requirements for these key resources.

The Master Production Schedule (MPS) then uses the forecast and actual orders as inputs, but works within the production plan to do some more detailed scheduling. The MPS generally (but not always) focuses on top-level items (finished goods) and will plan specific items or, in some cases, more detailed product families. The MPS is checked against Rough-Cut Capacity Planning to determine if there is adequate capacity of key resources to meet the MPS. The key resources in rough-cut capacity planning may be the same as the ones used in RRP, but would probably include additional resources.

Then, MRP uses the MPS to start generating planned orders. We then use Capacity Requirements Planning (CRP), to convert these planned orders and actual orders into the expected load for specific "work centers". A work center may be a work station, a set of work stations, a single machine, or a set of machines, used to complete an "operation". An operation can best be thought of as a step in the manufacturing process. For example, painting our bicycle frames would be a separate operation from welding the bicycle frame. CRP uses the "routing" to convert a planned order or actual order into the load for the work center. A routing includes all operations required to complete a manufacturing process. It also includes labor and machine requirements in the form of setup and run times for each operation. A routing is attached to an item much like a bill of materials is (each manufactured item will have a bill of materials and a routing).

Oh, but wait, there's more. Once the orders move out to the shop floor, we now have Production Activity Control (PAC), which consists of the detailed scheduling at the specific work centers. Here we have dispatch lists and input/output control and . . . well, you get the idea.

I think you can see how this can all seem intimidating to a small manufacturing company whose entire "materials division" consists of one guy named Larry. And while this standardized formal process for production planning certainly has its merits, I don't think it was ever intended that every company should follow this formal process to the letter.

Probably the greatest side-benefit to this standardized process is the standardized terminology that developed as part of it. While there is a lot of industry terminology thrown around that may mean different things to different people, almost all the terminology discussed here related to MRP is highly standardized and well-known throughout the manufacturing community (in great part due to the efforts of APICS). So as your careers take you from one manufacturing company to another, and from one software system to another, it is likely that planned orders, bills of materials, routings, operations, master production scheduling, capacity requirements planning, time fences, work centers, and MRP generations, will maintain the same definitions.

Finite versus infinite capacity scheduling.

The formalized process previously covered spent a lot of time checking capacity. The people creating the production plan needed to check it against resources requirements planning, the people putting together the master schedule needed to check it against rough-cut capacity, and then the MRP orders needed to be checked against capacity requirements planning. All this "checked against" language means someone is manually adjusting these schedules to work within capacity constraints.

So, if the computer can use the routings to calculate capacity requirements, and we know what our capacity is, why not just let the computer do all the scheduling and capacity checking and eliminate all this extra work? Well this is known as Finite Capacity Scheduling, and yes, it does exist. As the name implies, finite capacity scheduling involves scheduling within finite capacity constraints. Finite scheduling has been around for quite some time, and though it sounds like a great idea, very few manufacturers actually use it. Why? Well, for one, it's really hard to set up a finite capacity scheduling system, but the bigger reason is that our capacity probably isn't really finite. Well, let me restate that—our capacity probably is finite (there is a point at which we are truly at capacity) but most companies do have ways to adjust capacity at least a little.

I should note though that finite capacity systems are not "fixed capacity" systems. There's no reason why you can't change the capacity in your system to reflect any changes (even temporary ones) you make to your actual capacity. Therefore, there is no technical reason why finite capacity systems wouldn't work in any environment. It really comes down to a matter of practicality and personal preference. A finite capacity system puts hard constraints on how the system plans—that's kind of the whole idea. If the system thinks you don't have enough capacity to manufacture something, it won't create an order for it.

Here's a little analogy for the Star Trek nerds . . . er . . . I mean . . . fans. You recall all those times when Captain Kirk would want more power and Scottie would say "she can't take it, Captain" with that famous Scottie accent. Then Kirk would just do it anyway and they would miraculously escape impending doom. Well, if the Starship Enterprise had been set up with a control system that worked within the "finite" capacity of the ship (we'll assume Scottie set up the capacity parameters in the system), when Kirk goes to push the ship beyond its set capacity, the control system simply will not allow it. And subsequently, they all die. Yes, Spock too.

So the issues with finite capacity scheduling are:

1. You have to get the capacity right.
2. You have to get the labor, machine, and setup times right in the routings.
3. You have to be willing to work within these constraints.

In the real world, most companies find that not only can they not achieve all of those things, they probably cannot effectively achieve any of them. I want to make it clear that I am not dismissing finite capacity scheduling. I personally like the idea of finite scheduling, but I'm enough of a realist to acknowledge the difficulties of implementing these types of systems in the real world.

If we're not using finite capacity scheduling, we must be using infinite capacity scheduling, right? From MRPs perspective, the answer is, yes. MRP schedules planned orders based on need, and subsequently completely ignores any capacity issues. That's why we have Capacity Requirements Planning (CRP). CRP converts the schedule into loads on work centers, and if the load exceeds the capacity of a work center, it's up to you (a human being) to decide what to do about it.

More MRP stuff.

Nervousness in MRP.

We've talked about planned orders in MRP, but I want to do a quick review of planned orders and then talk about firm planned orders and some additional topics related to nervousness in MRP. When you run an MRP generation, MRP will use the bill-of-materials structure of your manufactured items to determine gross requirements for all components based on the date these components should be required. It then looks at your expected on-hand balances and inbound quantities (scheduled receipts) to determine if there are net requirements, and then uses your lot sizing rules to schedule planned orders to meet these net requirements. These planned orders are not only used as a "recommendation" for an actual production order, but are also used to calculate gross requirements for components further down in the bill-of-materials structure, which may subsequently create additional planned orders. For example, demand for a bicycle will create planned orders for the bicycle. The planned orders for the bicycle will create gross requirements— and subsequently create planned orders—for the wheels used in that bicycle. The planned orders for the wheels will then be used to create planned orders for the hubs, rims, spokes, nipples, and rim strips used to make the wheel. Planned orders for the hubs will then be used to create planned orders for the components that make up the hub.

The result is that you can have tens, or hundreds, or even thousands of planned orders for components that are all dependent on the demand for a single top-level item. So when demand for these top-level items change, these changes must be reflected in the gross requirements in all the lower-level components. Think of it this way, if we have a 13-week planning horizon, it means that our forecast for an end item 13 weeks from today is driving current planned orders for components. If you recall from the forecasting chapters, our week-13 forecast will likely be recalculated every week for the next 12 weeks using more current data. In addition, as real customer orders come in, these customer orders end up replacing the forecast and possibly changing demand in those periods. So every time we have these demand changes, MRP will recalculate gross and net requirements, and subsequently reschedule or change planned orders, or recommend changes to production orders or purchase orders already scheduled. These frequent changes in MRP are known as "nervousness", and can quickly become overwhelming for planners. Keep in mind that these changes are not only the result of MRP determining that you suddenly need more of something (or something sooner) because you had an increase in demand, but also the result of MRP determining that you don't need as much of something (or don't need it as soon) because demand turned out to be less than had been expected.

If you're running an MPS, you can use that to help control nervousness. Another partial solution to the problem of nervousness is the use of "firm planned orders". Unlike a planned order, which will be "re-planned" each time MRP runs—and subsequently change gross requirements for all lower-level components—a firm planned order is not re-planned by MRP. This doesn't completely eliminate nervousness since MRP can still create additional planned orders if there are net requirements beyond that of the firm planned order, but it does prevent all the de-expediting that occurs when actual demand turns out to be less than forecasted demand or when a forecast quantity is reduced. Firm planned orders are not really a separate type of planned order, instead, they are just a status you can use to prevent a planned order from being replanned by MRP.

This does bring up a flaw in MRP. More specifically, it's a flaw in how MRP and similar planning systems often deal with safety stock. If you recall, all reorder point calculations (MRP included) calculate reorder point as lead-time demand plus safety stock. And for the most part, this makes sense for determining when to place a replenishment order. However, what this means is your planning system may be planning as though safety stock cannot be used to cover demand. For example, if I have an item with a lead time of 10 days, a forecasted daily demand of 10 units, and a safety stock of 40 units, MRP will tell me to order when my inventory is at or below 140 units. So let's say I have 140 units on Monday and place a replenishment order to be received in 10 days. On Tuesday I ship 20 units to a customer, therefore I now have 120 units in stock. What my planning system sees, is that after it sets aside the safety stock of 40 units, I only have 80 available units, yet I have 9 days until my order comes in. It looks at my forecast of 10 units per day and thinks I will run out of inventory one day before my replenishment order comes in, so it may send me a message to expedite my order. It may also look to expedite pending orders for components. It does all this because it doesn't realize I can use my safety stock to cover this demand variability. It's not that MRP systems have to treat safety stock like this, only that some systems are designed to treat it this way.

A seemingly simple solution is to just have the planning system ignore safety stock when determining the need to expedite orders within the lead time of the item. While this helps some, it doesn't solve our problems related to planned orders scheduled out farther into our planning horizon that are driving orders for components. In these cases, we kind of do want MRP to use safety stock in the calculation, but at the same time, we kind of don't want it to be re-planning all components with small changes in demand. There are other ways to reduce some of this nervousness in MRP systems, but since they are not standardized, you will need to see what (if any) functionality your system may have in helping to reduce nervousness.

Time Fences.

In MRP, a time fence describes a time frame within which you want some control over changes to MPS and the production schedule. For example, you can say "we will not change the MPS within 30 days of the current date". The idea here is that if you determine there is a point at which changing the MPS or production schedule would result in more harm than the potential benefits of the change, you would want to have a policy to prevent (or at least limit) changes that occur in this time frame. Virtually every MRP implementation contains a discussion of time fences. Time fences are then set, and shortly after implementation it quickly becomes apparent that there really is not a commitment to these time fences and they eventually end up being ignored.

There are several problems with time fences, the biggest is that most companies don't have the discipline to stick with them. Sure, everyone will agree to a time fence but as soon as a big customer—or a little customer with a big mouth—needs something quick, well . . . you know what happens. The other problem with time fences is they assume all changes have the same impact. In many environments this just isn't the case. Some changes may have little or no negative impact, while others can be nearly catastrophic. So as much as I like the idea of time fences, the reality is that in most cases they are just guidelines. And not surprisingly, that is how MRP treats them. Though there is no reason why you can't program a system to prevent changes within a specified time frame, it's more likely you will just have a system give a warning when changes occur within a time fence.

My general recommendation here is that you educate your planners on the implications of schedule changes, provide some guidelines, and then monitor their performance to make sure they are making good decisions. You know, basic management stuff.

Regenerative MRP and Net Change MRP.

You often have choices on how to run MRP. Regenerative MRP is run as a batch program and will wipe out any existing planned orders (not firm planned orders) for all items, and pretty much start from scratch recalculating gross and net requirements and planned orders. On the other hand, net change MRP only recalculates gross and net requirements and planned orders for items (and components of items) that have had some type of change to planning data (change in on-hand balance, quantity on order, etc.). Net change MRP may be run as a batch program, or may be able to run real-time in a live environment (not all systems can do this).

I should note that running net change MRP real-time may not be the greatest idea in many environments. Planning data for a single item may change many times in a single day. Do you really want an item re-planned ten or twenty or a hundred times in a single day?

Regenerative MRP and net change MRP are not mutually exclusive. It's actually very common for manufacturers to run both. For example, a manufacturer may run net change MRP each night, and then run regenerative MRP once a week. Historically, a full regenerative MRP run could take many hours to run in an operation that had many SKUs and complex BOMs. This often made it impractical to run MRP frequently. Since net change MRP only runs for items that are impacted by recent changes, the processing time associated with running it frequently is much less. With significant increases in computer processing capabilities in recent years, this is not as much of an issue anymore for most companies running MRP, but it is still a consideration.

However, if you look at it another way, if net change MRP makes all the necessary changes without recalculating everything, why not just use it and eliminate regenerative MRP? Well, because (historically) MRP data tends to get a little funky over time. Some of this "funk" is either caused by or gets missed by net change MRP. Regenerative MRP generally does a better job of cleaning stuff up.

Scrap and yield rates.

The physical act of manufacturing something can lend itself to inconsistencies. These inconsistencies often result in scrap. Many (not all) MRP systems have functionality to include expected scrap into your inventory planning. I first need to clarify the difference between a scrap rate and a yield rate (note: these terms are not standardized and may mean different things in different systems). A scrap rate is generally the rate of expected scrap for specific components within the context of manufacturing an item. Therefore, a scrap rate would be attached to a specific component on the BOM for a specific item. For example, in assembling our bicycle wheels, we may have spokes and nipples that occasionally strip or fail to thread properly. What we would do here is try to estimate the expected scrap rate of these specific components, and then enter that as a scrap rate for these components on the bill of materials for each wheel assembly.

Yield rate, however, is used when you have situations where you must scrap the completed manufactured item. For example, if after we manufacture our bicycle frames we do an inspection and find that a certain percentage tend to be out of spec and are not worth reworking, we need a way to plan for this. In this case, we do not add the failure rate to the frames, but rather the percentage of good frames that are expected. And we do this at the frame level because it impacts the demand for all components used to make the bike frame.

So exactly what will scrap rates and yield rates do in your MRP system? This is where it gets a bit tricky because different systems handle this differently and may even have options that allow you to configure how this is handled. For example, scrap rates of components may be used to calculate gross requirements for components to be used in the planning process, but may or may not be reflected on the actual parts list that will be used to physically pick components when the manufacturing order is released to the floor. This is an area where you really need to consult the documentation for your specific system and do some testing before setting this up.

These scrap and yield rates are both directly related to the quantity being manufactured, but many manufacturing processes are also subject to setup scrap. Setup scrap is scrap that results from the act of starting up or setting up a production run, and therefore is not related to the quantity being run. For example, a printer may find that he generally needs to scrap the first 20 sheets that come off the printer as he tweaks settings and allows the ink to work through the printer. It doesn't matter if he is printing 500 or 50,000 sheets; he still generally needs to scrap 20 sheets. Once again, many MRP systems allow for planning of this type of scrap, but once again, check your documentation to see exactly how this works in your system.

Consumables and packaging materials on BOMs.

It's a bit surprising to see how many manufactures never consider incorporating consumables or packaging materials into their BOMs. For example, in our wheel and hub manufacturing process we add grease to the bearings of the hubs and use some type of thread compound on the threads of the spokes and nipples. If we then shipped our wheels to end-users or retailers, we would also require packaging materials for each wheel. Since the demand for these items is dependent demand that is directly related to the quantity of wheels being produced, why not use MRP to plan them? Some may say that they don't want to go through the bother of tracking inventory and entering transactions for these types of items, but many MRP systems have transactional methods that can do this automatically in the background (backflushing). So as long as you can determine with reasonable accuracy how much of this stuff you use to produce something, you may as well put it on the bills and take full advantage of your planning system.

Pseudo Bills, Phantom Bills, Planning Bills, Super Bills, Modular Bills?

There are some special types of BOMs that provide some very useful functionality. As far as all these different names for types of BOMs, I have to admit that I have a hard time remembering which is which (and I'm not sure there is even a difference between some of them). I'll use the names here the way I understand them, but the main point here is to understand the functionality available here, and then, if you find you could use such functionality, you can just check your system's documentation to see if it's available and how to set it up.

A Phantom bill of materials is a fictitious BOM created for common subassemblies or kits that you do not want to produce as separate items. For example, if you have a number of products that all use the same hardware, you can create a phantom bill for the hardware (as if it were a kit) and then just put the phantom item on the bills for all products that use it. Your MRP system will treat the phantom bill components as though they were part of the bill for the higher-level item (rather than treating it as a separate item that needs to be produced). Phantom items never actually exist, they are just a means for simplifying the management of your bills of materials.

For a more specific example, let's say I manufacture a whole bunch of items that all are assembled using 10 each of Bolt A, 10 each of Washer B, 10 each of Lock Washer C, and 10 Each of Nut D. Rather than having to duplicate this information on every one of those bills, I can create a phantom bill (and a phantom item), and then put the phantom item on the bills for all the other items. MRP will treat this as though you had the separate bolts, washers, and nuts on each bill. This not only makes the initial setting up of the BOMs easier, but also, if at some point in the future you change Bolt A to Bolt X and Nut D to Nut Y, you can just change it once on the phantom item rather than having to change all those bills.

Pseudo Bills, Planning Bills, Super Bills, Modular Bills are also types of fictitious bills of materials. However, in these cases, the bill is used to represent numerous products, or numerous configurations of products. For example, you may have a line of notebook computers where most of the components are the same, but some will have different hard drives, processors, memory, etc. Rather than creating separate bills for each possible combination, and then attempting to forecast each possible combination, you can create one large planning bill that contains all possible components but uses the "quantity per" to manage the options. If you expect half of the computers will use Drive A, 25% will use Drive B, and 25% will use Drive C, you would set up each drive on the bill, and use 0.50, 0.25, and

0.25 respectively as the quantity per. You would then proceed to do the same for all other options. Your higher-level forecast would then be for the total demand for all computers in this family. This way, you don't need to try to forecast how many will use the exact combination of Drive A, Processor B, and Memory C; or Drive B, Processor B, and Memory C; or Drive A, Processor A, and Memory C—which could be very difficult—but rather, just forecast how many computers will ship with each of these individual options.

When you go to manufacture these computers, you will need a means of creating the appropriate parts list showing the specific options chosen. This is sometimes accomplished through what is known as a "configuration processor". A configuration processor would be built into a sales order processing system, and allow the selection of the various available options (this assumes customer orders will drive the final assembly).

Planning Bill

Family - B2			Quantity 5,000	
	Item#	Desc	Qty. Per.	Qty. Rqd.
	FR7000SR	Mod 7000 Frame-Small-Red	0.04	200
	FR7000MR	Mod 7000 Frame-Med-Red	0.10	500
	FR7000LR	Mod 7000 Frame-Large-Red	0.02	100
	FR7000SB	Mod 7000 Frame-Small-Blue	0.06	300
	FR7000MB	Mod 7000 Frame-Med-Blue	0.14	700
	FR7000LB	Mod 7000 Frame-Large-Blue	0.04	200
	FR5000SB	Mod 5000 Frame-Small-Blue	0.15	750
	FR5000MB	Mod 5000 Frame-Med-Blue	0.35	1750
	FR5000LB	Mod 5000 Frame-Large-Blue	0.10	500
	BK001A	Build Kit Premium	0.30	1500
	BK001B	Build Kit Standard	0.70	3500

Figure 9H. Here we have an example of a planning bill for a product family (bicycles). What we have here or 2 frame models (7000 series and 5000 series). Each frame comse in 3 sizes, the 7000-series frame comes in 2 colors, while the 5000-series frame is only available in one color. Each frame model can be built up with either of the two build kits shown (a standard kit and a premium kit). Each build kit would have its own bill of materials, these build kits could be set up as physical kits, or they could be set up as phantom items.

If we look at the 7000-series small red frame, the quantity per of 0.04 means that we expect that 4% of our total bicycle sales for this family will use this frame (model, color, and size). If we then look at the premium build kit, we see that we expect that 30% of total bicycle sales for this family will use the premium build kit. We do not nead to know exactly how many small red 7000-series frames will use the premium build kit, only that 30% of the total bicycles in this family will use it. The Quantity Required column shows how we use the planning bill to calculate requirements for components based on a forecast of 5,000 units for the product family.

So what's the difference between pseudo, planning, super, and modular bills? Functionally, they are basically the same—or at least that's been my understanding. As best I can make out, sometimes one term is used over another to distinguish exactly how the bill is used. For example, if I create a bill for a specific model of computer that has various options, I may refer to it as a modular bill; however, if I create a higher-level bill that covers a whole family of computers (several models, each with options), I may call it a planning bill or a super bill. Once again, I suggest you focus on understanding the functionality you want, and then just check your system documentation to see how to set it up (and what your system supplier calls it).

The difference between BOMs and Parts Lists.

A parts list (also called a materials list) is a list of all components and quantities that are expected to be used to complete a specific production order. The parts list is used to allocate inventory, pull the parts to be used in the manufacturing process, and process the related transactions. The BOM is used to create the parts list, but once a parts list exists for a production order, it is an independent entity from the BOM. Therefore, you can change a parts list to reflect a temporary substitution for a component, or to customize a specific run of a product, without changing the BOM. Conversely, changes to the BOM do not affect any existing parts lists.

If this still sounds confusing, think of the BOM as a template that lists the components and quantities that you expect to use to manufacture something. Your planning system uses the BOM for planning purposes when a parts list does not yet exist. For example, when a planned order is created for a manufactured item, a parts list does not yet exist; therefore MRP will use the BOM to continue calculating demand of components. But, when a planned order is converted to an actual production order, the system will create a parts list based on the BOM and the planned order quantity. This parts list will be directly associated with the specific production order. From this point on, all planning and execution activities associated with this specific production order will use the parts list rather than the BOM.

Effective Dates.

BOMs (and routings) generally allow you to set effective dates on them. For example, if in our bicycle manufacturing operation we decide to start using a different headset on a specific model of bicycle starting in July, we can set the effective dates on the old headset to expire on Jun 30th, and then add the new headset with an effective date that starts July 1st. This not only allows you to set up changes to BOMs in advance of those changes occurring, but also provides a history of BOM changes. For example, many systems will allow you to inquire on a BOM by the effective date and see what the BOM was at that specific point in time. Note, we are not creating separate BOMs here, just putting different dates on the components on the same BOM.

Relationships between BOMs and Routings.

Each manufactured item will have a bill of materials and a routing attached to it. The BOM details the material requirements, while the routing details the labor and machine requirements. A routing is made up of one or more steps known as "operations". In many (not all) MRP systems, you can associate specific items on the BOM with specific operations in the routing. This can be useful when a significant amount of time occurs between starting the first operation in the routing, and the last operation in the routing, and different components are consumed at the various operations.

For example, let's say I "flattened" my bill of materials for manufacturing a bicycle. Rather than having a multi-level BOM where the bicycle was at the top level, and below that were subassemblies (such as the wheels and frame) that had their own BOMs, I would have all components on one BOM and have the wheel assembly and frame welding as steps in the routing (I just want to note this scenario is unlikely for bicycle manufacturing). By associating specific components with specific routing steps, I am able to associate my rim, spokes, etc. with the operation for wheel assembly, my frame components with the operation for frame welding, and purchased components such as the crankset, chain, pedals, and seat with the operation for final assembly. In doing this, MRP can more accurately plan the required dates based on the date the specific operation is expected to occur (this functionality may not be available in many MRP systems), but also assists in the physical processes of picking the materials for the specific routing steps, and performing the associated inventory transactions for these items.

Most manufacturers don't need to utilize this functionality, and many MRP systems (especially lower cost ones) aren't even capable of doing this, but I wanted to mention it because it can prove to be very useful in some environments.

Lot sizing in MRP.

Contrary to claims made by those pushing other methods, MRP does not cause large lot sizes. In fact, MRP and DRP have nothing to do with lot sizing other than executing the lot size you define. In other words, you tell MRP what you want to use for a lot size for each item, and it will then use that lot size.

What's wrong with MRP?

This is the part where I get to start telling you about all the little cheats and flaws in your MRP system. To be honest—with the exception of the occasional bug in a specific MRP software product and the previously mentioned problem with how it treats safety stock—MRP is functionally a very solid system for planning dependent demand items. As I mentioned earlier, MRP is just a whole bunch of simple math used to extend demand from manufactured items to the components used to manufacturer them.

BUT, there are a lot of companies that have experienced serious problems after implementing MRP. I'm not just talking about the typical problems associated with getting a new software program up and running, but also serious operational problems that occur as a direct result of their MRP system. When I say "their MRP system" I'm referring to the MRP software they are using, combined with the way they set it up. The latter is of particular importance here.

The main issue here is that MRP is highly dependent upon reasonably accurate data. This doesn't just mean that your inventory balances, forecasts, and BOMs are correct, but also that your routings are correct. As mentioned earlier, MRP uses the setup, run, and queue times from your routings and work centers to calculate manufacturing lead time. If you tell MRP there is a queue time of two days between welding and drilling, MRP will plan that every order will sit for two days between the welding and drilling operations. This should not surprise anybody.

Unfortunately, when people set up their shiny new MRP system, they tend to exaggerate queue times, setup times, and run times. Part of this is because the manufacturing folks do not want to be caught underperforming if they can't produce at the rate they set up in the system. The other part is just pure stupidity on how companies sometimes go about getting these numbers. "Hey Fred, how long does stuff usually sit between welding and drilling?" is not a very accurate way of determining queue times.

The result of these inaccuracies can be disastrous. After MRP adds up all the exaggerated queue times and setup times at each step of the routing and at each level in the BOM structure, it then schedules component receipts and manufacturing start dates accordingly. You soon find your storage areas and shop floor will quickly be overflowing with component and in-process materials, your inventory investment will be through the roof, your inability to meet your previous lead times will be creating friction with customers, your constant rescheduling and expediting will have your planners and shop floor personnel looking through the want-ads, and your local fire inspector is writing you up for code violations due to all that stuff being piled where it doesn't belong.

Then in walks a Lean consultant who starts preaching the evils of MRP and forecasting. He tells you that you're pushing when you should be pulling, and batching when you should be one-piece-flowing, and suddenly you're ready to chuck it all without ever truly understanding what went wrong. Well what went wrong here is your system did exactly what you told it to do. So what you need to do here is figure out what you really want it to do, and then set it up to do that. If you don't want piles of inventory sitting around for days before each operation, reduce the queue times you set up in the system. You just need to realize the stuff is sitting there because you told MRP you wanted it to sit there. If long manufacturing lead times combined with difficulty in forecasting demand that far into the future are creating problems for you, you need to look at ways of reducing setup times, run times, and lot sizes. It's not MRP that is creating these problems, it's your setup of MRP and your decisions related to your manufacturing processes.

Now there are some other problems that are common with MRP systems. I want to note that none of these problems are intrinsic to MRP, but rather they are just common in MRP systems. In other words, there is nothing in MRP that creates these problems. It's just a matter of the functionality in many of the software packages sold as MRP systems.

One of the big ones is that MRP systems tend to be better at planning than execution. So if you tell MRP what finished items you want and when you want them, MRP will tell you which components you will need and when you will need them. MRP does this very well (assuming you set it up correctly). However, when it comes to scheduling and coordinating the shop-floor activities required to manufacture these products, many MRP systems fall short.

In addition, MRP systems tend to assume that if they (the MRP systems) told you what components were needed and when they were needed (via planned orders), that these component would in fact be in stock and available on those dates. So when it comes to the recommended start date for assembling 50 units of a specific wheel, MRP tells you to start the order regardless of whether or not you have enough components in stock. It may be that you have enough components for 48 wheels and that you only really need 20 wheels (the quantity of 50 came from your lot sizing rules), but a typical MRP system does not have the functionality to work this out on its own. Instead, it will typically create a planned order for 50 units. The planner will then convert this to an actual production order and then run a shortage report. The shortage report will show that they do not have enough of a specific component to make the 50 units, and it will be up to the planner to decide what to do. I understand that it's difficult to create a system to make all these decisions, but my big gripe with this shortage situation is that almost every MRP system I've encountered does basically the same thing. It creates the planned order and doesn't provide any information to the planner about the shortage. Instead, the planner needs to go through the process of creating a production order and then running a shortage report before realizing that they need to change something.

As to the shop-floor-level execution issues, the reality is manufacturing processes can vary greatly and while these "generic" MRP systems can be configured to the inventory planning needs of diverse operations, it's a bit much to expect them to be configurable enough to meet the wide range of shop-floor execution needs encountered. Hence, the growing market for Manufacturing Execution Systems (MES).

I also want to briefly mention another common MRP setup issue. Just because the functionality exists, doesn't mean you have to use it. I had previously mentioned that you don't have to run a formal Master Production Scheduling (MPS) process if you don't need it. In addition, you don't need to setup complex routings or multi-level bills if they don't provide operational benefits for you. Routings can be especially dangerous in the wrong hands. For example, when setting up a routing for wheel assembly (I'm back to assembling the wheel as a separate item here), I can choose to have a routing with just a single operation called "wheel assembly", or I can get carried away and create one operation for "wheel preparation", another for "wheel assembly", another for "wheel dishing", another for "truing and tensioning", and another for "final inspection and packaging". I could then set up the system to require that I report production at each step in the routing because this allows me to track my costs at a greater level of detail. But in the process of doing this, I have added a whole bunch of additional production-reporting requirements that not only consume additional labor, but also may force me to change my wheel-assembly process to more accurately track these steps as separate operations. While this may have made sense to systems guys and accountants looking at flow charts, it creates a ridiculously cumbersome process on the shop floor. Similar problems can be created when the realization that you can now have multi-level bills is so exciting that you start creating multi-level bills where there isn't a real need for them.

DRP and Multi-plant MRP.

The "multi-plant" part of Multi-plant MRP is essentially the same functionality that makes up Distribution Requirements Planning (DRP). In other words, MRP+ DRP = Multi-plant MRP. To keep things simple here I'm just going to refer to this functionality as DRP, but will show how it integrates with MRP.

We have already covered how the main objective of MRP is to use the demand for higher-level items to drive the demand for lower-level (dependent) items. Similarly, the main objective of DRP is to use demand at downstream facilities to drive demand at upstream (supplying) facilities. The logic used in DRP is really just an extension of MRP logic.

We'll start with a simple example. Let's say I have a large centrally located distribution center (DC) that I use to supply several smaller regional distribution centers. Without a system like DRP, I would probably end up planning inventory separately at each DC. For example, each regional DC would have its own inventory planning system and place orders on the central DC when they needed replenishment. The central DC would have its own planning system and essentially treat the regional DCs as though they were separate entities (the same way it would treat a customer).

Subsequently, each regional DC and the central DC are likely forecasting demand in isolation of each other and there is no visibility between the DCs on inventory levels and actual demand. This is known as a "disconnected" supply chain, and while you may have no choice but to be disconnected with external customers and suppliers, there is no reason to be disconnected from your own internal customers and suppliers.

This is where DRP comes into play. Like MRP, DRP also calculates gross requirements and net requirements, and then uses the net requirements combined with lot-size rules to create planned orders. But where MRP would use planned orders to drive gross requirements of components based on a bill of materials,

DRP uses planned orders to drive gross requirements at a supplying facility based on a DRP relationship (sometimes called a bill of distribution). In its simplest form, a DRP relationship specifies a supply relationship between facilities, and a lead time. The supply relationship simply shows that Facility A supplies Facility B for this specific item, while the lead time generally represents the transportation lead time between facilities. This is really all DRP needs to "connect" the planning systems of these facilities.

As an example, if I set up Facility A to supply Item X to Facility B with a transportation lead time of one week, any planned order for item X in Facility B will automatically show up as a gross requirement in Facility A one week earlier. In addition, whenever a planned order for Item X in Facility B is converted into an actual order (a scheduled receipt), it automatically (in most DRP systems) creates an actual order (some type of shipping order) in Facility A. Therefore, DRP not only handles the planning across plants, but also the execution of transferring the materials.

Why DRP?

To better explain the advantages of DRP over a disconnected supply chain, we need to talk about visibility. If I'm a supplier in a disconnected supply chain, my visibility is pretty much limited to my shipping records (I know what I shipped), any current actual customer orders I have in my system, and my forecast. If demand is very stable this type of system can work reasonably well, but when demand changes at my customers' locations, my only way of seeing these demand changes is through the orders they place on me. However, depending on their ordering policies, that can take quite a bit of time, and, if they change their ordering policies, I might mistake those order policy changes for demand changes. For example, if a supplier changes their lot sizing rules and suddenly orders a larger quantity than they normally do, I may think that implies increased demand at their location, and subsequently increase my forecast (remember that whole "bullwhip effect" discussion), when all it really means is they changed their lot size and will be ordering less frequently.

On the other hand, if demand at a specific customer suddenly changes for one of the items I supply to him, I will not see that change in demand until he either places an order earlier than I expected, or doesn't place an order when I expected (based on my forecasts). Let me provide a more detailed example of this. Let's say I supply two retailers that compete with each other. At the beginning of October, I supply each retailer with 500 units of an item. This would generally cover about two month's demand for each of them. One month later, one of the customers is placing a rush replenishment order for 500 more units. In a disconnected supply chain I may assume this to be an increase in demand and adjust my forecast (and inventory) accordingly. But what I didn't know, was my other customer hadn't sold any of the 500 units I shipped to him. This was because the first customer dropped his sell price and subsequently everybody was now buying this specific product from him. So, although I do have an unexpected early shipment to this customer, my long-term forecast should not change, because overall demand for this product has not really changed (it just moved between my customers).

As another example, let's say that one of my items is primarily supplied to one customer and he generally orders the equivalent of three month's demand at a time. Immediately after filling an order for him, his demand suddenly drops off dramatically. Meanwhile, my planning system still plans as though I will be providing him with a similar sized order in about three months. So three months later, I have a bunch of inventory that I'm expecting him to buy, while he's still sitting on most of the last shipment I sent him and is probably thinking about returning some of it to me.

The problem in these scenarios is a lack of visibility. If I could see what is actually happening at my customers' locations, I can more quickly adapt to changing demand and eliminate reacting to perceived demand changes that are really just the result of their ordering calculations. To do this, I would need to be able to see their current on-hand inventory, inbound quantities, customer orders, safety stock requirements, lot sizes, and forecasts. Or would I? In a DRP scenario, the planned orders generated at the customer's location are actually the result of their current on-hand inventory, inbound quantities, customer orders, safety stock requirements, lot sizes, and forecasts. Therefore, by funneling their planned orders into my calculations for gross requirements, I am automatically taking all those things into account.

In fact, with DRP I don't need to adjust the forecast at the supplying facility, because there is no forecast at the supplying facility (in a typical DRP setup). The forecasts exist where the demand actually occurs, because theoretically, that is the best place to forecast demand. This isn't to say that the task of forecasting has to physically take place at the specific facility where actual demand occurs. You can still centrally manage your distribution and manufacturing inventory if you choose. In fact, I'm a big proponent of centrally managed inventory in distribution networks (can be trickier in manufacturing). My reasoning is primarily related to the skill set required for forecasting and related inventory management tasks. I find it's usually more effective to have a person or small group of people who are highly skilled at inventory management performing these critical tasks for all facilities using the facility-specific data, rather than trying to get individuals at each facility to do this independently.

Multi-directional DRP?

In a conventional DRP system, demand (for planning purposes) only flows in one direction. Therefore, if I tell DRP that DC#1 supplies Item X to DC#2 and DC#3, and end up in a situation where I am out of stock in DC#1 and DC#2, but have excess stock in DC#3, DRP is not smart enough to figure out that I can ship some of the inventory from DC#3 to DC#1 and DC#2 to meet their needs. This isn't to say that someone can't manually create interplant transfer orders to do this, and if they do, DRP will generally take these transfer orders into account in the planning process.

I should note here that the flow of demand between facilities is item dependent. So you can have DC#1 supply Item X to DC#2, and then have DC#2 supply Item Y to DC#1. So in that respect, DRP is multi-directional since different items can flow in different directions, but a single item can only have one direction of demand flow. You can, however, have many points in this flow of demand. For example, you could set up DC#1 to supply Item X to DC#2, then set up DC#2 to supply Item X to DC#3, then set up DC#3 to supply Item X to DC#4. What you can't have is what is known as a "circular reference". In the previous example, if I then tried to set up DC#4 to supply Item X to DC#1, I should receive an error (hopefully) since this would create a logic problem (think about it). What you also can't have is a facility being supplied by more than one other facility. Once again, this is a logic issue because DRP needs to know exactly where to flow the demand. But you obviously can have a facility supply multiple other facilities.

For the most part, this is exactly how you want DRP to work, but I think it's important to mention that there is no reason why you could not create a DRP-like system that had more advanced functionality. The key here would be to set "conditions" under which demand could flow in a different direction. As long as these conditions are clearly defined such that demand only flows in one direction within a specific set of conditions, there is no logical reason why you could not make such a system work. Though there is no "logical" reason why you can't make such a system, there may very well be some "practical" reasons. Putting together the logic for such a system could get very complicated, and I would not recommend it unless you feel you have a significant need for such a system.

Multi-plant MRP.

As I previously mentioned, multi-plant MRP is just MRP plus DRP. A typical example would be having demand flow from regional distribution centers back to the main manufacturing plant. In this example, DRP works exactly as it would in a distribution environment, except that once it hits the manufacturing plant, MRP takes over and the demand flows through the BOMs, creating gross requirements for components.

But, multi-plant MRP/DRP environments can be much more complex. For example, you can have a complex distribution network made up of large centrally located DCs supplying regional DCs, which then supply local retail locations. The centrally located DCs may then be supplied by multiple manufacturing plants, which may have subassemblies supplied between the manufacturing plants and may even have components supplied from the regional DCs that are also used to supply finished goods to the retail locations. Additional complexities may include an East Coast DC and a West Coast DC that receive items from overseas and subsequently supply back to the manufacturing plants and central DC as well as directly to some regional DCs and some local retailers. While this sounds extremely complex overall, the logical flow is rather simple when you look at it on an item-by-item basis. However, I should note here that there are sometimes glitches in MRP/DRP in these more complex setups. These "glitches" can usually be traced back to how the specific MRP/DRP program sequences its calculations. So as always, "test, test, and test some more".

Planned orders, firm planned orders, quantity on receipt, outbound quantity, quantity in transit.

In DRP, planned orders and firm planned orders generally work exactly the same as they do in MRP. However, once a planned order is converted to an actual order, things change. In DRP, these orders are usually called transfer orders. Once a transfer order is created it will show a quantity on receipt in the destination facility and an outbound quantity in the supplying facility. Once the order ships, it will still show as a quantity on receipt in the destination facility, but will move from an outbound quantity in the supplying facility to an in-transit quantity. Not all DRP systems use an in-transit quantity—though they should. Not only does the in-transit quantity allow for better visibility of where inventory is, but it is also used as part of the accounting system to track the value of this inventory, since it likely has been removed from the inventory account in the shipping plant once it ships.

Lot sizing in a multi-location distribution network.

Chapter 7 covered lot sizing, but focused on lot sizing where there was only a single point of distribution. When it comes to distribution networks—where the same product has several points of distribution—there are some additional factors that come into play. Primarily, you now have a situation where a lot-size decision in one facility can affect the costs at the supplying facility. Since both the destination facility and supplying facility are within the same business, these "new costs" are now part of our decision. So what are these costs? Well for one, the order costs now not only include the order processing costs at the destination facility, but also the order processing costs at the supplying facility. For example, the cost associated with physically picking the order and preparing it for shipment should now be included. Once again, this should only be the costs associated with the instance of an order, not with the quantity being processed. And while we're on order costs, I should note that the order costs associated with an internal transfer order are different from the order costs you would have calculated for a vendor-supplied item because the processing should be much simpler (no invoicing, payments, vendor communications, plus hopefully a more streamlined receiving process).

We calculated order costs before, so it really shouldn't be a problem to calculate order costs in our distribution network. The tricky part comes when we start looking at carrying costs. It's easy enough to calculate what the carrying cost would be at the destination facility, but does the order quantity at the destination facility change the carrying cost at the supplying facility? This is a tough question to answer since you have to look at the characteristics of the specific distribution network, ordering system used, and how lot sizes and safety stocks are calculated. It really does get very complicated. In fact, it gets so complicated, that I'm not even going to get into it here. Instead, I want to spend some time on a more practical approach to lot sizing in a distribution network that can provide some effective results.

First I want to describe how order quantities are frequently handled in distribution networks. Lot sizing at the main DC is generally handled either by an EOQ-type calculation or some subjective fixed-time-period supply calculation. But when it comes to the satellite facilities (regional DCs or retail locations), they will almost always go with a small fixed-time-period supply calculation that results in frequent very small quantity shipments.

For example, let's take a small distribution network that consists of one main DC feeding five satellite warehouses. We have an item that has forecasted demand at each satellite warehouse of 10 units per week, and we are using a two-week supply as our order quantity at the satellite warehouses. The main DC has an order quantity of 500 units. Subsequently, what we have here is a main DC ordering the equivalent of 10-week's supply at a time (500 units), then feeding the satellite warehouses smaller shipments every two weeks (20 units per shipment). When analyzing this policy, the most obvious question to ask is, if we are getting a 10-week's supply at the main warehouse, why not just split that into 10-week's supply for each of the satellite warehouses and send them each one shipment (a practice known as "fair-share distribution")?

Well here's why most companies don't do this. First, their planning software probably doesn't have the functionality to do this (though some do). And second, if they ship all the inventory to the satellite warehouses right away, then, if one of the warehouses has higher demand than forecasted, it will run out before the others and there will not be anything remaining at the main DC to resupply them.

That certainly makes a lot of sense, but now we need to think about the downside of using the smaller more frequent replenishment quantities to the satellite warehouses. The most obvious downside is that you are pouring more labor into the process since you will need to process 25 replenishment orders (planning time, order processing, picking, shipping, receiving, putaway) to the satellite warehouses instead of 5 (based on our example).

The other issue relates to the inherent buffer larger lot sizes provide against demand variability (this was covered in the safety stock chapter). Now you may be thinking that by keeping most of the inventory at the main DC, you are therefore providing a buffer that can be used to quickly resupply a satellite warehouse if it gets a spike in demand. And that is correct, but what is being traded off here is the immediate buffer this inventory could provide if it were already at the satellite warehouses. This is an aspect of small replenishment quantities in distribution networks that is very much underestimated.

Fair-share distribution.

I am a big fan of fair-share distribution, and think that it should be strongly considered for any distribution network where multiple facilities are being supplied the same items. However, implementing fair-share is not as simple as it sounds. First off, though I mentioned that some software systems have fair-share functionality, it may not be adequate to meet your needs. That's because the simple application of fair share distribution previously described is not the most effective. I recommend a slightly more complex (no surprise here) fair-share distribution method that takes into account variability and order cycles. This is sort of a compromise that allows you to get most of the benefit of fair-share distribution, but also allows some of the advantages of keeping some inventory at the main DC under certain circumstances.

In the earlier example where I received a lot size equivalent to a 10-week's supply at the main DC, I may want to immediately ship 8-week's supply to each satellite warehouse, then, when one of the warehouses starts running low (at reorder point), distribute the remaining inventory based on current conditions. This provides a buffer at the satellite warehouses immediately when the first shipment arrives, but leaves some buffer at the main DC that can be used to adjust the second shipment based on actual demand that occurred during the 8 weeks.

However, in this same operation, if I were to receive a lot size equivalent to just 3 or 4 week's supply at the main DC, I may want to distribute the entire quantity at once since I am dealing with a shorter order cycle. To complicate this further, this decision is not just related to the order cycle (the result of lot size) at the main DC, but also related to the variability of the specific item (or item group) relative to this order cycle. The greater the variability over the order cycle, the more likely I am to keep some inventory at the main DC. But also, the greater the variability over the order cycle, the more likely I am to keep a larger portion of the inventory at the main DC.

I'm not going to go into a whole new safety-stock-type calculation to be used for this, but similar logic would apply. Probably what you would end up doing here is to put together a relatively simple matrix that you would use as a cheat for the system to use to determine when and how to distribute the inventory. For example, you may decide to designate three demand variability groups (high demand variability, medium demand variability, low demand variability) then assign these groups to your items. You would then set distribution rules based on order cycles within each group. For example, in your high-demand-variability group, you may set it such that if you receive a quantity equivalent to four-week's demand or less, you distribute it all right away, but if it is greater than four-week's demand, you will initially ship 70% and hold the remaining 30% for a later shipment. However, in your low demand variability group, you may set it such that if you receive a quantity equivalent to ten-week's demand or less, you distribute it all right away, but if it is greater than ten-week's demand, you ship 80% and hold the remaining 20% for a later shipment.

I also need to describe fair-share distribution in a little more detail here since the previous example where you have five warehouses with equal demand and would just equally divide the receipt at the main DC between the satellite warehouses, is not very realistic. Plus, the calculation needs to take into account safety stock and current on-hand balances at each facility, along with forecasts, and then use this to calculate how much to ship to each facility to bring them up to the same level (expressed in time).

Let's try an example.

In Figure 9I, you can see an item forecast and requirements calculations for three retail locations. I've limited the detail shown in an effort to make the key inputs to our fair-share distribution calculation more obvious, but essentially what we are doing here is reducing the current on-hand quantity by the safety stock quantity for each retail location, then subtracting the forecast from each period from this to show our net requirements (once a net requirement shows up in a period, all subsequent periods will have a net requirement equal to the forecast). We then calculate a cumulative net requirement to show the total net requirements up to each forecast period.

We can now add up the cumulative net requirements for all retail locations to get our Total Cumulative Net Requirements. Now all we need to do is take our receipt quantity at the main distribution center and compare it to the total cumulative net requirements to see which period our receipt quantity matches (or comes close to). So, if we had a receipt of 500 units, we can see that it would cover all our expected demand through week #8. We can then look at the cumulative net requirement for week #8 for each retail location, and use this as our fair share distribution. Therefore, based on our example, we would ship 255 units to Retail Location #1, 120 units to Retail Location #2, and 125 units to Retail Location #3.

This assumes that we wanted a single (one-time) distribution of the total receipt quantity. However, had we set up a more complex system based on the order cycle and variability of this specific item, and therefore determined that we would initially only ship 70% of the receipt and hold the remaining 30% to be redistributed later, we now would be shipping only 350 units (70% of 500). There may be an inclination here to just take 70% of each quantity we were going to ship to each retail location, but this would not do what we want it to do (cover the demand for each location to a specific point in time). So instead, we again look at our total cumulative net requirements to see which period matches our quantity of 350 units. We can see that week #6 has a total cumulative net requirement of 355 units; since this isn't an exact match, we'll have to adjust our quantities a little bit. Subsequently, we would ship roughly 183 units, 78 units, and 89 units to retail locations #1, #2, and #3 respectively.

The remaining 150 units would be distributed when one of the retail locations reaches its reorder point. At that point, we would go through our calculation again, using the on-hand balances, safety stock, and forecasts as of that date.

Fair-share distribution

Periods (weeks)	1	2	3	4	5	6	7	8	9	10	11
Retail Location #1 (on hand = 60, Safety stock =20)											
Forecast	35	35	40	40	40	35	35	35	30	30	25
Net Requirements	0	30	40	40	40	35	35	35	30	30	25
Cumulative Net Requirements	0	30	70	110	150	185	220	255	285	315	340
Retail Location #2 (on hand = 100, Safety stock =15)											
Forecast	25	30	30	30	25	25	20	20	20	25	20
Net Requirements	0	0	0	30	25	25	20	20	20	25	20
Cumulative Net Requirements	0	0	0	30	55	80	100	120	140	165	185
Retail Location #2 (on hand = 40, Safety stock =10)											
Forecast	15	15	20	25	25	20	20	15	15	20	15
Net Requirements	0	0	20	25	25	20	20	15	15	20	15
Cumulative Net Requirements	0	0	20	45	70	90	110	125	140	160	175
Total Cumulative Net Requirements	0	30	90	185	275	355	430	500	565	640	700

Figure 9I. Here we have an example of how to calculate cumulative net requirements for an item sold through 3 retail locations. We can then use the total cumulative net requirements to identify the period in which our net requirement matches the inventory quantity we want to distribute among the 3 retail locations. We then use the cumulative net requirements for that period for each item to calculate our distribution quantities.

There are some other factors that need to be considered when determining how you distribute in this type of network. A significant one is space availability at the facilities. It's not unusual to set a max inventory level for specific items within specific facilities. You can still use the fair-share distribution calculation; you just need to add some programming to limit the quantity to prevent it from bringing the on-hand quantity to a quantity greater than the capacity at that facility.

Well I hope you enjoyed this little diversion into fair-share distribution. As I said before, I'm a big fan of fair-share distribution and see it as a very effective means of managing multi-facility distribution inventory. Though many systems have fair-share distribution functionality built into them, they likely don't have the type of functionality I described here. So until the software suppliers get around to reading my book and upgrading their systems accordingly, you'll likely need to modify your system to get this level of functionality.

And I guess I should mention that the fair-share functionality I described in this chapter is just another cheat. If you really want to "optimize" multi-facility inventory, you need to explore "supply-chain optimization". But even then, be prepared for a whole bunch of additional cheats because, for all practical purposes, true supply-chain optimization is a myth. Yes, it sounds great in theory, but at some point you're going to find that it's just impractical to accurately account for every variable in your supply chain.

Summary.

If you are a manufacturer, you either already are or probably should be using an MRP system. And while there are criticisms of MRP, there really isn't a practical alternative. The fact is, the logic used by MRP to explode and time-phase requirements from manufactured items to their components, makes perfect sense. Problems with MRP tend to be more related to decisions made in how MRP is set up in a specific environment, a lack of accurate data, or deficiencies in the specific MRP product being used.

Though this chapter should have provided you with an understanding of the logic used by MRP/DRP, there is much more you need to know before implementing an MRP system. First and foremost, you need to spend some significant time reading the documentation for the specific MRP/DRP system you intend to use. Though there are many similarities among various MRP/DRP systems, there are also plenty of system-specific peculiarities that you are going to need to be familiar with.

I would also recommend reading one or two more books that focus on MRP specifically. There are quite a few MRP books available, and don't worry if the books you choose were published ten or more years ago, because MRP really hasn't changed much over the years. You may also want to consider getting involved with your local APICS chapter (www.apics.org). APICS has had a very close relationship with MRP over the years and offers a variety of educational programs. In fact, the CPIM certification program they offer is so closely tied to MRP that it could easily be considered an MRP certification program.

10

Measurement and Analysis

Most businesses that carry saleable inventory will have some form of measurement relative to that inventory, but very few put adequate emphasis on analysis as a critical inventory management function. I've already come clean about being a bit of a data geek, so it shouldn't be any surprise that I'm going to spend some time promoting analysis over simple measurement.

Why analysis?

Analysis is where knowing happens (hey, that sounds kind of quote-worthy). Through analysis, you can validate or invalidate what you think you know about your operations. In addition, analysis can lead you to answers to questions you never even thought to ask. Your data represents a detailed factual account of your business, unaffected by personal biases or preconceived notions. Analysis of this data can provide a clear window into your operation that cannot effectively be achieved through any other means.

This doesn't mean analysis is always clean or "right". Most businesses will have some bad data, but even then, analysis is the best tool to identify and correct it. The larger danger in analysis comes down to a lack of understanding of the underlying data. Analysis isn't just about crunching numbers; it's about pulling meaningful information from your data. To produce this meaningful information, you need to have a clear understanding of the physical and transactional operations in your business that produce this data. For example, if you are analyzing raw sales data (actual sales orders) to accumulate inventory demand information, you need to know if your company does direct shipments, and, if so, how to segregate the direct-ship sales records from the ship-from-stock sales records. A failure to recognize the need to do this could result in some misleading analysis, and subsequently could result in incorrect decisions being made.

Not surprisingly, much of what we call "measurement" in the inventory management community is flawed. This isn't meant to imply that these measurements serve no purpose, only that to use these measurements without understanding their flaws and limitations can result in flawed decisions being made relative to these measurements. This will become more obvious later.

But first I want to talk a little about "management by exception". Earlier in this book I briefly talked about the changing role of inventory managers and how efforts need to migrate towards managing the system (system setup, item setup), and then letting the system handle most of the daily inventory planning tasks. However, it can be difficult to set up an inventory system that can handle every combination of variables that may be encountered; that's where management-by-exception comes in. Once you have your system set up to handle most of your inventory planning activities, you need to monitor your system and try to identify situations that could result in "bad" planning decisions or other types of problems.

And you achieve this through—yes, you guessed it—analysis. By analyzing the characteristics of your inventory and the outputs of the various calculations you are using, you will find situations where corrections or adjustments need to be made. By focusing your time on these exceptions, you can find ways to adjust your system (tweak your settings) to automatically handle them in the future, or, set up a formal process for manually dealing with them when they come up. In either case, you are making much better use of your time and achieving more effective and more consistent inventory planning

Keep this in mind as we progress though this chapter, since the primary purpose of measurement and analysis is to monitor processes. If your measurement/analysis would not result in an action if a certain result turns up, then there really is no reason to be doing it in the first place.

Service Levels.

Measuring service levels is incredibly important because it is the primary aspect of inventory management that directly affects your customers, and depending on the nature of your business, may have an immediate impact on your bottom line. In ship-from-stock operations (such as a retail fulfillment operation), service levels would likely be measured as some form of a fill rate. In make-to-order manufacturing operations, service levels would likely be measured as on-time delivery (OTD).

Fill rates.

Fill rates are measurements that calculate the percentage of line items, orders, pieces (also called units), or dollars that are filled complete on the requested date. I briefly covered this earlier but will run though it in more detail here. A line item is a detail line on an order that represents a quantity requested for a specific item on a specific date, while pieces are the individual units requested. Therefore, if I go online and place an order for 1 motherboard, 1 processor, 2 memory modules, and 2 hard drives, this would be considered 1 order, 4 line items, and 6 pieces. If this was the only order scheduled to be shipped and they were short one of the hard drives, their fill-rate measurements for the day would be 0% order fill rate (since the order could not be filled complete), 75% line fill rate (since only 3 of the 4 lines could be filled complete), and 83.3% piece fill rate (since only 5 of the 6 total pieces ordered could be filled). If the total ordered amount was $500, and the sell price for the hard drive that did not ship was $100, then the dollar fill rate would be 80%. Line fill tends to be the most useful fill-rate measurement, but that isn't to say order fill, piece fill, and dollar fill, don't serve a purpose. Since these are all easily calculated, I recommend measuring all of them.

Fill rates

		Quantity Ordered	Quantity Shipped	Backor- dered	Amount Ordered	Amount Shipped
Order#12345						
	Item A	5	5		$37.50	$37.50
	Item B	20	20		$55.00	$55.00
	Item C	2	2		$50.60	$50.60
	Item D	15	10	5	$52.80	$35.20
	Item E	7	7		$44.38	$44.38
Order #12346						
	Item B	10	10		$27.50	$27.50
	Item F	34	34		$43.18	$43.18
	Item G	3	3		$41.58	$41.58
Order #123457						
	Item A	2	2		$15.00	$15.00
	Item D	4	0	4	$14.08	$0.00
	Item H	1	1		$53.70	$53.70
Order #123457						
	Item C	1	1		$25.30	$25.30
Totals		104	95	9	$460.62	$428.94

Fill rates

Order fill rate	50.0%	4 total orders, 2 filled complete
Line fill rate	83.3%	12 total lines ordered, 10 filled complete
Unit fill rate	91.3%	104 total units ordered, 95 units shipped
Dollar fill rate	93.1%	$460.62 dollars ordered, $428.94 dollars shipped

Figure 10A. Here is an example of typical fill-rate measurements. In this example we have 4 orders with a total of 12 line items. Apparently we must have run out of stock of Item D during the day, so we had one line item partially filled and another that could not be filled at all. As you can see, each fill-rate measurement provides a very different result.

Though measuring fill rates seems fairly simple, there is one potential flaw in fill-rate measurements that has proven to be a significant problem in a growing number of businesses. That is, the measurement assumes you have a means of tracking line items that customers wanted, but there was inadequate inventory to fill. In the old days of mailed in, faxed in, or phoned in orders, this was possible by having your order department enter all line items regardless of whether or not they could be filled and whether or not your customers accepted backorders.

But with web-based ordering systems or other technology advances that allow your customers to check availability before completing or placing their orders, you may lose some or all visibility to instances where a customer wanted something but did not place an order because the item was out of stock. I have no doubt there are more than a few companies that blissfully sat back watching their fill rates gradually climb as their customer base slowly moved towards using their online ordering system. These companies may have never realized the "observed" increase in fill rates had no basis in reality. I'll cover this more later.

Tolerances are sometimes used in fill-rate measurements to allow a line item or order to be considered "filled" if the filled quantity or amount is within a pre-defined level. For example, if they were able to ship 90% of the quantity ordered on a line, they may consider it as filled even though they did not fill it complete. Personally, I'm not a big fan of using tolerances in fill-rate measurements. My preference would be to conduct your main fill-rate measurement without tolerances, and then provide some additional analysis that shows more detail on these partially filled lines or orders.

On-time delivery (OTD).

In its most basic form, on-time delivery is no different from the fill-rate measurements already described. However, OTD measurements often provide a greater emphasis on the requested date (or promised date) as a key portion of the measurement. Obviously, the requested date was already a key part of the fill-rate measurements we covered, but with OTD, the date portion of the measurement is sometimes taken to a whole 'notha level by breaking the measurement down further relative to time.

To start an OTD (or fill-rate) measurement, you need to have a date as a basis for the measurement. In typical fill-rate measurements, it's generally the requested date or a date within a period of time after the date the order was entered. For example, an online retailer may have a policy of shipping orders within two days of the order being entered. In this case, the fill-rate measurement would be based on the order date plus two days.

In manufacturing operations, this can get a bit more complicated. In some cases, the date is based on a published lead time for the particular item being ordered. This is similar to the previous example except that different items may have different lead times. In other cases, there may be a date that is essentially a mutually agreed upon shipping date. This is sometimes called a "promised date" and may be used on an exception basis when it is known in advance that they will not be able to meet the published lead time. For example, a company has a standard published lead time that they can generally meet, but due to capacity constraints they cannot always meet this lead time. Rather than just accepting the order with the standard lead time they know they can't meet, they provide the customer with another date that represents the date they expect to be able to ship the order.

This creates a bit of a dilemma since the promised date does not actually represent when the customer wanted the order, or when the customer had expected to get the order given your published lead time. Therefore, if you base your measurement on the promised date, you are not truly measuring your performance in respect to how it is perceived by your customers. On the other hand, the promised date does serve a purpose in that it represents the date the customer expects to get the shipment once he was informed of the delay, so it would make sense to measure to see how well you are performing to the promised date. So what you really need to do here is measure both.

We're not done yet. Knowing you missed a requested date or promised date is one thing, but don't you also want to know by how much you are missing these dates? I think most would agree there is a distinct difference between being a couple of days late filling an order versus being a couple of months late. Which brings us to breaking down OTD measurement by ranges. For example, in one division a fill rate is calculated as 95% based on the requested date, but it is 98% within 3 days of the requested date, 99% within a week, 99.5% within two weeks, and 99.99% within 30 days. In another division, the fill rate is still 95% based on the requested date, but within 30 days they are still only at 98%. You can see how even though both divisions are at 95% in the base measurement, there is a significant difference in how late the shipments are between the two divisions.

Web analytics, out-of-stock analysis, and lost sales due to out-of-stock analysis.

I briefly mentioned the problems fill-rate measurements have if you cannot accurately track the number of times a customer wanted something that was not available. Unfortunately, there is no easy way around this, but with a bit of creativity you can sometimes find ways of estimating this.

With growth in online ordering, there is growing interest in web analytics. Though this covers a lot of territory, we are particularly interested in analyzing data related to things like abandoned shopping carts, items deleted from shopping carts, or items viewed but not added to a shopping cart. I first need to make it clear there are many reasons beyond inventory availability that contribute to these occurrences, so don't even think that it is going to be this easy. But with some serious analysis, you may be able to get some useful information here. For example, if you can determine the rate at which an item is deleted from shopping carts when there is inventory available, and then compare this to the rate at which the item is deleted from shopping carts when inventory is unavailable, you may be able to conclude that the difference represents line items cancelled due to the inventory being unavailable. However, if a customer must add the item to the cart in order to check availability, you may also find that customers keep checking back periodically by adding the item to a cart and then deleting it; therefore you would have multiple instances that represent the same requirement.

If your customers can check availability by simply inquiring on the item (a click through or page view), the shopping cart deletions or abandons may not help you out at all here. But you may be able to get some information by doing similar analysis on the page views for the item page. You would need to do some analysis to see your rate of page views for an item compared to the actual sales that result from those page views when you have inventory available. Then compare that to page views when inventory is unavailable. Once again, you may also need to factor in that you get more page views due to the same customer repeatedly checking the same item for availability. As I said, this isn't easy and the accuracy of the resulting data is questionable to say the least, but sometimes this is all you have. I have no plans of going into any more detail on web analytics here, but I think you get some idea of the possibilities.

So let's move on to something a little more tangible. Since technology has made it more likely that your customers can check availability, and therefore not order something without you ever knowing they intended to order it, out-of-stock measurement becomes that much more important. Though I would hope this is obvious, out-of-stock measurement is the measurement of items that are currently not in stock OR are currently unavailable due to allocations equal to or greater than the on-hand inventory. More simply put, they are items that, if ordered, could not be shipped due to inadequate inventory levels.

It's pretty easy to create a report that shows you any items that are currently out of stock or unavailable. All you need to do is create an availability calculation, and then select all items with an availability less than or equal to zero. But that only takes you so far. You may find that you also want to know how long something is unavailable for sale. Since most inventory systems don't track this, it's probably going to require just a smidge of programming to get you this capability.

OK, so now you know how many items are currently unavailable for sale, and how long items have been unavailable for sale, what can you do with this info? It's easy to see how this information could prove useful for expediting inbound shipments, but we may also be able to use it to calculate the impact this has on service levels, and even attempt to calculate lost sales due to out-of-stocks. To do this, we need to combine this out-of-stock information with our forecast. For example, if I was out of Item A for the entire month of January and my forecasted demand for that item for the month of January was 200 units, it would be reasonable to conclude that had I not been out of stock I would have sold roughly 200 units. Now if I wanted to work that into a line-fill calculation, I would have to calculate the average order quantity for the item, and then divide 200 by this number to get an estimate of the number of line items I would have expected to be placed for that item in that period. If you have reasonably accurate forecasts, this can prove to be an effective way of estimating fill rates when you otherwise do not have visibility to instances when a customer decided not to order something due to unavailability of inventory.

Now that we've projected what we would have sold during that period if we had inventory available, we basically know our lost sales due to stockouts. Or do we? Sure, we have a pretty good estimate of how many of this particular item would have sold during the period were we not out of stock, but that doesn't necessarily mean these were all lost sales. Some of these sales may just end up being moved into a future period when we have inventory available. If customers enter the line item and accept backorders, you can easily track these, but it's a little harder when customers choose not to enter the line item, and instead, just keep checking back until you have inventory available. In this situation, you can go back to your forecast and determine if you had sales beyond your forecasted quantities for the period(s) immediately following the period when you were out of stock, and deduct these excess sales from the quantity you expected to sell during the time when you were out-of-stock. Once again, if your forecasts are reasonably accurate, you should be comfortable with using the result of this calculation as your lost sales—maybe.

Estimating lost sales

Period (weeks)	1	2	3	4	5	6	7	8	Totals
Forecast	200	200	200	200	200	200	200	200	1600
Actual shipments	183	204	0	0	321	243	185	193	1329
Difference	-17	4	-200	-200	121	43	-15	-7	-271

Figure 10B. In this example, we'll assume we ran out of this item at the beginning of week #3 and were out of stock for exactly 2 weeks. Therefore, we can estimate that we missed out on orders for about 400 units during the time we were out of stock. However, we can also see that in periods #5 and #6 we shipped significantly more than our forecast, therefore we can probably conclude that this unusually high demand was actually the result of us recouping some of the lost sales from the previous two periods.

So what exactly are our lost sales due to stockout? Well, there's no way to tell for certain, but if we net the variances for weeks #3 through #6, we would see that during those 4 weeks we sold 236 units less than our forecast. That sounds reasonable. However, as we look at the other periods, we can see that our sales seem to be running a little below forecast anyway, so our lost sales due to the stockout may be a little less than the 236. But then again, they could be more. I would say the number is probably somewhere between 225 and 250 units. Not an exact science, but still useful information to have.

There's one more big glitch here, and that's a little situation known as substitutions. If you have similar items, and your customer may have chosen to buy a similar item from you when they found you did not have the item they wanted in stock, you didn't actually lose a sale. Whether or not this applies to your business depends upon the nature of your products and your customers' buying habits. If your products are not ones that would lend themselves to substitutions, great, you don't have to worry about this. But, if substitutions are common in your business, this starts to get rather messy.

And this is the point where attempting to calculate this level of complexity is probably impractical for many businesses. However, if you feel this has a significant impact on your business, you can attempt to calculate it by expanding your calculation to include the forecasts and actual sales for items that would be likely substitutes.

How stockouts affect forecasting and safety stock calculations.

While we are on the topic of out-of-stock analysis, I wanted to mention that out-of-stock conditions can create serious problems with your forecast and safety stock calculations. This is especially true if you have been out of stock of an item for an extended period of time. You may need to increase your forecast for the period (or several periods) when you expect the inventory to be in stock and available. Otherwise, a sudden peak in sales that may result when your customers who have been waiting for the item, realize it is now in stock, may result in another out-of-stock situation. In addition, you may need to adjust your sales history to prevent an extended period of zero sales followed by a short period of greater-than-normal sales (all the results of your out-of-stock condition) from affecting your future forecasting and safety stock calculations. The "demand override" functionality I covered back in the forecasting chapters comes in pretty handy for stuff like this.

Inventory turns.

Inventory turns is a measure of the speed at which your inventory moves. It is generally calculated by dividing either the average inventory level during a period of time or the current inventory level at a point in time, by the annual cost of goods sold (COGS). If you're not familiar with cost of goods sold, it is the value (at cost, not sell price) of all inventory sold during a period of time (a year in this calculation).

In Figure 10C I show an example of calculating inventory turns for a group of three items. The "Value of Average Inventory" is calculated by multiplying the average inventory units by the unit cost. The "Value of Inventory Sold This Year (COGS)" is calculated by multiplying the units sold this year by the unit cost. Inventory turns is then calculated by dividing the COGS by the value of average inventory.

You can also see that the inventory turns for the group is calculated by totaling the value of the average inventory for each item, and then totaling the COGS for each item, and calculating inventory turns using these totals. Therefore, at the summary level, inventory turns is a measure of your overall inventory investment relative to overall sales, and does not necessarily reflect the average inventory turns of the individual items.

Though I previously mentioned that the current inventory level is sometimes used in the calculation, the preferred way is to use the average inventory level during the period of time the measurement is intended to represent. If you put together monthly inventory turns numbers, you would use the average inventory level during the month, and the COGS for the twelve-month period ending at the end of that month.

Inventory turns calculation

	Unit Cost	Average Inventory (units)	Value of Average Inventory	Units Sold This Year	Value of Inventory Sold This Year (COGS)	Inventory Turns
Item A	$1.53	142	$217.26	800	$1,224.00	5.6
Item B	$23.98	28	$671.44	350	$8,393.00	12.5
Item C	$0.37	1729	$639.73	5846	$2,163.02	3.4
Totals			$1,528.43		$11,780.02	7.7

Figure 10C. Here we show our inventory turns calculation for 3 items, and then again for the group of 3 items. We calculate it by dividing the annual COGS by the value of our average inventory. At the item level, we would get the same results by dividing the units sold this year by the average inventory in units, but at the group level, we would always use the value (not units) for our inventory turns calculation.

Although using the average inventory level is the preferred method, use of the current inventory level is probably the most commonly used method. The primary reason for this is that it's easier to use the current inventory level than it is to calculate an average inventory level. But the use of current inventory level is problematic. At the item level, it is just far too inaccurate since the calculation is based on the inventory level on a specific day, which probably does not even come close to representing the average inventory level. But even at the group level—where you would expect the number to be closer to the average—the calculation is still problematic, primarily because of how the inventory turns measurement is often used.

For example, it's very common for companies to use inventory turns as a performance measurement for their inventory planners. And they generally use the month-end inventory level (rather than the average) to calculate inventory turns for that month. Well, it doesn't take long for the inventory planners to figure out that if they can drive down month-end inventory levels by scheduling significantly more inbound shipments towards the beginning of the month, they will thereby drive up the inventory turns number they are being measured against. But this isn't really increasing inventory turns, it's just taking advantage of a flawed calculation, and in the process, creating unnecessary variability in the volume of receipts that must be processed and the amount of storage space required as the warehouse fills up to overflowing at the beginning of each month and then empties out by the end of the month. If you remember my discussion of self-induced seasonality—where internal business practices created demand variability—this is the inbound version of those same wasteful practices.

Well while I'm at it, I guess it's time for me to go into my rant on inventory turns. I consider inventory turns to be one of the most overused, misused, and abused calculations in business. I'm not saying the inventory turns calculation is fatally flawed or that it does not serve a purpose. What I am saying here is that somehow inventory turns has become the officially recognized primary measure of inventory performance throughout general industry despite the fact that it doesn't tell you a hell of a lot.

Inventory turns is simply a measure of the velocity of your inventory. You can also think of it as a measure of inventory investment relative to sales (at cost). But, no matter how you think of it, that's all it is. Unfortunately, there is this prevailing little nugget of "wisdom" in business that implies higher inventory turns are inherently better than lower inventory turns. This comes from the misguided assumption that having less inventory is always better than having more inventory.

This scenario is similar to using sales dollars as the primary measure of business performance. It's actually easy to increase sales in many businesses by simply adding more products or reducing prices. But the costs associated with increasing your product line combined with the reduced margins resulting from lowering your prices can easily result in lower profits even though you are experiencing sales growth. You can even "sales growth" yourself right out of business. The same goes with inventory turns. It's easy to increase inventory turns by simply ordering smaller quantities more frequently, but does that automatically translate into a more profitable business?

Here's the deal. Inventory turns can be a useful measurement provided it is used properly. Think of it this way. If your inventory levels are driven by sound inventory management decisions (such as using cost-based lot sizing calculations, statistical safety stock calculations, and effective forecasting methods), an increase in inventory turns would most likely represent an improvement in inventory performance (assuming they weren't the result of increases in sales). That's because, in order to increase inventory turns within this context, you need to do things like tweaking your safety stock calculations to allow you to determine the least amount of safety stock to get the service levels you require, or reducing safety stock by reducing lead times or increasing forecast accuracy, or finding ways to make it economical to order smaller lot sizes. If, however, your inventory levels are driven by the inventory turns calculation itself, an increase in inventory turns only means that your inventory is turning faster.

Let's use this book as an example. It's very possible that the inventory for this book will turn less than one time per year. That's primarily because the setup costs associated with printing a book are so significant that it makes it cost-prohibitive to run smaller quantities, and sales for this type of book are unlikely to be large enough to turn these large lot sizes more than once per year. Now if a publisher were to fall into the "more inventory turns is better" crowd, he could easily order much smaller quantities and end up with as many inventory turns per year as he likes. Hell, he may even get an article in a trade magazine covering his "success story" in increasing his inventory turns. But that doesn't change the fact that the costs involved are now greater, and subsequently his bottom line is shrinking.

On the other hand, if the publisher and printer were able to find ways to reduce the setup costs associated with printing the book, this change in costs would result in it making economic sense to order smaller quantities, and therefore result in more inventory turns and lower overall costs. But it's also important to note that if they were unable to reduce these setup costs, it simply does not make sense to reduce the order quantities. The reality is, the "appropriate" inventory turns for a specific item are relative to the characteristics for that specific item. And it's these characteristics that drive the performance of the inventory. Therefore, arbitrarily setting inventory turns that are not in line with the characteristics of the specific items, is simply bad business.

While I'm on the topic of inventory turns, I thought I would mention that you may occasionally run into someone bragging about having negative inventory turns. Now if we were to assume that more inventory turns are always better, we may come to the conclusion that negative inventory turns must be a bad thing. Well, at least that's what I like to say to the boneheads bragging about having negative inventory turns. What is actually happening here is these companies have changed the inventory turns calculation to account for payment terms (you would deduct the value of inventory you have not yet paid for from your inventory investment calculation before using it to calculate your inventory turns). So, if you regularly sell your inventory before you pay for it (not at all uncommon), you can get a negative result from the calculation. While I see some value in looking at this aspect of your inventory investment, I'm not sure this is the best way of doing it. But hell, since I already think people are kidding themselves when they use inventory turns as the primary measure of inventory performance, why not go ahead and funk up the calculation to the point where no one really knows what it means?

> *I consider inventory turns to be one of the most overused, misused, and abused calculations in business.*

Slicing and dicing your inventory.

Throughout this book I have referred to various groupings of items to assist in some of the calculations. For example, in the forecasting chapters we discussed grouping items that share similar seasonal patterns or trend patterns, grouping items by how fast they move, and grouping items by obvious product groupings (such as grouping riding lawnmowers separately from walk-behind mowers). This allowed us to fit the forecasting method and configuration to the specific group of products being forecasted. In the chapter on lot sizing, we discussed the possibility of using order groups, freight groups, storage groups, and risk groups, to more accurately assign costs in our lot-sizing calculations. Inventory classifications (groups) also play a key role in analyzing inventory and communicating the results of this analysis (measurement). And while you don't want to get too carried away with inventory classifications, you do need to make sure your classification system is in line with the complexity of the inventory being analyzed.

ABC stratification.

ABC classifications are generally based on the Pareto Principle (also known as the 80/20 rule), which states that a small number of causes are responsible for a great number of effects. For example, you may find that a small percentage of your customer base is responsible for consuming the majority of time of your technical support staff.

In the context of inventory management, this implies that a small number of items are responsible for a large portion of sales, or that a small number of items are responsible for a significant portion of the inventory investment, or that a small number of items are responsible for a significant portion of returns or scrap or backorders. The 80/20 rule attempts to add some more specificity to this by implying that 20% of causes are generally responsible for 80% of effects. Within the context of inventory management, this would imply that 20% of our items are responsible for 80% of our sales, or that 80% of our inventory problems are caused by 20% of our items.

And while I like using the 80/20 rule to help explain the Pareto Principle, I have to make it clear that the 80/20 rule does not mean that the ratio of 80 to 20 is an absolute. I would hope this would be obvious, but I have run into people who seem to think that an 80/20 relationship can be assumed in any situation. That said, it is rather surprising how often the breakdown actually does come close to 80/20.

So think of it this way, the Pareto Principle describes a common statistical situation whereby a small number of causes are responsible for a great number of effects. The 80/20 rule is a more specific example of what a pareto-type relationship might look like. But "analysis" is the key to determining if, and to what level, the Pareto Principle applies to a specific situation.

How does this help us in inventory management? Let's assume you are responsible for inventory planning for 1,000 items, and after some pareto analysis, you find that 300 of those items are responsible for 90% or your sales. Wouldn't it make sense to put greater emphasis on the planning activities associated with those 300 items? This isn't to say that you should totally ignore the other 700 items, but with limited resources, you will likely find you get more bang for your buck by focusing greater effort on the items that have a greater impact on the business.

It's not just about focusing efforts though. It's also about catering inventory management methods to groups of items that share similar characteristics. For example, being a "fast mover" is a characteristic, but there may be other characteristics that are common to fast movers. You may recall in the chapter on safety stock I mentioned that relative variability is often lower with fast movers than with slow movers. So given that variability is a key factor in how we calculate our forecast and safety stock, it may not be a bad idea to explore using different parameters or even different techniques for these calculations based on the item's fast-mover designation.

When you really start analyzing your inventory, you will likely find that a simple designation of "fast mover" or "slow mover" is not adequate. That's where ABC comes in. You can use ABC to rank your items into as many categories as you like. So rather than fast movers and slow movers, you have A items that represent your fastest movers, B items the represent your second fastest movers, and so on. And despite the term ABC, you are not limited to just three (A, B, and C) categories. In fact, I generally find that I need to go to E or F (A-B-C-D-E-F) in order to adequately break down a specific inventory characteristic.

ABC by Sales Dollars summary						
ABC	% of Sales	Cumulative %	SKUs	% of SKUs	Sales $	Average Sales $ per SKU
A	50.00%	50.00%	176	3.2%	$1,000,000	$5,681.82
B	30.00%	80.00%	952	17.1%	$600,000	$630.25
C	15.00%	95.00%	1586	28.5%	$300,000	$189.16
D	4.00%	99.00%	1230	22.1%	$80,000	$65.04
E	0.99%	99.99%	987	17.7%	$19,800	$20.06
F	0.01%	100.00%	643	11.5%	$200	$0.31
Totals			5574		$2,000,000	

Figure 10D. Example of the summarized output of an ABC breakdown.

In Figure 10D you can see an example of an ABC breakdown. The example is based on ABC by Sales Dollars (based on annual sales), and "A" items represent 50% of sales dollars, "B" items represent the next 30% of sales dollars, and it works its way down to "F" items, which represent the bottom 0.01% of sales dollars. The "Cumulative %" column just makes it easier to see cumulative level breaks. For example, the combination of "A" and "B" items account for 80% of sales dollars. The "SKUs" column shows how many items fall into each category. This is where you really start to get a feel for the Pareto Principle. In the example we have 5,574 SKUs, but only 176 SKUs (3.2% of SKUs) account for 50% of our sales, and another 952 items (17.1% of SKUs) account for another 30% of our sales. This falls right into the 80/20 rule since 20.3% of our SKUs result in 80% of our sales dollars. But to take things further, we can see that when we combine A, B, and C items, we have fewer than half of our SKUs (48.7%) representing 95% of our sales dollars.

I also want to use this example to help explain why I like to use more than just three categories (A, B, and C) to break down inventory. Some may say that since my A and B items already account for 80% of sales, why not just lump everything else into the C bucket? Or, keep the A, B, and C, as is, but then combine the D, E, and F into the D category since they only represent 5% of sales. Trust me, this is exactly what I hear when I start recommending ABCDEF breakdowns. But, when we start looking at the number of items that fall into D, E, and F, and also look at the "Average Sales $ per SKU" column for each category, we can see that there are distinct differences between these groupings of items.

For example, had I combined C, D, E, and F items into the C-item classification, I would have ended up with 4,446 SKUs in a single classification that resulted in $400,000 in sales (an average sales dollars per SKU of approximately $90). Sure, that tells me something, but is it as eye-opening as realizing I have 643 SKUs (my F items) that when combined, only brought in a total of $200 in sales (average annual sales dollars per SKU of only 31 cents)? Or, that my combined E and F items that represent almost 30% of my SKUs only resulted in 1% of my sales? Don't you think these revelations might spur some further analysis and hopefully some actions relative to these items?

As you can see, the beauty of an ABC breakdown is in the extremes. Those 176 A items in this example are so important to me that, among other things, I want to make sure I never run out of them, don't have quality issues with them, and have negotiated the lowest possible purchase costs (or manufacturing costs) associated with them. At the other end of the spectrum, I want to look good and hard at those F items and find out why I have them at all.

I didn't want to complicate the example too much, but in the real world, I would likely add some more columns to that breakdown. For one, average inventory investment (or current inventory investment) for each category. It's one thing to realize you have 643 items that only brought in a total of $200 in revenue last year, but you also want to know how much inventory you had to carry to get that 200 bucks. If the data was available, I may also want to include cube information to see how much physical space this stuff is taking up in my warehouse, or some gross margin numbers to get some idea whether there's any chance I'm even profiting from these items.

You can create ABC classifications for any inventory characteristic you feel is important to your business. Here are some examples:

- **ABC by Sales Dollars**. This is probably the most popular ABC ranking for inventory. ABC by sales dollars ranks your items by the gross revenue (sales dollars) they generate. Executives love it, accountants love it. Me? . . . not so much. Sure, sales dollars are very important, but when it comes down to practical uses for ABC analysis relative to operations management, I find that I just don't use this one all that much.

- **ABC by Sales Transactions (Times Sold).** Since a significant portion of my background is in fulfillment operations, this is my personal favorite because it drives many of my decisions related to order picking, slotting, and safety stock calculations. From a customer service perspective, ABC by times sold better reflects the items that have the greatest impact on your customers, and therefore is a better choice in defining parameters for safety stock service levels than ABC by sales dollars.

- **ABC by All Transactions.** Similar to ABC by Times Sold, however, this would also include any other transactions that occur for the item (receipts, issues to production, etc.). This can be used when making decisions that are impacted by how often the inventory is "touched".

- **ABC by Units Sold.** I don't think this is quite as useful as times sold, but it may be valuable in some environments.

- **ABC by Average Inventory Investment.** This one doesn't get used as much as it should, but it can be very useful since it shows you where your money is invested.

- **ABC by Gross Margin.** In this case, gross margin is represented as dollars (not a percentage) over a fixed period of time, so you can think of this as ABC by Gross Profit. Though gross profits do not always translate into net profits, this is still far more useful than ABC by Sales Dollars in giving you some idea of which items are making you the most money.

Some other examples of where you can use ABC in inventory management could include ABC by Cube if you wanted to rank your items based on how much space they take up in your warehouse, or ABC by Returns if you wanted to rank your items based on how many customer returns they generate. Once again, the choice to use an ABC designation needs to be based on your business needs. If you are in a retail business and returns are a significant part of your business, it may make sense to set up an ABC by returns classification (or some other type of returns analysis), but for most other businesses, an ABC ranking by returns would likely be overkill (though some occasional returns analysis may still be needed).

Determining the break points.

There are no real rules when it comes down to how many categories (A, B, C, D, etc.) you use, or exactly what percentages you use as break points for the categories. Some common mistakes (in my opinion) with applications of ABC would include using too few categories (just A, B, and C) or trying to get equal percentages or equal numbers of SKUs into each category. My approach is as much art as science (probably more science, but it feels like art when I do it). I start with a detailed ranking of all items, and essentially page through it looking for points that "feel right" to me.

Yeah, I know that's not all that helpful so I'll try to explain further. You first need to have a good understanding of how you will use the ABC classification. Then, you go through the data, and based on how you intend to use it and what you see in the data, you start to make groups of items that are similar enough to others in the group that you could make decisions related to them as a group. You can also think of it as placing a break where the data associated with the following items is different enough from the previous items to justify treating them differently. I like to start at both extremes and work my way towards the middle.

For example, if I were setting up an ABC by Times Sold, I would start by creating a report that sorted all items in descending order by annual times sold. I would include on that report a column for annual times sold, another column showing the cumulative times sold as the report progresses, another calculating the cumulative percentage of total times sold represented at this point in the report, and another representing the percentage of total SKUs this number represents. Starting at the top, I would likely see significant differences in times sold from item to item. For example, my top item may have an annual times sold of 2,375, and my next top item may only be 1,642. As the report progresses, I would see the differences between successive items to be smaller and smaller. I will generally quickly come to a point where there is a larger group of items with much more similar times sold numbers, but quite a bit fewer than the initial items on the report. At this point in the report, I can see that the previous SKUs represent a very small percentage of total SKUs, but a somewhat large percentage of total times sold. You essentially need to find the point at which you feel comfortable saying that everything above this point represents what you would consider to be your "fastest movers", and the movement of the item at the bottom of this point is still moving fast enough such that you could treat it similarly to the item at the top of the list. You may be surprised at how often there is a very clear point on the report where this makes sense. Based on those first two numbers (2,375 and 1,642) I would suspect that the times sold per item quickly drops to maybe somewhere around 300 or 500 times per year, and that may make a good place for a break. Though we often talk about ABC in terms of percentages, there is no reason why you can't set your breaks to the characteristic itself. For example, it can be easier for people to understand that an A item represents an item that sells at least 500 times per year.

Then, going to the bottom of the report; you sort of do the same thing in reverse. You're probably going to see a whole bunch of items that rarely if ever sell. Here you're looking to group the lowest of the low, so if you see enough items that sell one or fewer times per year, that's probably a good spot to place your break. If not, you want to progress up the report until you see a much larger group of items sharing similar times-sold numbers, and set the break just before (below) the point where these items start.

You then continue working from both ends towards the middle, keeping in mind at least a rough estimate of how many categories (breaks) you would like. Once you get through the first pass, you review all the points (set up a summary table like in the earlier example) and see how it looks. If you feel comfortable that the groupings and break points reasonably represent points where you would want to treat the groups differently, then you've done your job.

Though I like to use this somewhat subjective approach towards setting up an ABC breakdown, I will say that the earlier example (Figure 10D) I provided is fairly typical of the end result I receive.

The calculation itself.

If you're confused as to how you calculate ABC, I've included the following simple example:

In Figure 10E (on next page), you can see a listing of all SKUs (35 in total) sorted in descending order by annual times sold. There is a column for cumulative times sold that represents the sum of times sold for that item and all items above that item on the report. The "percentage of total" column then takes the cumulative times sold number at that level in the report, and divides it by the cumulative times sold for all items on the report. The "percentage of SKUs" column shows the percentage of total SKUs represented at that level in the report.

If you look at the fourth item on the list, you will see that it was sold 378 times in the last year. You'll also see that the top four items on the list (as a group) were sold 1,748 times last year and represent 53.13% of sales transactions. Since we have a total of 35 SKUs, those four fastest movers represent 11.43% of our total SKUs. To round these numbers out a bit, we can say that about 10% of our SKUs represent about half of our sales transactions. To see how close our data comes to the 80/20 rule, we go down the report to find the point at which 80% of our sales transactions are met. That occurs pretty close to the 8th item on the list where 79.97% of times sold is achieved with 22.86% of our SKUs. Well that's pretty damn close to 80/20.

So where would I set the break points in this example? That's a tough one to answer because it doesn't make a lot of sense to do an ABC breakdown if you only have 35 SKUs. With a much larger SKU base, it's easier to find break points because you will see much larger groupings of items with similar characteristics. So my answer is, I don't know.

Applying ABC and other logical product groupings in more complex analyses.

Though ABC can stand on its own as a form of analysis, you will also want to combine ABC and other logical product groupings in other forms of analyses. For example, when you do your service-levels analysis, it is likely you will want to break down your service levels by various ABC classifications or product groupings. I know I would want to see my service levels for my fastest movers (ABC by times sold) separately from those of my slowest movers. In fact, it's very rare that I would be satisfied with the simple output of a basic measurement (big surprise), so I will always look to see if there are logical groupings that can be applied to the measurement to assist in making decisions related to those measurements.

Calculating ABC

	SKU	Annual Times Sold	Cumulative Times Sold	Percentage of Total	Percentage of SKUs
1	546074	537	537	16.32%	2.86%
2	546373	431	968	29.42%	5.71%
3	546061	402	1370	41.64%	8.57%
4	546360	378	1748	53.13%	11.43%
5	546048	373	2121	64.47%	14.29%
6	546347	275	2396	72.83%	17.14%
7	546113	153	2549	77.48%	20.00%
8	546412	82	2631	79.97%	22.86%
9	546126	76	2707	82.28%	25.71%
10	546425	73	2780	84.50%	28.57%
11	546139	64	2844	86.44%	31.43%
12	546438	63	2907	88.36%	34.29%
13	546308	57	2964	90.09%	37.14%
14	546035	50	3014	91.61%	40.00%
15	546334	47	3061	93.04%	42.86%
16	546022	42	3103	94.32%	45.71%
17	546321	39	3142	95.50%	48.57%
18	546295	24	3166	96.23%	51.43%
19	546087	20	3186	96.84%	54.29%
20	546386	17	3203	97.36%	57.14%
21	546282	17	3220	97.87%	60.00%
22	546269	13	3233	98.27%	62.86%
23	546191	8	3241	98.51%	65.71%
24	546152	8	3249	98.75%	68.57%
25	546217	7	3256	98.97%	71.43%
26	546178	6	3262	99.15%	74.29%
27	546100	6	3268	99.33%	77.14%
28	546451	5	3273	99.48%	80.00%
29	546204	5	3278	99.64%	82.86%
30	546165	5	3283	99.79%	85.71%
31	546399	3	3286	99.88%	88.57%
32	546464	2	3288	99.94%	91.43%
33	546230	2	3290	100.00%	94.29%
34	546256	0	3290	100.00%	97.14%
35	546243	0	3290	100.00%	100.00%

Figure 10E. This is an example of the item-based data you would use to set your ABC breaks. See previous page for specifics on this example.

Gross Margin Return on Inventory Investment (GMROII).

GMROII is a nifty (yes, I said nifty) little calculation that shows your margin relative to your average inventory investment. It's calculated by dividing your annual gross margin (dollars) by your average inventory (dollars), and can be calculated for individual items or groups of items.

GMROII is particularly useful in determining which items provide the greatest profit potential relative to your investment in inventory. The term "profit potential" is important here because, as with all calculations that use gross margin as an input, the output may be flawed if other costs not included in the gross calculation vary significantly from one item to another.

To calculate GMROII, we first need to know how to calculate our gross margin. For the most part, gross margin is the difference between the sell price and the cost of an item. If I buy something for $3 and sell it for $10, and I sold 500 units last year, my gross margin is $7 per unit ($10 minus $3) times 500 units. If my average inventory for that item over the last year was 100 units, then my average inventory investment for that item was $300 (100 units times a unit cost of $3). I can now divide my annual gross margin ($3500), by my average inventory investment ($300) to get my GMROII of 11.67.

What this means is that for every dollar I have invested in inventory for this item, I received 11.67 dollars in gross margin last year. This is important because gross margin can be thought of as gross profit. Therefore, for every dollar I had invested in this item last year, I received a gross profit of $11.67. This is a far better measure in determining how your inventory is contributing to your bottom line. So, where I had previously mentioned how measuring performance solely based on sales dollars or inventory turns was a big mistake since you can easily increase either of these without necessarily increasing profits (and potentially decreasing them), GMROII looks to be a pretty sweet . . . I mean nifty, solution.

GMROII

	Unit Cost	Sell Price	Margin per Unit	Average Inventory (units)	Value of Average Inventory	Units Sold This Year	Gross Margin for Units Sold This Year	GMROII
Item A	$1.53	$2.75	$1.22	142	$217.26	800	$976.00	$4.49
Item B	$23.98	$29.95	$5.97	28	$671.44	350	$2,089.50	$3.11
Item C	$0.37	$1.43	$1.06	1729	$639.73	5846	$6,196.76	$9.69
Totals					$1,528.43		$9,262.26	$6.06

Figure 10F. Here I took the same 3 items from our previous inventory turns example (Figure 10C), added a sell price, and calculated the GMROII. All I did here is subtract unit cost from sell price to get my margin per unit. I then multiplied my units sold by the margin per unit to get my gross margin for units sold this year. Then I divide that by my average inventory (value) to get GMROII.

Note on calculating gross margin in the real world.

My example shows a gross margin calculation that assumes your unit cost does not change and you always sell at the same sell price. While this is fine to demonstrate the GMROII calculation, it isn't practical in most businesses. Therefore, most businesses will have to calculate their gross margin on an order-by-order basis, using the cost at the time of the order and the sell price on each specific order (would be calculated directly from your sales order data).

But GMROII is not without its flaws. Primarily, the reality that gross margins do not necessarily translate into net profits (the real profits after all costs are taken into account). Gross margin calculations generally don't account for item-specific costs such as storage costs, transportation costs, or risk of spoilage or obsolescence, any of which can potentially have a significant impact on the profit potential of the item. Nor does GMROII account for any general business costs that also affect the bottom line. For the purposes of decisions made relative to inventory management, the general business costs are not as critical here because they tend to be similar for all items, but we do need to look at the item-specific costs.

There's no reason why we can't improve upon GMROII by adding as many of these item-specific costs as is practical to the calculation. Lucky for us, we already know a lot of these costs because we used them when we earlier calculated our lot sizes. For example, we could go back to our "total annual cost" calculation from the lot-sizing chapter and divide the output by our annual demand to get a number we can use to adjust our unit cost in the GMROII calculation (you should 1st review the costs to make sure you really want them in this calculation). To even improve upon this further, we may want to see about including some sales-related operational costs to the items. For example, if we pay all or a portion of our outbound shipping costs, and/or if there are additional packaging costs involved in completing the sale to a customer, we may want to see if we can quantify these costs and add them into our calculation. This would be especially useful if these costs varied significantly across our various product lines. If returns are a big part of your business, and especially if some items are more likely to be returned than others, you may want to also see if you can apply these costs.

So now we have a modified gross margin return on inventory investment calculation (Should we call it MGMROII or maybe AGMROII for adjusted gross margin return on inventory investment? Nahh.), what can we do with it? Well, we can calculate it for all items and then sort them in descending order and see which items provide the greatest return on investment (those at the top of the report) and which provide the least return on investment (those on the bottom of the report). But this is only the beginning of our analysis. We're going to want to analyze the characteristics of our high-profit items and compare them to the characteristics of our low-profit (or loss) items. The basic idea here is to see if there is anything we can change to increase the profitability of those items at the bottom of the list.

Since there are many factors that go into this calculation, there are many factors that need to be considered here. For example, can we negotiate a lower cost with our supplier, or reduce various operational costs associated with the item? If not, can we increase the sell price? You may be surprised what you find here. For example, you may find that you have a fast mover that looks profitable when you just look at the gross margin, but when you factor in other costs, you find you are losing money on this item. Further analysis shows that due to overseas sourcing you are forced to order very large lot sizes and carry significant safety stock. In addition, this particular item is physically large and results in significant storage costs as well as significant inbound and outbound freight costs. Solution? Maybe you can find a domestic source that reduces your lead time and lot sizes, or maybe you can negotiate a lower lot size with your current supplier, or maybe you can negotiate a lower cost with your current supplier, or maybe you can exclude this item from your free outbound freight policy, or maybe you can do a combination of these. The important thing to note here is you would never have realized you had a problem had you not conducted this type of analysis.

You can also use the inputs to this calculation to create related calculations. For example, rather than calculating an adjusted gross return relative to our inventory investment, we can use the same data to calculate an adjusted annual gross profit for each item. This is actually a simpler calculation; just calculate your total annual costs associated with each item and subtract this from your annual sales dollars for each item.

Excess and obsolete inventory.

"What do you do about obsolete inventory?" This is one of the more common questions asked related to inventory management. While those asking the question are probably expecting some tips on how to convince the higher-ups to allow them to get rid of their obsolete stuff, or tips on the best ways to liquidate obsolete inventory, what they really need to understand is that the best solution is prevention.

Let's start with your current obsolete inventory. Sure, you could get the boss to sign off on sending it off to a liquidator, and feel like you've accomplished something. But eventually you will be doing this all over again. What you really want to do is analyze your current obsolete inventory and try to figure out how you ended up with it. This means going through it one item at a time and reviewing the item history to try to determine what went wrong. Yes, this is going to be tedious work, but it will be worth it in the end.

Here are some examples of what you might find.

- **Obvious ordering mistake.** This is common in manual ordering processes. A planner may have typed the wrong item number or quantity on the PO, and you subsequently end up with stuff you didn't need.

- **Cycle count or physical inventory error.** Cycle counting and physical inventories can be very dangerous in the wrong hands (you'll have to read my book on inventory accuracy for more on this) and it's very common to see an inventory adjustment that deducts all or a significant portion of an item's inventory. Then, the planner orders more, and later there is another adjustment when they find the inventory they previously deducted. Now you have way too much of something, and it eventually ends up in the obsolete category.

- **New item that never took off.** You introduce a new item and expect it to sell, but it just doesn't pan out.

- **Sales gradually dropped off, but forecast was slow to react, and order quantities were large and/or lead times were long.** Though this situation is common, it doesn't necessarily result in obsolete inventory since a gradual drop-off in sales often means you can still eventually sell the stuff. But sometimes, if your order quantities are very large and/or your lead times are really long, you can get stuck with some serious obsolete inventory here.

- **Sales suddenly dropped off.** This is very easy to identify by just looking at sales history. Figuring out why they dropped off requires a little more work.

- **An unusually large customer-order was placed and then later cancelled.** Basically what happened here is a customer placed an unusually large order (or series of orders) for an item, which resulted in you having to order more to fill this order. Then, before you fill the order, the customer cancels it. These can be tricky to try to track down after the fact because cancelled orders may not show up in the typical places you would look to track down demand.

- **A single large customer-order results in an increase in the forecast and order quantity.** Though not that common, I've seen this happen. You have a very slow mover and suddenly get a single very large order for the item (resulting in an out-of-stock situation). The planner then orders a whole bunch more, and you never sell them. This is because the large order turned out to be a one-time event (or mistake).

- **Customer returns.** It's not uncommon for companies that have generous return policies to receive returns of items that may already be obsolete or are very close to obsolescence. It may even turn out that the single-large-customer-order situation previously mentioned ended up being a mistake on the customer's part. He returns it. And now you are stuck with all the extra inventory you ordered after the big order, plus the customer return inventory. This situation is more common than you may think.

- **Someone stumbled into a "great deal".** Yeah, this really happens. One of your suppliers offers you a big quantity of something at a greatly reduced price and you bite. And in the process, your supplier has turned his obsolete inventory into your obsolete inventory. Well, it's good to see that someone is managing their inventory.

Now that you know how you ended up with obsolete inventory, you can start to look at ways to avoid it in the future. For example, a more automated ordering system can pretty much eliminate typos on purchase orders. Training and a better understanding of cycle counting and physical inventories can eliminate most of these types of counting and adjustment errors. Reevaluating your criteria for introducing new items may allow you to be more effective at picking winners, or at least allow you to better control the quantities purchased of certain types of new items that are at greater risk of obsolescence. Reevaluating your forecast parameters may allow you to tweak them to more quickly adapt to demand changes. Making sure you have adequately accounted for risks associated with obsolescence in your lot-sizing calculation should limit your lot-size exposure for high-risk items. You can also consider shorter lead-time options for higher risk items. And next time you see an unusually large order for an item, it may be worthwhile to call the customer and make sure the order is correct, and if it is, see if they can provide any information on whether or not they would expect to be placing similar orders in the future. Oh, and be wary of "great deals".

I think you can see how understanding the causes of obsolete inventory in your specific environment can open opportunities for prevention. I'm not saying that all obsolete inventory can be prevented, but you may be surprised to find out just how much of your obsolete inventory is the result of preventable causes.

So now that I've explained the importance of analyzing obsolete inventory, I want to move on pushing the importance of identifying and analyzing excess inventory. Excess inventory is often the result of the same conditions that create obsolete inventory. In fact, the inventory that is now designated as obsolete was probably previously identifiable as excess inventory. So by identifying and analyzing excess inventory, you are doing a bit of preemptive obsolete analysis (analyzing obsolete inventory before it is actually obsolete). This brings you closer (in time) to the actual causes and therefore makes it easier to identify them. In addition, by identifying the causes earlier, you can hopefully prevent additional excess and obsolete inventory.

While I like to emphasize prevention here, identifying your obsolete inventory before it becomes obsolete also provides more options in getting rid of it. For example, at the point it was identifiable as excess, you may still have been able to return some of it to a supplier, or you may have been able to sell the excess by promoting it or reducing the price. However, if you just sit back and let it collect dust for a few years until you are good and ready to classify it as obsolete, you have probably missed out on these opportunities.

And now you probably want to know how to identify excess and obsolete inventory. The definition of obsolete varies by industry and product group, but is generally defined as zero sales over a specific period of time. That period of time could range from weeks to years (or decades), so you'll have to figure out what works for your business.

When it comes to identifying excess inventory, the most common approach involves a simple time-based calculation. For example, Company A defines excess inventory as anything with greater than 10 week's demand in stock, Company B defines excess inventory as anything with greater than 26 week's demand in stock, etc. Well, based on what you've read so far, what do you think my opinion is of this keep-it-simple approach?

That's right; I have another more complicated calculation to throw your way. What we're trying to do here is identify our excess inventory, therefore we first need to define what excess inventory is. Simply put, excess inventory would be inventory that is greater than the "right amount of inventory". Since a significant portion of this book focused on determining the right amount of inventory, most of our work is already done. To recap things quickly, we developed forecasts to predict demand, and then used these forecasts (along with cost data and other information) as inputs to our safety stock, reorder points, and lot sizing calculations. The outputs of these calculations pretty much define what the right amount of inventory is.

So in the most basic calculation of excess inventory, if your current on-hand inventory is greater than your safety stock quantity plus your current lot size (order quantity), then you have excess inventory. Now you may be thinking that since you used these same calculations to determine safety stock and lot size when you ordered the inventory, you couldn't possibly end up with excess inventory. What you have to realize is that as conditions change, so will the output of your safety stock and lot sizing calculations. For example, if your demand has dropped off, your forecast will likely decrease, and subsequently, your lot size will likely decrease. Therefore, the right amount of inventory under current conditions will be less than the right amount of inventory was under previous conditions.

There are several problems with this simple calculation though. First, if you were to run a report based on this calculation, you would likely find that it spits out a whole bunch of inventory items that just have minor amounts of excess inventory. A lot of this is just due to small, normal changes in demand or costs; and while you now technically have excess inventory on these items, it probably isn't worth your time to have to review them all. To resolve this, you just need to set some tolerances for your calculation. For example, rather than defining excess as anything greater than the sum of safety stock and lot size, you can define it as anything greater than 120% of the sum of safety stock and lot size. I just used 120% as an example; you need to try various tolerances with your inventory to find the one(s) that work best for you. You also may need different tolerances for different product groups. Very slow movers are always tricky, so you may need to experiment with different types of tolerances (it doesn't necessarily need to be a percentage of the "right inventory") or a different calculation altogether.

The next issue with the calculation is a rather simple one. Since you may have current outbound orders in your system, you should probably incorporate these into the calculation. So rather than basing the calculation on your on-hand inventory, you would base it on your available inventory.

And finally, you may want to consider your open inbound orders. This is especially true if you have long lead times (and especially if these long lead times are due to manufacturing lead time). This may provide an opportunity to cancel a current open order that may eventually result in obsolete inventory, or delay orders that will eventually be needed but not as soon as you had originally planned. It would also be useful in catching those order mistakes discussed previously. But, in order to incorporate inbound orders into the calculation, you must also incorporate lead-time demand into it. What this means is that now, instead of comparing current on-hand inventory to the "right inventory", we are comparing current on-hand inventory plus inbound inventory minus lead-time demand minus outbound inventory, to the "right inventory" (defined as safety stock plus lot size, adjusted by a tolerance).

Figure 10G. Here's an example of our calculation for excess inventory. The "adjusted inventory" is calculated by adding the inbound quantities to the quantity on hand, then subtracting our lead-time demand and outbound quantities. The "right inventory" is the sum of our safety stock and lot size. The "adjusted right inventory" is the "right inventory" plus the tolerance.

The excess here is the result of the 500 units we show as an inbound quantity. We would need to do some research to try to figure out how we ended up with that quantity.

Calculating excess inventory		
Quantity on hand	153	
Inbound quantities	500	
Lead-time demand	164	
Outbound quantities	10	
Adjusted inventory		479
Safety stock	43	
Lot size	200	
Right inventory		243
Tolerance	15%	
Adjusted right inventory		279
Excess inventory		200

Now that's what I call an excess inventory calculation. Don't underestimate how useful this can be in identifying problems with your planning systems and preventing obsolete inventory. You can also adapt this calculation to try to segregate excess inventory that will likely eventually be used, from excess inventory that is at risk of becoming obsolete. Exactly how you go about this depends on the nature of your products and business, but would probably involve a combination of tolerances relative to the "right inventory", fixed-time-periods of demand, and product life cycle information.

Fun with ratios.

Ratios are a simple means of comparing two numeric factors or characteristics. I like to use ratios to evaluate obvious inventory characteristics as well as less obvious ones. In the case of the less obvious (or even obscure) inventory characteristics, I may just be using ratios to look for outliers and see if there is any significance to them. In other words, I may choose to do some quick analysis of a specific ratio without any predetermined purpose other than to just look for items that are "different" from most of my inventory, and then investigate these differences to see if there is anything to be learned from them. In fact, I take this same approach towards a lot of the analysis I do. I'm sort of playing around with the data and seeing if it leads me to anything meaningful. Yeah, I really am that much of a data geek.

Let's look at some examples of ratios. Keep in mind these are just a handful of examples to give you an idea of what you can do with ratios.

- **Ratio of sales to returns (or returns to sales).** This is a pretty obvious one that can help to provide information on items that are more likely to be returned. The results of this measurement may lead to further investigation of specific items and specific reasons for returns to see if there is a way of avoiding them in the future (resolving possible quality issues, problems with item descriptions, etc.) You may also use this to build return costs into certain item-level cost-based calculations you use.

- **Ratio of stockouts to receipts, or ratio of stockouts to sales.** These are just some additional ways of conducting out-of-stock analyses. For example, a high ratio of stockouts relative to receipts may lead you to a problem with vendor performance, lead times, forecasting, or safety stock calculations. However, it may also be an appropriate level of stockouts relative to receipts for that particular item. As you recall from the safety stock chapter, we may choose to carry very little safety stock for some items due to inherently high service levels that come from long order cycles (large lot sizes), or due to a lower requirement for service levels for that particular group of items (slow movers, for example). Therefore, it's important to look at these ratios within the context of other inventory characteristics.

- **Ratio of receipts to shipments (line items).** This is one I may look at when I'm evaluating warehouse operations. For example, in warehouse operations, the order-picking function tends to get the most focus, but if I have a high ratio of receipts to shipments, I want to make sure that the receipt/putaway function is adequately considered in warehouse layout, process, and slotting decisions. An obvious outlier that would be useful in inventory management would be if you found items that had more receipts than it had shipments. While there can be legitimate reasons for this, it's more likely that you will need to reevaluate your ordering practices for these items. Also, if you find you have items with a very low receipts-to-shipments ratio (like items with a 1:1 ratio), you may want to consider looking into having your supplier direct ship (drop ship) these items in the future. Why have him ship a quantity to you, only to have you turn around and ship that same quantity somewhere else.

- **Ratio of gross revenue (sales) to inventory investment, and ratio of net profits to inventory investment.** These are two different high-level measurements (company-based, not item-based) that give you a little glimpse of how your inventory is performing relative to sales or profits. Since there are numerous other factors involved here, you cannot count on these measurements to purely reflect inventory performance; however, you can use them to signal that something has changed. For example if my ratio of sales to inventory investment is going down, I would want to do some further investigation to try to figure out what has changed. It could be that I have experienced some price increases on my inventory, or that I am actually carrying more inventory, or that sales are down and inventory has not been adjusted accordingly, or that we have reduced our pricing. In the case of the ratio of net profits to inventory investment, there are many more factors at play so it does get even more challenging to narrow down the source of the change.

Again, these are just some examples of ratios that can be looked at when analyzing your inventory. For those of you not familiar with ratios, you calculate them by dividing one numerical factor or characteristic by another. Therefore, to calculate my ratio of receipts to shipments, I would divide the number of receipts I had for an item over a period of time (probably a year) by the number of shipments I had for the item over the same period.

Dock-to-stock cycle measurement.

Dock-to-stock cycle measurement involves measuring the amount of time it takes between the time something arrives at your dock, and the time it is in stock and available for sale or use. This is important to know because the supplier lead time you use when making ordering decisions is based upon the time it takes for the vendor to get the product to your dock. In other words, it does not include the time it takes you to process the receipt and get it into stock. If you have long dock-to-stock cycle times, you may need to incorporate a "safety lead time" (discussed previously) to compensate for this. Or better yet, evaluate your receiving process to see if you can shorten this time.

The big problem here is that it can be very difficult to measure dock-to-stock times. This is because most operations do not capture any data when the item arrives at the dock, therefore they don't have the information they need to calculate this. And for those of you who are about to run down to your receiving department and demand they start capturing this information, you need to realize that adding this task may result in even longer dock-to-stock cycle times.

If your suppliers can send Advanced Shipment Notifications (ASNs) and provided barcoded or RFID-enabled tags on the receipts that allow you to quickly scan them at the dock to capture this information, you may be able to measure dock-to-stock as a comprehensive ongoing measurement. Otherwise, your best option is likely some occasional audits. For example, you occasionally manually log stuff in as it arrives at the dock, then wait a while and compare the data you logged to "stock times" that you can likely pull from your system. While this isn't perfect, it should be adequate for inventory and operations-related decisions.

Forecast error/accuracy recap.

We discussed forecast accuracy earlier in the book (see Chapter 3), but I want to bring it up again here. Primarily, I want to re-emphasize the importance of maintaining a history of forecast data so you can measure forecast accuracy relative to how far into the future the forecast is. As you recall, we regularly recalculate our forecasts based on the most current information available. Therefore, my April forecast as of April 1st, is likely different from what my April forecast was as of January 1st. So, if I had to make planning decisions on January 1st based on my April forecast, I'm going to want a way of measuring the accuracy of the forecast that was in place at that time.

If your inventory system doesn't capture this data (it probably does not), you will want to find a way to do it. Fortunately, it's not all that hard. It's just a matter of creating a history file and writing your forecast data to it on a predefined schedule. You can then base your forecast accuracy measurement on this file and your actual sales history. Therefore, your forecast accuracy measurement would consist of multiple accuracy measurements based on the number of periods into the future the forecast represented at the time. Figure 10H shows an example of such a measurement.

The most important time period in a forecast is the time period equal to the lead-time of the item. Therefore, when you look at this type of measurement, you want to look at it within the context of your typical lead times. Technically, you could even create a measurement specific to the lead time for each specific item, but it does get a bit more complicated. And though the lead-time period is the most important time period in a forecast because it drives your when-to-order decision, the forecast is also used to calculate lot sizes, so you may also want to look at your forecast accuracy within the context of your typical order cycles. For example, if you have items that typically have order cycles of 26 weeks, and your

26-week forecast accuracy for the items is very low, you are at a greater risk of your lot sizes contributing to excess and obsolete inventory.

There are a couple ways of calculating the "periods into the future" accuracy measurement. One is to calculate the accuracy of that specific period; the other is to calculate a cumulative accuracy for all periods up to and including that period. For example, if I looked at my measurement for 26 periods into the future, the first method would compare the sales for that single forecast period to the forecast for that period, while the second method would compare the combined sales for periods 1 through 26 to the combined forecasts for periods 1 through 26. The second method is more reflective of how the forecast performs within the context of lead times and order cycles.

Forecast accuracy based on forecast history		
Periods (weeks) into the future	Period accuracy	Cumulative accuracy
1	95.0%	95.0%
5	89.0%	96.0%
26	76.0%	93.0%
52	73.0%	91.0%

Figure 10H. Here we show a measurement of forecast accuracy based on our forecast history. The "period accuracy" represents the forecast accuracy for that specific period, therefore, we show a 73% accuracy rate for a period 52 weeks into the future. The "cumulative accuracy" represents the accuracy of the period of time up to and including the referenced period. Therefore, we show a 91% accuracy for the 52-week period.

Notice how our cumulative 5-week forecast accuracy is actually a little higher than our 1st-week accuracy. This is the result of aggregate forecasts being more accurate. In this case, the 5-week period has less relative demand variability than a single one-week period. So we actually have two factors at play in our measurement. The aggregation of periods reduces relative demand variability and thereby increases accuracy, while at the same time our individual forecasts further into the future become less accurate.

And, of course, you will probably want to break down your forecast accuracy measurement by logical groupings of items (fast movers versus slow movers, major product groups, etc.).

Measuring supplier performance.

All the inventory planning in the world doesn't do a hell of a lot of good if your supplier doesn't get the product to you when you expected (planned) it. So it would seem obvious that you would want to monitor the performance of your suppliers. And it just so happens, a lot of business software comes with supplier-performance measurement functionality built right in. That's because, from a programmer's perspective, supplier performance measurement is really easy. You just take the requested date and quantity from the purchase order, and compare it to the transaction date and quantity of the receipt transaction(s). Then you can either report the early, late, over, and short shipments as raw data, or you can accumulate the data into a handy summary report or even a clever little supplier ranking system.

Normally I would be rather impressed when I encounter businesses actually making use of data they already have. However, when you look into the details, you may find that this seemingly logical use of existing data is providing misleading results. Let's start with the purchase order data. Here we have some of the same issues we ran into with our outbound service-level measurement. Primarily, the dates and even the quantities on purchase orders may be changed for various reasons. For example, let's say you ordered an item four weeks ago and it had a five-week lead time (you would now be expecting it to arrive in one week). Today, the supplier calls you to tell you that they had some type of a problem and won't be able to get the shipment to you for another three weeks (two weeks later than you expected it). You now change the purchase order to reflect the new date, and in doing so, unintentionally make that two-week late shipment appear to be on time in your supplier performance measurement system. So why not just leave the original date on the purchase order? Because someone else in your organization may need to know when the product is going to be in stock. Imagine if you are out of stock on the item in two weeks, and a customer calls wanting to know when he can expect you to have more in stock. Do you want the customer service representative to tell the customer "well, according to our system, it should have been here a week ago"? Yeah, that answers his question.

The solution here would be to have an additional date and quantity field on the purchase order record that allows you to enter an adjusted date or quantity. But even with this, you still need clear guidelines on exactly how these additional data elements and the original date and quantities are to be used. For example, if you choose to change a date or quantity on a purchase order due to reasons unrelated to the supplier's ability to deliver, you would want to change the original date or quantity fields as well as the "adjusted" date or quantity fields, otherwise this would show up as a vendor performance issue. Don't underestimate how difficult it can be to get consistency from your planners with these types of distinctions.

Unfortunately, that's only part of the problem. If you do some investigation of your receipt transaction data and your receiving process, you may also find that some of your "late" shipments were actually the result of delays in your receiving process. In other words, they were not the fault of the supplier. Hell, you may even find that MOST of your "late" shipments were actually the result of delays in your receiving area. In addition, you may even find that some of your early, late, over, or short shipments were the results of errors made in your receiving operation. The obvious solution here is to get better performance out of your receiving operation (and for many more reasons than just your supplier performance measurement), and that should be the focus here. But even with that, you still may occasionally have these types of discrepancies.

So what do you do? Well, you do the best you can. This is just one more imperfection in the imperfect world of inventory management. Most businesses simply don't need a highly accurate complex supplier performance measurement or ranking system. They just need to do enough monitoring to identify problem suppliers. So go ahead and do your flawed supplier performance measurement, keeping in mind the potential flaws and adjusting your processes to avoid them as much as is practical. You can also consider building in some human-generated performance measurement data. For example, have your planners keep track of how often a date is moved out or quantity changed due to a supplier's inability to meet the original request.

Another option is to see about having your key suppliers report their own performance to you. This is essentially asking them to provide you with their on-time delivery measurement for your account. Keep in mind that their measurement is possibly subject to the same flaws discussed earlier in this chapter. Although potentially flawed, this does achieve a couple of things. First, it gives you another source of supplier performance data to use to validate (or invalidate) your own measurement. And second, by requesting this information, you force your supplier to measure their performance (something they may or may not already be doing) and send a clear message that you are monitoring it and that it is important to you.

I also want to note that while late shipments and short shipments are of primary concern, don't ignore early shipments and over shipments. If you have a supplier that regularly ships early or over the quantity you ordered, you will end up carrying more inventory than you planned (or need).

Product data management.

Data drives our inventory systems, therefore we need to make sure our data is accurate. When I say "data", I'm talking about any piece of information you and your system use to make inventory-related decisions. While the obvious pieces of data would include things like lead times, current quantity data, item costs, and bills of materials, there is an enormous amount of additional data that drives these decisions. For example, all the product groupings that we use to drive variations in our forecasting, lot sizing, and safety stock calculations need to be accurate. In addition to basic item costs, all other costs that go into order costs and carrying costs need to be accurate. Weights, cube, and unit-of measure data need to be accurate if you use these in your inventory decisions. In addition to your basic quantity data (quantity on hand), you also need to make sure that other quantities used by your system are also accurate. It's not uncommon for inbound, outbound, and various allocation quantities to get out of whack over time in some inventory systems. Maintaining accurate vendor information such as email addresses, fax numbers, or addresses is incredibly important if you want your purchase orders to get where they need to go. Then there are all these obscure little "switches" used by your inventory system that must be populated appropriately or your inventory system may fail to do certain things.

Keeping your product data accurate generally requires several tactics. First, is to have a clean mistake-proof process for setting up new items and making changes to product data. These processes (and those who perform these processes) must be tightly controlled. Use programs, templates, or macros as much as practical to help prevent human error in setting up repetitive data. If your system comes with programs that "automatically" clean up data associated with known system problems, you should set them to run on a specific schedule (after testing, of course).

And now comes the analysis part. WHENEVER your system doesn't perform as expected, you need to figure out why. This means, if a planned order isn't automatically created when it should have been, or if an order quantity seems wrong, or if an item goes on backorder and you haven't experienced any unusual demand, you need to figure out why. And here's the real important part. Once you figure out what caused the problem, you need to see if this same set of circumstances or similar circumstances exists for other items. You need to do this because problems like this rarely happen just once. So if you find an order wasn't created because the item had somehow ended up with a stocking type that designated it as non-stock, you need to run some queries to see if there are other items that are also set up incorrectly. How do you do this? Well, you look for characteristics that are common to stock items that you can use to isolate stock items that are designated as non-stock. For example, you can start by reporting on any items that have inventory balances but are listed as non-stock. Or, if you have some type of electronic catalog that may have a separate designation for stock versus non-stock, you can compare that to the designation in your inventory system. There are almost always ways to run some quick queries to isolate these errors. You should also try to figure out how the errors occurred to see if there are any practical means of preventing them in the future.

Oh we're not done yet. You can't always count on errors being so obvious that they just jump out and bite you. You should also conduct some periodic audits of decisions made (or not made) by your inventory system and planners, to make sure they are in keeping with your expectations. This can be tedious, but it is a very important part of managing planning systems. You're basically going to somewhat randomly (not truly random since you want to use some logic here) pick some items and manually calculate forecasts, lot sizes, safety stock, and reorder points based on the same logic you think your system is using, and see if your results match that of your system. In addition, you should see if your results match your expectations. This is kind of a gut feel thing, but you essentially want to feel comfortable that the results make sense or seem right.

And so on . . .

I could easily keep going and knock out several more chapters on measurement and analysis, but this should be enough to get you on your way. As with many of my calculations, I treat measurement and analysis as part art and part science. You can't—and shouldn't—attempt to measure and analyze every minute aspect of your inventory systems on a continuous basis. Instead, you need to use what you know about your business and what you know about your systems to help guide you as you determine what to analyze and to what level you conduct your analyses. As I previously mentioned, if your measurement/analysis would not result in an action if a certain result turns up (an exception), then there really is no reason to be doing it in the first place. And, if the benefits gained from the action amount to less than the effort required to do the measurement and take the action, then again it does not make sense to do the measurement (at least in the form you are doing it). So while I'm a big supporter of measurement and analysis, I'm an even bigger supporter of being practical. Measurement and analysis is a tool, not a goal.

Before ending this chapter, I want to make it clear that when I talk about analyzing data, I'm not talking about sending a bunch of report requests off to the I.S. department. I firmly believe inventory managers must develop the skills to use whatever tools are available to directly analyze the data produced by their systems.

11

Wrapping Things Up

In this final chapter, I'm going to cover some miscellaneous topics that didn't quite fit into the other chapters, and then I'll wrap things up with a quick recap, some tips, and final comments.

Vendor managed inventory.

Vendor managed inventory (VMI) is just another example of an inventory practice that has been in existence for many decades (possibly centuries), yet is often touted as a shiny new concept that is poised to fundamentally change supply chain management. The idea is, why manage your inventory when you can have your supplier manage it for you?

When you get into the details, VMI covers a broad range of services offered by some suppliers. VMI may be as basic as your supplier showing up at your place of business, physically checking to see how much of his product you have in stock, then placing a replenishment order or replenishing immediately from stock he carries with him. In a more sophisticated application of VMI, your supplier may have direct access to data from your inventory system, and use that to plan replenishment activities. Additional services such as physically processing the deliveries directly into your stocking locations and maintaining accuracy of the inventory may also be performed by the supplier in some VMI arrangements. Other possible components of a VMI program may include special types of billing/ownership arrangements such as consignment inventory (covered later), or the consolidation of replenishments over a period of time onto a single purchase order/invoice/statement.

In some VMI arrangements, the supplier may be given total control over the planning decisions, while in others, the customer may place constraints on the planning parameters. Examples of constraints may include having a specific amount of storage space for the supplier's product, global inventory investment limits, or detailed item-based inventory quantity constraints.

What is all this really accomplishing? In some cases it simply moves certain costs from the customer to the supplier (possibly increasing overall costs in the process), while in others it results in more effective management of the supply chain. For those nickel-and-diming execs whose eyes widen at any opportunity to push costs out of their organizations and onto their suppliers, the first result is all they will likely receive. However, for those looking to increase supply chain efficiencies and drive costs out (not just move them) of the supply chain, there may be some opportunities here.

First, we need to look at why a supplier would offer to manage your inventory. Unfortunately, the most likely reason(s) a supplier would offer VMI as a service would be to either meet a specific customer requirement (mandate) for VMI, meet an industry expectation for VMI, or use it as a marketing strategy to gain new accounts. I said "unfortunately" because these reasons all pretty much fall under the "moving costs" category. While this may be a smart business decision for the supplier because it does result in him maintaining or increasing his current customer base, it doesn't necessarily result in better inventory management or a more effective supply chain.

There are, however, some potential supplier benefits to VMI beyond just "marketing". These fall into two categories—first, the supplier may be better at managing the customer's inventory, and through better inventory management the supplier may reduce costs and increase sales. Let's say we have a customer that totally sucks at inventory management, so not surprisingly, he is frequently out of the product we supply to him. As a result of these stockouts, he loses out on sales opportunities, and subsequently, we lose out on sales to him. In addition, his frequent stockouts result in constant expediting and "big favor" requests that disrupt our business. Beyond his stockout problems, he is also very inconsistent in his ordering practices. This results in very lumpy demand patterns being passed on to us even though the actual demand may not be lumpy at all. Oh, and let's not forget how his poor inventory management practices result in him building up stockpiles of inventory that eventually become obsolete, and sometime thereafter are returned to us under our very liberal return policy.

So here you can see how if we (the supplier) can do a better job at managing the customer's inventory, we can directly benefit from this improvement. But also, since we now have access to more information about our customer's inventory, we can use this information to better manage our inventory. Therefore, the other supplier benefit of VMI comes down to visibility. As you recall from the section on DRP earlier in this book, we covered the problems associated with a disconnected supply chain and how many of them were solved through integrated (through DRP) inventory planning. The exact same concept can be applied with external customers. If I have access to their inventory data and am doing their planning, I can be more effective at planning my inventory.

Now let's look at VMI from the customer's perspective. OK, there's the obvious why-should-I-do-it-if-my-supplier-will-do-it-for-me argument, but is that enough? Wouldn't you at least want to know that your supplier can manage the inventory at least as well as you could? Then there's the issue of how a supplier managing a portion of your inventory fits into your inventory system. You may find that you end up with a whole bunch of new tasks (and added costs) associated with fitting VMI into your system. Lastly, you need to consider the potential problems that can result in giving up control of certain aspects of your inventory to an outsider. A lot of this depends on exactly how far you go with VMI, but under some VMI setups, the supplier is given so much control that you (the customer) have no way to verify if you actually got what you are paying for. In addition, you may have given your supplier (and his employees) access to confidential information that could somehow end up in the hands of one of your competitors. Wait a minute; you say you had a representative of your supplier sign a confidentiality agreement? Well that changes everything . . . NOT.

Well there you go. VMI has some potential benefits for both the supplier and customer under the right circumstances, but also has some potential problems. I should note that I described VMI within the context of items being resold, but VMI is often used for consumed items as well. For example, your office supplies vendor may manage your inventory of office supplies, or a hardware (nuts & bolts) vendor may manage your inventory of hardware used in your manufacturing processes.

Consignment inventory.

Consignment Inventory is inventory that is in the possession of the customer, but is still owned by the supplier. In other words, the supplier places some of his inventory in his customer's possession (in their store or warehouse) and allows them to sell or consume directly from his stock. The customer purchases the inventory only after he has resold or consumed it.

The key benefit to the customer should be obvious; he does not have to tie up his capital in inventory. This does not mean there are no inventory carrying costs for the customer. He will still incur costs related to storing and managing the inventory. And, as I will discuss later, the seemingly obvious inventory investment benefits may not be all they're cracked up to be.

So what's in it for the supplier? This is where the benefits may not be so obvious—or may not even exist. Let's start with a classic consignment model that has significant benefits for the supplier.

Where Consignment Works Best.

A supplier has a product or group of products that he believes will sell if he can get them in front of end-users. The trick is that getting them in front of end-users means getting them stocked in retail establishments. Retailers are hesitant to stock the product because they do not have the same level of confidence in it as the supplier, and subsequently, they do not want to invest the money and risk getting stuck with something that may not sell. Because the supplier realizes in-store exposure is critical to getting his products sold, he offers to stock his product in their stores. This creates a condition of shared risk where the supplier risks the capital investment associated with the inventory, while the customer risks dedicating retail space to the product. This also creates a condition of shared benefit because neither the supplier nor the customer will benefit until the product is sold to an end-user. This shared-risk/shared-benefit condition will often be enough to convince a customer to stock the product.

For a more specific example, consider a bicycle manufacturer that produces a wide range of bicycles ranging in price from a couple hundred dollars to several thousand dollars. He has customers (local independent bicycle shops) that stock his low-to-mid-priced models but are hesitant to stock the more expensive bikes because they do not have the confidence that their customers are willing to pay that much for a bike. And if they do get a customer who wants a high-end bike, they could always special order it for him. The bicycle manufacturer strongly believes that getting his high-end bikes in the shops where customers can see and touch them is critical in driving up sales for these models, as well as helping to promote his brand, which ultimately drives up sales for the lower cost models. The solution? Well I think you can take it from here.

I consider this the classic consignment model because it is the best-case scenario for applying the consignment inventory model. It works well for:

- New and unproven products.
- The introduction of existing product lines into new sales channels.
- Very expensive products where sales are questionable.

The key to all these examples is the combination of a high-degree of demand uncertainty from the customer's point of view, and a high degree of confidence in the sales potential from the supplier's point of view.

The consignment inventory model can also be effective with service parts for critical equipment where the customer would not stock certain service parts due to budget constraints or demand uncertainty. In this situation, consignment inventory allows the supplier to provide a higher service level (by having the parts immediately available), save expedited freight costs, and ensure the customer does not procure a replacement part from a competitor.

There is a potential side benefit to consignment inventory in that some shared information that results from the consignment process could be useful to the supplier in his inventory management. This is pretty much what we covered under VMI.

Where consignment inventory is less effective or counterproductive.

I don't recommend using consignment inventory as a localized cost-cutting tactic. This is where a big customer decides that he is going to pressure his suppliers into providing consignment inventory to eliminate his investment in inventory (there go those nickel-and-diming execs again). In these situations, the customer was probably already stocking the product, and is simply using his leverage over the supplier to reduce his costs. While this may (not necessarily) reduce the customer's costs, it is actually just moving these costs from the customer to the supplier. In addition, consignment inventory will almost always add costs to the supply chain because there are additional costs associated with managing the consignment process. So in the end, the supply chain has to absorb more costs without any meaningful benefits.

I also want to point out that this "assumed savings" related to inventory investment may not even exist. I recently reviewed a situation where a BIG retailer forced a consignment requirement on a supplier, but as part of the consignment agreement, the retailer gave up the payment terms that the supplier normally provided with a normal purchase arrangement. Well, when I looked at the details of the actual shipments relative to when the product was sold by the retailer (and thus became payable to the supplier), it was evident that the retailer was actually paying for the product sooner than he would have been had he just stuck with the normal purchase arrangement. Well, remember when I warned you not to clever yourself into something really stupid? This retailer just 500-pound-gorilla'd itself into something really stupid.

And now for an annoying little problem associated with consignment inventory that the nickel-and-dimers often overlook. The nature of consignment inventory is that "change of ownership" is unrelated to the shipment/receipt processes. This is contrary to the basic design of most inventory/accounting systems' transactional processes. Because of this, most inventory systems do not handle consignment inventory very well. This forces many businesses to manage consignment inventory with manual off-line processes (sending reports back and forth, maintaining data in spreadsheets, etc.). Not only is this time consuming, but it also creates many opportunities for errors because the additional transactions necessary for consignment inventory can get rather complicated and are highly dependant on accurate information sharing. If this process is not monitored closely, you can end up in a situation where reconciling your consignment inventory becomes a nightmare.

If consignment inventory is a significant part of your business, you need to look for software that focuses on consignment inventory, or look into modifying your current system to add this functionality. It's very important to realize that consignment inventory will almost always add costs to the supply chain, so use it only when it provides benefits that surpass these added costs.

Collaborative planning.

I thought this would be a good place to jump in with a few words on collaborative planning. One of the previously discussed supplier benefits of VMI and consignment inventory is the opportunity to use the customer's inventory data to assist in planning the supplier's inventory. That's the basic concept behind collaborative planning. Rather than having a disconnected supply chain, we can share data between customers and suppliers and gain the same benefits we associate with using DRP in a distribution network.

In theory, collaborative planning should provide the ability to increase service levels while reducing overall inventory in the supply chain. From a technological standpoint, there's nothing standing in the way of achieving this. Data sharing is commonplace these days, and the planning logic used here is essentially DRP.

However, from a practical standpoint, there are some very real hurdles to overcome. Ideally, what we want to do here is net demand as we pass it up the supply chain (as we did with DRP). Again, there is nothing technologically too difficult here. You start with the furthest point(s) down the supply chain you can access, and use their forecasts, current inventory levels, and actual orders, to net demand. You then pass this netted demand up to the next level in the supply chain, where it is accumulated and netted against the current inventory levels and orders there, and passed up to the next level.

So the good news is, our inventory planning is now directly driven by the forecasts, inventory levels, and order data of our customers (or our customers' customers' customers). And the bad news is, our inventory planning is now directly driven by the forecasts, inventory levels, and order data of our customers (or our customers' customers' customers). That may sound a little scary because . . . well . . . it is a little scary. Earlier in the book I mentioned that most companies don't manage their inventory very well. I'm probably being a little kind with that statement. So before you hitch your wagon to the collaborative planning train, you need to be able to trust the data you will be using to make your planning decisions. If you don't really trust it, you probably won't really use it. Which means you will invest in the infrastructure required to do collaborative planning, but you won't really be doing collaborative planning.

You shouldn't underestimate how difficult it can be to trust data from your trading partners. Many companies don't even trust their own data. For example, it's not uncommon for a manufacturing company to have a formal sales forecast produced by their sales division, yet their manufacturing people create their own informal forecast and use that to drive production because they don't trust the "official" sales forecast. And that's just the forecast. You also need to trust the accuracy of their inventory levels, current orders, and possibly their allocation system. Once again, many companies don't even trust this data within their own facility. Just imagine what may happen when a single very large transactional error occurs. Many of us have experienced these in our own businesses; someone does a typo on a sales order or inventory adjustment and suddenly you have a million-dollar transaction that's completely wrong. Within the business in which this error occurred, it is likely that no one will take an action based on it because they (hopefully) will notice that this just can't be right. But what happens if, before they catch it, this data is passed up the supply chain. Is it going to be an obvious error at the next level in the supply chain? Or the next level above that?

I don't mean to be an alarmist here, but these are very real problems that you need to deal with in a collaborative planning environment. As a possible solution, you could build yourself a more sophisticated system that can use the data provided by your customers, but not be completely dependent upon it. For example, you can test the forecasts and demand being passed up to you against forecasts you have calculated yourself (yes, you are duplicating efforts here). If the customer-supplied forecast is within a tolerance, you use it, if not, you need a process to verify the customer's data or use your own. You can also build in some exception-handling rules to hopefully identify errors before they create further problems.

Postponement.

Postponement is really a simple concept. By delaying certain activities until the latest possible moment, you can reduce your inventory investment and some of the risks associated with carrying this inventory.

How does it work? Let's go back to my bicycle example. If I take all my components and immediately assemble them into complete (or partially complete) bicycles, box them up, and put them into storage, I am now carrying the cost of the labor associated with assembling those bicycles as part of my inventory. If a bicycle sits on the shelf for two months, that means that I paid for that labor two months earlier than I needed to.

But that's only part of the picture. Many of my components can be used on numerous different sizes, models, and colors of bicycles. If I assemble the bikes right away, I am dedicating these components to a specific size, model, and color. This means, I am carrying safety stock at the end-item level (which is normally a good approach). However, the variability at the end-item level is much greater than the variability at the family level, therefore, if I could carry my safety stock at the family level, I would need less safety stock. Unfortunately, I really can't carry safety stock at the family level; however, I can get similar results by carrying safety stock at the component level.

Here's a more specific example. Let's say I have one model of bicycle that has three frame sizes and two color choices. This means I have six different end items based on different frames, but all other components are the same. I'm confident that within this model (the six end items), I will sell somewhere between 4,000 and 6,000 bicycles over the next couple of months, but when I look at each specific size/color, the variability is much greater. For example, my Red Large bicycles may sell anywhere between 500 and 1000 units. If I were trying to be able to meet all demand for this period for each size/color, I would end up building 8,000 bicycles even though I don't expect to sell more than 6,000 bicycles in total. Once again, that's because I am covering the variability of each size/color combination.

However, if I choose to not build up the bikes right away, I would still need to have 8,000 frames manufactured to cover this potential demand, but I would only need components for 6,000 complete bikes. Not only that, but some of my components may allow for shorter lead times and smaller lot sizes, so I can have multiple smaller shipments of them arrive during this period rather than having them all arrive right away to build up all the bikes. To take it further, if I choose to not paint the frames right away, I could reduce the number of frames as well.

Another example of postponement involves branding or custom packaging. I may have a specific item that is sold under multiple brand names or even customer-specific branding. Once again, the variability at the specific brand level is greater than at the raw item (the unpackaged item) level. By putting off packaging this product until I receive the actual orders, I am able to reduce my inventory as well as reduce carrying my labor/machine investment in the packaging.

Lean, TPS, JIT, TOC, QRM, TQM, Six Sigma . . .

If you've spent even a small amount of time in operations management, and especially if you've spent time in a manufacturing environment, you have undoubtedly run into some of these terms. So what exactly are they? That's a little tricky to answer since different people interpret them differently and some are just chompin' at the bit to get into an argument over their interpretation. From my perspective, I view each of these as part strategy and part philosophy, but with a defined set of tactics and techniques used to achieve the strategy/philosophy.

When you look at the details, a good part of each of these is made up with what I would call commonsense business practices. Now don't get me wrong, I'm not saying that as a way of diminishing the value of these strategies; there is a lot of value in educating people on, and reinforcing the importance of, commonsense business practices. But in addition to these commonsense business practices, each strategy has its own unique hook. When I say, "hook", I mean that each has a very specific idea it focuses on, and all the tactics and techniques are built around this idea. For example, Lean, Toyota Production System (TPS), and Just-in-time (JIT) focus on eliminating waste, Theory of Constraints (TOC) focuses on bottlenecks, Quick Response Manufacturing (QRM) focuses on lead-time reduction, and Total Quality Management (TQM) and Six Sigma focus on quality. The common belief here is that by focusing efforts towards one specific objective, everything else will fall into line.

I should clarify that it is an oversimplification to say that Lean focuses on eliminating waste or that Theory of Constraints focuses on bottlenecks. For example, Lean very clearly defines what waste is and introduces a very specific way of thinking about waste, as well as very specific techniques for identifying and eliminating waste. Theory of Constraints takes a similar approach towards bottlenecks as do the others with their "hooks".

I'm not going to go into more detail on these because it's just not practical within the scope of this book. You can build an entire library on what has been written on these topics and I would strongly encourage you to start exploring each of these. Personally, I feel I have gained from my exposure to these strategies, but that doesn't mean I accept all their premises. My problem with these strategies is that they have often been packaged and sold as rather strict roadmaps that are expected to fit into any environment. And while each teaches you to think in new ways about your operations, they also expect you to accept certain premises of their strategy without question. Well let's just say that I'm not a big Kool-Aid drinker.

The make-or-buy decision.

I guess no book on inventory management would be complete without mentioning the make-or-buy decision. I'm not going to detail any specific formula here because, by now, you should know enough about inventory management to put together your own calculation. Plus, the thought process you will go through in developing your own calculation should help you to better understand the implications of the make-or-buy decision in your specific environment. I will help you get started though, and, of course, throw in some tidbits to help make things more complicated. Hey, I'm just doin' my job.

The make-or-buy decision generally starts out as a cost comparison—how much it costs me to make something compared to how much it costs me to buy it. If I currently manufacture something, I just go to the computer and look up the unit cost, then compare that to the unit cost on quotes I get from potential suppliers. Well hopefully, we all know better than that by now. There are obviously other costs that need to be considered. For the purchased items, we would need to look at transportation costs (or other landed costs, discussed next in the overseas sourcing section). We also need to look at lead times and lot sizes to determine expected inventory levels and their associated carrying costs, because the make-or-buy decision will likely result in changes in inventory levels.

But that's not all. We need to dig into our "make" unit cost to see what is included in it. How is the labor calculated? How is the machine time calculated? What set-up costs are included? What overhead costs are included? It's important to know these things because you need to be confident that you are doing an accurate comparison. Costing in manufacturing is tricky business, and like everything else in inventory management, it is often full of flaws and cheats. You need to make sure you include all the applicable costs, but also need to be certain that any costs included in the manufactured (make) cost would not exist should you decide to buy rather than make. If you recall from the chapter on lot sizing, we discussed how some storage costs don't change as the order quantity changes. Well, we can have similar issues with overhead costs that are often applied as part of manufactured costs. You also need to make sure you don't duplicate costs in your calculation. For example, if you put together a "total annual cost" calculation that includes order costs and carrying costs, you need to make sure you are not duplicating your setup cost by including it in both your order cost and your unit cost.

We also need to look at the component costs that make up the manufactured item. Since we logically decided to include inbound transportation costs in our "buy" calculation, shouldn't we also include the inbound transportation costs associated with our components in our "make" calculation? Yeah, we probably should. Now before this gets too scary, I want to note that depending on the nature of your components, you may be able to do a little cheating here by using some cost estimates or averages rather than trying to calculate actual inbound transportation costs for each component.

Then there are the really complicated issues. How is the make-or-buy decision affecting your manufacturing capacity, and, is that a good thing or a bad thing? If you are maxed out on manufacturing capacity and it would be very expensive to obtain more capacity, choosing to buy rather than make a product or group of products may have benefits beyond what you see in the simple cost comparison. On the other hand, if choosing to buy rather than make leaves you with excess capacity that is still incurring costs, this needs to be taken into consideration.

You want more? What if your reduced usage of components and raw materials that results from choosing to buy something you currently make, results in losing out on discounts on components or raw materials you use in other products you still manufacture? Or, what if choosing to buy something you currently make results in getting a greater discount on other products you currently buy?

As you can see, the make-or-buy decision isn't as much a calculation as it is an analysis-based decision-making process. Sometimes it will just come down to a simple cost comparison; other times it requires more extensive analysis and consideration of less tangible factors.

Implications of overseas sourcing.

Overseas sourcing (international sourcing) is an often highly debated topic and I thought I would hit on it briefly. Yes, there are deals to be had with overseas sourcing, but you need to do your homework to make sure you are actually saving money. I want to emphasize this point because there seems to be a growing number of nickel-and-diming execs who just assume they will save money by sourcing or moving their production overseas. Sure, it's easy to find an overseas supplier that quotes a lower unit cost, but when all other costs are considered, are you still saving money? That's the big question, and to answer it with a reasonable degree of accuracy you need to do some analysis. Let's look at some of the considerations here.

- **Landed cost.** Your first step when trying to do a comparison is to calculate (estimate) your landed cost. You can think of landed cost as your "delivered cost". In addition to the unit cost, it should include transportation costs, brokerage fees, and any import duties or taxes required. To be fair in your comparison, you would also need to calculate transportation costs associated with sourcing domestically.

- **Payment terms.** When sourcing domestically, it's rather common to get 30 or 60 days payment terms (you don't need to pay for the inventory until 30 or 60 days after the invoice date), but when sourcing internationally, it's not uncommon to have to pay in advance of shipment. When we're talking about transportation times of 30 to 60 days, that means you would be paying for the inventory one to two months before you receive it. In other words, you would have to pay for the inventory anywhere from two to four months earlier than you would if you sourced it domestically. Therefore, the cost associated with your money being tied up earlier (we discussed this in the lot-sizing chapter) needs to be calculated.

- **Exchange rates.** Fluctuating exchange rates can be a huge factor in overseas sourcing. You not only need to calculate your costs based on the current exchange rate, you also need to attempt to forecast changes in exchange rates. Good luck with that one.

- **Loss of intellectual property, knockoffs, counterfeiting.** You contract out with an overseas manufacturer to produce your product, and, in the process, you supply him with drawings, tooling, materials specs, and possibly even training. You later find that counterfeits or exact copies of your product with another brand on them are popping up around the world. You suspect your new supplier is behind these knockoffs, but what are you going to do? Sure, you can find another supplier, but that's not going to stop the first guy from continuing to produce the knockoffs now that you showed him how.

- **Lack of legal protection.** This partially goes along with the previous point, but goes beyond it as well. It's difficult enough (and costly) to have to pursue legal action against a supplier in your own country, but try doing it with a supplier in another country. Their legal system may not offer the same protections you are used to domestically, and even if they do technically offer the same protections, they may not enforce these protections.

- **On-time delivery, damage, and product loss.** The further you need to transport something, the greater the risk that something will go wrong along the way. In some cases this just means delivery delays due to bad weather or port congestions, but in others it means damage or product loss. In a recent USA Today article, it was estimated that between 2,000 and 10,000 ocean containers were lost at sea each year—they basically fell off the ship. Certainly, that's a small percentage of all containers shipped each year, but it's just one more thing that can go wrong. Besides, that's just a hell of a lot of cargo. Now add to that the damage that often occurs when the contents of a container are improperly secured and get tossed around in rough seas.

- **Increase in inventory.** Though this isn't an absolute, you can almost certainly expect your inventory to increase when you shift from a domestic supplier to an overseas supplier. Longer lead times and lower on-time deliveries will lead to greater safety stock requirements, while order and transportation costs combined with minimum buys will often lead to larger lot sizes.

- **Additional management costs.** This one is commonly overlooked. Dealing with longer lead times, communication difficulties, legal issues, accounting issues. and working with brokers, all take time. In addition, this time is often taken from your more capable employees since these are often complicated issues. You'll also likely find that it costs you more to process international receipts through your receiving department than it does to process domestic receipts. While some of these things seem minor, they do add up.

- **Bribes, paying protection.** Sure it's illegal or at least unethical, but it's commonplace in some countries. Not only is it an added cost, it's also an added risk. In recent years, some executives (I'm not saying which company, but let's just say their main product rhymes with zananas) have found out the hard way that they can be personally held responsible for these illegal activities. Yeah, nothing gets an exec's attention like the thought of doin' time in the big house.

- **Facilities costs.** This is not as big an issue as it used to be, because the current trend is to outsource production to an overseas supplier rather than building your own plant overseas, but some companies are still building plants overseas. Due to constantly changing economic conditions, the cheap labor that makes it cost effective to build a plant in a specific location today, may not exist five years from now (the labor may still exist, but it may cost you significantly more). Therefore, you really need to incorporate a rather aggressive depreciation model for the costs of your facilities.

Once again, I'm not trying to say there is not a business case to be made for overseas sourcing, only that there are many more variables that need to be considered in your decision.

The purchasing function.

This book focuses on planning activities, but I at least wanted to offer a quick intro to the purchasing function. Sometimes called procurement, the purchasing function involves sourcing (finding the right supplier for specific items) and negotiating agreements related to procuring products or services.

In some operations, purchasing and planning are done by the same people, while in others they are separate jobs (and possibly separate departments). There are arguments that can be made for either practice. For example, I could argue that the skill set that makes a good buyer is not necessarily the same skill set that makes a good planner. A good buyer needs to have above average people skills, needs to be a bit of a wheeler-dealer (negotiator), and may need specific industry or product knowledge, much like the skills you would look for in a good sales person. While a good planner needs to have above average computer skills and needs to be more analytical and efficient (good multitasking skills). This isn't to say that buyers don't need to be analytical or that planners don't need industry knowledge, only that the extent to which these skills are used is much different for a buyer versus a planner.

That said, there is also an argument to be made that there are problems that can result from separating the purchasing and planning functions. For example, decisions made by a buyer can have a significant impact on the planning function. If the buyer chooses to source from a supplier with long lead times and large lot size requirements, the planner is going to be stuck working within these less-than-desirable constraints. Therefore, if you do separate buyer and planner functions, the buyers must at least understand the impact of their buying decisions on the planning function. Well actually, they need to understand the impact of their buying decisions on the company (not just the planning function).

So let's look at some purchasing (buyer) responsibilities and related topics.

Finding suppliers.

Depending on the product being sourced, this may be as easy as a quick Internet search or may be as difficult as a multi-month odyssey traveling the globe searching for companies with the right capabilities. Locating potential suppliers is only part of the issue here, the buyer must also determine the capabilities of the supplier to meet your demand and quality requirements.

Negotiating prices and terms.

Technically, the seller sets the pricing and terms, but anyone that's been involved in buying or selling is quite aware that almost everything is negotiable. Pricing negotiations often involve committing to volume levels (units or dollar amount over a specified time period).

Terms fall into several categories. Payment terms determine at what point relative to the transfer of goods the seller must be paid, and if there are any discounts available for early payment. For example, 2/10 net 30 terms means that if you pay within 10 days of the invoice date you will receive a 2% discount, otherwise the full amount is due within 30 days of the invoice date. There may also be additional penalties for late payments.

Freight terms define who is responsible for paying freight from the supplier to the buyer. Freight terms can get complicated when special freight policies apply based on the amount of the purchase, quantity of purchase, weight of purchase, or shipment method chosen.

Terms are also used to determine when change of ownership occurs. This is a confusing area because there is very often a difference between the legal requirements of this and the actual practices that occur. For example, the official terms may state that change of ownership occurs when the shipment leaves the dock of the supplier (this is the most common practice), which means that anything that happens beyond that point is the responsibility of the buyer. However, should the shipment get lost or damaged, it's not at all uncommon that the seller would take responsibility for "making things right" even though he has no legal requirement to do so. Another confusing point here is related to the term FOB, which stands for Free On Board. Technically speaking, FOB defines the point that change of ownership occurs, AND the point at which the buyer takes responsibility for freight costs. So "FOB Shipping Point" would mean that change of ownership occurs when the shipment leaves the sellers dock, and that freight costs are the responsibility of the buyer. However, in my experience, most businesses treat freight policies completely separately from their FOB declaration, so they may list FOB Shipping Point in their terms, yet still prepay freight based on their freight policy.

Purchasing contracts.

The end result of the price-and-terms negotiations may be a purchasing contract or something less formal. A purchasing contract is a legal document agreed to by the buyer and seller on the pricing and terms that resulted from the negotiations. Let me first clarify that most purchasing transactions occur without ever entering into a formal purchasing contract (as described here). A formal purchasing contract is generally used when an agreement is made relative to the transfer of goods or services that amount to a significant value and are outside of the normal pricing and terms provided by the seller, or where a significant commitment is being made by the buyer and/or seller. For example, if I regularly buy ball bearings from a supplier and my purchase quantities fit right into his standard discount structure and terms, I'm probably not going to use a purchasing contract. However, if I want to commit to buy a significant quantity of ball bearings over a period of time, and in doing so want to negotiate a lower price and/or better terms and/or a specific service-level commitment from the supplier, I may choose to use a purchasing contract. Again, I don't absolutely need a formal purchasing contract to do this, but if either the buyer, or seller, or both, want the added protection of a formal legal document, it would make sense to look into a purchasing contract.

Purchasing contracts should not be entered into lightly. I once worked for a company that was stuck with a really bad multi-million-dollar purchasing contract that was agreed to by one of its buyers. The buyer no longer worked for them, but they were still stuck buying from this supplier for the next several years at prices that were above what they could negotiate with another supplier.

Purchase orders?

Technically, a purchase order is also a purchasing contract, but this is another area where actual business practices don't always treat it as such. For example, a purchase order should state the items and quantities ordered and the dates when the quantities should be filled, along with the pricing and terms. Technically, when the supplier accepts the purchase order, he is accepting all the terms stated on the purchase order.

The reality is that in many industries, the purchase order is just used as a notification and an instrument to track a transaction. Though it still technically is an agreement, it's very possible that no one is actually looking at the details of the terms stated on the purchase order. The seller just uses it to enter a sales/shipping order for the customer using the items and quantities on the purchase order, but applying terms and pricing based on the supplier's standard pricing and terms or any special agreement that has been put in place. I mention this because it's not unusual for a purchase order to state terms that are contrary to the actual terms that are in place. This is more common where the typical total value of a purchase order is rather small and the supplier has a somewhat transient customer base. In these cases, the supplier had decided it's just not worth the time to try to clarify these discrepancies on every purchase order because his customers generally are willing to accept his pricing and terms (the incorrect information on the purchase order is just a matter of laziness by the buyer).

I'm not saying this is right, only that it is rather common. Surprisingly (or not), there is a lot of this kind of thing going on in business, and while it's important to understand the technical legal implications and how things are "supposed to be", it is equally as important to understand the actual business practices you are likely to encounter in the real world.

I mention purchase orders here because I wanted to cover the legal and practical realities of them within the context of "purchasing". However, in an environment where buyers operate separately from planners, it is the planners that manage the purchase-order process.

Supplier liaison.

Buyers often also act as supplier liaisons. What exactly does this mean? It means that they often act as a go-between when certain types of issues come up between the supplier and the buyer's company. For example, if an order is late in arriving, the planner would generally just contact the supplier directly, however, if you are having repeated delivery problems, the buyer may be the one that would contact the supplier. Alternately, if the supplier has a past due invoice from the buyer's company, he would probably just contact their accounting department, but if he has a lot of past due invoices or has seen a pattern of late payments from the buyer's company, he may contact the buyer to work things out.

Every company has different requirements and therefore may operate a little differently when it comes to purchasing responsibilities. There are some businesses that will never enter into a purchasing contract, and others that have legal staff available just for this purpose. There are companies and industries where a purchase order is simply a number used to track transactions, and others where the terms detailed on a purchase order are gospel. There are businesses where their purchasing position is a low-level clerical position, and others where it's a very high-level strategic position.

If purchasing is a key part of your job, you may want to consider joining the Institute of Supply Management (ISM). Formally known as the National Association of Purchasing Management (NAPM), ISM has a strong focus on purchasing but also delves into inventory management and operations management in general. Go to www.ism.ws for more info.

Quick recap and tips.

Forecasting.

I dedicated three chapters to forecasting because I believe it is that important. Most businesses would do well to spend some serious time improving their forecasting process. While this doesn't necessarily mean that you have to start with your forecasting process, it's probably not a bad idea to at least do some work in this area fairly soon.

Safety Stock.

Since your forecast also drives your safety stock calculation, you are generally better off holding off on tweaking your safety stock calculation until you have a solid forecasting process in place. This is mainly to prevent you from having to repeatedly tweak your safety stock settings as you change your forecasting process. However, if you are having some serious problems with safety stock, it may make sense to go ahead and work on this right away. Just realize you will need to review it again after making changes to your forecasting process.

Lot sizing.

Though lot sizing is impacted by the forecast, you can pretty much implement a lot-sizing calculation at any time. I consider lot sizing to be the easiest improvement because once you spend some time up front working out the inputs (order cost, carrying cost), you are pretty much good to go. While you will want to watch the results and maybe do a little tweaking, it generally doesn't require the type of ongoing attention that you would give to forecasting and safety stock.

Do your initial development in a spreadsheet, and test, test, test.

I can't overemphasis this. A spreadsheet allows you to quickly and easily experiment with various calculations and options. It also allows you to test the calculation against your data, and provides a working formula a programmer can use as a blueprint should you decide to implement your calculation in the form of custom programming.

Use extreme examples as part of your testing.

I've used extreme examples throughout this book because that's the easiest way to demonstrate certain characteristics of inventory, or certain characteristics of methods used to manage inventory. Beyond demonstration purposes, extreme examples also help to identify potential problems with methods and calculations. A flaw that may be difficult to identify when running items with similar characteristics through a specific calculation, may jump out at you when you test with more extreme examples.

Plan your implementations.

This shouldn't need to be said, but since screwing up software implementations seems to be the norm, please take the appropriate time to plan any system changes. This not only means testing the changes, but also training people on them and projecting the potential impact of each change. For example, I had previously mentioned that changes to planning systems often result in short-term increases in inventory. That's because your "improved" planning setup will immediately start to increase any inventory levels that were too low under your previous settings, yet you are still stuck with any inventory that was too high under your previous settings. This can happen with changes to forecasting settings, safety stock calculations, and lot sizing. Whenever possible, you should try to phase in these implementations by applying them to smaller groups of products. This also allows you to confirm the results of the changes before having them affect your entire inventory.

Intellectual curiosity is a requirement.

At various points in this book, I took the opportunity to criticize and even ridicule certain practices and those who use them. This was not simply because I disagreed with these practices, but rather because I believe people use these practices out of pure intellectual laziness. There is really no other explanation as to how a practice like "order half as much, twice as often" can be accepted. So while I accept that we can't know everything about everything—or everything about anything or anything about everything—we at least need to try to know something about the field we choose to work in.

Intellectual curiosity does not mean you need to conduct endless analyses of your inventory practices, or expect to understand every academic paper ever written on inventory management. What it means is you need to at least invest a little time in thinking about the practices you are—or will be—using, to see if they are logical and provide effective results. If they don't, you need to consider how you may be able to change them to make them more effective, or determine what other options are available to achieve more effective results. This isn't asking a lot.

Add skepticism as a formal part of your decision-making process.

A good dose of skepticism can save you a lot of headaches (and money). There's always something "new" and "revolutionary" coming down the hype pipeline, but there are also well-established business practices that are all-too-often blindly accepted as "good" business practices. I say, question everything. Spend at least as much time trying to identify potential flaws as you do identifying potential benefits. Always explore alternate means of achieving the same objective. And please, don't believe something just because you read it in a book or magazine, or because it was recommended by an "expert". And yes, that includes everything in this book. If you blindly implement the calculations I described in this book, you obviously weren't paying attention.

Feel free to exercise cautious creativity.

Business practices are so diverse that you cannot just plug in standard solutions and expect them to work. For every rule, there are many exceptions; and while you should strongly consider standard business practices and standard solutions, you should not be constrained by them. If it makes sense in your business to carry safety stock for some component items, don't be afraid to do it just because the "rule of thumb" states that you should only carry safety stock at the finished-goods level. Or, if the output of your forecast or safety stock calculation is not what you want it to be, feel free to experiment with variations or develop your own cheats to get the output you want. But as I said before, be careful not to clever your way to something stupid. Think through your logic to make sure it is . . . ah . . . logical. And, of course, test it.

I just want to clarify my "clever your way into something stupid" comment. Unlike some other comments I've made in this book, I don't mean this one to imply stupidity on anyone's part. I mention it because it actually is very easy to clever yourself into something stupid—plus, I just like saying it. In fact, when I look back at the logic I used in the safety stock chapter, I'm not all that certain that I haven't been guilty of getting lost in my own logic. But through testing, I have found that even if my logic is flawed, the results I receive are effective in the environments I've implemented this logic.

Remind yourself to widen your view of solutions.

It's easy to get trapped into a narrow focus of solutions, or a narrow focus to what your problem is. For example, you may find you have a bulky, expensive, slow-moving item with a significant amount of variability. While you are racking your brain trying to figure out if you can forecast this variability or how you can justify the space requirements and inventory investment required to carry the safety stock to meet the variability, you overlook the possibility that your supplier may have a direct-ship program available that would allow you to not carry any inventory of this item, while still meeting or exceeding your fill-rate requirement. Other "wider view" solutions may include looking for ways to reduce or eliminate demand variability, or ways to reduce lead times and lot sizes rather than just planning around these factors.

Short lead times and excess capacity can be wonderful things.

Yes, I know I just mentioned lead times, but here I go again. Shorter lead times can take so much of the burden off your forecasting and safety stock calculations that they could almost be considered a miracle cure for inventory woes. When you shorten your inbound lead times, you should be able to reduce your safety stock levels while at the same time increasing your service levels. In addition, you may find you have savings related to less expediting (and the associated freight costs). Ultimately, shorter lead times will just plain make life easier for your inventory planners.

Having a little excess capacity can also provide some amazing results—and I'm not just talking about manufacturing capacity here (though that is the primary point). Having a little excess manufacturing capacity, processing capacity in your receiving and shipping departments, storage capacity in the warehouse, and even planning capacity, means you can have a more flexible production schedule, can get receipts into stock quicker, and don't have to short-change your planning processes. Though excess capacity certainly has costs associated with it, you will often find the benefits provided by excess capacity are well worth the investment in it.

I'm not saying you should blindly switch to shorter lead-time suppliers or add capacity, but I am saying you should strongly consider the advantages provided by these changes. While shorter lead times and excess capacity don't make you better at planning inventory, they do make it easier to plan and will provide better results given the same level of planning.

Don't get trapped in the "we're too small" mentality.

Yes, smaller businesses tend to have greater practical limitations than larger businesses, but that doesn't mean you have to settle for an ineffective inventory management system. Much of what I have covered in this book can be implemented without significant investments or resources. With a smaller business, it usually just means that you may not be able to automate your systems to the level a larger company could. On the plus side, smaller businesses can usually make these types of improvements much quicker than larger businesses.

Don't get trapped in the "we can just buy it" mentality.

There are plenty of software providers that are willing to take your money and provide you with the "latest and greatest" inventory management system. While some of these systems have some very useful functionality, you are unlikely to realize their full potential if you do not have skilled inventory managers setting them up, tweaking them, and knowing when human involvement is necessary.

Focus on inventory management, not inventory reduction.

There's nothing wrong with wanting to have less inventory, but if you blindly focus on inventory reduction—as many companies do—you just may develop the inventory management version of an eating disorder.

Know when to step in and make adjustments.

Timing is everything. I just happen to be putting the final touches on this book during October of 2008. In the past few weeks the world has found itself in a major financial crisis, the credit market is in turmoil, banks are closing, the stock market has plummeted, notices of facility closings and layoffs are on the increase, fuel prices have hit record highs, retail sales are struggling, and housing foreclosures are way up.

Well, if this kind of stuff doesn't affect your business, you certainly are in the minority. This is an excellent example of one of those times when it makes a lot of sense to step in and evaluate the setup of your planning systems. With expectations of capital shortages (due to the banking crisis), it may make sense to increase the cost-of-capital portion of your lot-sizing calculation. It likely also makes sense to increase your forecasting smoothing factor to allow your forecasts to more quickly react to changes in trend. It may even make sense to temporarily manually override your forecasts. I hate to sound like a recording here, but this is another one of those times when you will appreciate shorter lead times.

Exactly what you do under these conditions should be based on some analysis of how your business has been affected in the past by these types of economic changes. Don't panic, but don't just sit there either. Your inventory system needs human input, and you're it.

Know your inventory system.

Your knowledge of inventory management won't do you much good if you don't understand the capabilities, setup requirements, and peculiarities of your specific inventory system.

Keep at it.

Getting good at inventory management is an evolutionary process. Continue to improve your own knowledge and skills. Continue to tweak your settings and explore new ways of doing things. Continue to analyze your inventory data to identify changes that may be occurring. And remember, while you may never master inventory management, you can always be better at it.

Do you now know enough to be dangerous?

In keeping with a previous comment I made, I want to remind you that there may be some areas where you now know just enough to be dangerous. Though I went to great lengths to explain history-based forecasting techniques, statistics-based safety stock, economic-based lot sizing, and the key mechanics of common ordering systems, there were some related topics that I only briefly introduced.

For example, if your knowledge of regression analysis or optimization programs (like Excel's Solver) is based solely on what you read in this book, you now know just enough to be dangerous. In addition, while I spent a fair amount of time explaining the basic mechanics of MRP, this alone is not enough information to adequately prepare you to set up and operate an MRP system. And if you're thinking about blindly implementing the calculations included in this book, then not only are you dangerous, but you obviously weren't even paying attention.

Final comments.

I've thrown a lot of stuff at you in this book, including pointing out many flaws and misconceptions with what we refer to as our inventory systems. While I did introduce solutions or explanations to many of these, I did not resolve all of them. That's because there is no such thing as a perfect inventory system; they all currently have flaws and will continue to have flaws. Sure, you may have felt better about all this if—instead of reading this book—you had read one of those "simple" inventory books that fail to even come close to acknowledging the complexity of inventory management or the flaws and limitations of the simple calculations they advocate. With the right set of blinders or rose-colored glasses, you may have been able to go on thinking you really have a handle on this inventory management thing. Now you know otherwise, and there's no going back.

Being good at inventory management starts with understanding inventory management with all its flaws and complexities, but also understanding there is still stuff you don't completely understand, or there are certain solutions or calculations that are simply beyond your current skill set or practical business capabilities. That's what keeps us learning, improving, and hopefully prevents us from making big mistakes. We need to try to understand what we don't understand, and we need to try to find solutions for unresolved flaws, but we also need to realize that we can still effectively manage our inventory without having a perfect system.

In writing this book, my goal was to provide highly detailed explanations of some of the key principles of inventory management. I wanted to expose readers to the good, the bad, and the ugly aspects of forecasting, safety stock, and lot size calculations, and in the process, not only better prepare them to deal with these specific issues, but also, better prepare them to tackle other inventory-related topics not covered in this text. There simply is no way a single book—or even a library of books—can cover every potential issue you will encounter in the real world of inventory management. Therefore, a good inventory manager not only needs to be familiar with the ins-and-outs of "typical" inventory management situations, but also needs to be skilled at analyzing and developing solutions for atypical situations when they arise. In that respect, I'm hoping that you not only go away with an understanding of the topics covered here, but also an understanding of the logical and practical way I approached these topics. This approach has served me well over the years.

So spend the time to understand your problem before you start to develop possible solutions. When you have some possible solutions, take the time to identify their flaws, the potential implications of these flaws, and potential solutions for these flaws. And remember, while a perfect solution would be nice, it's probably neither necessary nor realistic. So the "best" solution for you comes down to the least-flawed solution you can implement within your practical limitations.

Glossary

80/20 rule—a more specific version of the Pareto principle. 80/20 implies that 80% of effects are the result of 20% of causes. *See also* Pareto principle.

ABC stratification—the activity of applying a ranking system (A-B-C-D. . .) to a characteristic. For example, ABC by times sold is frequently used to rank items based on how frequently they are sold.

Action message—in MRP, DRP, and related planning systems, action messages are notifications to planners that an action needs to be taken. For example, a notification to release or reschedule an order.

Adaptive smoothing—a variation on exponential smoothing that uses a calculation based on forecast error to automatically change the smoothing factor.

Advanced planning and scheduling—APS is a step beyond MRPII and is somewhat more difficult to define, but generally includes capabilities for finite capacity scheduling and reacting to rapidly changing demand.

Advanced shipment notification—a document used to notify a customer of a shipment. ASNs will often include PO numbers, SKU numbers, lot numbers, quantities, and pallet, carton, or container numbers. ASNs may be paper based, however electronic notification is preferred. Advanced shipment notification systems are usually combined with bar coded compliance labeling that allows the customer to receive the shipment into inventory through the use of bar code scanners and automated data collection systems.

Allocations—actual demand created by sales orders or production orders against a specific item.

Anticipation inventory—anticipation inventory can be thought of as "capacity inventory" because it is usually the result of a buildup of inventory in order to meet demand during a period of time when demand exceeds capacity.

APICS—The Association for Operations Management (previously known as American Production and Inventory Control Society). www.apics.org

ASN—See advanced shipment notification.

Available—refers to the status of inventory as it relates to its ability to be sold or consumed. Availability calculations are used to determine this status. Availability calculations vary from system to system but basically subtract any current allocations or holds on inventory from the current on-hand balance. *See also* Allocations.

Average forecast bias—the average of a series of forecast errors. *See also* Forecast error.

Backflush—method for issuing (reducing on-hand quantities) materials to a production order. With backflushing, the material is issued automatically when production is posted against an operation. The backflushing program will use the quantity completed to calculate through the bill of materials the quantities of the components used, and reduce on-hand balances by these quantities.

Backorder—a quantity on an order that was not filled on the required date due to inadequate inventory levels.

Best of breed—the term best of breed became widely used as people started realizing that certain modules within their software suite were inadequate to meet their needs, and started looking at separate software products to replace these modules. Software vendors, trade magazines, and consultants started using the term best of breed to categorize these highly functional, independent software modules (or sets of modules). The idea is that a single software suite cannot possibly have the best modules for every functional area of your business, therefore, rather than settling for the mediocre functionality in some modules just because you liked the functionality in other modules, you could build your system from the best modules from two or more software vendors.

Bias—See Forecast bias.

Bill of distribution—See DRP relationship.

Bill of materials—lists materials (components) required to produce an item. Multilevel BOMs also show subassemblies and their components. Other information such as scrap factors may also be included in the BOM for use in materials planning and costing. Commonly known as a BOM or just a Bill.

Black-box forecasting—an automated forecasting system that makes forecasting decisions without any human input.

BOM—See Bill of materials.

Bullwhip effect—a phenomenon where demand variation becomes amplified as it progresses up through the supply chain. It's based on the assumption that an increase in demand at a low level in the supply chain will trigger a series of overreactions at each subsequent level in the supply chain. Bullwhip is often used as a teaching tool in demonstrating the "potential" problems of a disconnected supply chain.

Capacity—the capabilities of a process, machine, location, or facility.

Capacity requirements planning—CRP is a capacity planning tool used to verify the ability of resources to meet scheduled production. CRP uses the routings to calculate loads on work centers, and then compares these loads to the capacity of these work centers. CRP is more detailed than either rough-cut capacity planning or resources requirements planning.

Carrying costs—the costs associated with having specific quantities of inventory. Carrying costs primarily include the cost of the inventory investment and the costs associated with storing the inventory. Carrying costs are used in cost-based lot sizing calculations such as EOQ.

Cheats—I use this term to describe mathematical calculations designed to provide a particular wanted result, but the means of getting that result may not be mathematically correct or even logical. In some cases these cheats are used because a mathematically correct means of getting the result is impractical due to significant data requirements, processing limitations, or a lack of mathematical knowledge by those setting up the system. In other cases, there simply is no mathematically correct means of getting the result. Cheats (as I describe them) are not necessarily bad things. In fact, they can be very useful and even necessary in inventory management. My point in referring to them as cheats, is to make it very clear that there likely is a lack of preciseness associated with them and they may even be completely wrong (or wrong for your application).

COGS—See Cost of goods sold.

Collaborative planning—describes a planning strategy where trading partners (customers and suppliers) share their inventory planning data.

Commodity classification—See Inventory classification

Component—any item used to produce another item.

Composite forecast—a forecast that is created by combining (through averaging or weighted averaging) the results of multiple forecasting methods.

Configuration processing—software functionality that allows a product to be defined by selecting various pre-defined options rather than having every possible combination of options pre-defined as specific SKUs. Placing an order for a computer and specifying hard drive, processor, memory, graphics card, sound card, etc. would be an example of configuration processing.

Configure-to-order—manufacturing strategy that exists somewhere between make-to-stock and make-to-order. In this strategy, all or most components are stocked in anticipation of customer orders. Partial processing—such as production of subassemblies—is often done in advance of customer orders. All that remains are the final assembly or final processing activities.

Consignment inventory—inventory that is in the possession of the customer, but is still owned by the supplier. The supplier places some of his inventory in his customer's possession (in their store, warehouse, or plant) and allows them to sell or consume directly from his stock. The customer purchases the inventory only after he has resold or consumed it.

Cost of capital—costs associated with having money tied up in inventory. Generally this would be the interest rate paid on business debt, but could optionally be the return on investment a company could expect if it had access to money to invest.

Cost of goods sold—accounting term used to describe the total value (cost) of products sold during a specific period of time. Since inventory is an asset, it is not expensed when it is purchased or produced, it instead goes into an asset account (the inventory account). When product is sold, the value of the product (the cost, not the sell price) is moved from the asset account to an expense account called "cost of goods sold" or COGS. COGS appears on the profit and loss statement and is also used in some inventory measurements (such as inventory turns).

CRP—See Capacity requirements planning

Cumulative forecast bias—the sum of a series of forecast errors. *See also* Forecast error.

Cumulative lead time—the longest sum of consecutive lead times. Calculated by tracking all lead time paths through the bill-of-materials structure, and using the longest one.

Current-demand inventory—inventory carried to meet immediate expected demand. For example, the inventory that will be shipping in today's orders. The definition of "current demand" is somewhat subject to interpretation since you must apply a period of time to determine what is considered "current demand" as opposed to "future demand".

Cycle count—any process that verifies the correctness of inventory quantity data by counting portions of the inventory on an ongoing basis. In other words, any process that uses regularly scheduled counts but does not count the entire facility's inventory in a single event.

Demand—the need for a specific item in a specific quantity.

Demand override—any adjustment that is used to supersede your demand history (usually for the purposes of forecasting or calculating safety stock). A demand override can be a fixed quantity that will be used to replace the actual demand, or it can be a factor that can be used to adjust the demand.

Demand planning software—software that includes forecasting capabilities and calculations for determining order quantities and safety stock.

Demand variability—changes in demand from period to period. Demand variability is the result of trend, seasonality, events, and noise.

Dependent demand—demand that is created as a direct result of another item's demand or demand from another facility. Demand for a component is an example of dependent demand since the demand for the component is a direct result of demand for the item(s) that are produced from that component.

De-seasonalize—to remove the seasonality effect on demand. *See also* Normalize.

De-trend—to remove the trend effect on demand. *See also* Normalize.

Direct shipping—a procurement strategy that allows a company to sell product without ever stocking or even handling the product. When a customer places an order with a seller, the order is passed on to the seller's supplier who will then ship the product directly to the customer.

Distribution inventory—distribution inventory is the result of a distribution network and the increases in inventory required to operate out of multiple distribution points. When you decide to have two or three or more strategically located distribution centers rather than a single centrally located distribution center, you will generally increase your overall inventory levels. The reason for this is you are now breaking up your demand among three locations. When demand is broken up (disaggregated) you will usually find greater variability in the demand at each location. This increase in variability results in increases in safety stock in order to meet desired service levels. This increase in safety stock is essentially your distribution inventory. Some practitioners consider all inventory in the distribution network to be distribution inventory. I disagree with that definition, since much of that inventory would exist regardless of the distribution network.

Distribution requirements planning—process for determining inventory requirements in a multiple facility environment. DRP may be used for both distribution and manufacturing. In manufacturing, DRP will work directly with MRP. DRP uses DRP relationships to allow demand to flow from one facility to another.

Dock-to-stock cycle measurement—measuring the amount of time it takes between the time something arrives at your dock, and the time it is in stock and available for sale or use.

Double exponential smoothing—forecasting method that uses exponential smoothing to smooth both the demand and the trend.

DRP—See Distribution requirements planning.

DRP relationship—sometimes called a bill of distribution, a DRP relationship specifies an item-based or facility-based supply relationship between facilities and a lead time, and is used by DRP to flow demand from one facility to another.

Eaches—term used to describe a unit of measure where each individual piece is tracked as a quantity of one in the computer system.

Economic order quantity—a calculation (or the result of a calculation) that determines the most cost effective quantity to order (purchased items) or produce (manufactured items) by finding the point at which the combination of order cost and carrying cost is the least. There is a specific calculation that has historically been known as EOQ, but any calculation (or variation of this calculation) that uses similar logic would also be considered EOQ.

Effective dates—dates on the detail lines of bills of materials and routings that let the system know when these lines should be included in planning and execution activities.

Effective lead time—a lead time that has been adjusted to take into account additional factors. For example, in a fixed-schedule ordering system (periodic review) you may adjust your lead time to include the time between ordering opportunities.

Engineer-to-order—a variation of a make-to-order manufacturing strategy. An engineer-to-order strategy is used when the end product is truly custom. In this strategy, design or engineering tasks must be completed as part of the order process. This strategy has the longest lead time to the customer, but is necessary since the detailed specifications of the product are not known in advance.

EOQ—See Economic order quantity.

ERP—enterprise resource planning. Software systems designed to manage most or all aspects of a manufacturing or distribution enterprise (an expanded version of MRP systems). ERP systems are usually broken down into modules such as financials, sales, purchasing, inventory management, manufacturing, MRP, DRP. The modules are designed to work seamlessly with the rest of the system and should provide a consistent user interface between them.

Event index—consists of a number (factor) for each specific forecast period that describes the relationship of each period's demand (excluding trend and seasonality) over the length of time demand is affected by an event (such as a promotion).

Excess inventory—inventory greater than the "right amount" of inventory.

Exponential smoothing—forecasting method that is essentially a variation of a weighted moving average. The data inputs to the exponential smoothing include the previous period's demand, the previous period's forecast, and a smoothing factor. The smoothing factor is a number between zero and one (0.01, 0.02, . . . 0.99) that is used to weight the most recent period's demand against the forecast for that period to produce the next period's forecast. The calculation is [Next period forecast]=([Previous period's demand]*[Smoothing factor])+([Previous period's forecast]*(1-[Smoothing factor]).

Exponentially smoothed absolute deviation (ESAD)—a variation of Mean Absolute Deviation (MAD) where instead of averaging the absolute values, you apply the exponential smoothing calculation to them. *See also* Mean absolute deviation and Exponential smoothing.

Exponentially smoothed forecast bias—application of exponential smoothing to a series of forecast errors. *See also* Forecast error.

Fair share distribution—a method of dividing a receipt or existing inventory at a supplying facility among the facilities being supplied, based on demand at those facilities.

Fill rate—a success rate in filling orders. Stated as line fill, order fill, unit fill, or dollar fill.

Finished goods—inventory that is in a salable or shippable form based upon its location within the supply chain. An item considered a finished good in a supplying plant might be considered a component or raw material in a receiving plant.

Finite capacity scheduling—a manufacturing planning system that schedules within the capacity constraints of work centers.

Firm planned order—a special status applied to a planned order that prevents MRP from replanning it.

Fixed reorder point—also called fixed order point, fixed reorder point is a preset (fixed) quantity that triggers the need for a new order being placed. *See also* Reorder point.

Fixed-schedule ordering system—a replenishment system where orders can only be placed based on a predetermined schedule. For example, you may have a supplier where you have a set "order day" and "delivery day", such as placing orders every Tuesday for a Friday delivery. *See also* Periodic review inventory system.

Flattening—when referring to "flattening your bills of materials", flattening implies you are removing levels from your bill-of-materials structure. It means that rather than making one item that is then later used to make another item, you make the first item as part of the manufacturing process for the second item (under the same production order in the same production run).

Forecast—an estimation of future demand.

Forecast basis—the data and information that is used to produce the forecast. In most cases, this is the historical demand for the product.

Forecast bias—the tendency of a forecast to be high or low.

Forecast consumption—the process of depleting the forecast as actual orders are received.

Forecast error—measurement that represents forecast error/accuracy. The most common base calculation is ([Forecasted Sales]-[Actual Sales]) / [Actual Sales]. But there are many variations and extensions of forecast error measurements.

Forecast horizon—the length of time into the future over which the entire forecast (all forecast periods) is based. As a general guideline, your forecast horizon must be at least as long as the cumulative lead time of the product being forecast. But, forecast horizons beyond the cumulative lead time may be needed to plan for lot sizing, manufacturing capacity, cash flow, facilities, labor, etc. Some definitions of forecast horizon would also include the period of time into the past over which historical demand was used to produce the forecast.

Forecast interval—the length of time over which each forecast period is based. Forecast intervals usually follow standard cumulative measures of time (years, quarters, months, weeks, days).

Forecast override—any adjustment that is used to supersede your normal forecast. A forecast override can be a fixed quantity that will be used to replace the forecast, or it can be a factor that can be used to adjust the forecast or an element of the forecast (such as a trend override factor).

Forecast period—a specific span of time described by a forecast quantity. For example, if I forecast demand of 500 units each week for the next six weeks, each week is a separate forecast period. Forecast periods are sometimes referred to as "time buckets", though that can get confusing since some systems have time buckets that are different from the forecast period.

Freight terms—an agreement between a supplier and customer that describes the responsibility for transportation costs.

Generic software—generic software (such as generic ERP systems) are products designed to work in a broad range of environments and tend to focus on standard business practices for general industry.

GMROII—See Gross margin return on inventory investment..

Gross margin—the difference between cost and sell price.

Gross margin return on inventory investment—GMROII is a calculation that shows your margin relative to your average inventory investment. It's calculated by dividing your annual gross margin (dollars) by your average inventory investment (dollars), and can be calculated for individual items or groups of items.

Gross requirements—the total demand (dependent and independent) for an item within a specific time period. Gross requirements are then used to calculate net requirements. *See also* Netting and Net requirements.

Group logic—methods used to manage inventory based on groups of items rather than single items

Hedge inventory—inventory that is purchased to protect against or take advantage of price fluctuations. The price fluctuations may be the result of seasonal or cyclical variations that result with imbalances in supply and demand (supply exceeds demand or vice versa), changes in exchange rates with international purchases, or even special promotions.

IF-THEN-ELSE—describes the most common logic used by software to make decisions. IF-THEN-ELSE is used to describe a situation and then describe what the program should do if the situation is true and what it should do if the situation is false. For example, for your computer to tell you when you have email, the software is programmed such that IF there is new mail in your mailbox, THEN execute the sound file that has the "you've got mail" message, ELSE do nothing.

IF statement—a calculation that uses IF-THEN-ELSE logic. When I use the term "IF statement", I am generally referring to a spreadsheet (Excel) formula that uses the IF function, but may be referring to any program where similar logic is used.

Independent demand—demand that is not created as a direct result of another item's demand or demand from another facility. Demand for customer orders is an example of independent demand.

Industry-specific software—software that is designed with a specific industry in mind, and therefore has functionality that focuses on the typical business practices of that specific industry.

Infinite capacity scheduling—a manufacturing planning system that completely ignores capacity constraints and schedules purely based on demand. MRP is an example of an infinite capacity scheduling system. It requires that planners check the production schedule against capacity and make adjustments accordingly.

In-transit quantity—a quantity that has been shipped from one facility and has not yet been received into another facility

Inventory—any quantifiable item that you handle, buy, sell, store, consume, produce, or track.

Inventory characteristic—any distinguishing trait that describes the types of inventory you are managing. The physical size, the form, demand patterns, and costs, are examples of inventory characteristics.

Inventory classification—any logical grouping of inventory based upon user-defined characteristics.

Inventory management—the control of inventory in a manner that best achieves the business objectives of your organization. It not only involves the physical management of inventory, but also the management of the data used to describe the inventory, and the systems used to process the data. Inventory management ultimately comes down to having the right inventory in the right form in the right quantity in the right place at the right time at the right cost.

Inventory system—the collection of programs and data used to plan and track inventory balances and activities.

Inventory turns—a measure of the velocity of inventory. It is generally calculated by dividing either the average inventory investment during a period of time or the current inventory investment at a point in time, by the annual cost of goods sold (COGS).

ISM—The Institute for Supply Management (previously known as National Association of Purchasing Management (NAPM). www.ism.ws

Issue—to reduce on-hand inventory and assign it to a specific document or process. Such as issuing raw materials to a production order or issuing finished goods to a sales order.

Item—any unique configuration of a material or product managed as part of your inventory. Item is used synonymously with SKU.

Item master—a collection of data that describes a specific item. Item master is also used to describe the database table that contains this data.

Item number—the identification number assigned to an item. Also called the part number, SKU number, or SKU.

Item numbering scheme—the format or template used for assigning item numbers.

JIT—just-in-time. Term usually thought of as describing inventory arriving or being produced just in time for the shipment or next process. Actually JIT is a strategy for optimizing manufacturing processes by eliminating all process waste, including wasted steps, wasted material, excess inventory, etc. JIT is often used synonymously with "Lean manufacturing" or "Toyota production system".

Kanban—replenishment system where a replenishment is triggered by emptying a container, and a physical notification such as a card or the empty container is sent up the line to the previous operation or supplier to be refilled. *See also* Multi-bin system.

Kit—items that are made up of multiple separate parts (not assembled).

Landed cost—you can think of landed cost as your "delivered cost" for an item. In addition to the unit cost, it should include transportation costs, brokerage fees, and any import duties or taxes required.

Last-period demand—forecasting method that uses demand from the previous period as the forecast for subsequent periods.

Last-relative-period demand—forecasting method that uses the relative period (usually from the previous year) to forecast demand. For example, where last-period demand would use January's demand to forecast February's demand, last-relative-period demand would use February's demand from the previous year to forecast February's demand for the current year.

Law of large numbers—a simple observation that with larger numbers you can generally expect lower variability.

Lead-time—amount of time it takes for a purchased item to be delivered after it is ordered, or the amount of time it takes for a manufactured item to be completed after it is ordered.

Lead-time demand—expected demand during the lead-time period. For example, if your forecasted demand is 3 units per day and your lead time is 12 days, your lead time demand would be 36 units.

Lead-time factor—a multiplier used to adjust a standard deviation based on forecast periods, to an estimated standard deviation based on lead time periods.

Lead-time offsetting—term used in planning systems such as MRP and DRP to describe the process of offsetting the demand of dependent demand items based on the lead time of the parent items or facilities. Or, the process of offsetting the planned order release date from the planned order receipt date by the lead time. Both definitions are commonly used.

Lean—see JIT.

Legacy system—implies an outdated computer system that is either a home-grown (custom built) system, a purchased system that has likely been modified over the years, and/or a hodgepodge of various disconnected software systems. It's actually a marketing term used by software vendors to convince you that your current system just isn't up to snuff any more.

Level—also known as normalized demand or base demand, level is your starting point for a forecast. It can be a confusing term because people sometimes think of it as a flat line, when in reality level changes over time (the result of trend). I find it's easiest to think of level as your current demand after seasonality and noise have been removed.

Line item—a single detail record. The term line item is most commonly used to describe the detail (each line that reflects an item and a quantity) on sales orders or purchase orders.

Lot-for-lot—a very basic lot sizing method that uses demand during the specified planning time period (time bucket) as the lot size. In most cases the planning periods would be your forecast periods, therefore your lot would be equal to the net demand in the forecast period in which the order is planned on being received.

Lot size—also known as order quantity, lot size represents the quantity of an item you order for delivery on a specific date, or manufacture in a single production run.

Lot-size inventory—lot size inventory is the result of ordering or manufacturing more inventory than is required to meet your current demand and safety stock.

MAD—See Mean absolute deviation.

Make-to-order—a manufacturing strategy where you do not manufacture your product until after you receive actual orders from your customers. The primary advantage to this strategy is that you do not have to carry finished goods inventory. This strategy does not necessarily result in zero inventories. Many make-to-order manufactures will forecast and procure some raw materials and components in advance of receiving orders in an effort to reduce the lead time to their customers.

Make-to-stock—manufacturing strategy where you must carry adequate finished goods inventory to meet upcoming forecasted demand. The reason this stocking strategy is so common is not that it is the most cost-effective inventory strategy overall, but rather it is a necessary strategy when market conditions require shipment of goods quicker than you can manufacture them.

Management by exception—a management strategy that consists of automating the majority of decisions and then monitoring for exceptions.

Manufacturing execution system—software designed to integrate with enterprise systems to enhance the shop floor control functionality that is usually inadequate in ERP and MRP systems. MES provides for shop floor scheduling, production and labor reporting, and integration with computerized manufacturing systems such as automatic data collection and computerized machinery.

Manufacturing lead time—the combination of setup time (the time it takes to set up equipment), run time (the actual assembly or manufacturing time), move time, and queue time (a buffer that represents the time stuff just sits around waiting to be worked on).

Master production schedule—MPS is a planning tool that exists as a layer between your MRP system and your demand (forecasting system and actual demand). MPS is used to balance demand with capacity by moving production from periods with inadequate capacity into periods with available capacity.

Mean absolute deviation—the average of the absolute values of a series of variances. MAD is used in forecast error measurement, safety stock calculations, and other applications of statistics.

MES—See Manufacturing execution system

Min-max—a slight variation on a fixed-reorder-point/fixed-replenishment-quantity ordering system. The "min" part of min-max is essentially your fixed reorder point. The "max" part represents a quantity you want to order "up to". When inventory drops at or below your min, you order enough to bring you to your max.

Modular bill of materials—See Planning bill of materials.

Moving average—forecasting method that calculates the average demand over a fixed number of time periods relative to the date the forecast is generated, and uses that as the forecast for subsequent periods. For example, if I am calculating a three-month moving average on July 1st, I will calculate the average demand over April, May, and June. Subsequently, on August 1st, I would use May, June, and July demand for the calculation.

Modification—a change to software that requires changing or adding to the software code.

Move time—the time it takes to physically relocate materials from one manufacturing operation (step in manufacturing process) to the next.

MRO—maintenance, repair, and operating inventory. Term used to describe inventory used to maintain equipment as well as miscellaneous supplies such as office and cleaning supplies.

MRP—material requirements planning (MRP) or manufacturing resource planning (MRPII). MRP was originally designed for materials planning only, and involved exploding demand through a bill-of-materials structure, calculating gross requirements and net requirements, and creating planned orders. MRPII is the consolidation of material requirements planning (MRP), capacity requirements planning (CRP), and master production scheduling (MPS). Today, the definition of MRPII is generally associated with MRP systems (when someone refers to a system as an MRP system, they are probably talking about an MRPII system).

MRP generation—describes the process where MRP uses the bill-of-material structure and other inventory data to calculate gross and net requirements, and create planned orders.

MRP explosion—describes the process where MRP expands demand through the bill-of-materials structure and offsets it by the lead time. The MRP explosion is part of the MRP generation process.

Multi-bin system—a simplistic replenishment system that uses two or more physical bins (or other type of container) for each item. When one bin is emptied, it is sent somewhere to be refilled. *See also* Kanban and Two-bin system.

Multi-level bill of materials—a bill-of-materials structure where components on one BOM have their own BOMs below them. Technically, a multi-level bill does not actually exist. Instead, you just have numerous single-level bills and your computer software figures out that if an item on one bill has its own bill, it can logically link these together for planning purposes.

Multi-period forecast error amplitude measurement (MPFEAM)—measurements that quantify the size of the forecast error over multiple forecast periods.

Multi-plant—environments where multiple facilities are managed.

Multi-plant MRP—MRP extended with DRP logic to plan inventory in multi-plant environments. *See also* Distribution requirements planning.

Nervousness—in MRP systems, nervousness describes frequent changes to planned orders for lower-level items, that result from minor changes in demand of higher-level items.

Net change MRP—a process that only recalculates gross and net requirements and planned orders for items (and components of items) that have had some type of change to planning data (change in on-hand balance, quantity on order, etc.). Net change MRP may be run as a batch program, or may be able to run real-time in a live environment (not all systems can do this).

Net requirements—the result of adjusting gross requirements by current on-hand, safety stock, and inbound quantities.

Netting—the process of adjusting gross requirements by current on-hand, safety stock, and inbound quantities.

Noise—the unpredictable variation in demand. Noise is demand variation that is not the result of trend, seasonality, or other predictable factors.

Non-stock inventory—inventory that is not tracked within your perpetual inventory system. Non-stock inventory will generally not have an item-master record or internal SKU number. An alternate meaning for non-stock inventory is order-as-needed inventory. In this case, you do have an item-master record and an internal SKU number, but do not carry stock of the item.

Normal distribution—term used in statistical analysis to describe a distribution of numbers in which the probability of an occurrence, if graphed, would follow the form of a bell-shaped curve. This is the most popular distribution model for determining probability and has been found to work well in predicting demand variability based upon historical data.

Normalize—to remove elements such as seasonality, trend, or effects of events from demand.

Obsolescence—the process by which inventory becomes obsolete.

Obsolete—the condition of being no longer of use due to passage of time. Usually associated with old, outdated designs.

On-time delivery—a fill-rate measurement generally used by manufacturers to describe the percentage of orders, lines, dollars, or units filled by the requested (or promised) date. Tolerances or time breakdowns may be used to adjust or add detail to this type of measurement.

Operation—in manufacturing, an operation is a step in the manufacturing process (a step in the routing). In more general terms, an operation is the combination of a physical facility and the processes that occur within that facility.

Optimization—the process of getting the "best" result from a stated problem. A typical optimization model would be made up of a value that you would like to optimize (minimize or maximize), one or more changeable values that have a mathematical relationship to the value you want to optimize, and one or more constraints (limits). Though optimization implies an optimal (best) solution, the reality is in most cases we are looking for the "best practical" solution, which is not necessarily the best solution.

Optimization algorithm—a series of steps used (usually by a computer program) to find an optimal solution to a problem.

Optional reorder point—also called optional replenishment point, is a separate reorder point that is a little higher than your normal reorder point, and can be used to avoid down-time on machines for manufactured items or meet minimum order amounts, discounts, or freight policies for purchased items. It's basically just a quick way of identifying items that are close to reorder point.

Order as needed—a replenishment method (and classification) that only triggers an order when actual demand is present. And generally will only order enough inventory to meet the actual demand.

Order cost—the sum of the fixed costs that are incurred each time an item is ordered or produced. Order costs are the costs associated with the instance, but not the quantity, of an order; which is not necessarily the same as all costs associated with ordering and receiving inventory. Order cost is used in cost-based lot sizing calculations such as EOQ.

Order cycle—the length of time between receipts of an item. You can also think of it as the length of time an ordered quantity should last.

Ordering system—any technique(s) or program(s) used to trigger and/or execute the ordering process. Fixed reorder point, min-max, multi-bin, MRP, and DRP are examples of ordering systems.

Order point—See Reorder point.

Outsourcing—the act of transferring responsibilities for a process to an outside supplier.

Overhead—indirect costs associated with facilities and management that are applied to the costs of manufactured goods through the manufacturing reporting process.

Override—any adjustment that is used to supersede the standard results of a decision or calculation. Overrides are sometimes used in forecasting, safety stock, and lot sizing calculations.

Pareto Principle—a principle that describes a common statistical situation whereby a small number of causes are responsible for a great number of effects. *See also* 80/20 rule.

Part number—See Item number.

Parts list—a listing of material required for a production order. The manufacturing planning system will use the bill of materials to calculate the material requirements for a manufacturing order, resulting in the parts list (also called a materials list). Parts lists can also be created or edited manually.

Payment terms—an agreement between a supplier and customer that describes how and when payment will be made for products or services.

Period order quantity—a method for stating an order quantity using time rather than units. When it comes time to order, your system will look at the immediate forecasted demand over the length of time designated by the POQ and use that as the order quantity.

Periodic review inventory system—a periodic review inventory system has two different (though related) definitions. When referring to inventory tracking methods, a periodic review system means that you do not keep track of inventory transactions and current inventory balances. Instead, you periodically physically count your inventory to see how much you have. When referring to replenishment systems, periodic review means that you have a fixed schedule (not daily) where you review inventory levels and place replenishment orders.

Perpetual inventory system—an inventory system that uses transactions to adjust on-hand balances to coincide with physical activities that are occurring.

Phantom bill of materials—a fictitious BOM created for common subassemblies or kits that you do not want to produce as separate items. For example, if you have a number of products that all use the same hardware, you can create a phantom bill for the hardware (as if it were a kit) and then just put the phantom item on the bills for all products that use it. Your MRP system will treat the phantom bill components as though they were part of the bill for the higher-level item (rather than treating it as a separate item that needs to be produced). Phantom items never actually exist, they are just a means for simplifying the management of your bills of materials.

Physical inventory—the process of counting all inventory in a warehouse or plant in a single event. Also called a wall-to-wall inventory.

Planned order—term used within MRP and DRP systems for system-generated order recommendations (recommended order dates and quantities). Planned orders only exist within the computer system and serve multiple functions. One function is to notify the materials/planner or buyer to produce or order materials, which is done by converting a planned order into a purchase order, production order, or transfer order. Another function is used by the MRP or DRP system to show net demand that is used by subsequent MRP and DRP programs to generate additional planned orders for lower level items.

Planned order receipt—term used within MRP and DRP systems to describe the date a planned order must be received in order to fulfill net requirements.

Planned order release—term used within MRP and DRP systems to describe the date a planned order must be released in order to meet the lead time. It is essentially the planned order receipt date offset by the lead time.

Planning bill of materials—a fictitious bill of material used to group a family of products or options of a family of products. For example, you may have a line of notebook computers where most of the components are the same, but some will have different hard drives, processors, memory, etc. Rather than creating separate bills for each possible combination, and then attempting to forecast each possible combination, you can create one large planning bill that contains all possible components but uses the "quantity per" to manage the options. If you expect half of the computers will use Drive A, 25% will use Drive B, and 25% will use Drive C, you would set up each drive on the bill, and use 0.50, 0.25, and 0.25 respectively as the quantity per. You would then proceed to do the same for all other options. Your higher-level forecast would then be for the total demand for all computers in this family. Planning bills are sometimes referred to as Super Bills, Modular Bills, or Pseudo Bills.

PO—See Purchase order.

POQ—See Period order quantity.

Postponement—a manufacturing /distribution strategy where specific operations associated with a product are delayed until just prior to shipping. Storing product in a generic state and then applying custom labels or packaging before shipping is an example of postponement.

Predictor variable—in regression analysis, a predictor variable is a set of data that is thought to be able to predict another set of data.

Procure-to-order—an inventory strategy where you do not procure your product until after you receive actual orders from your customers.

Procure-to-stock—an inventory strategy where you must carry adequate finished goods inventory to meet upcoming forecasted demand. The reason this stocking strategy is so common is not that it is the most cost-effective inventory strategy overall, but rather it is a necessary strategy when market conditions require shipment of goods quicker than you can procure them.

Product life cycle—the period of time in which a specific item is considered an active saleable item. Product life cycle starts when a product is first introduced, and ends when a product is removed from active status. Some definitions of product life cycle may also include the development time for a product.

Product life cycle index—consists of a number for each specific forecast period that describes the relationship of each period's demand (excluding trend and seasonality) over the complete product life cycle.

Production order—the document used to process a production run of an item. Also known as a job, work order, or manufacturing order, a production order is usually made up of a production order header, a parts list, and a routing.

Production plan—a very high-level long-term plan of what will be produced. It is generally stated in terms of families of products rather than specific products, and in large time periods such as months, quarters, or years.

Production run—the physical act of performing all tasks associated with a production order (or a group of production orders that require similar setup and processing).

Promised date—the date a supplier expects to be able to fulfill a customer order.

Pseudo bill of materials—See Planning bill of materials.

Pull system—an ordering or production scheduling system where production or procurement of a product is the direct result of actual customer demand. A pure pull system would be a make-to-order system where something is only manufactured after an actual customer order is placed. However, the term pull has been commonly used to describe other replenishment systems (such as Kanban) that arguably do not fit this pure pull definition.

Purchase order—document used to authorize, track, and process items purchased from a supplier. A purchase order is also a legal document that can include the terms of the sale.

Purchasing contract—a legal document agreed to by the buyer and seller on the pricing and terms of a sales transaction or a series of sales transactions. A formal purchasing contract is generally used when an agreement is made relative to the transfer of goods or services that amount to a significant value and are outside of the normal pricing and terms provided by the seller, or where a significant commitment is being made by the buyer and/or seller.

Push system—an ordering or production scheduling system where production or procurement of a product is triggered by expected (forecasted) demand rather than actual customer orders. Make-to-stock and procure-to-stock are examples of push systems.

Quantity discount—a price structure that involves lower prices for larger purchase quantities. Quantity discounts generally have specific "break points" that designate quantities at which the price changes.

Quantity per—the numeric representation of the quantity of a specific item required to make one unit of another item. Quantity per exists on the bill of materials and on the parts list associated with a production order.

Queue time—the amount of time inventory is staged prior to processing.

Raw materials—inventory used in the manufacturing process. Though some would categorize raw materials as very base materials in bulk form such as carloads of ore or unitized loads of paper, plastic, or steel, I generally consider anything used in the manufacturing process as a raw material. I use the term synonymously with the term "components".

Receipts—the materials or transactions associated with the receiving process.

Receiving—the process of placing materials into inventory. Also describes the department in which receiving activities take place.

Regenerative MRP—the process of completely regenerating (usually through a batch program) planned orders for all items. All existing planned orders (except firm planned orders) for all items are wiped out, and MRP starts all over calculating gross and net requirements and new planned orders.

Regression analysis—techniques used to determine a mathematical relationship between two or more sets of data where one or more sets of data is thought to be able to predict the other set of data. The data used to predict is known as the predictor variable.

Relevant history—data recorded under business conditions similar enough to current and future conditions, such that it can still be effectively used to forecast future demand.

Reorder point—the inventory level set to trigger an order of a specific item. Reorder point is generally calculated as the expected usage (demand) during the lead time plus safety stock.

Replenishment—within a warehouse or plant, replenishment is the process of moving inventory from secondary storage areas into fixed storage locations. Within a supply chain or a multi-plant environment, replenishment is the process of moving inventory between facilities or from suppliers to meet demand.

Requested date—the date a purchased item is requested to be received at a customer's location.

Requisitions—a way for people who don't have purchasing authority (authority to create purchase orders) to create purchase-order-like documents that specify item, quantity, cost, terms, and vendor information for something they require. These requisitions would then be reviewed by someone who does have purchasing authority, and if approved, would be converted to actual purchase orders.

Resources requirements planning—RRP is a capacity planning tool used to verify the ability of key resources to meet a production plan or business plan. RRP deals primarily with resources that require long-term planning, such as facilities, major equipment, capital, and workforce levels.

Rough-cut capacity—a capacity planning tool used to verify the ability of key resources (machines, labor) to meet the master production schedule. Rough-cut capacity exists at a level between resources requirements planning (RRP) and capacity requirements planning (CRP).

Routing—a list of operations (steps) used to complete a manufacturing process. A routing is used in conjunction with the bill of materials. While the BOM contains the material requirements, the routing will contain the specific steps (including labor and machine requirements) required to produce the finished items.

RRP— See Resources requirements planning

Run time—in an operation step in a routing, run time is the amount of time it takes to produce (run) a single unit. It does not include any setup time or queue time. The term can also be used to describe the accumulation of run time for multiple operations or multiple units (based on an entire production order).

Safety lead time—a means of adding some time to your lead time as part of your ordering calculations. Though safety lead time is used in the ordering calculation to determine when you need to order something, it is excluded from the calculation that then determines the "requested date" for the order.

Safety stock—quantity of inventory used in inventory management systems to allow for variation in demand or supply that cannot be effectively forecast.

Sales order—document used to approve, track, and process outbound customer shipments.

Scrap—inventory that must be discarded or recycled as a result of a manufacturing process or damage that occurs during storage or material handling.

Scrap rate—the rate of expected scrap for specific components within the context of manufacturing an item. A scrap rate would be attached to a specific component on the bill of materials for a specific item

Seasonality—fluctuations in demand that repeat with the same pattern over equivalent time periods. The most common representation of seasonality occurs with changing demand patterns measured weekly, monthly, or quarterly, that repeat annually.

Seasonality index—consists of a number for each specific forecast period that describes the relationship of each period's demand to the average demand over the complete seasonal cycle. The average demand is represented by the number one. If seasonality for a period results in demand greater than the average demand, it will be represented by a number greater than one. For example, if December's sales were, on average, 30% greater than the average monthly sales for the year, you would have a seasonality index of 1.3 (1 plus .30) for December.

Self-induced seasonality—term I use to describe repeating patterns of demand variability caused by internal processes and policies. For example, having a peak in sales at the end of each quarter because you have incentive policies for your sales people or customers that are based on three-month periods (quarters).

Semi-processed materials—stockable items (meaning they have their own unique item number) that have gone through some processing, but will be later pulled from stock and undergo additional processing.

Service factor—a number used as a multiplier (with the standard deviation) in statistical safety stock calculations. The service factor is associated with a desired service level.

Service level—service level has two meanings. It's a term used to describe a key input to statistical-based safety stock calculations. It's also a term used to describe fill-rate and on-time-delivery measurements. It's important to note that the service level used in safety stock calculations does NOT equate to any typical fill-rate measurement.

Setup costs—the costs associated with initiating a production run. May include labor and machine time to get equipment ready, as well as scrap or tooling associated with the setup process.

Setup time—the time it takes to prepare (equipment and materials) for a production run.

Shipping order—document used to approve, track, and process outbound shipments.

SKU—stock-keeping unit. Referring to a specific item in a specific unit of measure. Also refers to the identification number assigned to each SKU. Used interchangeably with the terms item and item number.

Smoothing—the act of removing variation from demand.

Smoothing factor—also called a smoothing constant, a smoothing factor is a number between zero and one (0.01, 0.02, . . . 0.99) that is used to weight the most recent period's demand against the forecast for that period to produce the next period's forecast in an exponential smoothing calculation. *See also* Exponential smoothing.

Sourcing—the activity of finding suppliers for products, materials, or services.

Spreadsheet modeling—the activity of creating a mathematical representation of a business problem (a set of circumstances that require a decision to be made) in a spreadsheet.

Square root trick—a statistical tool used to "soften" a ratio by taking the square root of the ratio.

Standard business practices—business practices that are typical for general industry or specific industries.

Standard deviation—a statistical term that describes a number (the result of a calculation) used to describe the "spread" of variation in a distribution. Note there are separate formulas for calculating standard deviation depending on whether you are basing the calculation on a sample or the entire population.

Stocking type—a classification used by planning and execution systems to identify the primary stocking characteristic of the inventory. Examples of stocking types would include classifications that distinguish manufactured inventory, purchased inventory, direct ship inventory, or order-as-needed inventory.

Stocking unit of measure—the unit of measure used to track inventory within a facility. Stocking unit of measure is usually, but not always, the smallest unit of measure handled.

Stockout—a situation where you have inadequate inventory levels to meet current demand.

Storage cost—the costs associated with the physical storage of inventory. This would include the cost of the physical space dedicated to the inventory, as well as storage equipment (racking, shelving) used to store the inventory.

Subassembly—a stockable item that has gone through an assembly process, but is also used in the assembly of other items. A subassembly is also a component.

Super bill of materials—See Planning bill of materials.

Supply-chain optimization software—generally implies considerable functionality related to inventory management, transportation management, and multi-facility planning. But, more importantly, it should include advanced optimization algorithms to optimize supply chain decisions by considering the key variables of a complex supply chain.

Terms—short for "terms of sale", terms is an agreement between a supplier and customer that describes the conditions of the sale. They would likely include payment terms, freight terms, change-of-ownership terms, and return policies.

Time fence—a time frame within which you want some control over changes to your production schedule. Time fences are typically implemented more as guidelines rather than firm restrictions.

Time-phased order point—describes systems that directly utilize the immediate forecast and actual customer orders to trigger order (reorder) decisions.

Total quality management—a management strategy that focuses on continuous improvement.

TQM—See Total quality management

Tracking signal—a calculation that describes the overall health of the forecast relative to trend, and can be used to initiate changes to the forecasting technique or parameters. There are numerous calculations used as tracking signals.

Transportation inventory—the amount of inventory that is currently in-transit. That is, it is the inventory that has left the shipper's facility (either an owned facility or a supplier's facility) and has yet to arrive at the consignee's facility (may be an owned facility or a customer's facility).

Trend—a gradual increase or decrease in demand over a period of time.

Trend adjustment—a mathematical calculation used to adjust future period's forecasts to account for trend (extend the trend).

Trend element—a specific aspect of trend. For example, changes in market share would be a trend element.

Trend lag—a forecast's inability to adequately account for trend. Usually the result of smoothing calculations reducing the impact of trend and/or a lack of a calculation to properly extend the trend.

Triple exponential smoothing—forecasting method that uses exponential smoothing to smooth the demand, the trend, and the seasonality index.

Two-bin system—a simplistic replenishment system that uses two physical bins (or other type of container) for each item. When one bin is emptied, it is sent somewhere to be refilled. *See also* Kanban and Multi-bin system.

Unfinished goods—items that are used to produce finished goods items. Unfinished goods are often called components, ingredients, raw materials, semi-processed materials, and subassemblies.

Units—describes the individual pieces of physical inventory that make up the quantity an item (assuming pieces is the unit-of-measure).

Unit of measure—the unit of measure describes how the quantity of an item is tracked in your inventory system. The most common unit of measure is "eaches," which simply means that each individual item is considered one unit. An item that uses "cases" as the unit of measure would be tracked by the number of cases rather than by the actual piece quantity. Other examples of units of measure would include pallets, pounds, ounces, linear feet, square feet, cubic feet, gallons, thousands, hundreds, pairs, dozens. *See also* Unit-of-measure conversion.

Unit-of-measure conversion—a conversion ratio used whenever multiple units-of-measure are used with the same item. For example, if you purchased an item in cases (meaning that your purchase order stated a number of cases rather than a number of pieces) and then stocked the item in eaches, you would require a conversion to allow your system to calculate how many eaches are represented by a quantity of cases. This way, when you received the cases, your system would automatically convert the case quantity into an each quantity.

Vendor managed inventory—phrase used to describe the process of a supplier managing his customers' inventory levels and purchases of the materials he supplies to them.

VMI—See Vendor managed inventory

Weighted moving average—forecasting method similar to a moving average, however different weights can be applied to the historical periods (the weights must add up to 1). Each previous period's demand is multiplied by the respective weight, then the results are added up to get your forecast. So where a four-period moving average used the same weight for all periods ($0.25 + 0.25 + 0.25 + 0.25 = 1$), a weighted moving average allows a variety of weights to be used, provided they total 1. For example, 0.15 for the first period, 0.20 the second, 0.30 the third, and 0.35 the fourth ($0.15 + 0.20 + 0.30 + 0.35 = 1$).

WIP—See Work-in-process.

Work-in-process—work-in-process (WIP) is a financial account that contains the dollar value of all inventory, labor, and overhead that has been issued to production but has not yet produced a finished product.

Work order—See Production order.

Yield rate—the expected "success" rate in the manufacturing process for an item. Yield rate exists at the parent-item level, as opposed to scrap rate that exist at the component level.

Index

On the web:

InventoryExplained.com

Inventoryexplained.com is the companion website to *Inventory Management Explained*. Here you can find updates, corrections, and additional information related to inventory management.

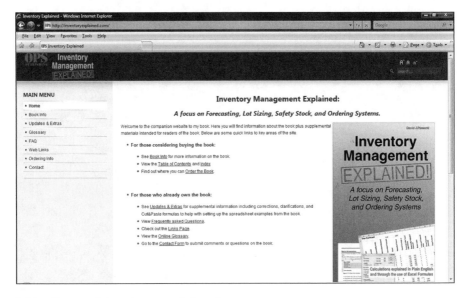

http://www.inventoryexplained.com

Code: EX7596